# Tax planni ⦚⦚⦚ ⦚⦚⦚ ou and your family

## 2018

| Editors-in-Chief | Editor |
| --- | --- |

**Nancy Belo Gomes,** CPA, CA
Toronto

**Paul Corupe,** BA
Toronto

**Luann Jones-Foster,** CPA, CA
Moncton

## Contributing KPMG Editors

**Line Arseneau,** MTax
Ottawa

**Ruth C. L. March,** CPA, CA, TEP
Halifax

**Anouk Leclair,** LL.L., LL.M. Fisc.
Montreal

**Stephen McHardy,** CPA, CA
Toronto

**Benita Loughlin,** CPA, CA
Vancouver

**Colin Miller,** CPA, CA
Lethbridge

**Paul Lynch,** CPA, CA
Toronto

**Justin Park,** MTax, CPA, CMA
Toronto

**David Magdalinski,** CMA, CPA
Edmonton

**Pam Prior,** CPA, CA, TEP
Vancouver

**Prepared by:**

ISSN 1207-5957
ISBN 978-0-7798-7829-1 (2018 edition)

**A cataloguing record for this publication is available from Library and Archives Canada.**

Composition: Imagineeringart.com Inc.

Printed in Canada.

**THOMSON REUTERS®**

THOMSON REUTERS CANADA, A DIVISION OF THOMSON REUTERS CANADA LIMITED

One Corporate Plaza
2075 Kennedy Road
Toronto, Ontario
M1T 3V4

Customer Support
1-416-609-3800 (Toronto & International)
1-800-387-5164 (Toll Free Canada & U.S.)
Fax 1-416-298-5082 (Toronto)
Fax 1-877-750-9041 (Toll Free Canada Only)
E-mail CustomerSupport.LegalTaxCanada@TR.com

# Contents

# Foreword

Many Canadians do not give much thought to how they can reduce their taxes until it's time to file their tax returns each spring. By then, many tax saving opportunities for the year may be lost. Filing your tax return is essentially a once-a-year accounting to the government to settle up your taxes owing or refund due for the previous year — it is the tax planning steps that you take throughout each year that will save the most money at tax time and in the years to come.

In this book our tax and financial planning professionals set out the most common rules and tax planning opportunities that may be available to individuals. A few hours invested in reading this book can pay off substantially in tax savings and in the organization of your financial affairs.

*This book cannot replace your tax adviser*

The income tax system is constantly changing. The discussions in this book reflect the law on the books at June 30, 2017. However, recent government proposals are set to significantly affect some tax planning that involves the use of private corporations (see Appendix I for a summary of these changes). Although these changes have not been enacted into law at the time of writing, you'll find cautionary notes in sections of the book that discuss legislation that may be changed by the proposals. Many of these changes would apply for 2018 and later tax years, while some could take effect as early as July 18, 2017.

It's a good idea to talk to your tax professional about the status of these proposals before you undertake any tax planning. Your tax professional can also update you on the status of other 2017 budget measures and tax proposals that were not yet enacted into law at the time of writing.

This book deals only in general terms. The Canadian tax system is extremely complex, far more than the book makes it appear. The details fill volumes, not a single book. If you carry on your own business, or manage a corporation, you will benefit greatly from personalized tax advice. Even if your affairs seem relatively simple, you should consult a qualified tax professional (not just a tax return preparer). You will likely find the savings far outweigh the fees.

# Chapter 1

## Tips for achieving your financial goals

- Create a financial plan and stick to it (1.1.1)
- Define your short-, medium- and long-term goals (1.1.1)
- Track your net worth and cash flow, and set an annual growth target (1.1.2 and 1.1.3)
- Save systematically by "paying yourself first" (1.1.3)
- Build an investment strategy that suits your unique circumstances and needs (1.1.4)
- Set benchmarks for measuring the performance of your investment portfolio and your investment manager (1.1.4)
- Contribute up to $2,500 annually to an RESP and earn a 20% government grant (1.2.1)
- Encourage your children to invest the money they earn (1.2.2)
- Think about using RRSP funds for a down payment on your first home under the Home Buyers' Plan (1.2.3)
- Increase the frequency of your mortgage payments to reduce your mortgage interest (1.2.3)
- Plan to minimize capital gains tax on dispositions of vacation homes (1.2.4)
- Set up an emergency fund or line of credit (1.3.1)
- Make sure you have adequate insurance and a current will (1.3.2 and 1.3.3)
- Consider a power of attorney (1.3.4)
- Shop around when choosing your financial and investment advisers (1.4)

*In this chapter, we offer a primer on financial planning with emphasis on the impact of taxes on your ability to meet your family's financial goals. We also point out tax planning ideas elsewhere in this book that may help you to achieve these goals. Given the importance of financial planning for your retirement, this area is discussed separately in Chapter 20.*

## 1.1 Developing your financial plan

For many Canadians, the very idea of financial planning is mystifying. It shouldn't be. Saving for retirement, financing your child's education or buying a house are within the reach of most of us—the purpose of financial planning is to clarify your objectives, set a realistic timetable for achieving them and marshal your financial resources to support your plan. Of course, the process may require changing your expectations, paring down your current lifestyle or simply prioritizing expenses and making choices. But having a sound financial plan will likely ease your financial anxiety by giving you a realistic picture of your family's finances and a clear path for satisfying your goals.

Tax planning to manage your family's overall tax bill should be an integral part of your family's financial plan. The balance of this book is full of ideas about how to save taxes; the rest of this chapter is an overview of the financial planning framework in which your tax planning should take place.

### 1.1.1 Define your financial and lifestyle goals

Create a financial plan and stick to it.

Putting your dreams on paper is the first step toward realizing them. Start by writing out what you want and when you want it. If you have a spouse or domestic partner, compile your list together, compromising where necessary to make sure that you are both committed to the same objectives. You might also include your children and have them develop their own plan as a teaching exercise.

Define your short-, medium- and long-term goals.

While your list should take into account your family's well-being and future financial security, be sure to include any desired lifestyle-enhancing items like vacation homes, major renovations, luxury cars or swimming pools. If you want to take a sabbatical from work to spend time with your children or eventually start your own business, write it down. As part of this exercise, consider the discussion of building your investment strategy in 1.1.4, common financial goals in 1.2 and important financial safeguards in 1.3.

When you have completed your list, divide it into short-, medium- and long-term goals and rank them in order of priority within each section. Set a timeframe for meeting each goal. Then do a bit of research and estimate the cost of achieving your goals, making sure to account for inflation. You may want to engage a financial planner or accountant to help you with the numbers. Don't let the amounts overwhelm you—over time the effects of compound growth can provide significant returns on your investments.

Nevertheless, you may need to revise your list by allowing more time to achieve a certain goal or by dropping items that are beyond your means.

As time goes by, your list will serve as a guide for directing your savings and investments and as an indicator of your progress. Since your personal and financial circumstances and goals are bound to change, it is important to revisit your list once or twice a year and revise it to reflect new priorities and achievements.

### 1.1.2 Track your net worth

Now that you have a better idea of where you want to go, the next step is to take a snapshot of where you are financially today—your net worth. Calculating your net worth is simply a matter of adding up your total assets (what you own) and total liabilities (what you owe), and then subtracting your liabilities from your assets. The resulting figure is the springboard for most aspects of financial management and planning.

It's also a good idea to separate your assets by ownership—whether your resources are owned by you, your spouse or jointly can help in determining potential strategies for income splitting (see Chapter 5) and estate planning (see Chapter 21).

A close look at your assets will show you whether most of your assets are personal items, such as your home or your car, or investment assets, such as savings accounts, shares and mutual funds. This review should also indicate how liquid your assets are and help you determine whether your investments are sufficiently diversified to balance expected rates of return with the degree of risk you are prepared to take (see 1.1.4).

Similarly, a close look at your liabilities may indicate whether your insurance coverage is adequate (see 1.3.2) and how your debts are affecting your bottom line. As we'll see in 7.2.3, interest incurred for personal reasons on credit cards, consumer loans and mortgages is not deductible for tax purposes, while interest on loans taken out to purchase income-generating investments or earn business income may be deductible. As a result, the interest on your consumer debts may cost you more than the return on your investments. Where possible, you should try to pay down your consumer debts, giving priority to those with the highest interest rates, and try to make sure that all loans you take out in the future are for a tax-deductible purpose.

Updating your net worth calculation once or twice a year is a good way to track your financial health and progress toward achieving your financial goals. For example, if you can increase your net worth by 8% each year, your net worth will double every nine years. Ways to increase your net worth include:

> Track your net worth and cash flow, and set an annual growth target.

- improving the rate of return on your investments
- investing more of your income by spending less on discretionary items and minimizing taxes

- reducing your debt by paying off your consumer and other high-rate loans and accelerating your mortgage and other debt payments.

### 1.1.3 Cash management and budgeting – the cornerstone of financial planning

The formula for accumulating the necessary funds to achieve your financial goals is no secret. Unless you expect to inherit money or win a lottery, the way to start building wealth is to save and regularly invest a portion of your income. Through the mathematical "miracle" of compounding, your investment assets can grow exponentially over time. The more savings you have to invest and the longer they are invested, the greater your net worth will be.

One way to increase your net worth is to gain better control over your savings and expenses with a personal or family budget. List the amounts of money you expect to receive through your pay cheque or other sources and the amounts you pay out monthly for living expenses, such as mortgage payments, groceries and entertainment. This will allow you to realistically assess your cash flow and help you prioritize your spending.

Considering this information and any non-recurring expenses, set your budget for the next month or the remainder of the year. Once your budget is set, review it regularly for reasonableness and compare your actual spending against it.

Without making lifestyle changes, there is usually little you can do about your mortgage payments, car payments and other fixed expenses. However, the exercise of preparing—and sticking to—a budget will probably reveal many opportunities to easily reduce your discretionary expenses such as travel, entertainment and gifts. For example, changing where and how you shop can reduce your expenditures. Though not required, there are plenty of excellent software packages available that can help you create and monitor your family budget.

*Save systematically by "paying yourself first".*

When preparing your budget, do not simply plan to save the amount left over at the end of each month—chances are there won't be as much left as you intended. Instead, get into the practice of saving a fixed amount of at least 10% of your income at the beginning of each month (or some other period) and using the balance for your expenses. Commonly known as the "pay yourself first" plan, this technique helps you to save systematically and to be less prone to making impulsive or needlessly expensive purchases. Although it may take you a few months to get used to having less cash readily available, you will probably be surprised at how quickly you will adjust. Consider having your financial institution automatically transfer your savings amount to a separate account, registered retirement savings plan (RRSP) (see Chapter 3) or Tax-Free Savings Account (TFSA) (see 4.1) on a monthly or other regular basis.

Once you have paid your maximum CPP/QPP and Employment Insurance premiums for the year, consider directing these amounts toward your savings or paying down debt (especially debt with non-tax deductible interest). Your take-home pay will stay the same, and you will be better off. Similarly, if you pay off a car loan, you could direct the amount of your payments to your savings.

### 1.1.4 Develop an appropriate investment strategy

Today's economic realities are forcing Canadians to take care of their own financial health. Even with professional advisers, most investors should take an active interest in their investment activities.

Modern investment wisdom suggests that it's not what you select but where you select it from. Known as "asset allocation", this process works as well for $10,000 as it does for $1 million. Simply put, asset allocation is the process of deciding how to invest a pool of resources among a broad array of assets. The process also helps you stick to your financial plan and avoid making rash decisions as rates of return go up or down. It is typically considered the single most important part of managing a portfolio.

> Build an investment strategy that suits your unique circumstances and needs.

Asset allocation involves three decisions. The first decision entails selecting between asset classes: cash, fixed income and equities.

The second decision includes determining market exposure—in many cases, you would be wise to diversify your investments geographically. Canada represents only a small portion of the world's capitalization, and substantial investment opportunities are considered to exist beyond our borders. Most Canadians are satisfied with owning some U.S. stocks, but this usually doesn't allow for enough diversification because the North American markets strongly influence each other. Today, global investments are available through a variety of mutual funds.

The last asset allocation decision is currency exposure. For example, if you held U.S. funds while the U.S. currency was depreciating against the Canadian dollar, you may have realized a loss if you converted to Canadian funds at a higher rate than you purchased the U.S. funds.

"Hedging" is an investment strategy through which an investor attempts to manage the various risks in a portfolio by holding different currencies in markets that are expected to move in opposite directions. Since hedging transactions require sophisticated knowledge of global markets, many investors ignore this strategy. Many investors instead choose to achieve additional diversification by investing in a hedge fund. Investing in U.S. currency may be advantageous for Canadians with recurring U.S.-denominated expenses for travel or vacation properties located in the United

States. Buying U.S. funds when the Canadian dollar is high relative to the U.S. dollar will save you money on paying future U.S. expenses when the value of the Canadian dollar declines.

Along with these three decisions, asset allocation comes in two forms: strategic and tactical. Strategic asset allocation takes a long-term view and divides a portfolio among several asset classes according to the inherent risks and rewards of each asset. Tactical allocation consists of short-term market predictions that could last an hour or a day. This type of allocation often proves difficult because variables used in selecting the asset mix continually change and the portfolio must be adjusted to keep up with market movements. Other disadvantages may include higher fees, lack of liquidity in esoteric markets like precious metals, and the potential to misread economic signals.

While there is no perfect asset allocation for any one person, there are definitely inappropriate allocations. The following are some tips for getting the right mix.

*Determine your objectives and risk tolerance*—Before you make any investment decisions, determine your objectives and risk tolerance and decide your asset allocation. Risk tolerance is influenced by factors such as your age, your family situation and investor personality. For example, a 55-year-old with two dependent teenage children may have a dramatically different risk tolerance than an empty-nester or single person of the same age. Also, if you have a defined benefit pension plan, the amount of risk you will accept with your RRSP may differ from that of someone whose RRSP is their only retirement savings vehicle.

Risk tolerance should also reflect your ability to replace losses. A person with a high net worth may be able to weather a loss of $50,000 in the market. But for the average retiree with a fixed pension, such a loss could be devastating. Asset allocation has to be a function of your investor profile and risk tolerance. If it's right, you should sleep well in any market environment.

For a discussion of revising your investment strategy as you approach retirement, see 20.2.2.

*Consider your total portfolio*—Many investors make a classic mistake at the outset by separating their registered from non-registered investments; whether investments are in an RRSP or other registered plan is irrelevant to an asset allocation decision. Your total investment portfolio should be considered so that the right proportion of asset types can be determined. Once you have completed your asset allocation, then you can decide, from a tax perspective, which investments are more effective to hold inside your RRSP (see 3.1.6) or TFSA (see 4.1).

*Plan for a long horizon and stay on course*—Once you have determined your asset allocation, plan to let your investments grow for at least five to seven years, long enough to go through a full market cycle. Average investors often make the mistake of buying what's hot because they think it's a great time to be in the market, then panic and sell as soon as the investment loses value. A disciplined approach to long-term asset allocation will probably give you higher returns in the long run.

*Pay attention to fees*—Be aware of management fees and commissions. A saving in fees of 1% per annum on a $100,000 investment earning a 6% annual return for 10 years could save you well over $15,000. You can't control the market, but you can control the fees and commissions you pay. If you do not know the amount of your fees, do not be afraid to ask your investment adviser or financial institution holding your investments.

*Inflation is a risk*—Inflation is another factor you cannot control, though you can plan for it. Depending on the rate of inflation, it can be a costly mistake to think of money in nominal terms instead of its real value. If your money isn't growing, you're losing it. Consider a $1,000 investment earning an average rate of return of 6% per year. After 10 years, the investment will be worth $1,790, but inflation will have eroded its real value. Assuming an annual inflation rate of 3%, this erosion will amount to $450 by the end of the 10th year, bringing the investment's real value down at that time to $1,340.

*Rebalance annually*—One of the most important steps in managing your investments is to regularly rebalance your portfolio according to your asset allocation. With discipline, this allows you to manage your investments for profit, by selling high and buying low.

For example, you may have decided originally that an investment mix of 40% in stocks and 60% in bonds met your objectives. However, due to a prosperous period in the economy, you find that the stock component of your portfolio grows to 55% while bonds now represent only 45% by value. In this case, the discipline of strategic asset allocation should force you to take profits and rebalance your original mix so that when the economy reverses—as it always does—you will be positioned to take advantage of the change.

*Choose the right investment firm and monitor your investments' performance*—Select an investment firm or adviser that fits your circumstances and needs and has consistently shown strong performance over the long term, compared to its competitors. Your written

Set benchmarks for measuring the performance of your investment portfolio and your investment manager.

investment policy should establish appropriate benchmarks that relate to your particular asset mix, such as market indices, to judge the performance of your investment portfolio and your investment manager. See 1.4 for general advice on choosing your professional advisers.

*Don't try to outsmart the market*—Focus your attention on getting the asset allocation right and then, within each asset class, try to keep your costs at a minimum. Make sure you are well diversified. Be consistent in your investment style and stick to your plan. Don't think that what happened in the past will happen in the future. In the financial market, history rarely repeats.

## 1.2 Some common financial goals

### 1.2.1 Planning for your children's education

Although post-secondary education may not be the route your children choose, having a college diploma or university degree can greatly expand their range of occupational choices and will probably enhance their future earning power. But with government support falling and tuition fees rising over the last decade, putting a child through college or university is becoming costlier. If your child decides to move away from home to study or attend an institution outside Canada, the cost would increase significantly. Most of us would be hard-pressed to finance these costs out of current income, so planning is crucial.

Like any financial planning endeavour, decisions about funding your child's education should be made with an eye toward the effects of taxation. Below are a few common options for reducing your family's overall tax burden so that more funds will be available to finance your child's education.

> Contribute up to $2,500 annually to an RESP and earn a 20% government grant.

Registered Education Savings Plans (RESPs) can be effective education savings vehicles, especially due to the availability of Canada Education Savings Grants (CESGs). Under this program, the government will provide a grant of 20% on the first $2,500 of annual contributions made in a year to an RESP. As such, the grant may be worth up to $500 each year for each beneficiary, giving you an easy extra 20% return on your first $2,500 of contributions each year per beneficiary. For low- and middle-income families, the CESG grant may be even higher. The maximum lifetime grant is $7,200 per beneficiary. The RESP rules are discussed at greater length in Chapter 4.

As an alternative or in addition to an RESP, you could invest in tax-efficient growth mutual funds in your child's name. Any income from these funds is normally taxed under the preferential rules for capital gains (see Chapter 6) or dividends (see Chapter 7). Any capital gains distributed by the fund or realized on the sale of the fund will be taxable in your child's hands at your child's lower tax rate (or not taxed at all if his or her income is low enough).

Until your child turns 18, the dividends and interest will be taxed in your hands due to the attribution rules discussed in 5.2.3; however, assuming you have selected a tax-efficient mutual fund, this will usually amount to a small proportion of the fund's overall return. Choosing a non-registered mutual fund provides some investment control and flexibility—there are no restrictions on the use of the funds and there is no limit on the amount that can be deposited.

If your child has a disability, you may be allowed to establish a Registered Disability Savings Plan to provide for his or her future financial needs, including education (see 4.6).

If you receive the new Canada Child Benefit (see 2.3.2) for 2017, consider depositing the payments to an account in your child's name. As with RESP funds, these deposits may add up to a significant investment over time and, since the anti-income splitting rules discussed in Chapter 5 don't apply, any investment income will be taxed in your child's hands, if at all. You may wish to withdraw the balance from the account annually and purchase higher-yielding investments on your child's behalf (see 5.3.12).

Another strategy to consider if interest rates are rising is to split income by entering a family loan with your child via a family trust (see 5.3.4 and 21.5.4).

## 1.2.2 Encouraging your child to invest

If you have a child who works part-time (e.g., summer employment) with an income below the federal basic personal credit amount ($11,635 for 2017—see 2.2) and the Canada Employment Credit amount ($1,178 for 2017) that can be earned tax-free, consider filing a personal income tax return for him or her. By reporting this earned income, your child will build up RRSP contribution room that may be useful in a later year when he or she becomes taxable (see 3.1.3). This can be especially helpful when your child is in the teenage years and can expect to earn much more income in the future, since any unused RRSP deduction room is carried forward indefinitely. If your child has cash available (and your financial institution agrees to set up a plan), he or she may contribute now to start enjoying tax-free investment growth but delay claiming the related tax deduction until a later year when your child has enough income to be taxable. Alternatively, if your child is over 17 and has a social insurance number, he or she could consider putting savings into a TFSA (see 4.1).

Instead of giving your child money that is easily spent, consider having him or her start an RRSP. The amount you can contribute may seem minimal—only 18% of the child's earned income from a summer or part-time job, plus the $2,000 lifetime overcontribution if the child turned 18 in the prior year (see 3.3.4). But the funds in the RRSP will enjoy tax-free compounding, which will accumulate significantly over time. For example, assuming a

6% cumulative rate of return, $1,000 a year invested in an RRSP each year beginning at age 16 will grow to $13,972 by the beginning of the year in which the child turns 26; at age 30, the RRSP will grow to $24,673, and if the annual contribution is made until the child retires at 65, the RRSP will be about $273,000.

To top up your child's earnings and help finance his or her education or other pursuits, consider lending your child, interest-free, an amount equal to what he or she earns over the year and would otherwise spend. Your child can use the loaned funds to pay for expenses such as tuition fees and invest his or her own income to earn investment income. That way, the anti-income splitting rules discussed in Chapter 5 will not attribute the investment income back to you and it will be taxed at your child's lower tax rate (or not taxed at all if his or her income is low enough). Later on, perhaps after graduating, your child can pay you back out of the invested funds, or keep the funds as "seed money" for his or her early working years. (This strategy is discussed in more detail in 5.3.11.)

| Encourage your children to invest the money they earn. | Chapter 5 discusses options for splitting income with children. These strategies can significantly lower your family's overall tax burden and help your child become financially independent. |

### 1.2.3 Buying a home

If you are renting your home, instead of buying, you may be missing out on a potential investment opportunity. A home can be a reliable hedge against inflation, a great retirement savings vehicle and a tax shelter—as we'll see in 6.5.2. If you own a home and sell it for a gain, the gain is usually tax-free as long as it has been your principal residence for income tax purposes.

So if you can afford to buy a home, don't rent. If you are renting while you are saving for a home, consider moving to less expensive rental accommodations and saving more toward your down payment. The sooner you start putting your money toward a mortgage instead of your landlord's pocket, the better off you will be. Below are a few tax planning and other issues for prospective home buyers to consider.

| Think about using RRSP funds for a down payment on your first home under the Home Buyers' Plan. | If you are buying your first home, you may qualify for a 15% tax credit on up to $5,000 of your costs (see 2.7.4). |
| | If you qualify, the Home Buyers' Plan can be a possible source of cash for financing your down payment. If you are saving to buy your first home, think about using your |

RRSP as your savings vehicle; if you qualify under the Home Buyers' Plan discussed at 3.3.6, you can generally withdraw up to $25,000 as a loan from your RRSP to buy or build a home, without counting the withdrawal as income for tax purposes. You must then repay the loan, without interest, over 15 years starting in the second year following the year of withdrawal.

If you do plan to withdraw RRSP funds under the Home Buyers' Plan, consider making your RRSP contribution for the year at least 90 days before you make the withdrawal to preserve your ability to deduct the contribution amount. If you are depending on your RRSP for retirement income, you should forecast the decline in income that would result from the loss of the tax-free compounding when you withdraw a large chunk of RRSP funds now and pay it back over 15 years. See 3.3.6 for a more detailed discussion of the Home Buyers' Plan.

Once you have a mortgage, consider accelerating your mortgage payment schedule to reduce the amount of interest you'll pay over the life of your mortgage.

Accelerating your payment schedule doesn't necessarily mean that you will be shelling out any more cash than you do now. Here's the trick: figure out how much you can or want to pay each month and multiply that amount by 12. This is your annual payment. Then divide this number by 52 to determine the amount to pay weekly. Over the course of a year, your total mortgage payments will be identical, but more frequent payments will reduce your principal more quickly and reduce your overall interest cost.

Another way to save on mortgage interest is to maintain your original payment level when your mortgage comes up for renewal, even if interest rates have fallen. Also, each time you renew, consider increasing your payment by whatever you can commit—even an extra $50 or $100 will save you money in the long run.

> Increase the frequency of your mortgage payments to reduce your mortgage interest.

### 1.2.4 Vacation properties

Buying a cottage, ski chalet or condo can provide years of enjoyment for your family. For a variety of reasons, a recreation property can also be a sound investment. You will probably save on your family's vacation costs. You may even find it easy to make up some of the property's costs by renting it out when your family is not using it. Market demand for desirable vacation properties (especially waterfront properties) within a reasonable drive from Canadian urban centres will probably remain steady, and, if historical trends continue, the value of your vacation home could rise significantly during the time you own it.

Whether you plan to keep the property in the family or sell it for future gain, bear in mind that capital gains tax (see 6.2.1) may apply on the difference between the property's cost when you bought it, plus capital improvements made, and its fair market value when you sell it or at the time of your death (or your spouse's death). The longer you own your cottage, the bigger the gain is likely to be.

To avoid leaving your survivors with a tax bill, which they may have to fund by selling the property, consider purchasing enough life insurance to fund the taxes that will arise on your death. You may be able to shelter some of the gain on the property's sale or on your death (or your spouse's) through the principal residence exemption (see 6.5.2). You may be able to protect future gains from tax by transferring the property to one of your children or to a family trust (see 5.3.7). Consider also our more general discussion of estate planning in Chapter 21.

Plan to minimize capital gains tax on dispositions of vacation homes.

If your vacation property is situated in the U.S. and you are a Canadian resident, the double hit of U.S. estate tax and Canadian income tax arising on death can carry a potentially high tax burden. The Canada-U.S. tax treaty may ease the potential for double taxation, but, as discussed at 19.4, some rather complex tax planning may be required and you should seek professional tax advice.

Whether your vacation property is in Canada or the U.S., it's important to keep track of the property's adjusted cost base and capital improvements for tax purposes (see 6.2.1).

## 1.3    Preserving your family's financial security

The achievement of your financial goals can be delayed or derailed by unexpected changes of circumstance. Your family's financial plan should include measures to address risk and protect your family's financial security.

### 1.3.1    Do you have a line of credit and/or an emergency fund?

Set up an emergency fund or line of credit.

In today's business environment, you cannot count on having a job for life. In addition to cash flow, job loss can affect your company-funded benefits and pension plan. Generally speaking, you should have an emergency fund large enough to handle the loss of a job for six months to one year. Canada Savings Bonds, money market or T-bill funds and cashable guaranteed investment certificates are good places to park emergency reserves.

Another way to provide an emergency fund is to establish a line of credit with your financial institution. Be careful to only use it when necessary, because the interest you'll incur will be non-deductible and you will have to repay it according to the line of credit's terms.

### 1.3.2    Do you have enough insurance?

Review your insurance needs with your financial advisers to determine the appropriate amount and form of your insurance coverage in various areas, including property loss, death, disability, sickness, personal liability and liquidity crisis.

A review should consider your need for life insurance. In the event of your death, life insurance may be critical for providing replacement income for your dependants and for funding your estate's tax and other liabilities. Life insurance plays many other important roles in estate planning. Some tax planning and other issues involving life insurance are discussed in 21.7.

> Make sure you have adequate insurance and a current will.

One of your most valuable assets is your ability to earn income through employment or self-employment. Review your need for disability or critical illness insurance—if you become disabled, the financial consequences can be devastating. Most disability insurance policies do not provide a level of income over and above what you need for basic ongoing living expenses. In the long term, this could leave you without enough funds set aside for your retirement since disability income usually stops at age 65.

Make sure you have sufficient insurance to protect you from significant financial loss due to damage or destruction to your home, automobile or other personal assets. Without adequate coverage, the emotional trauma of such losses could be compounded by irreversible damage to your family's finances. Depending on your occupation or circumstances, you should also assess your need for other forms of insurance such as health and professional or director's liability coverage.

### 1.3.3 Is your will up-to-date?

Have you and your family members reviewed your wills within the past two years, or has there been a change in your family circumstances? Are your wills effectively tax-structured? Remember that if you die intestate (without a will) your assets will be distributed according to provincial law, possibly differently from what you would have wished. Be sure to seek advice of a lawyer (or a notary in Quebec) to ensure your will is legally valid and accurately reflects your wishes. You should also consult a tax adviser for assistance in reducing your estate's tax liability, including probate fees and U.S. estate tax.

For a more detailed discussion of the role of your will in planning for the orderly distribution of your estate and the minimization of taxes on death, see 21.2.

### 1.3.4 Do you have a power of attorney?

A power of attorney allows you to designate a person who will take control of your financial affairs if you become incapacitated due to illness or injury. If this happens and you do not have a power of attorney, control will yield to a provincial public trustee, which may restrict your family's ability to access your financial resources.

Powers of attorney are usually limited to decisions regarding your property and finances. In some provinces (including Ontario and Quebec), you can empower a different person to make decisions about your health care and medical treatment.

*Consider a power of attorney.*

Like your will, your power of attorney should be prepared with professional advice—consider having both drawn up at the same time.

Note that a power of attorney operates only while you are alive. Once you die your will takes over, and your executor will manage your estate's affairs.

In some cases, a trust can be an effective alternative to a power of attorney (see 21.5.4).

## 1.4    Selecting your professional advisers

Financial planning is broad in scope, and you may need advice from professionals with expertise in different areas. For some financial decisions, it will be worth the expense to invest in professional advice, whether from a lawyer, tax adviser, insurance broker, investment counsellor or a personal financial adviser. And in some financial planning endeavours, such as estate planning, professional legal and tax advice is a must.

*Shop around when choosing your financial and investment advisers.*

Given what's at stake—your family's finances—you should take the time to shop around for advisers who are knowledgeable and experienced in their fields and with whom you feel comfortable. When interviewing prospective advisers of any profession, be sure to cover the following topics:

- Ask for client references, preferably from three or four people in circumstances similar to your own.
- Inquire into the professional's educational background, qualifications and level of experience.
- Ask whether the adviser belongs to any professional networks and associations to determine what sorts of resources are available to him or her.
- Make sure that you understand the fee arrangement and how the adviser is compensated.
- Be cautious of advisers whose objective may be to sell you investments, tax shelters, insurance or anything other than independent advice.

The level of your need for advisers depends primarily on the complexity of your affairs and your own knowledge of financial matters. You will get better value for the fees you pay to your advisers if you spend some time up front educating yourself. After all, it's your money and you must ultimately take responsibility for its handling and performance.

If you have a spouse, be sure that he or she is acquainted with your advisers, since your spouse will need to deal with them in the event of your death or disability. It is also a good idea to keep an up-to-date list of your advisers' names and phone numbers in one place, perhaps in the same place as your will and list of assets.

# Chapter 2

## Tips for claiming tax deductions and credits

- If you're unmarried and support a family member, don't miss out on the eligible dependant credit (2.2.1)
- Working parents and students—claim your child care expenses (2.3.1)
- Claim the tax credit for adoption expenses if you adopt a child in Canada or from another country (2.3.3)
- Take advantage of the tax credit for interest paid on student loans (2.4.6)
- If you're separating, co-operate to minimize your joint tax bill (2.6)
- Combine your family's medical expenses on one return (2.7.1)
- Choose your own 12-month period for medical expense claims (2.7.1)
- Plan for the timing of your family's medical expense payments (2.7.1)
- Take advantage of Canada's tax break for political contributions (2.7.2)
- Claim the tax credit for public transit passes used before July 1, 2017 (2.7.3)
- If you are buying your first home, claim the tax credit on up to $5,000 of the purchase price (2.7.4)

*In this chapter, we describe how your tax bill is calculated and highlight some commonly available and sometimes overlooked deductions and credits that can be claimed on your income tax return, depending on your family status and personal circumstances.*

## 2.1 Taxes, credits and deductions

### 2.1.1 Calculating your tax balance due or refund owing

To understand how deductions and credits work, you need to understand the basic tax calculation. We describe it briefly here. (For Quebec residents, the provincial tax calculation is completely separate and not as described below. See Chapter 17.)

You start by adding up your various kinds of income—employment, business, interest, grossed-up dividends, taxable capital gains, and so on. This gives you **total income**. From this figure you subtract certain deductions, some of which we'll look at in this chapter—to reach **net income**, a figure used for certain purposes later. Then some additional deductions are allowed, primarily losses carried forward from previous years, giving you **taxable income**.

You then calculate your **federal tax**, applying the federal **tax rates** and **brackets** to your taxable income using the formula shown on Schedule 1 of your tax return. Then you subtract various **non-refundable tax credits** (see 2.1.2), and certain others such as the dividend tax credit (see 7.1.1). This gives you **net federal tax**.

Your next step is to add your **provincial tax**. You compute your provincial tax in essentially the same way as your federal tax, using taxable income calculated for federal tax purposes but applying your province's tax brackets, rates and credits to your taxable income. Depending on the province, you may also have to add a provincial surtax and/or health care levy. Federal and provincial tax rates and brackets for 2017 are set out in Appendix II. Federal and provincial non-refundable tax credits for 2017 are set out in Appendix III.

If you are self-employed, you may also be required to add your Canada Pension Plan (CPP) contribution on your self-employment income at this point.

Finally, you record all source deductions of tax (withheld by your employer, for example) and instalments paid, both of which are credited to your account. Along with these are the **refundable credits**—including the employee or partner GST/HST rebate (see 2.9.4)—which are given the same treatment so that they can effectively be refunded to you even if you pay no tax for the year. (Some provinces also provide refundable tax credits.) The bottom line is your **balance owing** or **refund claimed**, and that will be the amount you remit by April 30 or receive when your return is assessed.

## 2.1.2 Deductions versus credits—what's the difference?

Before we get into the specific deductions and credits available, you need to understand the different effects of a deduction and a credit. You can refer back to the discussion in 2.1.1 as we go through this.

A **deduction** (or "write-off") reduces your taxable income, on which your federal tax is calculated. Bearing in mind that provincial tax rates and brackets vary, the combined effect of the federal and provincial taxes and provincial surtaxes means that, as long as you are still paying some tax, a deduction is worth about 25% where your taxable income is under $46,000; about 34% where it is from $46,000 to $92,000; about 42% where it is from $92,000 to $142,000; about 46% where it is from $142,000 to $203,000; and about 50% where it is over $203,000.

In other words, a $100 write-off (of, say, deductible moving or child care expenses) is worth about $25 to $50 in tax savings, depending on your tax bracket.

A **credit**, on the other hand, is a direct reduction in tax; $100 of a credit such as the credit for political contributions (see 2.7.2) is worth exactly $100 to you.

There is a twist, however. Under the federal-provincial tax collection agreement, provinces can top up the federal amounts or add their own credits if they wish, but at minimum they must offer the same basic credits as those available federally. As a result, the credits will be worth more, once you factor in the equivalent provincial credit. For example, for 2017, the maximum value of the basic personal credit (see 2.2) is $1,745 for federal purposes, but, if you live in Ontario, the value of the credit to you is actually $2,259 once the federal and provincial basic personal credit values are combined.

Finally, note the distinction between refundable and non-refundable credits. Because they are treated as having been paid by you, just like source withholdings and instalments, refundable credits are always worth what they say they are. Non-refundable credits, like deductions, become worthless once you reach the point of paying no tax at all for the year.

### 2.1.3 Transferring credits between spouses

Some of the non-refundable credits outlined below, such as charitable donations (see 8.1), can be transferred between spouses if not otherwise usable (see Schedule 2 of your tax return).

Where you have a choice as to which spouse will claim certain credits, credits are worth slightly more to very high-income individuals in some provinces. That is because some provinces impose additional surtaxes on individuals with high basic provincial tax. For example, in Ontario in 2017, the provincial surtax is effectively an extra 20% of Ontario tax over $4,556 plus an extra 36% of Ontario tax over $5,831.

If you are paying a surtax and your spouse is not, it is better for you to claim most of the credits that can be allocated between the two of you.

## 2.2 Personal, spousal and dependant credits

Every individual gets a basic federal credit, which allows you to receive a basic amount of income tax-free. In 2017, the basic federal credit is $1,745, which offsets the federal tax on your first $11,635 of income. (On your income tax return, you claim a "basic personal amount" of $11,635, which you later multiply by 15%.)

### 2.2.1 Spousal/partner and eligible dependant credits

If you are married, you can claim a further federal credit of up to $1,745 for 2017 if your spouse's net income is under the credit amount of $11,635.

If you are single, widowed, divorced or separated, and you support another family member (such as a parent or child) in your home, you can claim the eligible dependant credit for that person. This will allow you the same claim as if that person were your spouse.

A caregiver credit is available if you provide care for an infirm relative age 18 or over or if the person for whom you are claiming the spousal/partner and eligible dependant credit is infirm (see. 2.5.4).

If you're unmarried and support a family member, don't miss out on the eligible dependant credit.

Common-law spouses, including unmarried same-sex couples, who meet certain criteria (below) are treated identically to legally married couples for all purposes relating to income tax. This means that the spousal credit can be claimed for a dependent common-law opposite-sex or same-sex spouse. It also means that a taxpayer who has a common-law spouse cannot claim the wholly dependent person credit for a child.

Common-law spouses are treated as spouses if they are two people who "cohabit in a conjugal relationship", where either they have had a child together, or they have cohabited for at least 12 continuous months at the time the determination is made. Separation is considered to terminate this "cohabiting" if the couple separates for at least 90 days because of a breakdown in their relationship.

## 2.3 Children

### 2.3.1 Child care expenses

A special set of tax rules allows you to deduct child care expenses, within limits, if they have been incurred to allow you or your spouse to work, carry on business, attend school or carry on grant-funded research.

Working parents and students—claim your child care expenses.

You can claim child care expenses for your child or your spouse's child. You can also claim them for a child who was dependent on you or your spouse and whose net income in 2017 is less than $11,635. The child must be under 16 at some time in the year, unless he or she is mentally or physically infirm.

Eligible child care expenses include babysitting, day nursery services, day camps, boarding schools and overnight camps. The deduction is based on when the services are provided rather than when the amounts are paid, so prepaying in December does not give you the deduction a year earlier.

For two-parent families, child care expenses usually must be deducted by the spouse with the lower income. (The assumption is that the lower-income spouse would otherwise stay home with the children.) Single parents can deduct child care expenses from their own income. Common-law and same-sex couples who meet certain criteria are treated the same as spouses for purposes of calculating child care expenses (as well as for all other tax purposes—see 2.2.1).

The amount of child care expenses you can claim is subject to various limits, depending on the age of the child and whether the child has a disability. In addition to the limit for each child, your expenses are subject to an overall limit of two-thirds of the "earned income" (basically salary and wages) of the lower-income spouse or single parent.

The various limits on child care expense deductions are as follows:

| | Annual Limit Per Child |
|---|---|
| Child under age seven | $8,000 |
| Child age seven to 16 | $5,000 |
| Child over age 16 and infirm but not eligible for disability tax credit (see 2.5.1) | $5,000 |
| Child any age eligible for disability tax credit | $11,000 |
| Additional limitation | 2/3 of lower-income spouse's "earned income" |

Example

Mary and Adam are married and have two children under age seven. Mary earns $120,000 and Adam earns $28,000. They pay $12,000 in 2017 to a nanny to take care of their children while they are working.

Adam must be the one to claim the expenses, since he is the lower-income spouse. His deduction is the least of: (a) the amount paid—$12,000; (b) $8,000 per child—$16,000; and (c) two-thirds of his earned income—$18,667. He can therefore claim $12,000 as a deduction against his $28,000 of employment income. This will reduce his tax bill by about $3,000.

If Mary were a single parent, she could claim the same amount as a deduction against her own income of $120,000 and reduce her tax bill by about $5,040.

Different limits apply where one or both parents are attending school full-time or part-time (see 2.4.7).

Payments to a boarding school or overnight camp are subject to limits for each week that the child attends the school or camp. The weekly limit is $200 per child under age seven, $125 per child aged seven to 16 or over age

16 and infirm but not eligible for the disability tax credit, and $275 per child eligible for the disability tax credit (see 2.5.1).

There are special circumstances where the lower-income spouse is not expected to care for the children. These are: where the spouse is disabled, in prison or hospital, or confined to bed or a wheelchair, for at least two weeks; attending full-time high school or post-secondary school; or where the spouses have separated for at least 90 days. In such cases, the higher-income spouse can claim the deduction up to the above weekly limits for each week that the condition continues.

The tax treatment of child care expenses for Quebec purposes is discussed at 17.3.2.

### 2.3.2 Canada Child Benefit

The Canada Child Benefit provides non-taxable monthly payments to eligible families. This benefit replaced the Universal Child Care Benefit and the Canada Child Tax Benefit as of July 2017. The Canada Child Benefit provides a maximum annual benefit of up to $6,400 per child under the age of 6 and up to $5,400 per child for those aged 6 through 17.

To qualify for the benefit, you must be a resident of Canada, you must live with your child and be the parent who primarily cares for your child, or have shared custody of the child.

Entitlement to the Canada Child Benefit for the July 2017 to June 2018 benefit year is based on adjusted family net income for the 2016 taxation year. Benefit payments are recalculated each July based on information from your income tax return from the previous year.

If your family has less than $30,000 in net income, you will receive the maximum benefit. If your adjusted family net income is between $30,000 and $65,000, the benefit will begin to be phased out at a rate of 7% for a one-child family, 13.5% for a two-child family, 19% for a three-child family and 23% for larger families.

If your adjusted family net income exceeds $65,000, benefits will be further reduced and will be phased out at rates of 3.2% for a one-child family, 5.7% for a two-child family, 8% for a three-child family and 9.5% for larger families, on the portion of income above $65,000.

**Example**

Mary and Adam from our example in 2.3.1 have a family income of $148,000 for 2016. One of their children is two years old and the other is four. Their Canada Child Benefit amount for the July 2017 to June 2018 benefit year will be calculated as follows.

The maximum benefit amount for two children under age six is $12,800. The benefit will be reduced by 13.5% of Mary and Adam's income between $30,000 and $65,000, which equals $4,725. The benefit will be further reduced by 5.7% of their income between $65,000 and $148,000, which equals $4,731, for a total reduction of $9,456. As such, their annual benefit will amount to $3,344 ($12,800 – $9,456 reduction). Their monthly payments will be about $279.

If you have a child who is eligible for the disability tax credit (see 2.5.1), your Canada Child Benefit payments may include an additional amount of up to $2,730 per year. The phase-out of this amount generally aligns with the phase-out of Canada Child Benefit payments.

Amounts received under the Canada Child Benefit are not taxable and do not reduce benefits paid under the Goods and Services Tax credit (see 2.9.3). These amounts are also not included in income for the purposes of federal income-tested programs delivered outside of the income tax system, such as the Canada Education Savings Grant (see 4.4) and the Canada Disability Savings Grant (see 4.6).

### 2.3.3 Adoption expense tax credit

If you adopt a child under 18, a 15% non-refundable credit is available. For 2017, the maximum eligible expenses claimable are $15,670 per adoption. Eligible expenses include fees paid to licensed adoption agencies, court

> Claim the tax credit for adoption expenses if you adopt a child in Canada or from another country.

and legal expenses, reasonable travel and living expenses for the child and adoptive parents, translation fees and mandatory fees paid to a foreign institution. You can only claim the credit for the year in which the adoption is finalized, but at that time you can claim your adoption-related expenses incurred in previous years.

Quebec provides a refundable credit for adoption expenses (see 17.3.4).

## 2.4 Students

### 2.4.1 Tuition fees tax credit

Tuition fees qualify for a non-refundable 15% federal credit for 2017 if you pay them for yourself. You may be able to claim certain tuition fees paid for your child or another person under the transfer rules discussed below.

To be eligible for a credit, the fees must be paid to a Canadian university, college or other post-secondary educational institution, or to an institution certified by Human Resources and Skills Development Canada. Occupational skills courses that are not at the post-secondary level may also be eligible for the credit, as well as fees paid to institutions in other countries. Generally, any fees you claim must total more than $100 per institution.

Along with admission fees, eligible tuition fees include library and lab charges, examination fees, application fees, mandatory computer service fees, charges for certificates, diplomas and degrees, and the cost of books included in the fees for a correspondence course. Also eligible are mandatory ancillary fees for health services, athletics and various other services (but not student association fees or fees covering goods of value that you retain such as a computer or a cooking student's utensils).

Fees paid to an educational institution, professional association, provincial ministry or similar institution for an examination required to obtain professional status recognized by federal or provincial statute, or to be licensed to practise a profession or trade in Canada, are eligible for this credit.

Fees paid to private schools for grade-school or high-school education will not entitle you to a federal tax credit. However, religious private schools may be able to provide a tax receipt for some of your tuition fees, treating that amount as a charitable donation (see 8.1) made toward the school's religious instruction.

### 2.4.2 Education amount

Before 2017, as a separate credit from the tuition fees, you were entitled to a further non-refundable federal education tax credit of $400 (worth $60) for each month you were in full-time attendance at a post-secondary educational institution.

For part-time post-secondary students, the education tax credit was $120 (worth $18) per month if you met certain conditions. If you have unused education credit amounts carried forward from years before 2017, they remain available to be claimed in 2017 and later years.

### 2.4.3 Textbook tax credit

Before 2017, post-secondary students eligible to claim the education amount (see 2.4.2) could also claim a non-refundable textbook tax credit to help cover the costs of their textbooks. The amount you could claim for the credit was based on:

- $65 for each month you qualified for the full-time education tax credit amount (worth about $10 per month)

- $20 for each month you qualified for the part-time education tax credit amount (worth about $3 per month).

The textbook tax credit was eliminated effective January 1, 2017. If you have unused textbook tax credit amounts carried forward from years before 2017, they remain available to be claimed in 2017 and later years.

### 2.4.4 Transfer of unused student credits

If you are not able to use your tuition, education and textbook credits in 2017 (because you have no tax to pay), up to $5,000 (worth up to $750) in combined federal credits may normally be transferred to your spouse or to a parent or grandparent. Alternatively, you can carry forward any unused and untransferred tuition, education and textbook amounts and claim them against your taxable income in any later year. Note, however, that such amounts carried forward cannot be transferred—only the student can claim them in a later year.

### 2.4.5 Tax exemption for scholarships and bursaries

Scholarship, fellowship or bursary income is tax-free if the income is connected to a qualifying educational program that you were enrolled in as a full-time student in the immediately preceding or current taxation year, or if the income is connected to a specified education program (with not less than 12 hours in the month spent on courses in the program). Scholarships and bursaries provided to attend elementary and secondary schools are also tax-exempt. Amounts received for post-secondary programs up to and including doctoral degrees are exempt but post-doctoral fellowships do not qualify.

Such income is only exempt to the extent the award was intended to support your enrolment in the program.

If you receive a scholarship, fellowship or bursary in connection with a part-time program, the exemption is limited to the cost of tuition and course materials (unless you qualify for the disability tax credit or cannot attend full-time due to a mental or physical impairment).

### 2.4.6 Tax credit for interest on student loans

Students and former students can claim a 15% non-refundable federal tax credit in 2017 on their interest paid on student loans under the *Canada Student Loans Act*, the *Canada Student Financial Assistance Act*, the *Apprentice Loans Act* or equivalent provincial programs. The credit is available for interest paid in the year or any of the five preceding years. Although the credit is not transferable, it can be carried forward for up to five years.

> Take advantage of the tax credit for interest paid on student loans.

### 2.4.7 Other tax breaks for students

Single parents who are students and two-parent families where both parents attend school full-time may be able to deduct additional child care expenses, above the usual limits for child care expense deductions described in 2.3.1. For single students or two-parent student families, child care expense claims above the general limits are limited to two-thirds of your actual net income (instead of earned income). For each week that the single parent or both parents attend school full-time, the weekly limit is $200 per child under age seven, $125 per child aged seven to 16 or over 16 and infirm but not eligible for the disability tax credit, and $275 per child eligible for the disability tax credit.

For part-time students, the child care expense deduction is subject to these limits for each month (rather than week) for which the part-time education credentials are met.

For students claiming the child care expense deduction, "full-time" attendance at school means that you must attend a designated educational institution or a secondary school and be enrolled in a program of the institution or school that is at least three consecutive weeks long and requires you to spend at least 10 hours per week on course work. You are attending school "part-time" if the program lasts at least three consecutive weeks and involves at least 12 hours per month on course work.

In certain cases, students may also be able to deduct their moving expenses (see 13.1.2).

Students can also withdraw funds from their RRSPs (within limits) to help finance their education (see 3.3.7).

If you are a student who lives in Quebec, see 17.4.1.

## 2.5 People with disabilities

### 2.5.1 Disability tax credit

If you suffer from a severe and prolonged impairment in physical or mental functions, you can get an additional non-refundable federal tax credit of $8,113 (worth $1,217) for 2017. Depending on the nature of the impairment, your status must be certified by a medical doctor, nurse practitioner, optometrist, audiologist, speech-language pathologist, occupational therapist, psychologist or physiotherapist.

To qualify as having a severe and prolonged impairment, your ability to perform a "basic activity of daily living" must be "markedly restricted", and the impairment must have lasted or be expected to last for at least a year. People who must undergo therapy (e.g., dialysis) at least three times a week for an average of 14 or more hours of therapy in order to sustain their vital functions are also eligible for the credit.

The *Income Tax Act* has specific definitions to determine whether you qualify. The rules can be found on the Canada Revenue Agency's (CRA) Disability Tax Credit Certificate, Form T2201. If you have a disability and reside in Quebec, see also 17.9.

It is often difficult to determine whether a person qualifies or not, and the Tax Court of Canada has issued a slew of decisions interpreting these rules. In some cases, the court has found the CRA's view to be incorrect. Therefore, if you believe you fit within the *Income Tax Act*'s definition of disabled, you should consider pursuing your claim if it is denied.

You may also be able to claim a portion of your medical expenses for the medical expense credit (see 2.7.1).

If you have a dependent relative who qualifies for the disability tax credit but does not earn enough income to be able to use all of it, the dependant's unused credit can be transferred to your return. For this purpose, eligible dependants include your spouse, child, grandchild, parent, grandparent, sibling, aunt, uncle, niece or nephew.

If you support a dependent child age 18 or over who has a disability, you can also claim the Canada caregiver credit (see 2.5.4).

Additional assistance is available for children under 18 at the end of the year with severe disabilities in the form of a supplementary credit of $4,732 (worth up to $710) for 2017. The supplement amount is reduced by certain amounts claimed such as child care expenses (see 2.3.1), the disability supports deduction (see 2.5.2) and the medical expense tax credit (see 2.7.1).

### 2.5.2 Disability supports deduction

If you have a disability, you can deduct some or all of the costs of disability supports needed to allow you to earn employment or business income, carry on grant-funded research, or pursue your education, unless the costs have been reimbursed by a non-taxable payment (such as an insurance payment).

The disability supports deduction is limited to your "earned income" (which includes salary and business income), plus, if you attend school, the lesser of the difference between your net income and your earned income and $375 per week of school attendance (to a maximum of $15,000).

Eligible disability supports expenses include, among other things, amounts paid for sign-language interpretation services, job coaching services, real-time captioning services, teletypewriters that allow deaf or mute people to use telephones, and speech synthesizers, equipment and software that allows blind people to use computers or read print, note-taking services, tutoring services, talking textbooks and attendant care services provided in Canada.

Most of these expenses are eligible for the deduction, but only if a medical practitioner certifies the need for the items or services.

As an alternative, disability supports expenses can generally be claimed for purposes of the medical expense credit (see 2.7.1), whether or not you are earning income or attending school. In some cases, it may be more beneficial to claim these costs as medical expenses on your own or your spouse's tax return. To determine which option generates greater tax savings, calculate and compare the net tax results of claiming these costs through the disability supports deduction versus the medical expense credit.

### 2.5.3 RRSP withdrawals under the Home Buyers' Plan

Under the Home Buyers' Plan (see 3.3.6), you can withdraw up to $25,000 as a loan from your RRSP to buy or build a home and not pay tax on the amount as long as you repay it over 15 years beginning in the second year following the year of withdrawal. Since the Plan was originally intended to help first-time home buyers, you are generally ineligible if you or your spouse owned a home that you lived in as your principal place of residence in any of the five calendar years up to and including the current calendar year.

However, the five-year qualifying period under the Home Buyers' Plan does not apply to persons with disabilities and their relatives if the new home is more accessible to or better suited to the personal needs and care of a person with a disability who will reside there.

See 3.3.6 for a more detailed discussion of the pros and cons of participating in the Home Buyers' Plan.

### 2.5.4 Canada caregiver credit

If your spouse or common-law partner, minor child or eligible relative is dependent on you because of a mental or physical infirmity at any time in the year, you can claim the Canada caregiver non-refundable federal credit. You can also claim it if you provide care for infirm dependants of your spouse or common-law partner.

The dependant does not have to live with you for you to claim the credit. However, the federal credit is no longer available for non-infirm parents over 65 years of age who live with you.

The Canada caregiver credit is based on two maximum amounts: a high maximum amount and a low maximum amount. For eligible infirm dependants, the high maximum amount is $6,883 in 2017 (worth up to $1,032, unless the second amount applies).

The second, low maximum amount of $2,150 factors into the credit calculations for:

- an infirm dependent spouse or common-law partner for whom you claim the spouse or common-law partner amount (see 2.2.1)
- an infirm dependant for whom you claim the eligible dependant credit (see 2.2.1)
- an infirm child who is under the age of 18 years at the end of the tax year (see 2.5.1).

The maximum amount on which the credit is available is $4,732, or $6,883 if the dependant is infirm. This credit amount is reduced dollar-for-dollar by the dependant's net income above $16,163 and is completely phased out at an income of $20,895, or at $23,046 for infirm dependants.

If claiming the second, lower amount produces less tax relief than you would receive by claiming the higher maximum (i.e., $6,883 for 2017), you receive a top-up to offset the difference. No top-up is allowed for amounts claimed for an eligible dependant who is age 18 or younger at the end of the year.

Example

Line cares for her infirm spouse, Max, who has no income in 2017. Line's caregiver and spousal credits are calculated as follows:

Line's maximum regular spousal amount is $11,635, plus the low maximum $2,150 caregiver amount, for a total spousal amount of $13,785 (A). Because Max has no income in 2017, Line is entitled to the full high maximum caregiver amount of $6,883 (B). Because Line's spousal amount (A), exceeds her high caregiver amount (B), she receives no caregiver top-up or caregiver credit, but she is entitled to a spousal credit of $2,068 (15% of A).

As the table below shows, if Max earns $13,000, Line's 2017 spousal credit is $915 (15% of A) and her caregiver credit is $118 (15% of C), for combined credits of $1,033. As the table also shows, if Max earns $18,000, Line cannot claim a spousal credit (because her spousal amount (A) is nil), but she is entitled to a Canada caregiver credit of $757.

| Line's spouse income | $13,000 | $18,000 |
|---|---|---|
| **Spousal amount** | | |
| Base amount + low maximum ($11,635 + 2,150) | 13,785 | 13,785 |
| Less spouse's income | (13,000) | (18,000) |
| Amount (A) | 785 | — |
| **Canada caregiver amount** | | |
| Base amount + high maximum ($16,163 + 6,883) | 23,046 | 23,046 |
| Less spouse's income | (13,000) | (18,000) |
| | 10,046 | 5,056 |
| | claim max. of 6,883 | |
| Amount (B) (max. $6,883) | | |
| **Canada caregiver top-up amount** | | |
| Amount B | 6,883 | 5,056 |
| Less amount A | (785) | (0.00) |
| Amount (C) | 6,098 | 5,056 |
| **Canada caregiver credit** | | |
| 15% of Amount (C) | 915 | 757 |
| **Spousal credit** | | |
| 15% of Amount (A) | $118 | $0.00 |

### 2.5.5 Home accessibility tax credit

If you are 65 or older or you are eligible for the Disability Tax Credit and you renovate your home to make it safer, more accessible or more functional for you, you may be able to claim a non-refundable tax credit for up to $10,000 of eligible expenses per year (worth up to $1,500). Eligible expenses include wheelchair ramps, walk-in bathtubs and grab bars, among others.

## 2.6 Marital breakdown—Child and spousal support payments

*If you're separating, co-operate to minimize your joint tax bill.*

While marriage breakdown is often an occasion for bitter disputes, you and your spouse (through your lawyers, if necessary) should co-operate to minimize your joint tax bill and share the resulting savings.

Child support is not taxed as income to the recipient or deducted from income by the paying parent.

Spousal support payments are deductible to the payer and taxable to the recipient if they meet some well-defined and strict criteria.

To be deductible, the spousal support payment must be an *allowance*, which has been established in advance as a recurring payment. The amounts payable must be predetermined. (Amounts that are required to be adjusted for inflation can still be considered predetermined.)

Additionally, the allowance must be:

- paid under a written agreement or under a decree, order or judgment of a competent tribunal
- payable on a periodic basis for the maintenance of the recipient (your spouse or ex-spouse)
- paid at a time when you are living apart from your spouse or ex-spouse because of the breakdown of your marriage.

Payments to former common-law spouses may be deducted on the same basis, where the recipient is an individual who cohabited with you "in a conjugal relationship" or you are the natural parent of that person's child.

Note that the "periodic basis" requirement excludes one-time payments and transfers of property in settlement of rights of the marriage.

Payments made directly to third parties, rather than to your spouse or ex-spouse, are allowed in limited circumstances. Such payments can include medical bills, tuition fees and mortgage payments for your spouse or ex-spouse's home. Among other requirements, the court order or written separation agreement must specifically provide for the payments and must specifically provide that the relevant tax rules will apply, to make the payments deductible to you and taxable to your spouse or ex-spouse.

In general, you may deduct payments made before obtaining a court order or signing a written separation agreement, provided the order or agreement is signed by the end of the year following the year in which the payment is made, and the order or agreement specifically provides that the amounts paid earlier are to be considered as paid and received pursuant to the agreement.

If you are the support payer, you cannot deduct legal costs to establish, negotiate or contest the amount of support payments. However, if you are the recipient, you can deduct legal costs to obtain an order for child support, establish the amount for spousal support, enforce existing rights or have the support amounts increased.

Spousal or child support paid to a non-resident of Canada is deductible if the above criteria are met.

If you receive a lump-sum spousal support payment over $3,000 relating to prior years, you may ask the CRA to determine whether it is more advantageous to you to recalculate the tax on that income as if you received it in those prior years. This measure is intended to relieve the higher tax liability that may result if the entire lump-sum is taxed in the year of receipt, rather than year by year as the right to receive the payments arose.

Child support paid under arrangements reached before May 1997 is treated the same way as spousal support payments.

## 2.7 Other commonly available credits

### 2.7.1 Medical expenses

Medical expenses over a certain threshold entitle you to a non-refundable tax credit. The threshold is 3% of your net income, or, if your net income exceeds $75,600 in 2017, a flat $2,268. All qualifying medical expenses above this amount give rise to a 15% federal credit (if you live in Quebec, see also 17.8).

> **Example**
>
> Alison's net income is $50,000. She spends $2,500 on qualifying medical expenses in 2017. Given that 3% of Alison's net income is $1,500, the remaining $1,000 qualifies for the medical expense credit. The federal credit is 15% of that, or $150.

Medical expense claims made on behalf of dependent minor children are pooled with those of you and your spouse for purposes of the medical expense threshold of 3% of your net income and $2,268, whichever is less.

For amounts paid on behalf of any other close relative dependent on you for support, you can claim medical expenses that exceed the lesser of 3% of the dependant's net income for the year and $2,268. The list of qualifying medical expenses is very long, and you should refer to the CRA's Income Tax Folio S1-F1-C1 "Medical Expense Tax Credit" (see 2.10) if you need specific details. The list includes:

- payments to medical practitioners, dentists and registered nurses, hospital fees not covered by public health insurance and diagnostic procedures
- prescription drugs
- institutional care (e.g., nursing home)
- the care and supervision of persons with severe and prolonged disabilities living in a group home
- guide dogs (both purchase cost and upkeep cost)
- eyeglasses, hearing aids and dentures
- costs of moving to accessible housing, home renovations and driveway alterations required for someone with a mobility impairment
- sign language interpreter fees
- medical intervention to help conceive a child
- cost of disability supports not claimed for purposes of the disability supports deduction (see 2.5.2)

- a long list of specific devices, ranging from crutches to insulin needles, wheelchair lifts, speech synthesizers, visual fire alarm indicators and TDD devices for the deaf.

Expenses for purely cosmetic medical procedures that are aimed solely at improving your appearance, such as liposuction, hair replacement and teeth whitening, are not eligible for the medical expense credit.

Since self-employed individuals are allowed to deduct premiums to a drug or dental plan (see 11.2.11), these premiums are not eligible for the medical expense credit for those individuals.

Because of the threshold of 3% of net income, you should combine all of the family's medical expenses on one return. It is normally better for the lower-income spouse to make the claim, provided that spouse has enough tax to pay to use up the credit, since the 3% threshold will be smaller. On the other hand, the credit might be slightly more valuable to a high-income spouse because it will reduce the application of high-income provincial surtaxes levied in some provinces (see 2.1.3).

> Combine your family's medical expenses on one return.

When claiming medical expenses, you can pick any 12-month period ending in the year. If, for example, you made no claim for 2016, and you have large medical expense bills in February 2016, January 2017, and November 2017, you might be better off to use January 2016 as the end of your 12-month period, claim the February 2016 and January 2017 expenses for 2017, and leave the November 2017 expenses to be claimed on your 2018 return.

> Choose your own 12-month period for medical expense claims.

You can also plan for the timing of medical expenses, since they are based on when they are paid. If you are using a December end for the 12-month period, and you have pending expenses (perhaps for medical equipment purchases or large dental bills) that are due early in the new year, consider prepaying them so that you can claim them one year earlier.

> Plan for the timing of your family's medical expense payments.

## 2.7.2 Political contributions

If you are interested in the greatest bang for your buck, consider a contribution to your favourite federal political party or election candidate. Contributions to federal political parties and to candidates in federal election campaigns entitle you to a non-refundable federal tax credit. A donation of $400 will cost you only $100.

To encourage small political donations by many people, the federal credit is most generous at the lowest levels. The credit is 75% for the first $400

> Take advantage of Canada's tax break for political contributions.

of donation (worth $300); 50% for the next $350 (worth $175); and 33.33% for the next $525 (worth $175). There is no additional credit for donations beyond $1,275. As such, the maximum credit allowed is $650.

> **Example**
>
> Jacquelin contributes $500 to a federal political party in 2017. Jacquelin's political contribution credit for 2017 will be 75% on the first $400 ($300) plus 50% on the next $100 ($50), for a total of $350. There is no reduction in provincial tax resulting from this credit.

In addition, many of the provinces have their own credits for contributions to provincial parties and candidates. The Quebec credit for political donations is discussed at 17.7.2.

### 2.7.3 Public transit passes

*Claim the tax credit for public transit passes used before July 1, 2017.*

You or your spouse or common-law partner can claim a non-refundable tax credit for public transit passes. The credit has been cancelled, so your last chance to claim it is for passes that were used before July 1, 2017.

To qualify, the pass must be of at least monthly duration purchased for you, your spouse or common-law partner and any of your children under age 19. You can also claim the credit for weekly public transit passes, if you have purchased at least four consecutive passes that each grant you unlimited transit use for at least five consecutive days. Eligible transit includes local and commuter buses, streetcars, subways, commuter trains and local ferries.

The cost of electronic payment cards is also eligible, provided you use the card to take at least 32 one-way trips on public transit during a period of up to 31 consecutive days.

If you are entitled to claim this credit, be sure to keep your receipts or the transit passes themselves on file. For electronic payment cards, the receipt must set out the transit usage and cost of the trips in enough detail for the CRA to verify your claim.

### 2.7.4 First-time home buyers

If you are acquiring your first home, you may qualify for a non-refundable tax credit for first-time home buyers on up to $5,000 of the home's cost (worth up to $750).

*If you are buying your first home, claim the tax credit on up to $5,000 of the purchase price.*

The credit can be claimed by you or your spouse or common-law partner. To qualify, neither of you can have owned another home or lived in another home owned by your spouse or common-law partner in the year of purchase or in any of the four preceding years. A qualifying home is one that is currently eligible for the Home Buyers' Plan (see 3.3.6) that you or your spouse or common-law partner intend to occupy as your principal place of residence within one year of acquiring it.

You can also claim the credit for certain home purchases by or for the benefit of a disabled family member who is eligible for the disability tax credit (see 2.5.1).

### 2.7.5 Other credits

There are a number of other non-refundable credits with a provincial equivalent available when computing "basic federal tax" (and also reducing provincial taxes and surtaxes, as discussed in 2.1.2). These include the credit for donations to registered charities (see 8.1), the pension income credit (see 20.3.5), age credits (see 20.3.4), the dividend tax credit (see 7.1.2), and the credit for work-related expenses of employees (see 10.7.1).

Other federal-only credits include the investment tax credit, which is an incentive for those carrying on business to invest in particular regions or sectors of the economy (see 11.2.14) and the foreign tax credit (also available in Quebec), which offsets the impact of foreign tax paid on one's income from a foreign source, to reduce double taxation (see 18.2.2).

## 2.8 Other commonly available deductions

### 2.8.1 Legal fees

Whether you can deduct legal fees you have paid depends on why you paid them.

Legal fees are generally deductible if they are paid for the purpose of earning income from business or property. Legal fees to acquire or preserve a capital asset are normally not deductible, though there are exceptions.

Legal fees associated with an objection or appeal of your income tax assessment (see 9.5) are deductible. This includes the costs of negotiations with CRA officials prior to filing a formal Notice of Objection. The fees are also deductible if you are appealing a Quebec income tax assessment or an income tax assessment of a foreign government, or an Employment Insurance or Canada/Quebec Pension Plan decision.

Legal fees to collect unpaid salary or wages owed to you by your employer or former employer are deductible.

Legal fees generally can be deducted where they are incurred to obtain a "retiring allowance" (including severance pay) or a pension benefit (see 10.8.5), but generally only up to a limit of your income from those sources (in the current year or past years).

Finally, you may deduct legal costs to establish or enforce a right to child support. (See 2.6; see also 17.13.1 if you live in Quebec.)

### 2.8.2   Northern residents

If you live in northern Canada for not less than six consecutive months beginning or ending in a year, a special deduction is available to help offset the higher costs of living and the hardship and isolation relative to the more populated parts of the country. The deduction is limited to the lesser of 20% of your net income and, if you live in the "prescribed northern zone", up to $22 per day ($8,030 per year). If you live somewhat further south, in the "prescribed intermediate zone", you can only claim half as much. As well, if your employer pays the cost of travel for you and your family (e.g., an annual trip to southern Canada), a deduction is available to offset part or all of the taxable benefit that is thereby included in your income (see 10.8.9). A similar deduction is available for Quebec tax purposes if you live in northern Quebec.

### 2.8.3   Other deductions

Some other common deductions are covered in other chapters. See, for example, 3.1.3 (contributions to RRSPs), 6.2.3 (allowable business investment losses), 6.4 (capital gains deduction), 7.2.3 (interest paid), 10.8 (deductions available to employees) and 13.1 (moving expenses). Some of the deductions relating to self-employment (carrying on business) are discussed in Chapter 11.

## 2.9   Canada/Quebec Pension Plan Contributions, Employment Insurance and GST

### 2.9.1   CPP/QPP contributions and EI premiums

A federal credit of 15% of all Canada (or Quebec) Pension Plan (CPP/QPP) contributions and Employment Insurance (EI) premiums is available, effectively giving you back about 25% of these amounts when the equivalent provincial credit is factored in. If you are employed, these amounts are normally taken off your pay at source by your employer.

If you are self-employed, you will normally have to calculate and remit both the employer and employee portions of CPP/QPP (but not EI) contributions on your net self-employment income. Self-employed individuals may deduct the employer's portion (see 11.2.3).

### 2.9.2   EI clawback

If you receive Employment Insurance benefits and your net income exceeds a certain threshold, a portion of your benefits received during the year will be taxed back through a special tax, commonly called a "clawback", paid through your income tax return.

The clawback applies if your net income for 2017 exceeds $64,125. You must repay $30 for each $100 of net income over your threshold, up to a maximum of 100% of the benefits received. Benefits that are not clawed back are taxed as regular income.

The clawback does not apply if you are receiving EI benefits for the first time in the last 10 years or if you are receiving only maternity, parental, sickness or compassionate care benefits.

### 2.9.3 GST/HST credit

The Goods and Services Tax/Harmonized Sales Tax (GST/HST) credit is aimed at low-income individuals and families. It is designed to offset the GST/HST paid by consumers on most goods and services. For 2017, the annual credit is $280 per eligible adult and $147 per child under 19 in the family, reduced by 5 cents for each dollar that family net income exceeds $36,429. The credit is tax-free and is generally paid in quarterly instalments to qualifying families, based on their previous year's income. If your GST credit is less than $100, you should receive it in one lump-sum payment in July.

An extra GST credit supplement of up to $147 is available if you are single, separated, widowed or divorced and have no children. The GST credit supplement is the lesser of $147 or 2% of net income over $9,073. The total of the GST credit and the supplement are reduced by 5 cents for each dollar of income over $36,429.

Many provinces also have sales tax credits for low-income taxpayers. For the Quebec credit, which parallels the GST credit, see 17.13.4.

### 2.9.4 GST/HST rebate

In addition to the GST/HST credit described in 2.9.3, certain employees and members of partnerships can claim a GST/HST rebate on their income tax returns. The rebate is generally available to employees who claim income tax deductions relating to their employment expenses, and partners who claim deductions on expenses they incur outside the partnership to earn partnership income. (See 10.9, 11.3.7 and 12.3.2 for more details.)

## 2.10 References

The following publications and more information, including forms and brochures, can be obtained on the CRA's website at *www.cra-arc.gc.ca* or by telephone request at 1-800-959-8281 for individual income tax and trust-related enquiries or 1-800-959-5525 for business and self-employed individual enquiries.

> Booklet T4114, "Canada Child Benefit"
> Income Tax Folio S1-F1-C1, "Medical Expense Tax Credit"
> Income Tax Folio S1-F1-C2, "Disability Tax Credit"
> Income Tax Folio S1-F1-C3, "Disability Supports Deduction"

Income Tax Folio S1-F2-C1, "Education and Textbook Tax Credits"

Income Tax Folio S1-F2-C2, "Tuition Tax Credit"

Income Tax Folio S1-F2-C3, "Scholarships, Research Grants and Other Education Assistance"

Income Tax Folio S1-F3-C1, "Child Care Expense Deduction"

Income Tax Folio S1-F3-C3, "Support Payments"

Interpretation Bulletin IT-91R4, Archived – "Employment at special work sites or remote work locations"

Interpretation Bulletin IT-99R5 Consolidated, Archived – "Legal and accounting fees"

Interpretation Bulletin IT-513R, Archived – "Personal tax credits"

Interpretation Bulletin IT-523, Archived – "Order of provisions applicable in computing an individual's taxable income and tax payable"

Information Circular 75-2R9, "Contributions to a registered party, a registered association or to a candidate at a federal election"

Pamphlet P102, "Support Payments"

Pamphlet P105, "Students and Income Tax"

# Chapter 3

## RRSPs and other tax-assisted retirement plans

- Consider a self-directed Registered Retirement Savings Plan (RRSP) for greater flexibility (3.1.6)
- Think about transferring shares that you already own to your self-directed RRSP (3.1.6)
- Think about using your RRSP to shelter future gains on high-growth private company shares (3.1.6)
- Think about boosting your self-directed RRSP's foreign content (3.1.7)
- Contribute as much as you can to an RRSP (3.1.9)
- Contribute early in the year instead of the following February (3.1.9)
- Think twice before borrowing funds to contribute to your RRSP (3.1.9)
- Withdraw funds from your RRSP in low-income years (3.2.1)
- Contribute to your spouse's (or common-law spouse's) RRSP if your spouse's projected income on retirement will be lower (3.3.1)
- Make spousal RRSP contributions in December instead of the following February (3.3.1)
- Transfer pension commuted value, retiring allowances or severance pay to your RRSP (3.3.2)
- Top up your RRSP with a non-deductible $2,000 overcontribution (3.3.4)
- Consider shares of a labour-sponsored venture capital corporation for your RRSP (3.3.5)
- Consider Home Buyers' Plan withdrawals to buy or build your first home (but be sure to weigh the loss of RRSP growth) (3.3.6)
- Consider withdrawing RRSP funds under the Lifelong Learning Plan to help pay for training or post-secondary education programs (3.3.7)
- Consider contributing to your RRSP instead of a money-purchase RPP (3.5.1)
- Find out about the vesting of your pension benefits, especially before making a career change (3.5.1)
- Weigh the advantages of establishing an "individual pension plan" (3.5.2)

*Deferred income plans, particularly RRSPs and registered pension plans, are the most widely used tax shelters in Canada. Put simply, almost everyone should have one.*

*The concept of deferred income plans is simple, although the particular rules can be complex. In this chapter, we'll take you through the basic rules, so you understand the system in general. We also discuss the options you have and steps you can take for tax planning.*

*The rules are essentially the same for Quebec tax purposes.*

# 3.1 Registered Retirement Savings Plans—RRSPs

### 3.1.1 What is an RRSP?

Although RRSP stands for "registered retirement savings plan", these plans do not necessarily have anything to do with retirement. They can be used for a variety of purposes, such as financing your first home or training or post-secondary education, or simply as a tool for tax deferral.

The concept behind an RRSP is simple. If you agree to put some of your salary or self-employment income away and not have immediate access to it, the tax system will tax that income—along with all the interest and other income it earns—when it is *received* rather than when it is *earned*.

> If you earn $60,000, you pay tax on $60,000.
>
> Suppose you earn $60,000 but you put $2,000 of that into an RRSP. You will be taxed on only $58,000—the amount you have *received*.
>
> If, some years later, the $2,000 you put away has grown (in a tax-free environment) to $3,000, you can take the $3,000 out of your RRSP, and it will be taxed (added to your income) at that point.
>
> Again, the original $2,000, now grown to $3,000, is being taxed in the year it is *received* rather than when it was *earned*.

The rules governing RRSPs are more complex than the above example indicates, of course. The amount you can contribute to an RRSP is limited in various ways.

### 3.1.2 How do you set up an RRSP?

An RRSP can be set up easily at almost any bank or trust company or through an investment adviser, life insurance agent, mutual fund company or mutual fund distributor. Basically, you just fill out a form and contribute money to the plan. Some institutions will give you your official tax receipt immediately; others will mail it to you later, in time for you to file it with your tax return.

### 3.1.3 How much can you contribute?

Contributions to an RRSP are deductible for any given year if they are contributed in *the year* or *within 60 days after the end of the year*. So if you contribute by March 1, 2018, you can get a deduction for your 2017 tax return (and any resulting refund will come sometime in the spring of 2018 after you have filed your 2017 return).

Three factors limit the amount you can contribute to an RRSP: a dollar limit; a percentage of the previous year's "earned income"; and your "pension adjustment". We'll look at each of these in turn.

*Dollar limit*

The RRSP contribution limit rose to $26,010 in 2017 (from $25,370). For 2018 the limit will be $26,230.

*Percentage of previous year's earned income*

The annual deduction (subject to the $26,010 limit and pension adjustment) is limited to 18% of the *previous* year's earned income. That is, 18% of your 2016 earned income is used to determine your 2017 contribution (made by March 1, 2018).

"Earned income" for most employees is the same as "salary"—the gross amount of salary, before deductions for income tax, EI, CPP, etc., which are withheld at source. "Earned income" includes net business income, if you are self-employed or are an active partner in a business (see 16.2.4). It also includes:

- research grants, net of deductible related expenses
- royalties from works or inventions that you wrote or invented
- taxable spousal and child support received (see 2.6)
- net rental income from real estate
- disability pension income received under the CPP/QPP.

Earned income is *reduced* by:

- deductible alimony, maintenance and child support you pay
- most deductible employment-related expenses, such as union dues and travelling expenses (but not pension plan contributions)
- net business losses
- rental losses from real estate.

Earned income does not include most investment income, such as interest or dividends, or capital gains. Nor does it include pension benefits, retiring allowances, severance pay, death benefits or amounts received from an RRSP, RRIF or deferred profit-sharing plan.

If your 2016 earned income was more than $144,500, your 2017 contribution is limited to $26,010 (minus the pension adjustment as discussed below). Otherwise, you are limited by the 18% factor.

### Pension adjustment

Once you have calculated your maximum contribution limit as 18% of your previous year's earned income, subject to the dollar limits discussed above, you must subtract your pension adjustment for the previous year, if any. This figure represents the deemed value of your pension earned for the previous year. In other words, the more that has been put aside (by you and your employer combined) towards your retirement pension, the less you can contribute to an RRSP.

If you are *not* a member of an employer's pension plan or deferred profit-sharing plan, your pension adjustment is zero, and you can contribute the full 18% of your previous year's earned income (subject to the annual $26,010 limit).

Otherwise, your pension adjustment for 2016 should have appeared on your 2016 T4 slip, as well as on your Notice of Assessment received in 2017 following the filing of your 2016 return.

For "money-purchase" pension plans (see 3.5.1), the pension adjustment is the total contributions made to your pension by you and your employer combined. The same applies to deferred profit-sharing plans (see 3.6), except that the contributions are made only by your employer. For "defined benefit" pension plans, the pension adjustment is based on a calculation that takes into account the benefit you may receive on retirement based on your past year's employment.

> **Example**
>
> Melanie is a chemical engineer who belongs to her employer's pension plan. Her 2016 earned income was $60,000. Her pension adjustment for 2016, as reported to her on her 2016 T4 slip and her 2016 assessment received from the CRA in mid-2017, is $3,200.
>
> Before accounting for her pension adjustment, Melanie's contribution limit for 2017 is 18% of her 2016 earned income, to a maximum of $26,010. For 2016, 18% of her earned income is $10,800. From this amount she must deduct her pension adjustment for 2016 of $3,200. Melanie may therefore contribute up to $7,600 to an RRSP by March 1, 2018 for a deduction on her 2017 tax return.

In some situations, the calculation of your RRSP limit may also be reduced by a past service pension adjustment (PSPA). In general terms, a PSPA can arise when your pension benefits under a defined benefit pension plan are improved on a retroactive basis.

If you terminate your employment before retirement, you may be entitled to a pension adjustment reversal (PAR). The PAR is designed to give you back some of the RRSP contribution room lost due to pension adjustments (PA) while you were a member of a company pension plan.

If you were a member of a defined contribution plan or deferred profit-sharing plan, your PAR will be the total of all PAs reported by your employer since 1990 that have not yet "vested" (see 3.5.1). If you were a member of a defined benefit plan and you have not reported any PSPAs, your PAR will be equal to your total PAs since 1990 less the post-1989 portion of any lump sums paid to you or transferred to an RRSP or money-purchase pension plan (if you have reported any PSPAs, your PAR calculation will be more complex but, whatever your plan, your employer's pension plan administrator will figure it out for you). You will not be entitled to a PAR if you maintain any entitlement to periodic pension payments from the plan. The PAR is only available to you if you transfer the commuted value of your defined benefit plan to a locked-in RRSP, also known as a locked-in retirement account.

PARs increase RRSP room for the year of termination. If you have ended or will be ending company pension plan membership in 2017, you may want to encourage your employer to report your PAR shortly after your termination so you can make use of the related extra RRSP room as soon as possible. Your employer must report your PAR for your year of termination within 60 days of the end of the quarter in which termination occurred (or by January 31 of the following year if termination occurs in the fourth quarter).

### Carry forward of unused deduction room and undeducted contributions

If you contribute less than the maximum to an RRSP in any year, you can "carry forward" the extra deduction room and contribute that much more in any following year. You can also carry forward unused RRSP room created by a PAR. If you contribute an amount for a year but choose not to deduct the amount for that year, you can claim the deduction in any later year (provided you still have contribution room).

Example

Melanie, from the previous example, has $7,600 of contribution room for 2017. She chooses to contribute only $5,000 to an RRSP for the year.

Melanie has unused RRSP contribution room of $2,600 to carry forward. As a result, she may increase her contribution by that amount in any following year. If Melanie's contribution limit for 2018 is again $7,600, she can contribute up to $10,200 for deduction in 2018.

You should carefully review your assessment notice from the CRA to make sure the contribution limit reported is correct, before relying on it.

An incorrect statement from the CRA does not entitle you to deduct a contribution you would not otherwise be entitled to.

In some cases you might contribute more than you can actually deduct. We discuss overcontributions in 3.3.4.

### 3.1.4   What's your contribution worth?

What is your contribution worth in tax savings? It depends on your marginal tax rate. Tax rates and brackets vary among the provinces (see Appendix II), but for 2017 they are approximately:

- 25% on income from $12,000 to $46,000
- 34% on income from $46,000 to $92,000
- 42% on income from $92,000 to $142,000
- 46% on income from $142,000 to $203,000
- 50% on income over $203,000.

In the example above, if Melanie's taxable income (after other deductions) is between $46,000 and $92,000, her contribution of $5,000 to an RRSP would save her about 34% of that amount, or $1,700, in tax for 2017. For someone whose taxable income stays over $203,000 even after making the RRSP contribution, the same $5,000 contribution would be worth about $2,500. Clearly, RRSPs are more tax-effective for those with higher incomes.

You should keep the value of your deduction in mind and try to take maximum advantage of the carryforward mechanism in claiming your RRSP deductions. In a low-income year, for example, it may be advantageous to make your maximum RRSP *contribution*, but to defer claiming the *deduction* until a later year when your income is taxed at a higher marginal rate.

### 3.1.5   What happens to the funds in the RRSP?

While your funds are in the RRSP, they are not subject to tax at all. No matter what amounts of interest, dividends, capital gains—or losses—result, there will be no tax effect until you withdraw the funds. (As we shall see in 20.4, you must close out the RRSP by the end of the year in which you turn 71, but even then, the tax effects can be partially deferred.)

The effects of having income compound without tax are quite dramatic. Compare the following two situations: Scenario 1, where you invest $5,000 of your salary in an RRSP for 10 or 20 years at 6%, and Scenario 2, where you earn the same 6% but it is subject to tax. (The example assumes a 50% marginal tax rate.)

| | Amount invested *2017* | After 10 years *2027* | After 20 years *2037* |
|---|---|---|---|
| *Scenario 1:* | | | |
| Invest $5,000 before tax in an RRSP | $5,000 | $8,954 | $16,036 |
| Tax on withdrawal | | (4,566) | (8,178) |
| After-tax amount following withdrawal (A) | | 4,388 | 7,858 |
| *Scenario 2:* | | | |
| Invest $5,000 less current tax of $2,500 outside an RRSP (B) | 2,500 | 3,360* | 4,515* |
| **Additional after-tax return from investing in RRSP (A − B)** | | $1,028 | $3,343 |

\* Net of annual tax on investment income earned.

In Scenario 1, you pay 50% in tax when you withdraw the funds, but they have grown substantially in the meantime. After 20 years, your $5,000 is worth $8,018 *after* tax. In Scenario 2, since the annual 6% interest is taxed, you have only 3% to reinvest for compounding purposes. The fact that you can use the $4,515 (after 20 years) directly in Scenario 2, without having to pay 50% tax on it as in Scenario 1, doesn't come close to making up for the tax-free compounding of interest.

Of course, if you are paying non-deductible interest such as mortgage interest, that interest also effectively compounds on a pre-tax basis, and you might be better off to pay down your mortgage rather than contribute to an RRSP. In such a case, you can generally use all your unused RRSP contribution room by making and deducting a "catch-up" RRSP contribution in a later year, when you have the funds to contribute.

As we mentioned earlier, your RRSP can be invested in many different forms. The simplest, and usually lowest-paying, is a deposit account that pays interest monthly or twice a year. Many people invest instead in longer-term Guaranteed Investment Certificates (GICs) and term deposits. Equity mutual funds are popular as a method of indirectly investing RRSP funds in a range of different equity investments, but they can entail a higher level of risk. See 1.1.4 for tips on choosing investments and advice on developing an appropriate investment strategy.

### 3.1.6   Self-directed RRSPs

If you're a do-it-yourselfer who would like a wider range of investment choices and you're willing to take a little more risk with your funds, you can set up a self-directed RRSP and gain hands-on control over the investment of funds in your RRSP. This

Consider a self-directed RRSP for greater flexibility.

is normally done through a financial consultant with a brokerage firm or financial services institution, and is typically subject to an annual fee in the $100 to $150 range (plus normal commissions on any stock trades or mutual funds, where applicable). Some financial institutions offer a low- or no-fee self-directed plan—it pays to shop around to find the plan that's right for you.

With a self-directed plan, you decide what to invest in within your RRSP. There are restrictions—the system tries to ensure that your money, while not necessarily "safe", is at least invested in reasonable places. "Qualified investments" for an RRSP include:

- cash
- government, Crown corporation or municipal bonds
- GICs, term deposits and treasury bills (T-bills)
- certain government-insured mortgages
- shares or bonds of corporations listed on Canadian stock exchanges
- RRSP-eligible mutual funds and segregated funds
- shares listed on certain foreign stock exchanges, bonds of certain foreign governments and mutual funds and segregated funds invested in foreign markets (see 3.1.7)
- certain small business shares
- gold and silver bullion (under certain conditions)
- a debt obligation that has an investment grade rating and is part of a minimum $25 million issuance
- any security (other than a futures contract) that is listed on a designated stock exchange.

The rules governing the details (e.g., which mortgages and small business shares are qualified investments) are extremely complex, and you should consult a professional adviser if you wish to do more with your self-directed RRSP than simply buy, say, government-backed T-bills and government bonds (which are generally regarded as good, safe investments). If you have the time to give it the attention it needs, a self-directed RRSP can prove to be much more rewarding in the long run. The control you will gain over investment decisions can diversify your risk and give you the flexibility to pursue a different range of investment opportunities—including some that are generally only possible through self-directed RRSPs, like strip bonds, mortgage-backed securities, index funds and other less common RRSP investments. If you only plan to invest in mutual funds and GICs, a self-directed RRSP may not be required; in this case, you may be better off using a regular plan to save on annual administration fees.

The broader range of investment options you may acquire with a self-directed RRSP comes with a higher level of risk. The financial markets are volatile, but they tend not to move in step with each other, so you may be able to minimize the level of overall risk in your portfolio through diversification—holding a mix of different types of investments (i.e., cash, fixed income and equities) and ensuring that at least a portion of them have fixed rates of return, such as GICs or strip bonds.

Your investment mix or asset allocation should also be a function of your age, family situation and risk tolerance. When determining your investment mix and allocating your assets, be sure to consider your total portfolio, and not just those investments inside your RRSP. See 1.1.4 for details on developing an appropriate investment strategy.

Consider contributing shares (or interest-bearing investments) that you already own to your self-directed RRSP in lieu of cash contributions. Shares in small businesses can be contributed in limited circumstances (for example, you, your spouse and other related persons, either individually or collectively, cannot own 10% or more of the corporation's shares). Also, most shares of Canadian public corporations are fair game, as long as you don't own 10% or more of the company's shares. If you have shares that you intend to hold for a long time, you can contribute them to your RRSP and get a tax deduction without any cash outlay.

> Think about transferring shares that you already own to your self-directed RRSP.

A transfer of investments to your RRSP can trigger a capital gain (see 6.2.1), since the transfer is deemed to take place at fair market value. However, you are prohibited from claiming a capital loss (see 6.2.2) on the transfer of investments to your RRSP. Professional advice should be obtained before entering this type of transaction.

If you have shares that have declined in value, you cannot transfer the shares to your RRSP to trigger a capital loss to use to offset any capital gains you may have realized—the tax law won't let you claim a capital loss on the transfer of investments to your RRSP.

However, you can sell the shares on the open market, contribute the proceeds in cash to your RRSP and, after 30 days, have your RRSP acquire a similar position. This strategy will permit you to trigger the capital loss on the shares, which you can apply against other taxable capital gains, while effectively transferring ownership of the shares to your RRSP so that any future growth will be tax-sheltered.

Previously, you could swap investments owned outside your RRSP with assets inside your plan. Under the RRSP anti-avoidance rules (see 3.4), these swaps are no longer allowed, except in limited circumstances.

Note that capital gains and dividends are effectively fully taxed when withdrawn from an RRSP, since you're taxed on the total amount withdrawn. So if you contribute shares (or buy shares inside your RRSP), any capital gains and dividends will eventually be taxed at a higher rate than if you earned them directly (see 6.2.1 and 7.1.2). However, if you leave the funds in the RRSP for long enough, the deferral of tax and tax-free compounding of interest should more than make up for the tax rate differential. Nonetheless, consider holding fixed income investments inside your RRSP and equities outside your RRSP as part of your overall asset mix.

When considering investments within your RRSP, bear in mind the one major drawback of long-term investments such as five-year GICs. If you decide to withdraw the funds sooner for tax purposes (see 3.3.4), or to use the Home Buyers' Plan (see 3.3.6) or Lifelong Learning Plan (see 3.3.7), you may find that you cannot get access to your investment due to GIC restrictions.

**Think about using your RRSP to shelter future gains on high-growth private company shares.** If you are a shareholder of a start-up company or a company that has high growth potential, you may want to consider owning part or all of the shares through your RRSP or transferring such shares to your RRSP early in the company's life cycle when the shares have relatively low value. Future gains on the shares will then be sheltered from tax inside the RRSP and you will be able to diversify your investment base by having your RRSP sell the shares and acquire a broader range of investments. (Bear in mind our comments above on capital gains and dividends. Also, note that the shares will not qualify as an RRSP investment if you own more than 10% of the company.)

It is even possible for you to arrange for your RRSP to hold your own mortgage—in other words, you put funds into your RRSP, receive a tax deduction, and lend the funds to yourself. This is not easy to do, however; the mortgage must be federally insured, and various other restrictions apply.

Investing in your own mortgage may make you feel good, but does not always make sense financially. Since the investment must be at the market rate, you may be no better off depending on the size of the mortgage, once all fees (legal, insurance, appraisal, etc.) are taken into account. As a rule of thumb, to be a worthwhile investment, the mortgage's principal should be in the $50,000 to $100,000 range with a term of at least five years. Alternatively if you don't have that much cash in your RRSP, some financial institutions offer a program through which the mortgage is "shared" between your RRSP and your institution. You should also consider whether holding a mortgage in your RRSP is consistent with your overall investment strategy.

### 3.1.7 Self-directed RRSP investments in foreign properties

**Think about boosting your self-directed RRSP's foreign content.** There is no limit to the amount of property held by your RRSP that is invested in foreign property, allowing you more scope to diversify your self-directed RRSP's holdings in foreign content, such as shares listed on certain foreign stock exchanges, certain foreign government bonds and other foreign properties.

Don't let periodic downturns in foreign markets scare you away from increasing your RRSP's foreign holdings. As long as you plan to invest for the long term, your RRSP's foreign content will increase the diversity of your investment mix and thus reduce your overall investment risk. See 1.1.4 for details on the importance of diversifying your investments geographically as part of your overall investment strategy.

### 3.1.8   RRSP fees

Administration, trustee and investment management and counselling fees related to your RRSP are not deductible. However, you can use funds already deposited in your RRSP without having to pay tax on the amount as you would if you withdrew the money for another purpose. Alternatively, you can pay these fees from funds outside your RRSP and the amount will not count as part of your contribution for the year.

If you have not used all of your available contribution room and you do not foresee doing so in the future, consider contributing the amount of the fees and paying them with funds inside the plan so you get a regular RRSP deduction for that amount. On the other hand, if you have or will be maximizing your RRSP contributions, you are better off paying the fees with other funds so you do not erode the amount of RRSP funds available to grow tax-free.

### 3.1.9   How to make the most of your RRSP

If you have cash in the bank earning interest, even if you are young and not yet concerned about retirement, you should contribute as much as possible to an RRSP. The example we saw in 3.1.5 above shows how valuable it is to have your funds earning tax-free income.

> Contribute as much as you can to an RRSP.

If possible, you should contribute early, rather than waiting until the deadline. Your 2017 contribution, for example, may be made any time before March 1, 2018 if you intend to deduct it on your 2017 tax return. If you contribute at the beginning of 2017, all of the income earned for that extra year will accumulate tax-free. The effect of early contributions over several years will be dramatic. Do ensure, however, that you have enough contribution room before you commit your contribution for the year, and remember that each year's contribution will be limited to 18% of your previous year's earned income (less your pension adjustment).

> Contribute early in the year instead of the following February.

You can store up any unused RRSP contribution room if you can't afford to make a contribution now, and make your contribution and claim the deduction in later years.

Think twice before borrowing funds to contribute to your RRSP.

If you're behind on your RRSP contributions, you might be thinking about taking out an RRSP loan. Generally, this strategy only makes sense if you can repay the borrowed funds within about a year, or if your income for the current year falls into a higher tax bracket than usual. Otherwise, the non-deductible interest that you will pay on the loan may negate the tax benefits of your contribution. Instead, consider making regular catch-up payments later when you have the funds to contribute.

If you have the cash and the contribution room, but do not want to claim a deduction in the current year because you are already in a low tax bracket, make the contribution but delay the deduction. As discussed in 3.1.3, you can claim the deduction in any later year. If you are confident of being in a higher tax bracket within the next year or so, this strategy can maximize the tax-free growth of funds while also maximizing your tax savings.

For cash-flow purposes, you may wish to set up a monthly transfer of a few hundred dollars from your regular bank account to your RRSP account. That will ensure steady contributions to the RRSP over the course of the year.

## 3.2     How do you get money out of an RRSP?

At any time, you may withdraw cash from your RRSP. The amount will be included in your income for that year and taxed as ordinary income, just as if it were salary, even if some of the value of the RRSP represents capital gains (which outside an RRSP are normally only partially taxed and, in some cases, could be entirely exempt).

A percentage to cover tax will be withheld at source by the financial institution and remitted to the CRA (and Revenu Québec if appropriate) on your behalf. For federal purposes, a withdrawal of up to $5,000 is subject to 10% withholding; over $5,000 and up to $15,000, 20%; and over $15,000, 30%. In Quebec, a single RRSP withdrawal is subject to one-half of the federal withholding plus a 16% Quebec withholding, regardless of the amount of withdrawal. You will then report the income and amount of tax withheld on your annual income tax return and either receive a refund or, if not enough tax was withheld, pay the difference. Keep in mind that an administration fee may also apply to the withdrawal.

The government allows you to make tax-free RRSP withdrawals (within limits) if you use the funds for certain purposes, such as buying a new home (see 3.3.6) or financing training or post-secondary education for you or your spouse (see 3.3.7). Generally, you must repay the amount withdrawn under these plans over a certain amount of time or it will become taxable.

You must wind up your RRSP by the end of the year in which you turn 71. At any time before then, you can transfer your RRSP funds tax-free to an annuity, a registered retirement income fund or a life income fund (for locked-in retirement accounts only). Your various options for maturing your RRSP are discussed in 20.4.

### 3.2.1 Early withdrawals—your RRSP as a tax averaging tool

As discussed in 3.1.5, the funds in your RRSP are not taxed until the year in which you withdraw the funds. As a result, RRSPs can be used as a tax averaging tool rather than just a mechanism for retirement saving. If you are still fairly young and not too worried about retirement income, you can withdraw funds from your RRSP whenever there is a tax advantage to doing so.

Suppose you plan to take some time off to care for your young children, for example, or to go on an extended vacation or take up some other activity. During such years, where your

*Withdraw funds from your RRSP in low-income years.*

employment income will be low, you can withdraw funds from your RRSP and perhaps pay tax at the low tax rate of about 25% (depending on your province) instead of the middle or high rates. The advantage of low-rate taxation will have to be balanced against the advantage of tax-free growth available by leaving the funds in the RRSP.

In an anticipated low-income year following a high-income year, you can even consider contributing in February, claiming a deduction (say at the middle rate of about 35%) for the previous year, and withdrawing the funds later in the current year, to be taxed at the low (25%) rate for the current year.

You will need to plan around the withholding tax on RRSP withdrawals discussed in 3.2, however. You may be able to arrange withdrawals so that they incur the least possible withholding tax, leaving you with the use of the funds until you file your tax return the following April. Bear in mind, however, that you may have a tax liability to settle in the following April to the extent that your tax rate on all sources of income exceeds the withholding tax rate.

## 3.3 Special RRSP rules

A number of rules deal with special situations relating to RRSPs. We will refer to them only briefly; you should consult your professional adviser if you are in these situations.

### 3.3.1 Spousal plans

**Contribute to your spouse's (or common-law spouse's) RRSP if your spouse's projected income on retirement will be lower.**

The RRSP rules allow you to contribute to an RRSP for your spouse, and claim the deduction yourself. Your total contributions (to your own and your spouse's plans) are still subject to your normal limits (18% of your previous year's earned income or $26,010 for 2017, minus any pension adjustment). The advantage is that your spouse will be the one who ultimately reports the income for tax purposes, when the funds are withdrawn on retirement or otherwise. If your spouse has less income than you, either on retirement or at some earlier time (including, for example, due to expected parental leave), this can result in significantly less tax on the income.

Spouses can split certain pension income, which may reduce the need for spousal RRSPs to accomplish retirement income splitting (see 20.3.6).

If you are over 71 (the age at which you must mature your RRSP; see 20.4) and have "earned income" in the previous year, this will create new RRSP room for you in the current year. As long as your spouse is 71 or younger, you can still claim a deduction for a spousal RRSP contribution.

**Make spousal RRSP contributions in December instead of the following February.**

To prevent spousal RRSPs from being used for "income splitting" (see Chapter 5), the amount you contribute will be taxed back to you (rather than your spouse) to the extent any amount is withdrawn by your spouse in the year in which you contribute or in the next two calendar years (see 5.3.9).

This rule does not apply if the spouses are separated or divorced. We explore this rule in more detail at 5.3.9, in the chapter on income splitting.

> *Example*
>
> Jon and Nancy are married. Jon contributes $5,000 to Nancy's RRSP in February 2018, and claims the deduction on his 2017 tax return.
>
> If Nancy withdraws the funds at any time up to the end of 2020, $5,000 of the amount withdrawn will be treated as Jon's income, not Nancy's. (If, however, Jon's contribution had been made in December 2017, this would only be the case until the end of 2019.)

In general, there will be little effect on the real ownership of the funds under provincial law if you and your spouse separate or divorce. The rule in most provinces is that such funds will be pooled and shared between the spouses. There are rules in place to allow a tax-free division of RRSP funds in such situations.

### 3.3.2 Transfers to and from RRSPs

RRSPs can generally be transferred, with no tax consequences, to other RRSPs, registered retirement income funds (RRIF) or annuities, by simply filling out a government form.

> Transfer pension commuted value, retiring allowances or severance pay to your RRSP.

Under pension legislation you may be prevented from immediately withdrawing pension benefits (known as the "commuted value") from your employer's plan on your departure from the company. This legislation is commonly referred to as "locking-in" legislation. Pension benefits subject to these rules may be transferred to a locked-in RRSP, also known as a "locked-in retirement account" (LIRA).

Locked-in RRSPs are essentially subject to the same restrictions on withdrawal of funds as the original pension plan. For example, depending on the applicable pension legislation, you cannot usually access the locked-in plan funds until you are within 10 years of the retirement date set out in the plan documents. Even then, you can only use the plan funds to purchase an annuity or a special RRIF that will provide a lifetime income, called a "life income fund" (LIF) or, in some provinces, a "life retirement income fund" (LRIF) (see 20.4.5). With a LIF or an LRIF, you have more flexibility in deciding how to invest the funds.

Where the pension legislation permits a transfer from a registered pension plan to a locked-in RRSP, LIF or LRIF, there are generally no tax consequences to such transfers, though the tax rules may restrict the amounts that can be transferred from a "defined-benefit" pension plan.

Special rules allow a "retiring allowance" (which, for tax purposes, includes severance pay and amounts received for wrongful dismissal as well as unused sick leave credits) to be transferred tax-free to an RRSP, rather than taxed as income when received. The amount that can be transferred is normally limited to $2,000 for each calendar year (or part year) of employment before 1996, plus $1,500 for years of employment before 1989 for which employer pension contributions or deferred profit sharing plan contributions have not vested.

### 3.3.3 Death

On death, a taxpayer is normally taxed on the entire amount of any RRSPs or RRIFs, except where the funds are left to the taxpayer's spouse or financially dependent child, in which case they are included in the spouse's or child's income. See 22.4.1 for details.

### 3.3.4 Overcontributions

The RRSP contribution limits are discussed in 3.1.3. What happens if you contribute more than the maximum?

First, bear in mind that your financial institution will not prevent you from overcontributing. Your financial institution is not obliged to tell you how much you can or cannot contribute.

Second, any contributions over the maximum are non-deductible. However, once the funds are in your RRSP, they are taxable when withdrawn (whether on retirement or earlier), just like the funds that were deductible when you contributed them. Therefore, there is double taxation—once when you earn the income (and receive no deduction despite putting the funds into the RRSP), and again when you withdraw the funds from the RRSP.

If you are facing double taxation because of an overcontribution, you may be able to correct the problem if you act quickly to file a prescribed form and withdraw the overcontribution.

Third, in certain rare circumstances, overcontributing might be valuable despite the double taxation, because of the beneficial effect of tax-free compounding (as illustrated in the table in 3.1.5). Also, you can often deduct an overcontribution in a later year as new contribution room is created.

There is a rule preventing excessive overcontributions. At any one time, up to $2,000 can be overcontributed without penalty. Above the $2,000 level, the excess is subject to a penalty tax of 1% per month until the excess is withdrawn. If you are not generating new contribution room from year to year (e.g., because you have no earned income in the prior year), your overcontributions should be withdrawn in the year of making the contribution or the next year to avoid tax on the withdrawal.

Top up your RRSP with a non-deductible $2,000 overcontribution.

The $2,000 figure is designed to catch those cases where you might have miscalculated your pension adjustment (see 3.1.3) and contributed a little too much. However, as long as you are certain about your pension adjustment, you can use the $2,000 deliberately if you wish. So if you are already contributing your maximum for 2017, consider making an additional contribution of up to $2,000 to further benefit from the compounding of tax-free growth.

### 3.3.5 Labour-sponsored venture capital corporation shares

In some provinces, a combined federal/provincial credit of 30% to 35% (depending on the province) may be available for an investment of up to $5,000 per year in shares of a "labour-sponsored venture capital corporation", or LSVCC. Since 2016, the federal LSVCC credit is 15% for purchases of provincially registered LSVCCs.

However, the federal tax credit for federally registered LSVCCs decreased to 5% in 2016 (from 10% in 2015) and is eliminated for 2017 and later years.

You can buy shares in a labour-sponsored venture capital corporation and contribute them to your RRSP. You can also generally have the shares bought directly by your self-directed RRSP (see 3.1.6), provided the RRSP uses "new" or previous contribution funds (but not earnings). Either way, you claim the credit on your personal income tax return.

Consider shares of a labour-sponsored venture capital corporation for your RRSP.

When combined with the deduction for the RRSP contribution, a $5,000 investment in a provincially registered LSVCC may cost you as little as $1,000 after tax (assuming a 15% provincial credit). Particularly if you are not otherwise making the maximum possible RRSP contribution, an investment in an LSVCC for your RRSP may be worth considering. Before taking the plunge and investing in an LSVCC, make sure you evaluate the relative merits from an investment perspective, as they are generally a higher risk and possibly illiquid investment.

### 3.3.6 The Home Buyers' Plan

Under the Home Buyers' Plan, if you qualify, you are allowed to withdraw up to $25,000 as a loan from your RRSP to buy or build a home, without counting the withdrawal as income. You must then repay the loan, without interest, over 15 years starting in the second year after the year of the withdrawal.

*Who may use the Home Buyers' Plan?*

The Plan may only be used by what the government calls a "first-time buyer". You are not a "first-time buyer" if you have owned and lived in a home as a principal place of residence at any time during the five calendar years up to and including the current year. (For the current year, you can use the Plan up to 30 days after you acquire a home.) If your spouse has owned and lived in a home during that period, and you have inhabited that home during the marriage, you also do not qualify. (Remember that "spouse" includes a common-law spouse as outlined in 2.2.1.)

Past participation does not prevent you from participating in the Plan again, as long as you have fully repaid to your RRSP the amounts previously withdrawn and you have not owned a home in the past five calendar years (including the current year).

As noted in 2.5.3, the five-year qualification test is waived for disabled persons and their relatives for purchases of new homes that are more accessible or better suited to the personal needs and care of a disabled person who will reside there.

*How does the Plan work?*

You can borrow (withdraw) up to $25,000 from your RRSP under the Plan. If you and your spouse each have RRSPs, you can borrow up to $50,000 between the two of you if you are taking joint ownership in the property. A qualifying home must be acquired before October 1 of the year following the year of the withdrawal. You must also begin or intend, to use the home as a principal place of residence no later than one year after its acquisition. No tax will apply to the withdrawal.

When you withdraw the funds, you fill out Form T1036 (TP-935.1-V for Quebec purposes), certifying that you have entered into a written agreement to purchase a home and stating its address. Once you have done this, the financial institution will not withhold tax when it pays the funds to you.

Note that the Home Buyers' Plan does not give you any right to withdraw funds from your RRSP if you didn't already have that right. If your RRSP funds are invested in term deposits or other long-term obligations, you will still need to negotiate with the financial institution to have the funds released as cash. Similarly, if your RRSP funds are in your employer's group RRSP or a LIRA ("locked-in RRSP"), you may not be able to get them out.

Once you borrow the funds, you must normally complete the purchase by September 30 of the *following* year. (A one-year extension may be available if the deal falls through and you buy a replacement property.) If you withdraw less than the $25,000 maximum, you can in many cases withdraw a further amount up to the following January 31 and treat the total as one withdrawal.

The requirement to repay the funds begins in the second year following the withdrawal. You can opt to make any year's repayment up to 60 days after the end of the year.

Example

Olivia has $30,000 in her RRSP. She signs an agreement in September 2017 to purchase a new home. In November 2017 she completes Form T1036 and withdraws $15,000 from her RRSP. The purchase closes in January 2018.

No tax will be withheld from the $15,000 that Olivia withdraws, so she can use the full amount towards the home purchase. Since she withdrew the funds in 2017, Olivia must repay $1,000 (1/15 of the total) to her RRSP during 2019 or by March 1, 2020. If she chooses to repay only $600, she will have to include $400 in income for 2019 and pay tax on that amount.

If Olivia repays no more than $1,000 in 2019 (or by March 1, 2020), she would be required to repay 1/14 of the balance, another $1,000, in 2020 (or by February 28, 2021). Suppose she repays $8,000 in 2019, leaving a balance owing of $7,000. For 2020, she would still be required to repay 1/14 of the balance, or $500. The fact she has prepaid more than required reduces but does not eliminate her obligation to continue paying the balance in later years.

If you do not make repayments as required, you must include the shortfall in income for tax purposes, like Olivia in the example above when she repays only $600. In effect, the shortfall is treated as a permanent withdrawal from your RRSP and you're taxed on it.

### Contributions in the year you use the Plan

If you contribute to an RRSP and withdraw the same funds within 90 days under the Home Buyers' Plan, you cannot deduct your contribution. For purposes of this rule, any balance that was already in your RRSP can be considered as withdrawn first. Thus, it is only to the extent the amount of your new contribution is needed for the withdrawal (within the 90-day period) that a deduction will be disallowed.

### Some special situations

The Home Buyers' Plan may be used for building a new home on an existing lot that you own. Instead of an agreement to purchase the home, you must have an agreement in place to construct it.

Consider Home Buyers' Plan withdrawals to buy or build your first home (but be sure to weigh the loss of RRSP growth).

If you withdraw the funds but your home purchase does not close, you can generally cancel your participation in the Plan and return the funds to your RRSP with no adverse tax consequences. Alternatively, if you buy another qualifying home as a replacement, you can remain in the Plan.

If you have contributed to a spousal RRSP, your spouse must normally wait two to three years before withdrawing the funds or they will be taxed back to you (see 3.3.1). However, with the Home Buyers' Plan, your spouse can borrow the funds to purchase a qualifying home, and to the extent they are not repaid over the 15-year repayment period, it is your spouse that must include the difference in income, not you. If your spouse withdraws the funds and does not purchase a qualifying home, so that the full amount withdrawn is taxed in the current year, the attribution rule *will* apply and you, not your spouse, will be taxed on the withdrawal.

If you become a non-resident of Canada, you must repay the entire outstanding balance to the RRSP within 60 days of leaving Canada. Otherwise, the balance will be included in your income for the year that you became non-resident.

If you should die while you have an outstanding balance to repay, that balance will be included in your income for the year of death and tax will be payable by your estate (see 22.2.1). However, if you leave a surviving spouse, your executor and your spouse may make a special election to have your spouse take over the obligation to repay the funds over the remainder of the repayment period, and the balance will not be included in your income for the year of death.

### Should you use the Home Buyers' Plan?

At first glance, the Plan seems attractive, since it gives you ready access to a potentially large amount of cash. However, there are three costs to consider.

First, you lose the tax-free compounding in your RRSP (see the example in 3.1.5). Balanced against this cost is the fact that you have probably reduced the mortgage interest expense you would otherwise have to pay out of after-tax dollars. Even still, the value of the RRSP may be much less at your retirement than it would be otherwise. If you are depending on your RRSP for your retirement income, you will want to forecast the reduction in income that will result from withdrawing a large amount of the funds now and repaying it to the RRSP over 15 years starting in the second year after the year of withdrawal.

Second, you have to be able to sustain the cash flow to repay the RRSP; if you cannot, you will end up being taxed on the funds you have withdrawn. When figuring out the cash you need to handle your mortgage and property tax payments, don't forget the 1/15 minimum repayment to the RRSP in each year beginning with the second year after the withdrawal (due by 60 days after the end of the year). Of course, since you are simply repaying borrowed funds and not contributing new money to the RRSP, no deduction is available for the amounts you repay.

Third, you may not be able to claim a deduction for your RRSP contribution for the current year if you make your contribution and withdraw it for the Home Buyer's Plan within 90 days. This will depend on the balance in your

RRSP. If your withdrawal does not exceed the value you had in the RRSP 90 days before the withdrawal, you have no problem.

Nevertheless, if you need the funds to help you purchase your first home, the Home Buyers' Plan may be a significant help.

### Planning for the Home Buyers' Plan

If you're thinking about tapping your RRSP to purchase your first home but your RRSP is not yet at $25,000 and you intend to use the Home Buyers' Plan to its fullest, make your contribution early enough so that it can sit in the RRSP for 90 days before you withdraw the funds. Then the amount you contributed can be withdrawn as well without affecting your deduction for the contribution.

If you are planning to buy a new home and you are close to the four-year cutoff that will re-qualify you as a "first-time buyer", consider waiting and making your purchase at a time when you can use the Home Buyers' Plan. For example, if you sold your last home in 2013, you can use the Plan as of January 1, 2018.

If you are about to be married and your future spouse owns a home that you will be living in, consider borrowing funds under the Home Buyers' Plan before your wedding. Once you are married, you will not be able to do so. However, you are not restricted by a previous home owned by your spouse, as long as you do not live in it while married. Therefore, if you plan on buying a new home after your wedding, you should not (romantic considerations aside) move into your spouse's current home until you have made your withdrawal under the Plan.

The same applies if you have been living in a common-law relationship (and have not had a child together) or a same-sex relationship for less than 12 months. Once you reach 12 months of living together, you are considered "married" for income tax purposes (see 2.2.1). If your partner owns your present home, but you plan on moving up to a larger home, consider withdrawing funds under the Home Buyers' Plan before you have lived together for 12 months. However, you will have to take ownership (or at least part ownership) of the new home in your own name.

### 3.3.7 The Lifelong Learning Plan—RRSP withdrawals for education

You can tap your registered retirement savings plan to help finance your own or your spouse's education. Under the Lifelong Learning Plan, students in full-time training or post-secondary education and their spouses can withdraw up to $10,000 per year from their RRSPs over a four-year period, as long as the total amount does not exceed $20,000.

> Consider withdrawing RRSP funds under the Lifelong Learning Plan to help pay for training or post-secondary education programs.

Withdrawn amounts must be repaid to an RRSP in equal instalments over 10 years, or they will be included in the income of the person who made the withdrawal. The first repayment will be due 60 days after the fifth year following the first withdrawal at the latest (or earlier in certain circumstances such as failure to complete courses).

There is no limit on the number of times you can participate in the Plan over your lifetime. Starting the year after you repay all of the withdrawn amount, you can participate in the Plan again and withdraw up to $20,000 over a new qualifying period.

If you die or emigrate from Canada, outstanding amounts will be included in your income in the year of death or emigration. In the case of emigration, you can avoid the income inclusion by repaying the outstanding amount within 60 days of emigration. In the case of death, your surviving spouse and your executor can make a special election to take over the obligation to make the repayments over the remainder of the 10-year period and the balance will not be included in your income in the year of death.

## 3.4 Anti-avoidance rules

As we saw in 3.1.6, you can hold only certain types of qualifying investments in your RRSP. Special anti-avoidance rules prevent individuals from holding prohibited investments in their RRSPs and from using these accounts in tax planning arrangements that the government considers unacceptable.

If the anti-avoidance rules apply you'll be subject to harsh penalties, so it's important to ensure that your RRSP investments comply with the rules.

Under these rules, some investments that previously qualified for RRSPs became prohibited as of March 23, 2011 and are not "grandfathered". As a result, you may have investments in your RRSP, such as certain private company shares, that were qualified investments when your RRSP acquired them but are now prohibited investments under the anti-avoidance rules. If you made a special election by March 1, 2013, you do not have to remove these investments from your RRSP but you will have to withdraw any income or capital gains from these investments from your RRSP within 90 days after the end of the year in which the income or capital gains are earned or realized. You will then pay tax on the income or gains at your regular rate for this RRSP withdrawal.

## 3.5 Registered pension plans—RPPs

### 3.5.1 Ordinary RPPs

A registered pension plan (RPP) is set up by an employer for its employees. Large companies, and many smaller ones, have such plans. These are quite different from the Canada Pension Plan (or, in Quebec, the Quebec Pension Plan), to which all employed and self-employed taxpayers must contribute.

The employer contributes (and deducts for tax purposes) an annual amount on behalf of each employee. Unlike most other employment benefits, these amounts are not taxed as benefits from employment in the year they are contributed. Instead, employees are taxed on the income from the pension when they *receive* it, which is normally after retirement.

In some cases, employees may be required or permitted to make additional contributions to the plan, which they can deduct for tax purposes in the year contributed.

There are two general kinds of pension plans: money-purchase and defined benefit. Money-purchase plans are analogous to RRSPs, in the sense that the amount of the pension payments is determined by the contributions and the investment income they earn.

Contributions to a money-purchase plan are generally limited to the lesser of 18% of your pensionable earnings for the year or $26,230 for 2017.

Many large and public employers provide defined benefit plans. With such plans, you know from the beginning how much your pension will be, usually based on a percentage of your actual salary over a specified number of years. It is up to the employer to contribute enough, and to the pension fund management to invest wisely, to make sure that the plan remains sufficiently funded to make those payments.

Once an employee retires and starts receiving pension income, the pension income is taxed as regular income as it is received. Up to $2,000 per year may be eligible for the pension income tax credit (see 20.3.5).

If you receive a lump-sum pension payment relating to prior years, you may ask the CRA to determine whether it is more advantageous to you to recalculate the tax on that income as if you received it in those prior years. This measure is intended to relieve the higher tax liability that may result if the entire lump-sum is taxed in the year of receipt, rather than year by year as your right to receive the income arose. Eligible payments must total at least $3,000 in the year and include superannuation or pension benefits (other than non-periodic benefits), wrongful dismissal and other employment-related payments arising from a court order or similar judgment, and certain other amounts.

If you have terminated your employment but are not yet eligible to receive pension income, you can transfer lump-sum amounts from the RPP to a locked-in retirement account or a locked-in RRIF (see 20.4.5). Generally, locked-in funds cannot be withdrawn in a lump sum; they must be used to provide a lifetime income. (In some provinces, if the amount of pension is below a certain threshold, it may be paid as a taxable lump sum. Other circumstances such as shortened life expectancy or financial hardship can also give rise to commutation of a pension.)

The amount you can transfer from a defined benefit RPP to an RRSP or RRIF is limited to the amount of annual pension given up under the RPP multiplied by a factor based on your age at the date of the transfer. The factor is 9.0 if you are under 50, gradually rising to 12.4 at ages 64 and 65. Generally, any amount over this limit must be paid to you in cash and is taxed as income in the year received.

If you are a member of a money purchase RPP, the plan may allow payouts in the form of the same income stream currently permitted under a RRIF. If the relevant pension legislation and the plan allow it, you would have to withdraw from your money purchase account a minimum amount each year (corresponding to the existing RRIF rules—see 20.4.4), beginning no later than the year in which you turn 72.

This rule allows members of money purchase RPPs to benefit from the same advantages as RRIF-holders without taking on greater investment management responsibilities or higher investment management fees. If you are a former member of a money purchase RPP who previously transferred your money purchase account to an RRSP or RRIF, you can transfer the funds back into the RPP if you wish. Contact your RPP's administrator to determine whether your plan accommodates this option.

Consider contributing to your RRSP instead of a money-purchase RPP.

If you've been making voluntary contributions to your registered pension plan under a money-purchase provision, consider contributing to an RRSP instead. Though the amount you can contribute is normally the same and your administration and investment management fees may be higher, the RRSP may give you much greater flexibility in terms of your investment choices.

Find out about the vesting of your pension benefits, especially before making a career change.

If you are a member of a company pension plan, find out how long it takes for your employer contributions to "vest". Once they are vested, the pension you have earned becomes yours and, if you change jobs, many plans will permit the transfer of your pension benefit to your new employer's plan. If they are not vested, you get your own contributions back with interest when you leave—but no pension down the road. The vesting of your pension benefits can be a major factor in career change decisions.

You may have the option to receive pension benefits from a defined benefit RPP while still working part-time or full-time, with certain restrictions—see 20.2.6.

### 3.5.2 Individual pension plans—IPPs

An individual pension plan (IPP) is exactly what the name implies—a defined benefit registered pension plan designed and structured for one individual member. Sometimes a spouse or other family member can also be a member of the IPP. Some owner-managers may also qualify to have this type of pension plan registered with the CRA.

As a defined benefit pension plan, the benefit payable at retirement is specified and IPP contributions are made accordingly. The amount needed to provide a defined benefit rises at ages closer to retirement since less time is available to accrue investment income in the plan.

An IPP may be worth considering if you are already in your employer's group RPP but the benefits from that RPP are less generous than you would like.

In contrast to RRSPs, which can be cashed in any time, contributions made to the IPP will be locked in under applicable pension benefits legislation until retirement, when they must be used to provide retirement benefits (usually in the form of a life annuity or life income fund). Annual minimum withdrawals from an IPP are required, similar to a RRIF (see 20.4.4), once the plan member reaches age 72. An RRSP, on the other hand, provides a variety of options on termination or retirement (see 20.4).

In the past, the main advantage of the IPP was that you and your employer would usually be allowed to make higher annual contributions than you would otherwise be entitled to under the RRSP route.

Weigh the advantages of establishing an "individual pension plan".

Keep in mind that past service contributions made after March 22, 2011 must be funded first out of a plan member's existing RRSP assets or by reducing the individual's available RRSP contribution room before new deductible contributions for the past service can be made.

Your employer will be required to top up the funds in the IPP if investment performance is poor and there will be insufficient funds (as determined by an actuary) to pay you the defined benefit pension promised under the plan (which could be a point of concern to your employer). A further advantage is that an IPP is generally creditor-proof, while many RRSPs are not.

In addition, start-up and ongoing costs of administration of an IPP are higher than those of your RRSP. This is due to the complex regulatory environment governing pension plans. For example, an actuarial valuation is required at start-up and for the next three years and certain forms must be filed annually.

The rules regarding IPPs are complex. Consult your professional tax adviser for more information.

## 3.6 Deferred profit-sharing plans—DPSPs

Deferred profit-sharing plans (DPSPs) are less common than registered pension plans. They operate the same way in that contributions are made by the employer and are only taxed in the employee's hands when received, normally on retirement.

Employer contributions to DPSPs are based on current or accrued profits but may have a defined minimum contribution. Such plans may be used, for example, by smaller companies that are not sure of profits and do not wish to commit themselves to large pension contributions, especially if they end up losing money for the year.

Employer contributions to DPSPs are generally limited to the lesser of 18% of your earnings for the year or $13,115 for 2017. Employee contributions to a DPSP are not permitted. Contributions to a DPSP are reported as a pension adjustment on your T4 slip and so they reduce the amount you can contribute to an RRSP in the following year (see 3.1.3). Employer contributions vest in an employee after 24 months of plan membership.

DPSPs cannot be set up for employees who are also major shareholders (over 10% of any class of shares) in the employer corporation, or for members of their families. They therefore cannot be used for owner-managers of small businesses.

## 3.7 References

The following publications and more information, including forms and brochures, can be obtained on the CRA's website at *www.cra-arc.gc.ca* or by telephone request at 1-800-959-8281 for individual income tax and trust-related enquiries or 1-800-959-5525 for business and self-employed individual enquiries.

Guide T4040, "RRSPs and Other Registered Plans for Retirement"
Guide RC4112, "Lifelong Learning Plan (LLP)"
Income Tax Folio S3-F10-C1, "Qualified Investments – RRSPs, RESPs, RRIFs"

Income Tax Folio S3-F10-C2, "Prohibited Investments – RRSPs, RRIFs and TFSAs"

Information Circular 72-22R9, "Registered retirement savings plans"

Information Circular 77-1R5, "Deferred profit sharing plans"

Information Circular 78-18R6, "Registered retirement income funds"

Also, see the following selected topics on the CRA's website:

"What is the Home Buyers' Plan?"

"Contributing to your spouse's or common-law partner's RRSPs"

# Chapter 4

## TFSAs and other tax-assisted savings plans

- Contribute up to $5,500 annually to your Tax-Free Savings Account (TFSA) to enjoy tax-sheltered growth (4.1)

- Consider the potential family income splitting benefits of a TFSA (4.1.1)

- Determine your best tax strategy for dividing your investments among TFSAs, RRSPs and RESPs (4.2)

- Consider a Registered Education Savings Plan (RESP) for education cost planning, tax deferral and income splitting with the plan's beneficiary (4.3)

- Consider making large lump-sum payments to an RESP to take full advantage of tax-sheltered growth within the plan (4.3.1)

- Think about establishing a self-directed RESP to increase your investment options (4.3.2)

- Determine which type of RESP best suits your needs—individual, family or group (4.3.2)

- Contribute up to $2,500 annually to an RESP and earn a 20% government grant (4.4)

- If your child does not pursue higher education, consider transferring up to $50,000 to your own or your spouse's RRSP (4.5.2)

- If you have a child with a disability, consider setting up a Registered Disability Savings Plan (RDSP) to provide for his or her future financial security (4.6)

*TFSAs, RESPs and RDSPs are tax-assisted savings vehicles similar to RRSPs discussed in Chapter 3 but their purposes are quite different. TFSAs can earn tax-sheltered investment income you can withdraw at any time, RESPs are education investment vehicles, and RDSPs can help you save for a disabled family member's long-term financial security.*

*In this chapter, we discuss the rules governing contributions to and payments from these plans and compare their benefits to help you decide where you should invest your savings.*

## 4.1 Tax-Free Savings Accounts—TFSAs

Tax-Free Savings Accounts (TFSAs) are a tax-assisted savings plan introduced in 2009. TFSA

> Contribute up to $5,500 annually to your Tax-Free Savings Account to enjoy tax-sheltered growth.

contributions, which can include investments you already own, are not tax-deductible, and you can withdraw the income earned in the TFSA and your contributions to it at any time tax-free.

### 4.1.1 How much can you contribute?

You can contribute up to $5,500 per year to a TFSA (reduced from $10,000 for 2015), as long as you are 18 or older and resident in Canada. If you have made no contributions to date and you are 26 or older in 2017, you can contribute a total of $52,000. You can carry forward unused contribution room indefinitely. You can hold more than one TFSA, subject to your contribution limit.

| Years | TFSA contribution limit | Total |
|---|---|---|
| 2009–2012 | $5,000 per year | $20,000 |
| 2013–2014 | $5,500 per year | $11,000 |
| 2015 | $10,000 per year | $10,000 |
| 2016–2017 | $5,500 per year | $11,000 |
| | | $52,000 |

Unlike the $2,000 overcontribution allowed for RRSPs, there is no cushion for excess contributions to a TFSA and the penalty for overcontributions is harsh. If you have an excess TFSA amount at any time in a calendar month, you are liable for a penalty tax of 1% of that month's highest excess amount. Because the test applies at any time in a calendar month, withdrawing the excess amount will only stop the penalty from applying in the month after the withdrawal.

Like an RRSP, interest on funds borrowed and fees incurred to invest in a TFSA are not tax-deductible. Unlike an RRSP, however, you may be able to use your TFSA as collateral for a loan.

#### Income splitting benefit for families

**Consider the potential family income splitting benefits of a TFSA.**

TFSAs may offer an opportunity for income splitting for families in which one spouse has more income than the other. You can give funds to your spouse to contribute to his or her own TFSA, as long as your spouse has available contribution room, and the normal income attribution rules that would tax the investment income in your hands will not apply (see 5.2.2).

### 4.1.2 Withdrawing funds

You can make a tax-free withdrawal from a TFSA at any time. The amount withdrawn is added to your contribution room, but not until the next year. You can re-contribute the amount you withdrew in the next year or later.

**Example**

Scott contributed $46,500 to his TFSA before the end of 2016. In January 2017, he contributes $5,500 so that he has contributed the maximum amount of $52,000. He decides to withdraw $5,000 in June 2017 so that only $47,000 of his contributions remains in his TFSA. In this case, he cannot re-contribute the $5,000 he withdrew until 2018. At that time, he can re-contribute the $5,000 withdrawal along with his new $5,500 contribution limit for 2018, for a total of $10,500.

Investment income earned in Scott's TFSA is treated the same way. If Scott's $5,500 investment in 2017 earns $275 and he withdraws the $5,775 in December 2017, he can re-contribute the entire $5,775 in 2018 along with his new $5,500 contribution limit for that year, or $11,275 in total.

In a similar vein, if you invest some of the funds in your TFSA in the stock market and your share investment appreciates rapidly, say from $20,000 to $30,000, you could sell the shares and realize the $10,000 tax-free capital gain in the TFSA, withdraw the $30,000 cash proceeds and still be able to re-contribute the full $30,000 amount to the TFSA along with any other unused TFSA contribution room in the following year or later.

As a result, you could potentially contribute much more than the contribution limit annually, and therefore earn more tax-free investment income.

Consider putting investments that are expected to increase significantly in value over a short time in a TFSA. You can withdraw the income and capital gains earned tax-free at any time, and any withdrawals you make will create additional contribution room.

When choosing your investments, keep in mind that capital losses realized in a TFSA cannot be claimed against capital gains realized outside the TFSA.

### 4.1.3 Which investments qualify?

TFSAs are generally allowed to hold the same qualified investments as RRSPs (see 3.1.6), such as cash, guaranteed investment certificates (GICs), term deposits, mutual funds, government and corporate bonds, publicly traded securities, and in certain cases, shares of small business corporations.

You can transfer investments you already own into your TFSA. The rules are similar to those for transferring investments into your RRSP (see 3.1.6).

Note that your TFSA cannot hold investments in "non-arm's-length entities", which are generally companies in which you, your spouse and other related persons, either individually or collectively, own 10% or more of the shares.

Special anti-avoidance rules apply harsh penalties to income from prohibited investments held in TFSAs and from deliberate over-contributions, so it's important to ensure your TFSA investments comply with the rules.

### 4.1.4 Special situations

Various rules apply to special situations, including the death of a TFSA holder and ceasing Canadian residency. Some violations of the TFSA rules may trigger penalties.

*Death*—Generally, investment income earned in the TFSA after the account holder's death is no longer tax-exempt. Special rules apply if there is a surviving spouse (see 22.4.2).

*Non-residents*—If you become non-resident, you can maintain your existing TFSA and your investment income and withdrawals will remain exempt from Canadian tax. While you are non-resident, however, no new contribution room will accrue. You must also consider foreign tax implications of TFSA income and withdrawals, if they apply.

For example, earnings in a TFSA are tax-free for Canadian tax purposes, but they are taxable for U.S. tax purposes. U.S. citizens may still benefit from establishing a TFSA if they have enough foreign tax credits to offset the additional U.S. taxable income (see 18.3.3). However, don't overlook onerous reporting requirements in the U.S. because the TFSA may be considered a foreign trust (see 18.7.4).

Withholding tax does not apply to a non-resident's withdrawals from a TFSA but it may apply to payments to a non-resident beneficiary of income earned in a TFSA after the account holder's death.

## 4.2 Where should you invest your savings?

Determine your best tax strategy for dividing your investments among TFSAs, RRSPs and RESPs.

With all its advantages, you'll want to consider making a TFSA an important part of your tax and financial planning. Of course, you'll need to weigh these advantages against the benefits of other tax-assisted savings plans such as RRSPs (see Chapter 3) and RESPs (see 4.3) and other financial priorities such as paying down your mortgage.

Whether you should choose to save your money in an RRSP, TFSA or RESP depends on your circumstances. Generally, if you have enough resources, you should invest in all the relevant plans. Though TFSA savings are initially limited, as contribution room increases, a TFSA may become a much more significant supplement to your RRSP.

### RRSPs versus TFSAs

A TFSA is like a mirror image of an RRSP: RRSP contributions are tax-deductible but the contributions and investment earnings are taxed when you withdraw them. TFSA contributions are not tax-deductible but withdrawals of contributions and investment income are tax-free.

As such, your best tax strategy for dividing your investments between TFSAs and RRSPs may depend on any differences between your current tax bracket and the one you expect to be in when you start withdrawing funds from your RRSP.

If you expect your future income to fall into the same tax bracket as your current income, the tax benefits of a TFSA and an RRSP will be similar. That is, the value of the tax deduction for an RRSP contribution will generally equal the value of withdrawing funds tax-free from a TFSA.

If you expect your future income to fall into a lower tax bracket than your current income, an RRSP investment can provide a tax advantage because the tax deduction you get today will be more than the tax you will pay when you withdraw the money from your RRSP.

If your income falls into a lower tax bracket now but you expect it to be higher in the future, a TFSA offers a greater tax benefit because you would pay a higher tax rate on RRSP withdrawals than you will pay today on the income you contribute to the TFSA.

### TFSAs for seniors

Unlike an RRSP, which has to be wound up when you reach age 71, you can maintain your TFSA for your entire lifetime and so your TFSA should be integrated with your retirement income plan (see 20.4.7).

### RESPs and TFSAs

If you're saving for your child's education, keep in mind that, unlike a TFSA, an RESP offers an annual guaranteed rate of return of $500 (20% on $2,500 annual contributions) via the federal government's Canada Education Savings Grant (see 4.4).

Once your children turn 18, you may want to consider giving them funds to invest in their own TFSAs to help finance their post-secondary education or other expenses.

### TFSA versus mortgage paydown

If you're considering whether to invest in a TFSA or pay down your mortgage, it probably makes sense in most cases to reduce your non-deductible mortgage interest as soon as possible.

*Funds earning interest*

Assuming you have TFSA contribution room, it almost always makes sense to invest in a TFSA if you have money sitting in a bank account earning taxable interest.

# 4.3 Registered Education Savings Plans—RESPs

Registered Education Savings Plans (RESPs) can help you build an education fund for your child or grandchild (or a friend's or relative's child) by allowing you to earn investment income in a tax-deferred environment. You can set up an individual plan with organizations such as life insurance companies, mutual fund companies and financial institutions or you can enroll in a group plan offered by a non-profit scholarship or education trust foundation. If the child goes to college or university, the RESP provides funds to help cover the child's expenses.

Consider an RESP for education cost planning, tax deferral and income splitting with the plan's beneficiary.

Unlike RRSPs, contributions to an RESP are *not* tax-deductible to the contributor. However, the income in the plan grows tax-free, so RESPs enjoy the effect of tax-free compounding of investment income, which we illustrated in 3.1.5. When the child withdraws the funds, the income portion will be taxable to the child. As a student, the beneficiary will probably not have much other income and will be eligible for the tuition tax credit (see 2.4), so he or she will likely pay little or no tax. The investment income payments from an RESP are all taxable as regular income, even if the investment income was earned as dividends or capital gains, which are normally taxed at a lower rate.

## 4.3.1 How much can you contribute to an RESP?

The overall lifetime limit for RESPs contributions is $50,000 per beneficiary. Overcontributions are taxed at a rate of 1% for each month that they remain in the plan.

Income generated in an RESP may be sheltered from tax for a maximum of 35 years (or 40 years if the beneficiary has a disability). You can make contributions to the plan for up to 31 years (35 years if the beneficiary has a disability). The plan can exist and earn tax-sheltered income for four more years, after which the plan must be wound up.

If an RESP contributor dies, his or her estate can continue to contribute to the plan.

Since there is no annual contribution limit, you may want to consider making a large lump-sum payment to the RESP to take advantage of the tax-sheltered growth. This tax savings needs to be weighed against the Canada Education Savings Grant you may lose if you do not make annual contributions (see 4.4). The best approach is to start investing in an RESP in the first years after your child is born to maximize the benefit of government grants (see 4.4) and earn potentially higher returns from making earlier investments.

> Consider making large lump-sum payments to an RESP to take full advantage of tax-sheltered growth within the plan.

Determining how much your child's education will eventually cost can be daunting; software tools are available that can help you project how much you need to save today to meet your child's future education costs.

If you wish, you can withdraw your own contributions to an RESP without any tax consequences since you did not get a tax deduction when you contributed the funds. However, you cannot withdraw the income earned by the RESP tax-free. You may also be required to repay some or all of any Canada Education Savings Grants upon a RESP withdrawal for non-education purposes (see 4.4).

### 4.3.2 Choosing the right type of RESP—Group and individual plans

If you choose to set up an individual plan rather than enroll in a group plan, the investments can be self-directed and tailored to your circumstances. The types of investments that may be held in an RESP are the same as those that may be held by an RRSP (see 3.1.6). Keep in mind that your financial institution may charge additional fees for this flexibility.

> Think about establishing a self-directed RESP to increase your investment options

You can choose between a single-beneficiary and a multi-beneficiary plan. Under a single-beneficiary plan, the beneficiary does not have to be related to you—he or she can be anyone you choose. You can also set up a single-beneficiary RESP for yourself if you're planning to pursue post-secondary education in the future.

If you are saving for the education of more than one person, you may want to consider a multi-beneficiary or family plan. The beneficiaries under a multi-beneficiary plan may only include your children, brothers, sisters, grandchildren or great-grandchildren. You cannot contribute to the plan for a beneficiary after he or she reaches age 31. Although you can usually change the beneficiaries after you set up either a single or multi-beneficiary plan if you wish,

> Determine which type of RESP best suits your needs—individual, family or group.

certain plans may have conditions restricting the changing of beneficiaries. Understanding the terms of any plan contract you consider is critical.

If you have set up single-beneficiary plans for siblings, you can transfer assets among these plans without tax penalties and without triggering the repayment of Canada Education Savings Grants (see 4.4), as long as the beneficiaries of the plans receiving the transfers were under 21 when the plans were opened.

Group plans tend to be more restrictive in terms of required scheduled contributions and the contributor usually has no say in how the contributed funds are invested.

Group plans may require that children be enrolled in the plan before they reach a certain age. They generally allow only one beneficiary to be named and may not allow you to change the beneficiary after he or she reaches a certain age. Again, make sure you understand the terms of the plan before entering into an RESP contract.

## 4.4 Canada Education Savings Grant

Under the Canada Education Savings Grant (CESG) program, the federal government will provide a direct grant to an RESP of 20% of the first $2,500 of annual contributions made to the RESP in a year (with enhanced rates on the first $500 of contributions of lower and middle income families—see below). The grant will be worth up to $500 per year for each year the beneficiary is under 18, to a maximum of $7,200 per beneficiary. The grant amount will not be included in the annual and lifetime contribution limits for the beneficiary.

*Contribute up to $2,500 annually to an RESP and earn a 20% government grant.*

If the maximum contribution is not made in a year, entitlement to the grant can be carried forward to a later year (within restrictions). The total CESG per beneficiary per year is capped at $1,000 or 20% of the unused CESG room, whichever is less.

> **Example**
>
> Robin contributes $1,000 in 2016 to an RESP for her newborn son. This contribution earns a CESG of $200 (20% of $1,000), leaving $1,500 in CESG contribution room available for carryforward in future years.
>
> In 2017, Robin contributes $4,500 to the plan. In this year, the contribution for the CESG is limited to the $2,500 of new contribution room arising in the year, plus the $1,500 carried forward. However, the CESG is only 20% of $4,000, or $800.

Note that only unused CESG contribution room can be carried forward; in our example, even though a CESG was earned on only $4,000 of Robin's

$4,500 contribution, the extra $500 of contribution could not be carried forward and claimed for CESG purposes in later years. If you expect your annual contributions to vary, consider deferring your "excess" contributions to the next year to secure maximum grants.

CESG contribution room accumulates at the rate of $2,500 per year ($2,000 per year for 1998 to 2006), whether or not the child is currently an RESP beneficiary. So even if you do not start making CESG-eligible RESP contributions in your child's first year, you can make catch-up payments eligible for the grant in later years (subject to the lifetime limit of $7,200 per beneficiary and the annual limit per beneficiary of $1,000 or 20% of the unused CESG room).

The CESG rate on the first $500 of contributions is 40% for families with income under $45,917 in 2017 and 30% for families with income between $45,916 and $91,832. The maximum contribution eligible for the CESG remains at $2,500, while the $500 maximum CESG payable for a year is increased for low and middle income families to accommodate the enhanced CESG rates. For example, a lower income family that contributes $2,500 in a year could receive a CESG totalling $600—that is, 40% on the first $500 ($200) and 20% on the remaining $2,000 ($400). Unused access to the enhanced CESG rates cannot be carried forward to future years.

To qualify for the CESG, the RESP beneficiary must be a resident of Canada under age 18 and must have a Social Insurance Number (SIN) (see 4.8). You can apply for a SIN for your child by contacting Service Canada. Bear in mind that SIN processing may take several weeks.

If you have already set up an RESP, you should confirm that it qualifies for CESG purposes. If you want to receive a CESG for 2017 but you do not have a plan, you'll need to set one up and make a contribution before December 31, 2017. To qualify for the CESG, the contributions must be new—money cannot be withdrawn from existing RESPs and recontributed to a new plan to qualify for the grant. If you change the plan's beneficiary, the grant funds can stay in the RESP if both the old and new beneficiaries are under 21 years old and are related to you.

There are special rules for beneficiaries in the years they become 16 or 17. RESPs for beneficiaries aged 16 and 17 are eligible for CESGs only if:

- Contributions to all RESPs for the child totalled at least $2,000 before the end of the calendar year in which the child turned 15 and the contributions remain in the RESPs, or
- There were contributions for the child of at least $100 per year in any four years before the end of the calendar year in which the child turned 15 and the contributions remain in the RESP.

If your child chooses not to pursue post-secondary education, you will have to repay the CESG funds received but you will only have to pay back the principal amount of the grant. You do not have to pay back the income earned on the grant funds; however, the income will be taxed when it is withdrawn from the RESP (see 4.5.2).

## 4.5 Payments from an RESP

### 4.5.1 If the beneficiary pursues higher education

Your RESP can begin making educational assistance payments to the plan's beneficiary once he or she enrolls as a full-time student in a qualifying educational program at a qualifying post-secondary institution. Part-time students aged 16 and over are eligible to receive up to $2,500 of educational assistance payments for each 13-week semester. Students with disabilities can also receive educational assistance payments for part-time study.

Payments from the plan can be used to cover the student's living expenses and educational expenses such as tuition fees and books, although certain plans may restrict which expenses payments can cover. A beneficiary cannot receive more than $5,000 during the first 13 weeks of his or her post-secondary education unless pre-approved by Human Resources and Social Development Canada. After the first 13 weeks, there is no limit on the amount that can be paid, as long as the student continues to qualify. If there is a 12-month period in which the student is not enrolled in a qualifying education program for 13 consecutive weeks, the $5,000 maximum applies again.

You can decide whether to let the student use the principal amount contributed to the plan or only the income accumulated in the plan. You can also decide how much is paid out of the plan and when the payments are made, subject to what the plan you choose allows. You may want to spread the payments over the duration of the student's program to minimize taxes. If your RESP received CESGs, in most cases, a part of each income payment will be attributed to the CESG funds received by the plan. Bear in mind that managing these different income streams can be complex, especially where group RESPs are involved.

If you contributed to a group RESP, the principal you contributed to the plan will be the first year's payment to the student. The plan administrators will determine the student's share of the income from the pooled funds in the plan and start making those payments in the student's second year of post-secondary education.

For an educational program to qualify, generally it must be at least three weeks long, require at least 10 hours per week of instruction (or 12 hours per month for part-time students) and be at a designated educational institution. Correspondence courses and other distance education courses may also qualify, as well as universities outside Canada if the student is enrolled in a course of at least 13 weeks leading to a degree.

Some group RESP plans may have other restrictions, such as prohibiting the beneficiary from changing schools or requiring the beneficiary to meet a minimum academic standard.

Special rules apply if the beneficiary becomes a non-resident of Canada, for example, to attend an institution in another country (see 13.3.6).

### 4.5.2 If the beneficiary does not pursue further education

What happens to the RESP funds if the intended beneficiaries decide not to enroll in college or university? In the past, if none of the intended beneficiaries went on to higher education, the family would only get back the original amounts contributed to the RESP, while the income earned over the years would be forfeited. However, these rules have been eased in cases where none of the RESP's intended beneficiaries are post-secondary students by age 21 and the plan has been running for at least 10 years. (If a beneficiary is mentally impaired, these conditions may be waived.) Under the current rules, you may transfer up to $50,000 of RESP income to your RRSP (or your spouse's) during your lifetime to the extent you have available RRSP contribution room. This allows the RRSP deduction to offset the inclusion of the RESP funds in your taxable income.

> If your child does not pursue higher education, consider transferring up to $50,000 to your own or your spouse's RRSP.

If you do not want to contribute the income to an RRSP or you do not have enough RRSP contribution room to do so, you will be subject to an extra tax of 20% of the excess RESP income, on top of your regular taxes on the amount (the extra tax is designed to make up for the taxes deferred while the funds were in the plan). You must wind up the RESP before March 1 of the year following the year in which you first withdrew income from the RESP.

Family plans are subject to the same contribution limits per beneficiary as single-beneficiary plans but, if one of your children decides against post-secondary school, the funds you have contributed for this child and the income earned on those contributions can be re-directed to benefit your other children who do pursue post-secondary education. If your plan received CESGs, the remaining beneficiaries can use up to $7,200 of CESGs funds each.

Group RESPs will return your contributions, but the income earned will remain in the plan to be distributed to the plan's beneficiaries who go on to post-secondary education.

## 4.6    Registered Disability Savings Plans—RDSPs

If you have a child with a disability, consider setting up a Registered Disability Savings Plan to provide for his or her future financial security.

Registered Disability Savings Plans (RDSPs) can help you save for the long-term security of a child with a disability who is eligible for the disability tax credit (see 2.5.1). These plans are similar to RESPs in that contributions to RDSPs are not tax-deductible, but investment income can be earned in the plan tax-free. Investment income, but not contributions, will be taxable to the beneficiary when it is paid out of the RDSP.

Anyone can contribute to an RDSP and there is no annual limit on the amount you can contribute. Contributions on behalf of any one beneficiary are capped at a lifetime maximum of $200,000. Contributions can continue to be made until the end of the year the beneficiary turns 59.

RRSP funds can be transferred tax-free on death to the RDSP of the RRSP holder's financially dependent infirm child or grandchild, subject to the beneficiary's lifetime contribution limit.

If you saved in an RESP for your disabled child and he or she does not pursue post-secondary education, you may be able to transfer the investment income in the RESP tax-free to your child's RDSP.

The beneficiary must begin receiving payments from the plan by the end of the year he or she turns 60, subject to maximum annual limits based on life expectancy, the age of the beneficiary and the value of the plan's assets.

These plans qualify for Canada Disability Savings Grants (CDSG), which are similar to Canada Education Savings Grants (see 4.4). Under this program, your RDSP contributions earn CDSGs at matching rates of 100%, 200% or 300%, depending on family net income and the amount contributed. An RDSP beneficiary can receive up to $3,500 of CDSGs in their RDSPs annually and up to $70,000 of CDSGs in their RDSP over their lifetime. CDSGs can be paid to an RDSP until the end of the year in which the beneficiary turns 49. Unused entitlements to CDSGs can be carried forward for up to 10 years.

Lower-income families may also be entitled to receive Canada Disability Savings Bonds (CDSB) of up to $1,000 per year (to a maximum of $20,000 over the beneficiary's lifetime). CDSBs can be paid into an RDSP until the end of the year in which the beneficiary turns 49. Eligibility for CDSBs is linked to family net income, rather than amounts contributed. Like CDSGs, you can carry forward unused CDSB entitlements for up to 10 years.

## 4.7    Anti-avoidance rules

As with RRSPs (see 3.4), you can hold only certain types of qualifying investments in your RESP or RDSP. As of March 23, 2017, special anti-avoidance rules prevent you from holding prohibited investments in these accounts or using them in tax planning arrangements that the government considers unacceptable.

If you have prohibited investments in an RESP or RDSP, you have until April 1, 2018 to make an election to pay the regular amount of tax on distributions of investment income. Otherwise, harsh penalties may apply.

## 4.8    References

The following publications and more information, including forms and brochures, can be obtained on the CRA's website at *www.cra-arc.gc.ca* or by telephone request at 1-800-959-8281 for individual income tax and trust-related enquiries or 1-800-959-5525 for business and self-employed individual enquiries.

> Guide RC4466, "Tax-Free Savings Account (TFSA), Guide for Individuals"
> Information Sheet RC4092, "Registered Education Savings Plans"
> Information Circular 93-3R2, "Registered Education Savings Plans"
> Information Sheet RC4460, "Registered Disability Savings Plan"
> Information Circular 99-1R1, "Registered Disability Savings Plans"

Information about RESPs, CESGs and how to apply for a Social Insurance Number is available on Service Canada's website at *www.servicecanada. gc.ca*.

# Chapter 5

## Reducing your family's tax bill through income splitting

- Watch out for the income splitting tax on certain income received by minor children (5.2.4)

- Beware of the "general anti-avoidance rule" (5.2.6)

- The higher-income spouse should pay household expenses (5.3.1)

- Pay your spouse's tax bills with your own funds (5.3.1)

- Pay the interest on your spouse's third-party investment loans (5.3.1)

- Give your spouse up to $5,500 annually to invest in his or her Tax-Free Savings Account (5.3.1)

- Pay a salary or consulting fee to your spouse and/or children (5.3.2)

- Think about loaning business assets to your spouse or child (5.3.3)

- Consider making spousal investment loans when interest rates are rising (5.3.4)

- Have your spouse or child earn income on income from loaned or transferred funds (5.3.5)

- Shelter future gains by transferring property at fair market value (5.3.6)

- Shelter future gains by transferring capital assets to your children (5.3.7)

- Transfer shares that will pay capital dividends (5.3.8)

- Contribute to your spouse's RRSP (5.3.9)

- Make spousal RRSP contributions by December 31 (5.3.9)

- In the year your children turn 17, give them funds they can invest (5.3.10)

- Let your children invest their own earnings (5.3.11)

- Deposit Canada Child Benefit payments to your child's bank account (5.3.12)

- File a joint election to split pension income with your spouse (5.3.13)

- Claim baby-sitting wages paid to your adult children as child care expenses (5.3.14)

*"Income splitting" is a term used to describe strategies to save taxes by shifting income from the hands of a family member in a higher tax bracket to the hands of a second family member in a lower tax bracket so that the same income is*

*taxed at a lower rate of tax—or not at all if the second family member's income is low enough. In this chapter, we discuss the tax rules that are in place to prevent many forms of income splitting and point out some of the income splitting opportunities that remain available.*

> *Caution: The tax planning ideas discussed in this chapter may be affected by the federal government's proposed new tax regime for private companies, as outlined in the Department of Finance's July 2017 consultation paper and draft legislation. See Appendix I for details.*

## 5.1 Why income splitting?

The Canadian tax system uses progressive tax rates, whereby the marginal rate of tax (tax on additional income) increases as taxable income increases.

Marginal rates of tax, tax brackets and surtaxes vary widely from province to province, but are *approximately*:

- 25% on income from $12,000 to $46,000
- 34% on income from $46,000 to $92,000
- 42% on income from $92,000 to $142,000
- 46% on income from $142,000 to $203,000
- 50% on income over $203,000.

As you can see, the tax payable on two $75,000 incomes will be significantly less than that on one $150,000 income. The tax savings can range from about $6,700 to about $12,500, depending on the province you live in. Taxpayers, therefore, have an incentive to "split" income between, for example, a high-income earner and a non-working spouse or children.

The federal *Income Tax Act* contains measures to prevent the most obvious kinds of income splitting (similar rules apply for Quebec purposes). However, some opportunities are available. We review the rules here, so you understand the context in which to plan, and then discuss the planning opportunities that remain.

Note that most of this chapter will be irrelevant to you if you do not have funds invested that are earning taxable income. One of the best general tax planning techniques is to channel extra cash into paying off any loans incurring non-deductible interest expenses such as your mortgage or credit card balances.

## 5.2 Rules that prevent income splitting

### 5.2.1 Indirect payments

The *Income Tax Act* provides that a payment or transfer made "pursuant to the direction of, or with the concurrence of" a taxpayer to some other person is to be included in the taxpayer's income to the extent it would have been if paid to the taxpayer. So, for example, if you arrange for your employer to pay part of your salary to your spouse, the income will still be taxed in your hands and you will not have accomplished anything.

### 5.2.2 Attribution between spouses

Suppose you earn $150,000 per year and your spouse earns $25,000. Your marginal tax rate (tax on any additional income) is 46% and your spouse's is 25%. Assume you have $10,000 in bonds that generate $1,000 per year in interest and decide to give, or lend, the bonds to your spouse. As a result, you hope to pay only $250 tax on the income instead of $460.

This is the kind of transaction that the attribution rules cover. These rules attribute income from property (in our example, the $1,000 of investment income each year) back to the person who transferred or loaned the property.

The attribution rules that apply to spouses provide that where property (including money) is *transferred or loaned, directly or indirectly* by you to your spouse (or a person who has since become your spouse), then all *income or loss from the property*, and any *capital gain or loss* on the disposition of the property will be *attributed back* to you. So, in our example, the $1,000 income on the $10,000 investment that you gave to your spouse must be reported on your tax return, not your spouse's—and so will be subject to tax of about $460 rather than about $250. This will be true year after year—as long as you and your spouse remain together, any income from the bonds will be taxed in your hands. If you transfer shares, for example, and your spouse sells the shares at some later time, any capital gain or capital loss relative *to your* original cost must be reported as your capital gain or loss, subject to the usual rules for capital gains (see Chapter 6).

Note that common-law and same-sex couples who meet the criteria outlined in 2.2.1 are considered spouses for tax purposes, and are therefore subject to these attribution rules as well.

There is an exception to these attribution rules; an exception that also applies to the other attribution rules we will see later. If you transfer for fair market value consideration (for example, sell the bonds to your spouse for $10,000 cash) and report the resulting gain, the attribution rule will not apply. (If you realize a loss on the transfer, a special rule deems the loss to be zero. However, the denied loss can be added to your spouse's cost for tax purposes.)

If the consideration includes indebtedness (for example, you sell the bonds for a $10,000 promissory note), or if you simply lend funds or property to your spouse, then you must charge and report interest on the loan to avoid these attribution rules. The interest rate must be at least equal to the lesser of the CRA's prescribed interest rate at that time (see 9.3) and a commercial rate of interest. For this exception to apply, the interest must actually be *paid* in each year or by the following January 30. If the January 30 deadline ever passes without the interest being paid, that year's income and *all* future income from the loaned property will be attributed back to you as the lender.

---

**Example**

On January 1, 2017, you lend $10,000 cash to your spouse, who puts the money in an investment and earns $400 interest over the year.

If you do not charge interest, then the $400 will be attributed back to you and taxed in your hands. Suppose you do wish to charge interest. The minimum rate required to prevent the attribution rules from applying would have to be the lesser of:

- the rate that would apply between two arm's-length parties (assume 3% for this example); and
- the CRA's prescribed rate at the time the loan was granted (assume 1%—see 9.3).

If your spouse is required to pay interest on the anniversary date of the loan and actually pays you at least $100 in interest by January 30, 2018, then the $400 interest will not be attributed back to you in 2017. Your spouse can deduct the interest paid to you and the amount will be taxable to you as interest income.

Setting up a system for automatic payment, such as an automatic bank transfer between you and your spouse, can help ensure that the interest payments are not inadvertently missed.

---

The CRA's (and Revenu Québec's) prescribed rate is set quarterly (see 9.3).

### 5.2.3 Attribution between parents and children

Suppose you give $10,000 in bonds to your daughter, who is in high school and can earn $1,000 in interest without paying any tax at all.

Where property is transferred or loaned to a child, there will be attribution of income (or loss), but usually not of capital gains or losses. The attribution rules apply only for years in which the child is still under 18 *at the end* of the year (though the attribution rules discussed in 5.2.5 will apply once your child turns 18).

Not all children under 18 are caught by the rule. It depends on the child's relationship with the taxpayer who transfers or lends the property. Attribution applies where the taxpayer and the child "do not deal at arm's length", a phrase that is defined to include all persons who are "related" as defined in the *Income Tax Act*. Generally, this covers one's child, grandchild, great-grandchild (including one's spouse's child, one's child's spouse, etc., where "spouse" includes a common-law or same-sex spouse as outlined in 2.2.1) or brother or sister (including brother-in-[common]-law and sister-in-[common]-law). This rule also specifically applies to nieces and nephews. For other relationships, it is a "question of fact" whether two taxpayers deal at arm's length.

Although the attribution rule for minors does not usually apply to capital gains and losses, the transfer of the property itself to the minor is generally deemed to take place at fair market value. Any capital gain or loss accruing up to the time of the transfer is triggered immediately in the transferor's hands, and it is only the gain or loss accruing *after* the transfer that, when realized, is taxed in the child's hands.

As a result of the attribution rules, the $1,000 of income transferred to your daughter in our example above would be taxable to you. You may also have to pay capital gains tax (if any) on the deemed disposition of the $10,000 in bonds transferred, though future capital gains or losses will accrue to your daughter.

The exceptions that we saw in 5.2.2, where the transferred property is acquired for fair market value or where interest is paid on any indebtedness or loan, also apply to this attribution rule.

### 5.2.4 Income splitting tax on certain income received by minor children

Some income splitting arrangements with minor children attract a special "income splitting tax" (sometimes called the "kiddie tax") in the minor child's hands. The tax neutralizes the benefits of certain arrangements, including some plans involving the use of family trusts (see 21.5.4), by subjecting certain types of dividend, partnership or trust income received by, or used for the benefit of, minor children to tax at the top marginal tax rate, instead of the lower rate that would usually apply on income received by a minor child. Certain capital gains as described below are also subject to this tax.

The types of income subject to this tax include:

- taxable dividends and other shareholder benefits from private Canadian and foreign company shares (received directly by the minor or through a trust or partnership)
- income from a partnership or trust derived by the partnership or trust from the business of providing property or services to a business carried on by a relative of the minor or a business in which the relative participates
- capital gains realized by a minor from the disposition of a corporation's shares to a person who does not deal at arm's length with the minor and capital gains allocated to a minor by a trust, if taxable dividends on the shares would have been subject to the tax on split income. These capital gains will be treated as dividends and thus

will neither benefit from the capital gains inclusion rates (see 6.2.1) nor qualify for the capital gains exemption (see 6.4)

- income that is directly or indirectly paid or allocated to a minor from a trust or partnership where the income has been derived from a business or rental source and a person related to the minor is actively involved in these activities. These rules also apply if a person related to the minor has an interest in the partnership, whether directly or indirectly, through another partnership.

Parents are jointly and severally liable for the tax on split income if they were active in the business from which the income was derived. The only deductions allowed against income subject to this tax are the dividend tax credit and foreign tax credit.

The tax does not apply to income earned by minors from property acquired on the death of their parent or income earned by minors who have no parent resident in Canada for tax purposes in the year.

Watch out for the income splitting tax on certain income received by minor children.

These rules do not apply to trust income distributed to your spouse or child who is 18 or older at the end of the year, so income splitting can still be accomplished by allocating the above types of income to older family members, provided the attribution rules discussed in 5.2.2 and 5.2.6 do not apply.

### 5.2.5 Attribution on loans to adult family members

One further rule applies to loans (but not transfers) of property to other persons with whom the taxpayer does not deal at arm's length—such as, for example, one's children who are over 18, or one's in-laws or grandparents. If one of the main reasons for the loan was to achieve income splitting and thereby reduce taxes, the income is attributed back to the lender. So, if you lend $20,000 to your adult son who is in university, and the purpose is to allow him to earn $600 interest and pay little or no tax on it (rather than, say, to allow him to use the $20,000 to pay for his tuition), the $600 of interest is attributed back to you. The exception where interest is charged and paid, as outlined in 5.2.2, applies in this case.

### 5.2.6 Special anti-avoidance rules

If you are creative, you may have thought of some possible ways around the attribution rules we have just described. Don't bother. The federal and Quebec tax laws contain special rules designed to thwart the loopholes that some taxpayers exploited in years past. We summarize them here only briefly; basically, anything you can think of has probably been thought of before.

*Substituted property.* If property is substituted for transferred or loaned property, the attribution rules apply to income or capital gains from the substituted property, and so on *ad infinitum* (to the extent that attribution would have applied to income from the original property). If you give $10,000 in bonds to your spouse, who then sells them and buys $10,000 in stocks, any dividends and capital gains on the stocks is attributed back to you.

*Transfers to a trust or corporation.* In general, transfers to a trust cause the attribution rules to apply in the same way as if the transfers were made directly to the beneficiaries of the trust. Transfers to a corporation that result in a benefit to a "designated person" (spouse or related minor children, using the same definition we saw in 5.2.3) are also caught in most cases. For example, if you and your spouse each own half the shares in a corporation, and you give $10,000 to the corporation so that your spouse will benefit, you are taxed as though you had received a specified amount of interest from the corporation. This attribution rule does not apply where the corporation is a "small business corporation" (see 6.2.3).

*Back-to-back loans and transfers.* If you lend or transfer property to a third party, who then lends or transfers it to a "designated person" (your spouse or related minor children), it is treated as though you had lent or transferred the property directly.

*Guarantees.* If you arrange for a third party (e.g., a bank) to lend funds to a "designated person" on the strength of your guarantee, it is treated as though you had lent the funds directly.

*Repayment of existing loan.* If you lend funds to a "designated person", and they use the funds to pay off another loan that they used to buy property, your loan will effectively be treated as if it had been used to buy that property. (This is the flip side of the "substituted property" case covered above.) For example, if your spouse borrows $10,000 from a bank to invest in bonds, and you then lend your spouse $10,000 that is used to pay off that bank loan, the interest from the bonds is attributed back to you.

*Reverse attribution.* The attribution rules can be ignored if you try to use them to turn the tables on the CRA and have them apply in the opposite direction from that intended.

*General anti-avoidance rule.* The *Income Tax Act* provides a general anti-avoidance rule (GAAR), applicable to all transactions. If you come up with

Beware of the "general anti-avoidance rule".

a way of avoiding the attribution rules that is not caught by the existing rules but is a misuse or abuse of the *Income Tax Act*, it may be caught by GAAR.

## 5.3 Income splitting opportunities

In this section, we discuss the planning opportunities available to achieve income splitting. For many of these to work, you need to keep careful documentation. Separate bank accounts for spouses will allow you to trace each one's funds properly. (Under provincial family law, this will not normally affect either spouse's rights to the family's funds on marriage breakdown.)

### 5.3.1 Increasing the lower-income spouse's investment base

*The higher-income spouse should pay household expenses.* The simplest technique is to make sure that daily living expenses (such as groceries, mortgage or rent payments, and credit card bills) are paid by the higher-income spouse. This allows the lower-income spouse to maintain a larger investment base for earning future income that is taxed at a lower rate.

*Pay your spouse's tax bills with your own funds.* Another way to effectively transfer funds is for you to directly pay your spouse's income tax liability—both in April and any instalments that are due during the year. Simply make sure that the payment for your spouse's taxes is drawn on your own account. Since the amount you pay goes directly to the government and is not invested by your spouse, there is no property from which income can be attributed. The result is that any funds your spouse would otherwise use to pay income taxes can be invested without the income being attributed back to you.

*Pay the interest on your spouse's third-party investment loans.* If your spouse has taken out an investment loan from a third party, consider providing him or her with the funds to pay the interest. There is no attribution provided you do not pay any principal on account of the spousal loan. (Since the amount you pay is not actually invested by your spouse, there is no property from which income can be attributed.) The interest payment will be deductible on your spouse's tax return. This technique preserves your spouse's assets and thereby increases his or her investment income.

*Give your spouse up to $5,500 annually to invest in his or her Tax-Free Savings Account.* You can give your spouse up to $5,500 annually to invest in his or her own Tax-Free Savings Account (TFSA), provided he or she has available contribution room. Since the attribution rules do not apply to amounts transferred to a TFSA, any investment income earned within your spouse's TFSA is not attributed back to you. See 4.1 for details.

### 5.3.2 Employing your spouse and children

If you carry on a business, either personally or through a corporation, consider paying a salary to your spouse and/or children. The salary must be "reasonable" in light of the services they perform for the business. Such services might include bookkeeping, filing, other administrative work, business development planning and acting as a director of the corporation. The CRA and Revenu Québec auditors can be fairly flexible in interpreting what constitutes a "reasonable" salary, provided services are genuinely being provided. To help you determine a reasonable amount, consider how much you would pay an arm's-length person for the same services.

The cost of payroll taxes, Canada Pension Plan contributions and Employment Insurance premiums should be weighed against any potential tax savings.

> Pay a salary or consulting fee to your spouse and/or children.

Consider also whether your spouse can provide services on a contract (consulting) basis rather than as an employee. This would allow your spouse the advantages of self-employment income (see Chapter 11), including writing off expenses. This plan should only be implemented with appropriate professional advice.

Another possibility is to bring your spouse into partnership with you. Taxation of partnerships is discussed in 11.3 and 16.2.

### 5.3.3 Transfers of business assets

The attribution rules, as we have noted, apply to income from *property*—such as interest, dividends, rent and royalties. They do not, however, apply to income earned from a *business*.

> Think about loaning business assets to your spouse or child.

If you can transfer or lend business assets in such a way that your spouse or child carries on business on a regular and continuous basis to earn income from business rather than from property, there is no attribution. Such a step should only be undertaken with proper professional advice, to ensure that the legal steps required to effect the transfer are properly completed and minimize the possible application of the general anti-avoidance rule.

Note that this generally cannot be done for a passive interest in a partnership (including an interest in a limited partnership). Income from the partnership's business is technically business income, but it is deemed to be property income for purposes of the attribution rules unless the taxpayer is actively engaged in the partnership's business or is carrying on a similar business.

### 5.3.4 Spousal loans

Consider making spousal investment loans when interest rates are rising.

As we saw in 5.2.2, the attribution rules do not apply where property or funds are loaned and interest is charged at a minimum rate, provided the interest is actually paid. Where assets are expected to produce a return that is well above the minimum rate (the lesser of a reasonable commercial rate and the CRA prescribed rate), it may make sense to lend the funds or assets and charge a rate of interest sufficient to avoid triggering the attribution rules. The excess yield from the assets over the amount of interest charged is then effectively transferred to the lower-income taxpayer and not attributed back to the lender.

If interest rates are rising, the current CRA prescribed rate may be relatively low, since there is a time lag before it is set each quarter. Where such an opportunity arises, consider making a loan to your spouse (or other family member) on which interest is charged, "locking in" at the low prescribed rate, and having your spouse use the funds to invest at current market rates. (At the time of writing, the CRA's prescribed rate is at a historic low—see 9.3.)

### 5.3.5 Reinvesting attributed income

We have seen that attribution applies to the income from property that is transferred or loaned. But what about the income from that income (secondary income)? Suppose you give $20,000 to your spouse, who earns $600 in interest in the first year, and the $600 is attributed back to you. In the second year, your spouse invests the $600 as well as the $20,000, and the $600 generates a further $18 in interest.

Have your spouse or child earn income on income from loaned or transferred funds.

This "secondary income" of $18 is not attributed back to you, as it is not income from the property that was transferred. It is thus taxed in your spouse's hands. Over time, a significant stream of such secondary income can be built up. However, accurate records must be maintained. You may wish to have your spouse keep two bank accounts, one for the income that is attributed back to you and one into which all income from the first account is deposited. Only the income from the first account would be reported on your return.

### 5.3.6 Transfers for fair market value

Shelter future gains by transferring property at fair market value.

As we have seen, the attribution rules also do not apply where property is transferred in exchange for consideration equal to the property's fair market value. (Where the consideration includes indebtedness, such as a promissory note, interest must be charged as outlined above.) A transfer at fair market value may be beneficial where the assets are expected to produce a high yield or to increase in value in the future. (Bear in mind, however, that the transfer may trigger a capital gain or loss subject to the rules discussed in 5.2.2.)

### 5.3.7 Transferring capital property to children

As we saw in 5.2.3, the attribution rules for minor children do not usually apply to capital gains. If you have assets that are expected to increase substantially in value (such as shares of

> Shelter future gains by transferring capital assets to your children.

a corporation), consider transferring them to your children or to a trust for your children. Any dividends will be attributed back to you as long as your children are under 18 at the end of the year in which the dividend is paid, but capital gains on the sale of the assets will not be.

For example, suppose you own shares in a public corporation. You invested $10,000 originally, and they are now worth $20,000. You expect the corporation to do well over the coming years. If you give the shares to your children, you will be deemed to have disposed of them at $20,000 and will realize a $10,000 capital gain. If, a few years later, your children sell the shares for $100,000, the $80,000 capital gain will be taxed in their hands, not yours, and possibly taxed at a lower marginal rate.

Other assets that might be appropriate for transfer to children are those that normally generate capital gains but not income. Examples include jewellery and art.

Transfers to children should be done with proper professional advice. In some provinces, there is a question as to whether minors can legally own property such as shares. You may need to set up a trust for this purpose.

### 5.3.8 Payment of capital dividends

Normally, dividends that are paid on shares you transfer to your spouse or minor children are attributed back to you. However, the tax system provides for "capital dividends", which are always tax-free. Such dividends include a distribution of the untaxed half of a corporation's capital gains. (For an example, see 14.2.4.)

If you transfer shares of a private corporation, and the shares later pay capital dividends, there is no attribution of the income because it is not taxed in anyone's hands in the first place. As well, any

> Transfer shares that will pay capital dividends.

income earned from reinvesting the capital dividends is not attributed.

Keep in mind that if one of the main purposes of the share transfer is to pay a capital dividend to the new shareholder, the dividend may be subject to an anti-avoidance rule that would deny the capital dividend treatment and treat the dividend as a taxable dividend, resulting in attribution.

### 5.3.9 Spousal RRSP

A contribution to your spouse's RRSP, as we saw in 3.3.1, is specifically allowed for federal and Quebec tax purposes. When the funds are turned into an annuity or RRIF on retirement, no income is attributed back to you as long as your spouse withdraws no more than the minimum amount from the RRIF in the year of the RRSP contribution or the next two years.

**Contribute to your spouse's RRSP.**

Contributions to your spouse's RRSP, if withdrawn by your spouse, are taxed back in your hands to the extent you have made any spousal contributions in the year of withdrawal or in the two previous years. This means that you can split income, provided you can wait 24 to 36 months and make no spousal contributions in the meantime. It also means foregoing the benefits of leaving the funds to grow tax-free in the RRSP (see 3.1.5).

**Example**

On December 31, 2017, you make a first-time contribution of $26,010 to an RRSP for your spouse.

This entitles you to a deduction of $26,010 for 2017 (assuming you have adequate contribution room—see 3.1.3—and have made no contributions to your own RRSP for 2017). Any withdrawals of up to the limit of $26,010 from your spouse's RRSPs in 2018 or 2019 will be attributed back to you, but on January 1, 2020, your spouse can withdraw the full $26,010, which will be taxed in your spouse's hands provided you make no further spousal RRSP contributions in 2018, 2019 or 2020.

**Make spousal RRSP contributions by December 31.**

Of course, when you contribute to a spousal RRSP you use up your own RRSP contribution room, so the tax advantages of this technique are somewhat limited, but it does achieve income splitting over the long term. You must also consider whether your spouse having a higher income at retirement will affect eligibility for the age credit (see 20.3.4) or trigger the Old Age Security clawback (see 20.3.2).

Note that in this example, if you contributed for 2017 on January 1, 2018 rather than December 31, 2017, your spouse would have to wait until January 1, 2021 to withdraw the funds without attribution back to you. Contributions to spousal plans should thus not be put off to January or February, as is often done with one's own contributions.

### 5.3.10 When your children turn 17

**In the year your children turn 17, give them funds they can invest.**

Consider giving your children funds that they can invest. If your child turns 17 in the year you make the gift, the funds can be invested in a one-year (or longer) term deposit or certificate, with the first interest payment being made in the year in which the child turns 18, and no attribution will result. (If the investment is for more than one year with compounding interest, the interest earned must still be reported annually—see 7.2.1.) Do not simply lend the funds without considering the special attribution rule discussed in 5.2.5.

You might also consider a gift of enough funds so that the income earned on the funds will cover the child's university tuition and residence over four (or more) years. Of course, you must be prepared to lose the funds, since they will legally belong to your child and not to you. Consider using a trust (with proper legal advice) if this is a concern.

### 5.3.11 Your children's employment income

Consider lending your child, interest-free, an amount equal to what he or she earns over the summer and would otherwise spend. This will allow the child to earn investment income on his or her own earnings, and the investment income will not be attributed back to you.

Let your children invest their own earnings.

Suppose you have a daughter who attends university and earns $20,000 over the summer, and your normal arrangement with her is that she uses her income to pay for her tuition and basic expenses. If you lend her $20,000 interest-free instead, she can use the funds you lend her to pay her tuition and living expenses, and invest her summer earnings. Since the $20,000 invested represents her own funds, the income earned on that amount will not be attributed back to you and will be taxed at her marginal rate (or not taxed at all if her income is low enough). You could then repeat this process through several years of university, and have your daughter pay back the entire amount of the loan when she graduates, using the funds she has invested from her own earnings. Alternatively, you could lend her less money each year, as she will have her investment income available as an additional source of funds.

### 5.3.12 Canada Child Benefit

The attribution rules do not apply to payments your family receives under the Canada Child Benefit (see 2.3.2).

Deposit Canada Child Benefit payments to your child's bank account.

As a result, you can direct these payments to an "in trust" bank account for your child so that the investment income earned on these amounts will be taxed in your child's hands. You may wish to withdraw the balance from the account annually and purchase higher-yielding investments on your child's behalf.

### 5.3.13 Splitting pension income and CPP/QPP benefit payments

If you earn income eligible for the pension income tax credit (see 20.3.5), you may be able to split this income with your lower-income spouse by filing a joint election with your personal income tax returns. See 20.3.6 for details.

*File a joint election to split pension income with your spouse.*

You can also split income by directing that up to 50% of your Canada or Quebec Pension Plan (CPP/QPP) benefits be paid to your spouse, provided both of you are over 60. If either of you does this, a portion of the other spouse's CPP/QPP is assigned automatically back to the first spouse and the attribution rules will not apply. See 20.3.1 for details.

### 5.3.14 Paying children over 18 for child care

*Claim baby-sitting wages paid to your adult children as child care expenses.*

The deduction for child care expenses was discussed in 2.3.1. No deduction is allowed for payments you make to a person related to you who is under 18. Once your older children turn 18, if you are the lower-income spouse you can claim amounts paid to them for child care or baby-sitting services that permit you to earn employment or business income. Your adult child will need to give you a receipt and report the income for tax purposes.

## 5.4 References

The following publications and more information, including forms and brochures, can be obtained on the CRA's website at *www.cra-arc.gc.ca* or by telephone request at 1-800-959-8281 for individual income tax and trust-related enquiries or 1-800-959-5525 for business and self-employed individual enquiries.

Guide T4040, "RRSPs and Other Registered Plans for Retirement"
Interpretation Bulletin IT-295R4, Archived – "Taxable dividends received after 1987 by a spouse"
Interpretation Bulletin IT-307R4, Archived – "Spousal or common-law partner registered retirement savings plans"
Interpretation Bulletin IT-335R2, Archived – "Indirect payments"
Interpretation Bulletin IT-369RSR, Archived – S.R. – "Attribution of trust income to settlor"
Interpretation Bulletin IT-510, Archived – "Transfer and loans of property made after May 22, 1985 to a related minor"
Interpretation Bulletin IT-511R, Archived – "Interspousal and certain other transfers and loans of property"

Also, see the following selected topics on the CRA's website:

"Contributing to your spouse's or common-law partner's RRSPs"
"Withdrawing from spousal or common-law partner RRSPs"

# Chapter 6

## Capital gains and losses

- Consider delaying the sale of all or part of an asset until after year-end to defer capital gains tax (6.2.1)

- If you have unused net capital losses, carry them back or forward to offset taxable capital gains (6.2.2)

- Carry over unused "allowable business investment losses" to reduce taxable income (6.2.3)

- Classify your gains as capital gains and your losses as business losses, where possible (6.3)

- Make the Canadian securities election to ensure capital treatment for gains on your stock market transactions (6.3)

- "Purify" your corporation to create qualified small business corporation shares eligible for the lifetime capital gains exemption (6.4.1)

- Plan around your CNIL balance when using the capital gains exemption (6.4.3)

- If you've sold an asset but not received all of the proceeds, claim a capital gains reserve (6.5.1)

- Consider changing principal residence ownership to shelter gains on recreation properties (6.5.2)

- Make the election to treat rented-out property as your principal residence (6.5.2)

- Look into the tax deferral benefits for capital gains on investments in eligible small businesses (6.5.3)

*Capital gains and losses are given special treatment in the federal income tax system. Capital gains are effectively taxed at a lower rate than regular income; and individuals are entitled to an exemption for capital gains on certain kinds of property.*

*The rules are substantially the same for Quebec purposes. In this chapter, we'll describe the rules in general and take a look at some of the planning opportunities that are available.*

> *Caution: The tax planning ideas discussed in this chapter may be affected by the federal government's proposed new tax regime for private companies, as outlined in the Department of Finance's July 2017 consultation paper and draft legislation. See Appendix I for details.*

## 6.1 What is capital?

Before we get into the rules that apply to capital gains and losses, it helps to understand what we mean by "capital". Capital property is property that, if sold, will lead to a capital gain (or capital loss). The alternative is property that, when sold, leads to full income inclusion of any gain as income from business. For example, if you speculate on real estate, and you buy and sell a number of properties, your gains on the sales will probably be business income rather than capital gains.

*There are no clear rules defining capital property.* The *Income Tax Act*'s only comment is to define a "business" as including "an adventure or concern in the nature of trade". The courts have developed guidelines over the years, from which a general picture emerges. If you buy property with the intention of reselling it, and particularly if you sell it quickly and engage in many such transactions, your profit is likely to be considered income from business. If you buy property with the intention of earning income (e.g., rent or dividends) from it, and particularly if this is an isolated transaction and you hold the property for a long time, any gain on a sale is likely to be a capital gain.

As we'll see in 6.2.1, most capital gains are only one-half taxed and gains on certain small business shares and farm or fishing property may be eligible for the lifetime capital gains exemption (see 6.4). So it is much better to have capital gains than regular income. On the other hand, capital losses are of limited use since they can only be used to offset capital gains (see 6.2.2), while business losses can be deducted against other income.

## 6.2 Capital gains and losses

### 6.2.1 Ordinary capital gains

Capital gains occur only when property is sold (or is deemed to be disposed of under special rules, which we'll see in 6.5.4). If you own, say, a rental property that has increased in value tenfold, you do not pay any tax on the increase until you actually sell the property. The capital gain is taxed only in the year of the sale.

The basic calculation of a capital gain is easy to understand: proceeds of disposition (normally the sale price), minus any selling expenses (e.g., real estate commissions), minus the "adjusted cost base", equals the capital gain. In most cases the adjusted cost base is simply your cost of the property, but this figure is "adjusted" in various ways. (For the adjusted cost base of an interest in a partnership, see 11.3.5.) Where you have used an election to trigger part of your capital gains exemption (see 6.4), your adjusted cost base will be higher than the actual cost.

Capital gains are, in effect, taxed at a lower rate than regular income. This is done by including in income only the taxable portion of the capital gain, which is one-half of the capital gain.

> **Example**
>
> Alison paid $5,000 (including commission) for shares of the Capital Bank in 2009. On March 1, 2017, she sells the shares for $6,100, of which her broker keeps $100 as commission.
>
> For 2017, Alison has a capital gain of $1,000. The taxable capital gain is one-half, or $500, and this amount is included in her income for tax purposes.

We have mentioned in earlier chapters the marginal tax rates on ordinary income. With one-half taxation of capital gains, the effective tax rates are approximately:

| Income level | Salary income | Capital gains (1/2) |
|---|---|---|
| $12,000–$46,000 | 25% | 12.5% |
| $46,000–$92,000 | 34% | 17.0% |
| $92,000–$142,000 | 42% | 21.0% |
| $142,000–$203,000 | 46% | 23.0% |
| $203,000 and up | 50% | 25.0% |

The exact tax rates and brackets vary by province (see Appendix II).

If you have very large capital gains, minimum tax may apply (see 7.6).

Consider delaying the sale of all or part of an asset until after year-end to defer capital gains tax.

If you sell an asset after the end of the year, any tax on the capital gain will be payable one year later, giving you the use of the funds for an extra year, except to the extent you are required to make quarterly tax instalments (see 9.2.2). A sale on December 31, 2017 will require tax to be paid by April 30, 2018; a sale on January 1, 2018 will require tax to be paid by April 30, 2019.

Note that most stock and bond market transactions normally settle three business days after the trade is entered. (This is standard practice in the brokerage industry and is recognized by the CRA.) Because weekends and public holidays may affect the determination of "business days", if you intend to do any last-minute 2017 trades, consider completing all trades before Christmas and be sure to check the settlement date with your broker.

In some circumstances, you may wish to sell half of an asset at the end of December and the other half at the beginning of January. Doing this will split your capital gain across the two years. This can be beneficial for two reasons. First, you may be able to reduce the marginal rate that applies in both years by keeping your total taxable income below the high tax bracket threshold for each year (which is about $203,000 for 2017). Second, you may be able to avoid minimum tax, due to the $40,000 minimum tax exemption available for each year (see 7.6).

### 6.2.2 Ordinary capital losses

A capital loss occurs when the capital gain calculation produces a negative amount; that is, the adjusted cost base is greater than the proceeds of disposition minus the selling expenses. Just as capital gains are less heavily taxed than regular income, capital losses are less useful to you than regular (business) losses.

An allowable capital loss is *one-half* of a capital loss. This amount can only be offset against taxable capital gains. In normal circumstances, if you have no taxable capital gains, the loss *cannot* be used against other income.

> **Example**
>
> Brent earns an annual salary of $90,000. In October 2017, Brent sells some shares of a bank, which cost him $2,000 several years before, for $5,000 after commission. In November 2017, he sells some shares of an Internet-based company he bought in 2000 for $18,000, and receives only $9,000 since the price of the stock has come down.
>
> Brent has a $3,000 capital gain on the bank shares, which is a $1,500 taxable capital gain. He also has a $9,000 capital loss on the Internet company shares, which is a $4,500 allowable capital loss. This allowable capital loss wipes out the taxable capital gain, but the extra $3,000 of allowable capital loss cannot be used to reduce his salary income of $90,000. This loss can only be used against taxable capital gains of other years, as outlined below.

If you have unused net capital losses, carry them back or forward to offset taxable capital gains.

Allowable capital losses that cannot be used in any given year, as in this example, can be carried back and applied against taxable capital gains of any of the previous three years, subject to whether the capital gains exemption was used in that prior year. They can also be carried forward indefinitely; this balance is known as "net capital losses" and can be used against taxable capital gains in any future year. The inclusion rate for loss carryovers (e.g., for losses occurring before October

20, 2000, when the inclusion rate was higher) is adjusted to match the inclusion rate of the taxation year in which they are used.

If you have any net capital losses that cannot be used in the current year, look into whether you can carry them back to any of your three prior years' returns. The CRA and Revenu Québec are required to reopen and reassess your return when you make such a claim. Make sure as well that you keep track of any such losses that you cannot carry back, and carry them forward to use in future years.

### 6.2.3 Allowable business investment losses

There is an exception to the general rule that allowable capital losses cannot be used against ordinary income. The exception applies to allowable business investment losses, which arise when there is a loss on shares of, or debt owing by, a small business corporation.

The term "small business corporation" has a very specific meaning in the *Income Tax Act*. It need not, in fact, be small. The corporation must meet a number of tests, such that it be resident in Canada, a private corporation, not controlled in any manner by non-residents or public corporations, not listed on a Canadian or any of about 25 foreign stock exchanges, and, most importantly, that substantially all (taken by the CRA to mean 90% or more of the value) of its assets be used in an active business carried on primarily in Canada. Shares and debts in other small business corporations can qualify as such assets.

A capital loss on the shares or debt of a small business corporation (including, in some cases, simply determining that the debt has gone bad and will not be repaid) is called a "business investment loss". One-half of this amount is the "allowable business investment loss" (ABIL), which can be deducted against any other income such as employment income or investment income. However, the amount of the ABIL that can be deducted against other income must be reduced by any capital gains exemption claimed in prior years. The amount of this reduction is treated as an allowable capital loss, which you can use to offset any taxable capital gains. In addition, if an ABIL is deducted against other income, you must realize an equal amount of taxable capital gains in later years before you can use the capital gains exemption again. The availability of an ABIL is an extra incentive to invest in private Canadian businesses.

> **Example**
>
> Janet carries on business as the proprietor of a clothing store, from which she nets $120,000 per year in business income. In 2001, Janet invested $20,000 in shares in XYZ Jewellery Inc., a corporation run by her brother that meets the definition of "small business corporation". In December 2017, the corporation goes bankrupt and Janet's shares become worthless.
>
> Janet has a $20,000 business investment loss in 2017, resulting in a $10,000 allowable business investment loss. She can use this against her $120,000 business income, and so will be taxed in 2017 as if she had earned only $110,000.

**Carry over unused ABILs to reduce taxable income.**

Allowable business investment losses that cannot be fully used (because you have already wiped out all of your income) are treated similar to business losses (see 11.4.1). That is, they can be carried back and used to offset income in any of the three previous years (even though you have already filed returns and paid tax for those years), or they can be carried forward and used to offset income in any of the next 10 years. Any unused balance remaining after the 10th year is reclassified as a net capital loss.

## 6.3 Capital gains vs. income

Depending on the nature of your activities, there may be some question about whether your gains or losses from disposing of property are capital in nature or instead are fully taxable as business income or deductible as business losses.

**Classify your gains as capital gains and your losses as business losses, where possible.**

To the extent possible within the law, you should try to classify your gains as capital gains and your losses as business losses. For example, if you buy and sell a commodity on the stock market, how you classify the transaction may depend on whether you have a gain or a loss. Where you are near the borderline between income and capital, you have some leeway to classify the transaction as either. Of course, you should be consistent; you could not take two essentially identical trades and call one a capital gain and the other a business loss.

For example, if you are buying and selling real estate and doing well at it, try to gather data for your files that will support your claim to be engaging in capital transactions. Evidence that you are purchasing properties purely for their investment value as rental properties, and that any sales were not originally planned but were required by a change in circumstances, can support capital gains treatment.

If you are audited, the CRA may reassess you on your classifications. Then you would have to decide whether to fight the assessment via a Notice of Objection (see 9.5.1) or to accept it and pay the tax that you would have paid in the first place, plus interest. If you are unsure as to whether property you own is capital property or not, you should consult your professional adviser.

If you wish to ensure that your current and future trades on the stock market will always result in capital gains rather than business income, you may file an "Election on Disposition of Canadian Securities" (federal Form T123) with your tax return. This will prevent the CRA or Revenu Québec from claiming that you are buying securities for the purpose of selling them and therefore earning business income rather than capital gains.

Once you do so, all "Canadian securities" you ever own will be considered capital property for the rest of your life. This includes, generally, shares in Canadian corporations, investments in mutual funds, and bonds, debentures or other debt issued by individuals or corporations resident in Canada (except a corporation related to you). Certain taxpayers, such as traders and dealers, are not allowed to make this election.

> Make the Canadian securities election to ensure capital treatment for gains on your stock market transactions.

The downside of making the election is that you will never be able to claim losses on Canadian securities as business losses in the future. Since this is generally hard to do for shares anyway, this may not be a problem. You should consider your entire financial position and obtain professional advice to determine the likely effects of the election.

## 6.4 The lifetime capital gains exemption

Every individual (but not a trust or corporation) is entitled to a lifetime "capital gains exemption" of up to $835,716 for 2017 on certain small business shares. This exemption amount is indexed for inflation annually.

For certain farm and fishing property, the exemption is $1 million (see 6.4.2).

Technically, under the *Income Tax Act* and on the CRA's forms, the exemption is called the capital gains *deduction*. Where it applies, the taxable capital gain is still included in income for tax purposes (see 6.2.1), but an offsetting deduction from net income is allowed when computing "taxable income", the last step on the tax return before calculating tax and tax credits (see 2.1.1).

Note that your $835,716 or $1 million exemption is limited to the *total* gains on both small business shares and family farming and fishing businesses over your lifetime. If in 2017, for example, you have already claimed an exemption for $600,000 of gain on small business shares, the maximum exemption available to you for other small business shares would be $235,716. For eligible farming and fishing property, the amount available would be $400,000.

### 6.4.1 Qualified small business corporation shares

Up to $835,716 of capital gains on "qualified small business corporation shares" can be tax exempt.

The meaning of "small business corporation" was discussed in 6.2.3. The definition of "qualified small business corporation share" is very complex. In very general terms:

- substantially all (considered by the CRA to mean 90% or more of the value) of the business's assets must be used for carrying on an active business in Canada or be shares and debt in other small business corporations (or any combination thereof);
- nobody but you or a person "related" to you can have owned the shares for the two years before you sell them; and
- throughout the two-year period, more than 50% of the corporation's assets must have been used principally in an active business carried on in Canada or invested in other small business corporations (or any combination thereof).

Consult your tax adviser for details as to how these rules apply to any shares you own.

> **Example**
>
> Arnold has not used any of his capital gains exemption in the past. He owns all the shares of a corporation. The shares, which are "qualified small business corporation shares", originally cost him $20,000. On March 1, 2017, Arnold sells the shares for $200,000.
>
> Arnold's capital gain is $180,000. One-half of the gain, or $90,000, is included in Arnold's income for 2017, but an offsetting capital gains deduction of $90,000 is allowed in computing his "taxable income"— so he pays no extra tax, except possibly for minimum tax (see 7.6). Of his $835,716 lifetime exemption that is fully available in 2017, Arnold still has $655,716 ($835,716 minus $180,000) of capital gains, or $327,858 of taxable capital gains, that can be exempt in the future.

As you can see from the example, it doesn't matter whether you think of the exemption as covering $835,716 (in the example, $180,000 plus $655,716) of capital gains, or $417,858 ($90,000 plus $327,858) of taxable capital gains. It comes to the same thing.

If you own shares in a small business, and are considering selling them or transferring them to a family member, you should investigate whether the corporation's shares qualify for the capital gains exemption. There may be steps you can take to "purify" the corporation so that it meets the criteria discussed above. However, this planning may be affected by the federal government's proposed new tax regime for private companies (see Appendix I).

> "Purify" your corporation to create qualified small business corporation shares eligible for the lifetime capital gains exemption.

It is also possible to transfer the assets of a business that you carry on personally (as a proprietor) into a corporation on a tax-free basis in order to take advantage of the exemption. This procedure, known as a "section 85 rollover", requires professional advice, as do other mechanisms for "crystallizing", or locking in, the exemption (see 14.1).

There is also a special election that lets you take advantage of the exemption for qualified small business corporation shares if the corporation goes public, without having to actually sell the shares. (Once the corporation becomes a public corporation, the shares no longer qualify for the exemption.)

With indexing increasing the exemption amount annually, you may benefit by disposing of shares early in a year rather than later in the previous year if it makes sense from a business perspective.

## 6.4.2 Qualified farm and fishing property

The lifetime capital gains exemption generally applies to property used in a family farming or fishing business that meets certain conditions. In general terms, the property will qualify if you have owned the property for at least two years before you sell it, have used the property in the business of farming or fishing on a regular and continuous basis, and have earned more gross income from farming or fishing than from other sources. (If you acquired a farm property before June 18, 1987, it will be qualified farm property if it was used in the business of farming by you or a family member either in the year you sell it or in any five previous years.) Similar rules allow the exemption to be claimed for gains realized on the sale of shares of a family farm or fishing corporation or an interest in a family farm or fishing partnership.

If you own farm or fishing property that you are considering selling, you should obtain professional advice to determine whether you are eligible for the lifetime capital gains exemption.

### 6.4.3 Restrictions on use of the exemption

The *Income Tax Act* provides rules to prevent people from taking what is considered unfair advantage of the capital gains exemption. The exemption is supposed to exempt capital gains from being taxed. If, however, you are able to use the system of capital gains taxation to claim capital-related losses against other income, the rules prevent you from getting the exemption as well. We'll look at the details in this section.

*Allowable business investment losses*

If you have allowable business investment losses (see 6.2.3), you will lose your capital gains exemption to the extent that the losses are or can be written off against your ordinary income. The idea is that such losses should effectively be netted against your taxable capital gains first. In other words, you cannot both have a gain that is sheltered by the capital gains exemption and also use allowable business investment losses against your other income.

*Cumulative net investment loss (CNIL)*

As discussed in 7.2.3, interest paid on a loan is deductible if you use the loan to invest in shares. Even though your reason for buying the shares may be to obtain capital gains, the fact that the shares *could* pay dividends (which are income from property) is generally considered enough to make the interest on the loan deductible as interest on funds borrowed to earn income from property.

Tax policy-makers consider it unfair for people to be able to take out large loans, write off the interest, and use the funds to buy shares that would increase in value, giving them a capital gain that is tax-free due to the capital gains exemption. This kind of "double-dipping" is not allowed.

Your capital gains deduction (normally taken, as we have seen, when calculating your "taxable income") is therefore *reduced* by the amount of your cumulative net investment loss, or CNIL (pronounced "see-nile"). The basic idea is that if you borrow money, buy an investment and the investment goes up in value, you should not be able to get both the capital gains exemption and your interest expense write-off.

The actual calculation is rather more complicated. Your CNIL is the total of your investment expenses minus all your investment income, cumulative since January 1, 1988. "Investment expenses" include interest you have deducted, investment counsel fees, partnership losses (except where you are an active partner), losses from rental property, and most tax shelter write-offs. Investment income includes interest, dividends ("grossed-up" as explained in 7.1.2), rental income and income from a partnership where you are not an active partner.

**Example**

Arnold has not used any of his capital gains exemption in the past, but has claimed a total of $10,000 in net investment expenses since 1995, so his CNIL balance is $10,000. He owns all the shares of a corporation. The shares, which are "qualified small business corporation shares", originally cost him $20,000. On March 1, 2017, Arnold sells the shares for $200,000.

Arnold's capital gain is $180,000. One-half of the gain, or $90,000, is included in Arnold's income for 2017. Because of his $10,000 CNIL balance, the offsetting capital gains deduction is only $80,000, not $90,000.

In effect, Arnold must "eat through" his CNIL balance and pay tax on the $10,000 before he can start to use his capital gains exemption.

Note that the CNIL limitation applies even though the investment expenses and the capital gain are unrelated. However, taxable capital gains that are actually taxed, because you cannot or do not offset them with your capital gains exemption, effectively reduce the impact of the CNIL balance.

Note also that the calculation of the exemption (and CNIL) is done at the end of the year. It is therefore possible to realize a capital gain that you think is exempt, but for which you cannot claim the exemption because you create a CNIL balance later on in the same year. So if you have a CNIL balance, consider reducing or eliminating it before the end of the year. This can be done by increasing your investment income. For example, if you are the owner-manager of an incorporated business (see Chapter 14), you may be able to reduce your salary and increase your dividends from the corporation to use up your CNIL balance. There may also be situations where you can advance interest income receipts before the end of the year, or defer deductible interest payments until after December 31, to reduce your CNIL.

*Plan around your CNIL balance when using the capital gains exemption.*

## 6.5 Special cases

### 6.5.1 Reserves

If you sell a property for a capital gain but do not receive all of the proceeds right away, you may be able to claim a reserve, to defer recognition of the gain for tax purposes.

Suppose, for example, you sell a house you have been renting out. The house cost you $200,000 and you sell it for $400,000. But you take back a mortgage for $200,000. You can normally claim a reserve on the capital gain, reflecting the fraction

*If you've sold an asset but not received all of the proceeds, claim a capital gains reserve.*

of the sale price that you haven't yet received. In this case, since you haven't received half of the sale price, you would only have to recognize half of the gain in the year of sale.

Under the reserve rules, you must recognize at least 1/5 of the gain each year (cumulatively), so that the entire capital gain must be accounted for by the fourth year after the year of sale. (A longer capital gains reserve period is allowed when you sell farming and fishing property to your child—see 15.4.3.)

Claiming a reserve might not be beneficial where you may be in a higher tax bracket in later years.

### 6.5.2  Principal residence

A gain on selling your home is normally completely exempt from taxation. The exemption is based on the definition of "principal residence". This term includes, among other things, a house, a condominium and a share in a co-operative housing corporation. It also includes the land around the house, but normally only up to 1/2 hectare (about 1.2 acres).

You, or your spouse or child, must have "ordinarily inhabited" the residence for it to qualify, so you can't use the exemption on property you rent out without ever having lived in it, or for vacant land. However, it need not have been your "principal" residence in a literal sense. It can be a cottage, for example.

Since 1982, each family unit is limited to one "principal residence" at a time. For this purpose, the family unit means you, your spouse (including a common-law or same-sex spouse as outlined in 2.2.1) and any unmarried children under 18. So if you designate your house as your principal residence for a period of several years, your spouse cannot also designate your cottage as a principal residence over the same period. (The designation is only made when you file your tax return for the year in which you sell the property, so you can decide at that point which property to claim the exemption on.)

Consider changing principal residence ownership to shelter gains on recreation properties.

Before 1982, each taxpayer was entitled to a principal residence exemption. So if you and your spouse or another member of your family unit have owned two residences (such as a regular home and a summer cottage) since before 1982, it may be possible to structure your holdings so that the pre-1982 portion of the capital gain on the second residence will be exempt. Consult a professional adviser on this matter.

If you have adult children, consider giving them the ownership of a second residence. If you own your house and your 19-year-old son owns the cottage, he can designate it as his principal residence when he sells it. However, at the time you transfer it to him, you generally will have to recognize any increase in value since you purchased it. You should also be sure you are satisfied with the legal effect of what you are doing—giving away your cottage—before you embark on such a transaction for tax purposes.

An exemption is also available in some cases where you rent the property out, either before or after you use it as your own residence. If you move out of your home and rent it out, you can continue to designate it as your residence for up to four years (provided you do not claim any other property as your principal residence and you file a special election with your tax return for the year in which you begin to rent the property). If you move due to relocation of your or your spouse's employment, the four-year period can normally be extended indefinitely, provided you move back to the home upon leaving that employment.

> Make the election to treat rented-out property as your principal residence.

If you acquire property and rent it out, and then move in at some later date, you can file a special election with your tax return for the year in which you move in to defer the capital gain that would normally apply when you change the property from income-earning to personal-use. If you do this, you may be able to get an exemption for four years during which you rented the property.

### 6.5.3 Capital gains rollover for investments in eligible small businesses

Under a tax incentive to encourage investments in small business corporations, individual investors may defer capital gains on a small business investment where the proceeds from the investment are used to make other small business investments. The deferred gain reduces the tax cost of the new investment, which may be subject to tax when it is disposed of later.

> Look into the tax deferral benefits for capital gains on investments in eligible small businesses.

Example

On March 31, 2017, Will sells an eligible share investment in Bio Ventures Inc. for $100,000. Since Will had initially invested $40,000 in the company, he realizes a capital gain of $60,000. If only $90,000 of the total proceeds is reinvested in shares of the replacement investment, Agri Tek Inc., then 90% of the gain can be deferred, or $54,000. Will's capital gain, one-half of which will be subject to tax, is equal to the portion that cannot be deferred, or $6,000. The deferred gain of $54,000 reduces the adjusted cost base of the Agri Tek Inc. shares to $36,000, resulting in a potentially larger gain when the shares are sold in the future.

There are currently no limits on the total amount that can be reinvested. You do not have to deal at arm's length with the corporation you are investing in.

To qualify for the rollover treatment, an investment must be ordinary common shares issued from the treasury of an eligible "small business corporation" (see 6.2.3). At the time of the share issue, the total carrying value of the corporation's assets and the assets of any related corporations cannot exceed $50 million. Throughout the period the investor holds the shares, the issuing corporation must be an eligible "active business corporation" (that is, the company must essentially meet the tests for a small business corporation, except that it does not need to remain a private corporation).

Among other requirements, you must hold the eligible investment for six months before a gain can be deferred. You must acquire the replacement investment at any time in the year of the disposition or within 120 days after the end of that year. For example, if you sell an investment in 2017, you must acquire another by April 30, 2018 to qualify for the deferral.

### 6.5.4 Other rules

*Death*—When you die, you are generally deemed for tax purposes to have sold your capital property for its current fair market value, thus triggering a capital gain on all of the increase in value that has accrued since you purchased it. The treatment of capital gains on death is discussed in detail in 22.2.3.

*Non-arm's-length transfers*—When you give or sell property to a member of your family, you are normally deemed to have received fair market value for it, triggering recognition of any accrued capital gain (or loss) for tax purposes. However, if you transfer property to your spouse, it is normally deemed to have been sold at your cost unless you elect to realize a gain. This rule also applies to common-law spouses and same-sex spouses who meet the criteria outlined in 2.2.1.

*Personal-use property*—No capital loss is available on personal-use property, except for "listed personal property" (jewellery, works of art, stamps, coins and rare books) losses that can be used only against listed personal property gains.

As well, the adjusted cost base and proceeds of disposition of personal-use property are deemed to be $1,000, which essentially means that capital gains on personal-use property only apply to the extent the sales price exceeds $1,000. The $1,000 deemed adjusted cost base and deemed proceeds of disposition do not apply if the property is acquired as part of an arrangement in which the property is donated as a charitable gift.

If you change a property from personal use to income-earning use, you are normally deemed to have sold it at its fair market value, requiring you to recognize for tax purposes any accrued capital gain.

*Options*—Special rules apply to determine capital gains where you purchase or grant options (e.g., on the stock market).

*Superficial loss*—If you sell property (e.g., shares) to trigger a capital loss, and you or your spouse or a corporation controlled by either of you acquire identical property within 30 days before or after your sale, the capital loss will be a "superficial loss" and ignored for tax purposes. The denied loss will be added to the cost of the identical property.

*Insurance or expropriation proceeds*—If property of yours is lost or destroyed or expropriated, any insurance settlement or expropriation payment is considered proceeds of disposition for purposes of the capital gains calculation described in 6.2.1.

*Charitable donations*—If you donate certain capital property to a registered charity, you may not have to pay tax on any inherent capital gain but you can still get a tax credit for the full value of the donation (see 8.3.2).

*Pre-1972 property*—If you have property that you have owned since before 1972, when capital gains were not taxed at all, only the gain accruing after 1971 will be taxed. For publicly traded shares, valuation is easy; for real estate and shares in private businesses, valuation as of December 31, 1971 may be difficult to accomplish. When you report such a gain, you will need to estimate the value of the property on that date, and use that as the cost of the property (assuming it is higher than your actual cost).

## 6.6 References

The following publications and more information, including forms and brochures, can be obtained on the CRA's website at *www.cra-arc.gc.ca* or by telephone request at 1-800-959-8281 for individual income tax and trust-related enquiries or 1-800-959-5525 for business and self-employed individual enquiries.

Guide T4037, "Capital Gains"
Income Tax Folio S1-F3-C2, "Principal Residence"
Interpretation Bulletin IT-170R, Archived – "Sale of property—When included in income computation"
Interpretation Bulletin IT-218R, Archived – "Profits, capital gains and losses from the sale of real estate, including farm land and inherited land and conversion of real estate from capital property to inventory and vice versa"
Interpretation Bulletin IT-232R3, Archived – "Losses—Their deductibility in the loss year or in other years"

Interpretation Bulletin IT-387R2 Consolidated, Archived – "Meaning of identical properties"

Interpretation Bulletin IT-456R, Archived – "Capital property—Some adjustments to cost base"

Interpretation Bulletin IT-459, Archived – "Adventure or concern in the nature of trade"

Interpretation Bulletin IT-479R and 479RSR, Archived – "Transactions in securities"

Interpretation Bulletin IT-484R2, Archived – "Business investment losses"

# Chapter 7

## Investments

- Consider acquiring preferred shares instead of debt to reduce the overall tax rate (7.1.2)
- If you're the higher-income spouse, consider electing to report your spouse's dividend income on your own return (7.1.6)
- Look into the potential benefits of investing in a dividend reinvestment plan (7.1.7)
- Defer tax by acquiring investments that mature shortly after year-end (7.2.1)
- Structure your investments to make interest deductible (7.2.3)
- Consider the merits of acquiring an exempt life insurance contract (7.3.3)
- Consider investing in tax shelters—but don't let tax write-offs drive your decision (7.5)
- Before investing in a tax shelter, obtain its identification number (7.5.1)
- Be aware of the possible impact of minimum tax on otherwise tax-free capital gains (7.6.3)

*In this chapter, we look at how investment income is taxed, how interest expense can be written off, and a few types of tax shelters, along with a number of tax planning ideas that you should keep in mind. We also discuss special tax rules that apply to foreign investments. The chapter concludes with a discussion of Canada's alternative minimum tax, which may apply depending on the nature of your investments. For advice on developing an appropriate investment strategy, see 1.1.4.*

## 7.1 Dividends

### 7.1.1 What is a dividend?

A dividend is a distribution of after-tax profits to the shareholders (owners) of a corporation. A corporation may have many classes of shares. Preferred shares often have priority over common shares on the payment of dividends and also have priority over common shares on the winding-up of a corporation.

Preferred shares typically pay a fixed annual or quarterly dividend. In some ways, they are similar to bonds or other debt, since the return is a fixed percentage. However, in certain situations a corporation may not be *required* to pay dividends on its preferred shares as long as it does not pay dividends on its common shares. If the corporation suffers losses, its board of directors may well decide not to pay dividends on preferred shares.

From a tax point of view, for individuals, preferred shares are identical to common shares (which typically pay dividends that bear some relationship to the corporation's profits).

### 7.1.2 How is a dividend taxed?

Dividends received by individuals from Canadian corporations are taxed in a rather peculiar manner, designed to reflect the fact that the corporation paying the dividend has already paid tax on its profits. The amount included in the individual's income is "grossed-up" to notionally reflect the total amount of pre-tax income that the corporation is presumed to have earned. The individual then receives a credit to offset the tax the corporation is presumed to have paid. In no case, however, is the *actual* income earned or tax paid by the corporation taken into account.

"Eligible" Canadian dividends received by individuals from public corporations and Canadian-controlled private corporations (CCPCs) that have been paid out of business income taxed at the high corporate tax rate are grossed-up by 38% for 2017. That is, you add 38% to the amount received and show the total as income from dividends on your tax return. The offsetting federal dividend tax credit for 2017 is 15% of the grossed-up dividend (i.e., 20.7% of the actual dividend). Similar credits are available at the provincial level.

Dividends received from CCPCs that pay tax at the small business rate (see 14.1) are treated differently. These "non-eligible" dividends are grossed-up by 17% for 2017, and the federal dividend tax credit for 2017 is 10.5% of the grossed-up dividend (i.e., 12.3% of the actual dividend).

In 2017, assuming the highest marginal tax rate applies, eligible dividends are taxed at combined federal and provincial/territorial rates ranging from 24.81% to 42.62%. Non-eligible dividends are taxed at rates ranging from 35.72% to 46.97%, depending on your province or territory of residence.

Example

Melissa earns $80,000 per year. She also owns shares in Canadian Inc., a public company, which pay her a dividend of $1,000 in 2017.

Melissa's income for 2017 will be $80,000, plus the $1,000 dividend, plus a gross-up of 38% of the dividend, or $380. Her tax will be calculated on this income of $81,380. From the tax, she will deduct her regular credits (see Chapter 2) and a federal dividend tax credit of $207 (20.7% of the actual dividend). Melissa then calculates her provincial dividend tax credit in a similar fashion. The net result is that the dividend is taxed at a significantly lower rate than the marginal rate of about 34% that applies to her ordinary income.

(See 14.2.1 for more detail on the dividend tax credit from the perspective of the corporation.)

Remember that this information applies only to dividends from Canadian corporations. Dividends from foreign corporations are taxed as ordinary income.

Since preferred shares pay dividends rather than interest (which is taxed like regular income, as we'll see in 7.2), preferred shares may offer a better after-tax rate of return than many interest-earning investments while still coming close to a guaranteed yield. While the yield is never completely guaranteed, many major public companies will continue to meet preferred share dividend expectations even when they suffer losses.

> Consider acquiring preferred shares instead of debt to reduce the overall tax rate.

The yields on preferred shares usually reflect the fact that dividends are less heavily taxed than interest (as well as the fact that dividend payments are not deductible to the corporation). You or your investment adviser will have to monitor preferred share distributions and prices on the market to find the best yields.

### 7.1.3 Stock dividends

A corporation will sometimes pay a stock dividend by issuing new shares to pay the dividend rather than giving you cash. In such a case, the gross-up and dividend tax credit still apply, and you must pay tax on the stock dividend even though you have received no cash. The amount of the dividend on which the gross-up is calculated is the increase in the corporate paid-up capital resulting from the issue of new shares. If you sell the stock in order to produce cash to pay the tax, you may also have a capital gain or loss.

### 7.1.4 Capital dividends

> **Caution:** *The tax planning ideas discussed in this section may be affected by the federal government's proposed new tax regime for private companies, as outlined in the Department of Finance's July 2017 consultation paper and draft legislation. See Appendix I for details.*

You may also receive capital dividends from private corporations. They are completely tax-free (see 5.3.8). A capital dividend is generally a distribution of the untaxed one-half of capital gains realized by the corporation. As we saw in 6.2.1, that fraction of the capital gain is not taxed at all. The capital dividend mechanism is used to distribute the untaxed portion without any tax consequences to the shareholder. (For an example, see 14.2.4.)

### 7.1.5 Dividends received by a corporation

Intercorporate dividends are normally tax-free. The assumption is that once a corporation has paid tax on its income, its profits can be distributed through a chain of holding corporations with no further tax consequences until an individual receives a dividend at the end of the chain. However, a special refundable tax—"Part IV tax"—can apply to intercorporate dividends in some circumstances, including most dividends received on investments in public corporations. The Part IV tax rate for certain corporations is 38-1/3%. Since intercorporate dividends may be taxable in certain other circumstances, professional advice in this area is strongly recommended.

### 7.1.6 Election to transfer dividends from spouse

Since the dividend tax credit is a credit against tax owing, it is worthless if there is no tax to pay. If your spouse's income is very low, remember that any income your spouse earns in the year reduces the spousal credit amount dollar for dollar and that no spousal credit is available for 2017 once your spouse's income is approximately $11,635 or more. Thus any amount of the grossed-up dividend income reported on your spouse's return can reduce your spousal tax credit. At the same time, since your spouse does not pay any tax, the dividend tax credit is of no use.

*If you're the higher-income spouse, consider electing to report your spouse's dividend income on your own return.*

In such a case, you may elect to report all of your spouse's dividend income on your own tax return. While this may result in the income being taxed at a higher rate, it will avoid the erosion of the spousal tax credit. You will have to calculate tax both ways to see which is better. This election is done by including the dividends directly on Schedule 4 (Investment income) of your tax return, not Schedule 2 (Amounts transferred from spouse). If you live in Quebec, you do not need to make the similar election for Quebec tax purposes. Quebec taxpayers can claim the unused portion of their spouse's non-refundable tax credits, including the dividend tax credit (see 17.2).

### 7.1.7 Dividend reinvestment plan (DRIP)

Dividend reinvestment plans may offer a cost-effective way of building your investment portfolio. DRIPs give investors the opportunity to automatically reinvest their cash dividends by purchasing additional shares or fractional shares

> Look into the potential benefits of investing in a dividend reinvestment plan.

directly from the company on the dividend payment date. The additional shares are usually purchased at a discount from the current share price and without brokerage commissions.

Many of these plans allow you to periodically purchase more shares of the company with cash at a discount for nominal or no fees. (Depending on the nature of the plan, the discount may trigger a taxable shareholder benefit—check with your broker or the plan's administrator to avoid surprises.)

Bear in mind that you will still be liable for tax on the dividends in the current year. Because the dividend income is reinvested, you will have to pay the tax with other funds (or sell some of your investment). Amounts reinvested will also incrementally increase the cost base of your investment, which will affect the average cost of the shares for capital gains tax purposes when you sell them (see 6.2.1).

## 7.2 Interest income

Interest income is taxed at the same rates as employment or business income.

### 7.2.1 Accruing interest

Suppose you acquire a five-year GIC for $1,000 that will return $1,160 after five years (assuming a compound interest rate of 3%). When do you report the $160 in interest?

Each year you must declare the interest accrued to the anniversary date of when you acquired it. Your financial institution should issue you a T5 slip showing the interest accruing on all such long-term investments, regardless of whether you receive the cash.

> **Example**
>
> In 2012, Christine lent $10,000 to her cousin, Ben, who is attending university and needed the funds for tuition and residence. Ben agreed in writing to pay 6% annual interest (not compounded) on the loan, but that he will not pay back the loan or the interest until after he has graduated and secures a job.
>
> Christine is required to report and pay tax on $600 of accrued interest income each year beginning in 2013. If, in 2017, Ben pays her $13,000 to cover the loan and all interest, she will only report $600 as income in 2017, since she will have already reported $2,400 over the previous four years (2013–2016).

**Defer tax by acquiring investments that mature shortly after year-end.** The accrual rules apply to almost all kinds of investments, including strip bonds (see 7.2.2 below), Canada Savings Bonds, and mortgages or loans to third parties or to relatives on which interest is allowed to accrue.

As a general tax deferral strategy, acquire investments that mature shortly after year-end rather than just before. For example, if you are investing in T-bills on July 15, 2017 and you can choose between maturity dates of December 29, 2017 and January 2, 2018, then you should choose January 2 if all else is equal. That way you will defer reporting and paying tax on the income by one year. Of course, tax considerations should not override normal investment considerations, such as the available rates of return and the question of when you will need access to the funds.

### 7.2.2 Strip bonds and clipped coupons

Strip bonds are long-term government or government-backed (e.g., provincial hydro) bonds that pay interest when their coupons are cashed in. A typical bond might have a 20-year term, have a face value of $100,000, and come with coupons paying $2,500 in interest, cashable every six months. At the end of the 20 years one simply redeems the bond for $100,000.

Brokerage firms often acquire such bonds and split up the bond and its coupons, selling them separately. The $100,000 bond maturing in 20 years, in our example, might be sold for $10,000, while the forty $2,500 coupons would be sold at prices reflecting the length of time until their maturity.

For tax purposes, the difference between the discounted price of the bond (or coupon) and the amount you receive when it is redeemed is considered interest. Because of the annual accrual rule, such bonds generally are unattractive to many taxpayers—you have to pay tax annually on interest that you will not receive for some time. However, they can be excellent investments for self-directed RRSPs and other tax-deferred plans (see Chapters 3 and 4).

Be cautious when acquiring strip bonds or clipped coupons—or, for that matter, any long-term bond. If you need to sell them before they mature, you will find that their value may fluctuate considerably due to trends in interest rates. If interest rates in general have gone up, the resale value of your bond or coupon will likely have gone down.

### 7.2.3 Deductibility of interest expense

As a general principle, interest is deductible for tax purposes as long as the loan was used for the purpose of earning income from a business or property. Such expenses are also called "carrying charges".

If you borrow money to buy common or preferred shares on the stock market, or to invest in a business, the interest you pay is generally deductible. Similarly, if you buy an investment with a fixed interest rate, you generally can deduct interest on your loan.

Interest is not deductible if the loan is taken out for some purpose other than to earn income subject to tax. Examples include:

- home mortgage, except to the extent you use a home office for business purposes (see 11.2.10)
- car loan, where the car is used solely for personal use
- credit cards, except to the extent the charges are for business expenses
- loan to contribute to an RRSP, TFSA or RESP
- interest on late income tax or instalment payments.

If you dispose of the property that you borrowed money to acquire, you can continue to deduct the interest in certain cases even though the underlying source of income has been lost. The rules in this area are complex, and professional advice may be required if you are in this situation.

For Quebec purposes, you may only deduct expenses paid to earn income from property from your investment income earned in the year (see 17.11.1).

Interest on a car loan, where the car is used for your employment or business purposes, is limited to the employment or business portion of $300 per month (see 12.3.1).

Since interest on consumer loans and home mortgages is normally not deductible, while interest on loans taken out to purchase income-generating investments is generally deductible,

> Structure your investments to make interest deductible.

you should try to ensure that all loans you take out are for a deductible purpose. For example, if you have funds that you could put towards either a home mortgage or investments and you plan to do both, you will probably be better off to use the funds towards the mortgage and take out a loan to purchase the investments.

The CRA often pays special attention to deductions for interest expense. It is wise to keep on file, along with your tax return, accurate records showing the amount of the loan, the purpose of the loan and the interest paid during the year, along with the relevant financial statements and possibly a confirming letter from your financial institution. It may be appropriate to file this information with your tax return if you have claimed a deduction for interest in the current or previous year.

For minimum tax purposes, interest expense must be added back to your income if it relates to tax shelters or other "tainted" deductions. See 7.6.2.

## 7.3 Other tax-effective investments

### 7.3.1 Mutual funds

Mutual funds are pools of assets that are invested by professional managers, either in general investments or in a particular sector (such as real estate or natural resources). Investors purchase units if the mutual fund is a trust or purchase shares if the fund is a corporation.

Mutual fund trusts are flow-through entities for tax purposes—taxable income earned inside the entity is treated as if you held the investments directly, instead of through the fund. As such, the income retains its character for tax purposes (e.g., as dividend income, capital gains or interest) when it is distributed to you during the time you own the units, and taxed accordingly. A management fee, also known as a management expense ratio, is paid from income earned by the fund to compensate the fund's professional managers. Although the fee is a cost of the fund itself, the amount of the fee will affect your rate of return.

When you redeem or sell the units or shares, you are taxed on the capital gain, if any, according to the regular treatment of capital gains discussed in 6.2.1.

### 7.3.2 Income funds

Income funds have been popular as tax-effective investments. However, the government announced a new tax regime for these vehicles on October 31, 2006. The new rules eliminated many of the current tax benefits for most existing income trusts at the end of 2010.

Income funds came in a variety of forms, but were generally publicly traded mutual fund trusts that owned businesses, such as real estate, resource properties (oil, gas, and mining) and other assets, which typically produced a stable stream of cash flow. Cash flowed from the operating business to the income fund, and the fund made distributions to its investors at regular intervals.

Under the previous rules, distributions from the fund to investors were generally a mix of income and capital payments. Amounts paid or payable to an investor as income were taxed according to the regular rules for interest, dividends or capital gains, depending on the payment's nature (provided the fund made the appropriate designations). But, as we will see in 14.2.5, an amount received as a payment of capital may be treated as a return of funds that the investor initially used to buy the asset, so no tax should have applied to the capital payment.

For certain remaining income funds, these rules may still apply.

A special tax applies to distributions from publicly traded income trusts (and certain limited partnerships, see 7.5.3) established after October 31, 2006. Trusts already in existence on that date became subject to the new tax in their 2011 taxation year. Under this regime, the tax treatment of income trusts is more like that of corporations and investors in income trusts are taxed on their distributions as though the distributions were dividends.

Amounts received as repayments of capital from an income fund reduce the "adjusted cost base" of your investment (see 6.2.1), which is subtracted from your sales proceeds when you sell the investment to determine your capital gain. Though you will not pay current tax on a portion of investment income received during the year, you may eventually pay tax on a larger capital gain on the investment when you sell your income fund units.

Income fund investors should also be aware of the potential application of the minimum tax (see 7.6).

### 7.3.3 Exempt life insurance contracts

The life insurance industry has developed attractive and highly sophisticated products that can help you meet two objectives at once: having insurance coverage and providing retirement income from tax-sheltered growth.

These policies allow you to pay insurance premiums and make deposits to a tax-sheltered investment account at the same time. You can choose between more conservative investments, such as GICs, or investments that involve more risk, such as equity indices. Unlike RRSP contributions, which are tax-deductible and thus are made with before-tax dollars, insurance premiums are not deductible. In both cases, the income earned is tax-sheltered until maturity of the plan or policy. Funds withdrawn from the policy during your lifetime are taxable to the extent the amount withdrawn exceeds its adjusted cost basis. On death, the entire amount (that is, the original insurance amount plus the accumulated cash value) is received tax-free as a death benefit. Alternatively, funds withdrawn may be treated as a loan against your policy that is repaid from the death benefit.

> Consider the merits of acquiring an exempt life insurance contract.

If you have maximized your TFSA and RRSP contributions, this type of life insurance policy may provide another opportunity for you to shelter your savings from tax.

Keep in mind that new rules reduce the maximum amount of tax-exempt savings allowed inside new insurance policies, starting January 1, 2017. These rules generally do not apply to existing policies.

There are many issues to look at when considering whether to acquire such a contract, such as the underlying mortality costs and administrative expenses, a guaranteed minimum rate of return compared to a similar return in a non-tax sheltered environment, your required life insurance coverage, your income objectives, investment management fees, the financial reserves and strength of the insurance company and so on. Professional advice is a must when assessing the merits of this type of "investment". Insurance policies are, however, a potential opportunity for those who cannot otherwise find alternative tax deferral arrangements.

Life insurance is discussed in more detail at 21.7.

## 7.4 Special rules for investments in foreign property

Over the past few years, tax rules and reporting requirements have been introduced to address the government's perception that many Canadians are avoiding Canadian tax by transferring their assets and income outside of the country. Some of these rules are discussed below.

The tax rules in this area are complex and penalties for non-compliance may be onerous. If you own investments outside of Canada, you should consult with a tax adviser to make sure your Canadian tax obligations are met.

If you own assets or other property in the U.S., see Chapter 19. If you contribute to or are a beneficiary of a trust resident outside of Canada, see 7.4.3.

### 7.4.1 Reporting rules for foreign investment property

You have to file an annual information return with the CRA if you own or have interests in foreign property where the aggregate cost is more than $100,000 at any time in the year. For these reporting purposes, foreign property includes:

- ʳfunds in foreign bank accounts
- rental property outside Canada
- Canadian securities held outside Canada
- investments in foreign corporations, trusts, partnerships or other foreign entities.

Excluded from these rules are interests in foreign affiliates (see below), property used in an active business, property held in RPPs, RRSPs, RRIFs and TSFAs, and personal-use property such as a vacation property.

Form T1135, "Foreign Income Verification Statement", is due at the same time as your personal tax return and can be filed electronically. To complete the form, you must:

- describe each foreign property
- provide the country location of the foreign property held
- disclose the maximum cost amount during the year
- disclose the cost amount at the end of the year
- identify whether any income (or loss) was earned from the property during the year
- identify whether any capital gain (or loss) arose on the property's disposition.

You are still required to report your foreign property even if you receive a T3 slip or a T5 slip for the property.

If you hold your foreign property in the account of a Canadian registered securities dealer or a Canadian trust company, you may be able to use a streamlined reporting option. Under this option, you can choose to report the total aggregate value of all such property on a country-by-country basis instead of reporting the details of each property separately.

If you have specified foreign property that is valued at more than $100,000 but less than $250,000 throughout the year, you may also be able to use a simplified form to report the property.

New immigrants to Canada do not have to file this information return in the year in which they become resident.

The CRA can extend the three-year reassessment period for your taxation year to six years if you failed to report income from a foreign property on your income tax return and did not file Form T1135, filed it late or reported incorrect information on the form.

Similar reporting rules apply if you own (together with related persons) 10% or more of a foreign corporation, if you transfer or lend property to a non-resident trust (or a corporation controlled by it), or if you receive distributions from, or are indebted to, an offshore trust.

The information required is extensive and the penalties for non-compliance are severe. You should seek help from your tax adviser if you own or have an interest in such foreign property.

### 7.4.2 Foreign investments

If you own certain types of foreign investments, you may have been affected by proposed tax rules applying to "foreign investment entities" (FIE) that the government first announced in 1999. The broad objective of these proposed rules was to accelerate a Canadian tax liability in the hands of taxpayers owning an interest in a FIE.

These proposed rules created much controversy until the government eliminated them in the 2010 federal budget. Instead, the government has made some limited enhancements to the existing rules in the *Income Tax Act* that apply to offshore investment funds. These changes generally apply to 2010 and later years.

If you have an interest in any form of non-resident entity, you should ask your tax adviser whether the rules apply to your foreign investments.

### 7.4.3 Trusts resident outside of Canada

If you are a Canadian resident contributor to a non-resident trust or a Canadian resident beneficiary of a non-resident trust, you may face a substantial tax liability as a result of tax rules regarding the taxation of income earned by non-resident trusts.

These rules generally apply to non-resident trusts that have a Canadian resident contributor, or a Canadian beneficiary and a contributor with a significant connection to Canada.

Since these rules were first proposed in 1999, they changed several times and finally became law in 2013, with retroactive effect.

If the rules apply, the trust is deemed to be a resident of Canada and will be taxed in Canada on its income and capital gains that are connected with Canada.

If you have an interest in or are involved in any way with a non-resident trust, contact a tax adviser for help in determining the potential impact of these rules. (For a general discussion of the taxation of trusts, see 21.5.)

## 7.5 Tax shelters

Tax shelters are no longer as important to tax planning as they were some years ago. For a variety of reasons, there are now relatively few publicly offered vehicles for sheltering your ordinary income from tax.

Consider investing in tax shelters—but don't let tax write-offs drive your decision.

You should only invest in a tax shelter if, after taking the tax benefits into account, there is a reasonable expectation of profit from the shelter. The CRA is extremely aggressive in challenging tax shelter-related deductions. The tax benefits alone should not control your investment decision.

Strict rules are in place that make many tax shelters unattractive. For example, "at-risk" rules prevent you from writing off more than the original cost of your investment (that is, in a limited partnership tax shelter—see 7.5.3). Other rules take aim at certain types of tax shelter investments that have rights to receive future income, such as limited partnership structures involving mutual fund limited partnerships, curtailing the tax benefits of such investments.

The federal government also wants to discourage taxpayers from participating in certain charitable donation tax shelters. If you participate in such a tax shelter, the CRA may disallow a deduction or tax credit you claim as a result of that participation and assess tax, interest or penalties. If you object to this reassessment, the CRA is allowed to collect up to 50% of the assessed income taxes, interest or penalties in dispute. Normally, the CRA cannot collect amounts in dispute if an objection or appeal is outstanding (see 9.5.4).

When investing in tax shelters, you must be aware of the possible application of the minimum tax (see 7.6). Finally, you must always be aware of the possible application of the general anti-avoidance rule discussed in 5.2.6.

For details on RRSPs, TFSAs and other tax-assisted plans, see Chapters 3 and 4.

### 7.5.1 Tax shelter identification number

Anyone selling an interest in a tax shelter must obtain an identification number from the CRA (and Revenu Québec, in some cases) and provide that number on all documents and financial statements relating to the shelter. *If you do not have the identification number, or if any penalties relating to the identification number are payable by the promoter and have not been paid, you will not be able to claim the benefits of the shelter.*

The identification number does not indicate approval by the CRA or Revenu Québec of the proposed benefits. It merely ensures that the shelter has been registered for administrative

> Before investing in a tax shelter, obtain its identification number.

purposes, making audit and reassessment easier for the CRA and Revenu Québec if they eventually decide to disallow some or all of the tax benefits.

If the promoter of a tax shelter you invest in has not filed its required information return as part of the registration process, the CRA can extend the normal three-year reassessment period for your tax return until three years after the information return is filed.

### 7.5.2 Information reporting for aggressive tax planning

Along with the tax shelter registration rules described above, the federal government has requirements for reporting aggressive tax planning transactions. Under these rules, you may be required to report a transaction if it contains at least two of the following hallmarks:

- The promoter or tax adviser of the transaction is entitled to contingent remuneration.
- The promoter or tax adviser requires confidentiality protection for the transaction.
- You obtain contractual protection for the transaction.

If you are required to report a transaction, you will have to file the prescribed form RC312 by June 30 following the calendar year in which the transaction first became reportable.

Like the tax shelter rules, the CRA can extend the normal three-year reassessment period to three years after the form reporting an aggressive tax planning transaction has been filed.

A similar aggressive tax planning reporting regime applies in Quebec.

### 7.5.3 Tax shelters involving limited partnerships

Tax law changes over the years have curtailed the benefits of tax shelters involving the purchase of an interest in a limited partnership.

A limited partnership is a partnership, in that you share the profits of the business with the other partners, and report a percentage of the partnership's income (or loss) directly as your income—whether or not you have received any of the profits. This flow-through concept is in contrast to corporate profits, which are reported only when distributed as dividends, as we saw in 7.1.2. However, a limited partnership is similar to a corporation in that you have limited liability—you cannot be sued for the partnership's debts, provided you are a passive investor. In general, you can only lose your original investment.

Because you can report partnership losses directly on your own tax return, limited partnerships used to be an attractive investment where the partnership business was expected to have losses in its initial years (either real losses due to start-up costs, or tax-created losses due to high write-offs available on certain kinds of investments).

However, you may not write off more than the original cost of your investment. The "at-risk" rules in the *Income Tax Act* do not allow you to deduct more than the amount you have at risk in a limited partnership. Other rules severely restrict the use of limited partnerships to create losses where there is "non-recourse" debt (i.e., you are required to contribute amounts to the partnership, but cannot be forced to do so from your own funds, only from the profits from your partnership interest).

Losses from limited partnerships must be added back to income for minimum tax purposes (see 7.6.2).

The tax on income trusts (see 7.3.2) also applies to distributions from certain publicly traded limited partnerships established after October 31, 2006. Limited partnerships that existed on October 31, 2006 had until their 2011 taxation year before this tax applied.

## 7.6 Minimum tax

### 7.6.1 What is the minimum tax?

The minimum tax was enacted as a political solution to the perception that many high-income taxpayers were paying little tax through the use of tax shelters and other so-called tax preferences. It is relatively narrow in focus, concentrating on specific shelters and credits.

The minimum tax is an alternative tax calculation. You must calculate your tax both normally and under the minimum tax rules, and pay the higher of the two.

In simplest terms, you calculate minimum tax by taking your taxable income, adding back "tainted shelter" deductions (such as resource write-offs and tax shelters) and 60% of the untaxed one-half of capital gains, taking a $40,000 exemption and then calculating federal tax at 15% for 2017. Most personal credits, but not the dividend tax credit or investment tax credits, are then allowed as with regular tax.

A similar calculation is required at the provincial level, with provincial minimum tax rates (except Quebec) ranging from 33.7% to 57.5% of federal minimum tax (with possible adjustments for provincial credits and provincial surtax, depending on the province). The Quebec minimum tax generally mirrors the federal system but with its own rules and calculations. The Quebec minimum tax rate is 16%.

Minimum tax paid can be recovered in the next seven years to the extent your regular tax exceeds your minimum tax (see 7.6.2). Minimum tax does not apply to the year of death.

### 7.6.2 Calculating the tax

Somewhat simplified, the calculation is as follows:

1. **Start with your taxable income** (after all deductions allowed for regular tax purposes).

2. **Add back the deductions** that you are not allowed to claim for minimum tax purposes:

   - losses from any investment that requires a tax shelter identification number (see 7.5.1)
   - losses from a partnership that is a tax shelter (see 7.5.3)
   - certain resource-related deductions

- certain carrying charges, including interest expense relating to any of the above (see 7.2.3)
- employee home relocation deduction (see 10.3)
- 60% of amounts claimed under the employee stock option deduction (see 10.4.1 and 10.4.2).

These are sometimes called "tainted" deductions, since you cannot claim them for minimum tax purposes.

3. **Add 60% of the untaxed one-half of capital gains**, whether the rest of the gain was eligible for the capital gains exemption or not. (The exemption is still allowed for minimum tax purposes.)

4. **Deduct the gross-up on dividends** (see 7.1.2). Since the dividend tax credit is not allowed for minimum tax purposes, you are only taxed on the actual dividend received, rather than on the grossed-up amount.

5. **Deduct $40,000** as your basic minimum tax exemption.

6. **Calculate federal tax at 15% for 2017.**

7. **Deduct personal credits** (see Chapter 2), such as your basic credit, other dependants, old age, disability (for self or spouse only), CPP/QPP contributions, EI premiums, tuition, education, medical and charitable. Do not deduct investment tax credits (see 11.2.14), political contribution credits (see 2.7.2), pension tax credits (see 20.3.5), transfer of unused tax credits from spouse (see 2.1.3), tuition and education credits transferred from a child (see 2.4.4), dividend tax credits (see 7.1.2) or labour-sponsored venture capital credits (see 3.3.5).

8. If the resulting tax is higher than your federal tax calculated normally, you must **pay the minimum tax**.

Provincial minimum tax is then generally calculated by multiplying the federal minimum tax amount by the applicable provincial minimum tax rate.

If you find that you have to pay minimum tax in any given year, the excess of your minimum tax over your regular tax becomes a "minimum tax carryover", which can be used in any of the next seven years.

In a future year, you can use the carryover to the extent your regular tax exceeds your minimum tax.

Riley's 2017 regular federal tax is $30,000. His 2017 minimum tax (federal) is $35,000.

Riley must pay the $35,000 tax and provincial taxes (about, say, $53,000 in total). However, he has a $5,000 federal minimum tax carryover. If, in 2018, his regular federal tax is $32,000 and his minimum (federal) tax is $22,000, Riley can deduct the carryover from his regular federal tax and pay only $27,000 basic federal tax (before calculating provincial tax).

### 7.6.3 Tips for minimizing minimum tax

#### Exempt capital gains

The minimum tax can have a serious impact on capital gains, particularly where the lifetime capital gains exemption would otherwise eliminate your regular tax entirely.

Be aware of the possible impact of minimum tax on otherwise tax-free capital gains.

Max sells the shares of his small business corporation for a $480,000 capital gain, which is fully exempt under the lifetime capital gains exemption of $835,716 for 2017 (see 6.4.1). Max has no other income in 2017.

Max will pay no regular tax. For minimum tax purposes, however, his adjusted taxable income will be about $144,000 (one-half of $480,000 x 60%), minus the basic $40,000 exemption. His federal minimum tax will therefore be 15% of $104,000, or $15,600. The federal minimum tax of $15,600 (net of personal credits) may be carried forward for seven years and applied against regular federal tax payable in those years.

#### Interest expense and business losses

Two important deductions are not affected by the minimum tax. The first is deductible interest paid (see 7.2.3) on loans not used for tax shelter purposes. The second is business losses and loss carryforwards (see 11.4) other than loss carryforwards that are attributable to "tainted" shelters (see 7.6.1). Where it otherwise makes sense from a business perspective, you can claim such deductions without triggering any minimum tax liability. Keep in mind, however, that high interest expense may give you a high cumulative net investment loss (see 6.4.3) and thus make the capital gains exemption unavailable to you, to the extent you would otherwise want to use it (see 6.4.1 and 6.4.2).

### Tax shelter deductions

Be aware of possible minimum tax implications when planning for large tax shelter claims, particularly on resource funds such as drilling funds and flow-through shares. Resource expenses that exceed your total income from such funds (and are therefore claimed as losses) must be added back for minimum tax purposes.

To the extent you have loss carryforwards from previous years that are attributable to "tainted" shelters, they must also be added back to your taxable income for minimum tax purposes.

## 7.7  References

The following publications and more information, including forms and brochures, can be obtained on the CRA's website at *www.cra-arc.gc.ca* or by telephone request at 1-800-959-8281 for individual income tax and trust-related enquiries or 1-800-959-5525 for business and self-employed individual enquiries.

Income Tax Folio S3-F2-C1, "Capital Dividends"
Income Tax Folio S3-F6-C1, "Interest Deductibility"

Also, see the following selected topics on the CRA's website:

"Tax shelters"
"Minimum tax"

# Chapter 8

## Charitable donations

- Combine two or more years of charitable donations into one year (8.1)
- If you have a spouse, combine your charitable donations and claim them on the higher-income spouse's return (8.1)
- Consider donating publicly traded securities or other assets to charity (8.1)
- Claim the first-time donor's super credit (8.1.1)
- Consider planned charitable gifts and bequests (8.2)
- Think about donating publicly traded securities instead of cash (8.3.3)

*Canada's tax system provides special incentives to encourage Canadians to donate to charities. In this chapter, we provide an overview of these incentives and discuss ways of planning your gifts to make the most of the available tax benefits.*

## 8.1 Tax credit for charitable donations

Charitable donations entitle you to a three-tier credit. The first $200 of donations for the year (total to all charities) gives you a 15% federal tax credit, worth about 25% when provincial tax is taken into account. Donations above that level give you a 29% federal tax credit, worth about 46% when provincial tax is factored in (see 17.7 if you live in Quebec). If your income is above about $203,000, you will get a 33% federal tax credit, worth about 50% including the provincial credit, for the portion of your donation above $200 that equals your income over $203,000.

> **Example**
>
> Elizabeth's income for 2017 is $218,000 and she makes a charitable donation of $20,000. She will claim a 25% federal and provincial tax credit for the first $200, which equals $50. Elizabeth will be able to claim the top tax credit rate of 50% for $15,000 of her donation, which matches the amount of her income over $203,000. This credit equals $7,500. For the remaining $4,800 of her donation, she can claim a tax credit of 46%, which equals $2,208, for a total federal and provincial tax credit of $9,758.

The 33% federal donation tax credit applies for 2016 and future years. Donations carried forward from 2015 or earlier years are not eligible for this higher credit rate.

For federal purposes, charitable donations above $200 for the year are therefore given the same treatment as if they were deductible, if you are in the top two federal tax brackets. If you are in a lower bracket, the credit for large donations is worth far more than a deduction.

To claim charitable donations, you must have official receipts that show the recipient organization's charitable registration number. You may claim receipts made out in either your name or your spouse's.

The maximum amount of donations you can claim in a year is 75% of your net income. To the extent you have receipts for more than this amount, or if you choose not to claim a donation for any other reason, you can save the receipts and claim the credit in any of the following five years.

The annual limit for donations in the year of death and the year before (including bequests and legacies) is 100% of net income for the year (see 8.2 below for more on making charitable bequests in your will).

**Combine two or more years of charitable donations into one year.** If you donate only small amounts over a year, consider combining two or more years of donations into one year to put yourself over the $200 threshold. A $100 donation above the $200 level for the year can cost you between about $50 and $54 after tax, depending on your tax bracket, instead of about $75 below the $200 level.

Once you are over the $200 level, consider making extra contributions in December rather than early in the new year. Your tax saving through the donations credit will come one year earlier.

**If you have a spouse, combine your charitable donations and claim them on the higher-income spouse's return.** If you and your spouse donate separately, you should combine your receipts and claim them all on one return to avoid having to get the low-rate credit on $200 twice. If your province levies a high-income surtax (see 2.1.3), the higher-income spouse should claim all the donations.

Donations made by one spouse can also be split between the two spouses in whatever proportion they choose. Further, spouses are able to claim each other's unused charitable donation carryforwards from a prior year.

**Consider donating publicly traded securities or other assets to charity.** Instead of donating cash, you should also consider the potential benefits of donating property such as publicly traded securities, employee stock option shares, artwork or real estate. The tax treatment of donations of property—or "gifts in kind"—is more complex but may result in greater tax savings for you and may enhance the value of your gift to the charity. Gifts in kind are discussed in 8.3.2.

Note that the government discourages investments in certain charitable donation tax shelters. As a result, if you object to an assessment from the disallowance of a deduction or tax credit claimed for a tax shelter that involves a charitable donation, you may have to pay 50% of the disputed tax, interest or penalties to the CRA, pending the outcome of your objection (see 7.5).

### 8.1.1    First-time donor's super credit

A first-time charitable donor's super credit is available for donations made after March 20, 2013 and before 2018. If neither you nor your spouse or common-law partner have claimed a charitable donations tax credit in any year after 2007, you may be able to claim an additional 25% federal tax credit on up to $1,000 in donations.

If you meet these qualifications as a first-time donor, you are entitled to a 40% federal credit for donations of $200 or less, and a 54% federal credit for the portion of donations over $200 but

Claim the first-time donor's super credit.

not exceeding $1,000. If your income is over $203,000, this tax credit could be 58%. Only donations of money qualify for this credit. You can claim this temporary credit only once in 2013–2017.

## 8.2    Charitable bequests

Charitable gifts can be made through your will. New rules for bequests made in 2016 or later years provide more flexibility than the previous rules for claiming tax credits related to donations

Consider planned charitable gifts and bequests.

made on death. A donation in your will may be allocated between your final tax return, your tax return for the year prior to death, the estate's tax return for the year the donation is made by the executors, or a previous tax return of the estate. The estate can also claim any unused donation tax credits in its tax returns for five years after the donation is made.

To be able to carry back donations to the deceased's tax returns or to a prior year of the estate, the estate must qualify as a "graduated rate estate" (see 22.2.2) and the donation must be made within 60 months of death.

The charitable donations limit in the year of death and the immediately preceding year is 100% of the deceased's "net income". If the donations are claimed in the estate's tax returns, the donations will be limited to 75% of the net income of the estate for federal tax purposes. Donations made in your will cannot be claimed by your spouse, unlike donations made during your lifetime.

If you name a charity as the beneficiary of your life insurance policy (or your TFSA, RRSP or RRIF), the death benefit (or value of your TFSA, RRSP or RRIF at death) can be claimed as a charitable donation in the same manner as donations made in a will as noted above. Naming a charity as a beneficiary can also save probate fees (see 21.4) on the value of the policy (or TFSA, RRSP or RRIF) if the proceeds would otherwise be paid to your estate.

It is possible that large bequests in your will (or large donations during your lifetime) may become unusable for tax purposes, if they far exceed the allowable threshold. You may therefore want to consider other options to maximize the tax credits and the funds available to your beneficiaries—both family members and charities.

Proper will planning can help ensure that your bequests will be made as you intend and provide significant tax savings for your estate.

Careful planning together with an informed adviser can ensure your philanthropic goals are met and the tax benefits are available when you need them most.

## 8.3    Types of charitable gifts

In this section, we look at some ways you can structure charitable gifts, both during your life and through your will, to further your philanthropic and estate planning goals and make the most of the available tax credits. The options are much broader than simply donating cash or leaving a sum of money to a charity in your will.

There are many ways to make gifts to charitable organizations—including gifts of property (such as securities, artwork, real estate), life insurance and annuities—with significant tax benefits. These benefits depend on the type of gift, the timing of the donation and the nature of the charitable organization.

A gift made today can provide a current tax saving and, in addition, a charitable insured annuity (see 8.3.6) will allow you the continued use of, or income from, the property itself.

### 8.3.1    Gifts to the Crown
The federal limit for claiming gifts to the federal or a provincial government ("Crown gifts") is 75% of net income, the same limit that applies to gifts made to other charities.

### 8.3.2    Gifts in kind
Both during your lifetime and on your death, you can donate property to a charity as an alternative to money. A gift of property is called a gift in kind. Examples include artwork, shares and real estate, as well as some more esoteric gifts we discuss below, such as life insurance. (You cannot "give" services, however—only property.)

A gift in kind is normally valued at its fair market value. For purposes of determining the tax credit for your donation, it will be the same as a gift of cash. Thus, the tax credit will generally be worth about 46% to 50% of the value of the property. However, at the time of the donation you are deemed to have disposed of the property at its fair market value—meaning that you must recognize any capital gain or income that would apply had you sold the property for that price.

If you have large capital gains in a year from other dispositions, gifts that trigger significant gains could result in a liability for alternative minimum tax (see 7.6). Before you make such a donation, run the numbers to ensure that minimum tax will not result.

For purposes of the tax credit, the 75% net income limit is effectively increased to 100% of net income for:

- gifts of ecologically sensitive lands to municipalities and certain charities (with no income inclusion for resulting capital gains—see 8.3.4)
- gifts of "certified cultural property" (and capital gains on such property may not be taxable—see 8.3.4).

For donations of capital property resulting in taxable capital gains and donations of depreciable property that trigger recapture of capital cost allowance (see 11.2.7), a mechanism is in place to increase the 75% net income limit so that 100% of the taxable capital gain and recaptured CCA are included in the donation limit.

Individuals and corporations who donate securities listed on prescribed stock exchanges, mutual funds and segregated funds of life insurance companies to charities do not have to include any portion of the resulting capital gain in their income.

These rules apply to donations of securities to private foundations as well as public charities, though private foundations are subject to some restrictions on the amount of stock they can hold in a corporation.

Similarly, if you exercise an employee stock option and donate the shares (or mutual fund units), you do not need to include any amount of the resulting employee benefit in your income. To be eligible for this treatment, the shares must qualify for the employee stock option deduction discussed in 10.4.1 and meet the criteria for donations of publicly listed securities noted above. The stock option shares must be donated in the year and within 30 days of the option being exercised. If the value of the stock option shares declines between when you exercise the option and when you donate the shares, the amount of your employee stock option deduction will be reduced accordingly.

If your corporation donates securities, its capital dividend account (see 14.2.4) will be increased by the non-taxable portion (or 100%) of the capital gain; this amount can then be paid to the corporation's shareholders tax-free. However, this planning may be affected by the federal government's proposed new tax regime for private companies (see Appendix I). (If you live in Quebec, see 17.7.)

Special rules apply to restrict the tax advantages on donations of publicly listed flow-through shares.

If you make a gift of capital property to a charity, you can file an election with your tax return to use a lower amount than the fair market value, for purposes of determining both your proceeds of disposition of the property and the value of your donation. You can elect any amount between the adjusted cost base (see 6.2.1) and the actual fair market value.

Whether the election is useful depends on a number of factors, including your tax bracket, your other sources of income and deductions, and your prospects for income in future years against which to use up the charitable donation carryforward.

The election described above can also be used by artists for gifts of work they have created (which is inventory rather than capital property).

### 8.3.3 Shares vs. cash from sale of shares—which should you donate?

Think about donating publicly traded securities instead of cash.

Say you want to make a $2,000 donation to a favourite cause and you have publicly traded securities that originally cost you $1,000 and that are now worth $2,000. Should you sell the securities and donate the proceeds, or should you simply donate the securities? Assuming your income is taxed at the top marginal rate of about 50% and you have already donated $200 in the year, the tax effects of both choices are as follows:

- If you sell the shares and donate the before-tax proceeds, a $1,000 capital gain will arise on the securities' sale. You would then have to pay $250 in tax on the taxable portion of your gain (one-half of $1,000 × an assumed 50% tax rate). Your $2,000 donation will give you a tax credit of $1,000 (50% × $2,000). In the end, the donation will result in net tax savings of $750 ($1,000 tax credit – $250 capital gains tax).
- If instead you donate the shares directly, the charity will still get the full $2,000 value of the shares. The taxable portion of the $1,000 capital gain will be zero, and you will get the same tax credit for the donation, producing net tax savings of $1,000 (50% × $2,000).

As you can see, you will come out ahead if you donate the securities directly. You give up property of the same value but your tax savings are $250 more ($1,000 vs. $750) than they would be had you sold the securities and donated the proceeds.

### 8.3.4 Gifts of cultural property and ecologically sensitive land

Gifts of "cultural property" to certain public authorities or institutions (such as museums) also produce tax benefits. If the property being gifted is certified as being of cultural significance to Canada, the donation will be equal to the property's fair market value for purposes of the credit but no taxable capital gain will arise. Any capital loss that may arise may be deductible in some circumstances.

The same treatment applies for gifts of ecologically sensitive lands to Canadian federal or provincial governments, municipalities or approved registered charities.

### 8.3.5 Gifts of life insurance

If you have a "permanent" life insurance policy (see 21.7), such as whole life or universal life, you can donate it to a charity by transferring the ownership of the policy to the charity and having the charity become the beneficiary of the policy. For tax purposes, the value of your donation will be the policy's fair market value, minus any policy loan outstanding. However, to the extent that value exceeds the tax cost of the policy to you, you must recognize the excess as income, as if you had cashed in the policy.

Once you have donated the policy to the charity, if you continue to pay the premiums on the policy, each such payment will be considered an additional charitable donation entitling you to a tax credit.

If you make the charity a beneficiary of a life insurance policy that you continue to own, the payment of the death benefit to the charity is considered a donation made by your estate. The donation can be claimed on your final tax return, on your return for the prior year or on the estate's tax returns as noted in 8.2.

### 8.3.6 Charitable insured annuity

Another option is to set up a "charitable insured annuity". You buy an annuity from a life insurance company and use part of the monthly payments to pay the premiums on a life insurance policy with a charity as the owner and beneficiary. Thus, you receive an income stream over your lifetime (from the annuity) and donation tax credits for the insurance premiums you pay. On your death, the charity receives the insurance proceeds.

## 8.4 References

The following publications and more information, including forms and brochures, can be obtained on the CRA's website at *www.cra-arc.gc.ca* or by telephone request at 1-800-959-8281 for individual income tax and trust-related enquiries or 1-800-959-5525 for business and self-employed individual enquiries.

Interpretation Bulletin IT-226R, Archived – "Gift to a charity of a residual interest in real property or an equitable interest in a trust"

Interpretation Bulletin IT-244R3, Archived – "Gifts by individuals of life insurance policies as charitable donations"

Interpretation Bulletin IT-288R2, Archived – "Gift of capital properties to a charity and others"

Interpretation Bulletin IT-297R2, Archived – "Gifts in kind to charity and others"

Interpretation Bulletin IT-407R4 Consolidated, Archived – "Dispositions of cultural property to designated Canadian institutions"

Pamphlet P113, "Gifts and Income Tax"

# Chapter 9

## Dealing with the tax collectors

- File your return on time even if you can't pay your taxes owing (9.1.1)
- Pay your taxes owing by April 30 even if you're filing later (9.1.1)
- NETFILE or EFILE your return for a quicker refund (9.1.2)
- Consider prepaying instalments to reduce deficient instalment charges (9.2.2)
- Be aware of the CRA's interest rates and compounding of interest (9.3)
- If you know you owe interest on late or deficient instalments, think about paying an estimate with your final payment (9.3)
- Sign a waiver only if necessary (9.4.3)
- If you've neglected to file returns, report income or make tax payments, consider making a voluntary disclosure to reduce penalties and interest (9.4.5)
- File a Notice of Objection to preserve your right to appeal (9.5.1)
- When your return is reopened on reassessment, consider requesting other adjustments (9.5.1)
- Be sure you understand the legal issues when appealing (9.5.2)
- Consider paying the amount owing even if you are filing an objection (9.5.4)

*In this chapter, we deal with the administrative side of the tax system—how tax is collected, how your return is assessed and what you can do if you disagree with the Canada Revenue Agency or Revenu Québec as to the amount of tax you owe.*

## 9.1 Tax returns

### 9.1.1 Filing your return

Most individuals are required to file their federal and Quebec tax returns by April 30 each year. When the due date falls on a Saturday, Sunday or public holiday recognized by the CRA, your payment is considered paid on time and your return to be filed on time if the CRA receives it or if it is postmarked on the next business day.

The deadline for individuals who have business income and their spouses (including common-law and same-sex spouses—see 2.2.1) is June 15. Even though the return may not be due until June 15, any balance of tax owing for the year is due on April 30.

If you have no tax to pay for the year (as distinguished from no balance owing in April), no return is required unless you disposed of capital property or realized a capital gain in the year or unless the CRA or Revenu Québec requests one.

In all provinces except Quebec, you file a single return with the CRA to cover both federal and provincial tax. Quebec residents and taxpayers with business income from operations in Quebec must file a Quebec provincial tax return as well (see Chapter 17).

The return must be postmarked or transmitted electronically by the due date. If the return is late, an automatic penalty of 5% of any tax still owing applies. This penalty is increased by 1% of the unpaid tax for each full month that the return is late, to a maximum of 12 months. Repeated failures to file a return on time results in higher penalties.

| File your return on time even if you can't pay your taxes owing. | To avoid the 5% penalty, you should file your return on time even if you are not able to pay your balance owing. Interest will accrue on the unpaid balance, but the penalty will not apply. |

| Pay your taxes owing by April 30 even if you're filing later. | Conversely, if you are unable to get your return completed (or your return is not due until June 15) but you have a rough idea of how much tax you owe, it is a good idea to pay that amount to the CRA or Revenu |

Québec by April 30. Make sure to have it credited to the correct taxation year (and not as an instalment for the subsequent year, for example).

When you're preparing your return or providing your information to a tax return preparer, check carefully to ensure you have all your information slips such as T4 slips from your employer or other slips reporting investment or trust income such as T3s and T5s. If you fail to report income of at least $500 from a T-slip more than once, you may face a penalty of up to 10% of the unreported income.

Using the CRA's new "Auto-fill my return" service can reduce the likelihood of errors and the chance of missing information from T-slips. This service allows you and your representative to automatically fill in parts of a current-year income tax return.

If you have to file Form T1135 to report owning more than $100,000 in foreign property (see 7.4.1), remember that this form is due at the same time as your personal tax return. Even if you don't file your tax return on time, you should submit your T1135 form on time to avoid a penalty for late-filing it.

### 9.1.2   Electronic filing

The CRA offers two options for most taxpayers to file their returns in electronic form: NETFILE and EFILE. NETFILE (which is also offered by Revenu Québec) allows you to file returns prepared on your personal computer via the Internet. To use NETFILE, you will need CRA-approved tax preparation software and a web browser that meets the CRA's security standard. An access code is no longer required.

Taxpayers who cannot use these electronic services due to CRA guidelines must file a paper return.

The EFILE system allows authorized tax return preparers or transmitters to file returns directly to the CRA using tax return preparation and transmission software. Most professional tax return preparers offer this service in addition to preparing the actual tax returns. If you prepare your own return, most EFILE preparers will charge a small fee to transmit it. The Quebec government also allows electronic filing for Quebec provincial tax returns.

The main benefit of these electronic filing options to taxpayers is the ability to have the return assessed and a refund paid in as little as two to three weeks, as opposed to a somewhat longer wait using the conventional paper filing method. If you are expecting a refund, electronic filing should speed up the processing of your return and the delivery or electronic deposit of your refund.

> NETFILE or EFILE your return for a quicker refund.

Further, you do not need to file paper returns or receipts with the return. (You must keep your receipts and other supporting documentation for any later review by the CRA.) This reduces the paper burden on you and the tax authorities.

If you are concerned about reassessment of your return down the road, electronic filing will normally get your return assessed sooner and start the three-year reassessment period (see 9.4) earlier.

If you have a balance due, you can use NETFILE or EFILE before the deadline but you will have until April 30 to mail in your payment. (You may also be able to pay your taxes electronically—see 9.2.3.)

## 9.2   Payment of tax

### 9.2.1   Source withholdings

Tax is withheld at source and remitted to the CRA and Revenu Québec by employers and others. Tax withheld from a payment to you is considered to have been paid by you to the tax authorities, even if your employer never remits it. It is also considered to have been paid to you in the sense that it forms part of your income.

Source withholding applies to the following kinds of payments, among others:

- employment income
- pension benefits
- Employment Insurance benefits
- withdrawals from an RRSP
- annuity payments
- Old Age Security benefits
- payments of passive income to non-residents (interest, dividends, rent, royalties, etc.)
- purchase of real estate from a non-resident (unless the non-resident has a certificate from the CRA and Revenu Québec, where applicable).

Note that there is no withholding of tax on interest, dividends, rent or royalties paid to Canadian residents. Self-employment income such as consulting fees (see 11.1) is also received without source deductions.

### 9.2.2  Instalments

You must pay instalments if the difference between your tax payable (including provincial tax except Quebec tax) and amounts withheld at source is more than $3,000 in both the current year and either of the two preceding years. For Quebec residents, since provincial tax is not collected by the CRA, the threshold is $1,800 of federal tax (see 17.1.3).

Quarterly instalments are due on the 15th of March, June, September and December.

There are four possible ways to determine your instalment obligations.

The first method is for your total instalments, paid in four equal payments, to equal the tax owing for the year on your sources of income from which tax is not withheld. In other words, your instalments should equal the balance owing at the end of the year.

The second method is for your quarterly instalments to equal the tax owing on your previous year's sources of income for which tax was not withheld. In other words, take the balance you had to pay last year after accounting for source withholdings, and pay that amount over the year in quarterly instalments.

The first method requires you to estimate your current year's income. If you guess low, you will end up not paying enough. The second method lets you use the previous year's income, but on March 15, when the first instalment is due, you might not yet have calculated your previous year's total tax. For this reason, the third method was introduced.

Under the third method, your March and June instalments are each one-quarter of the *total* tax owing on income from which tax was not withheld for two years ago. Your total instalments for the year must still equal the total amount for one year ago, as with the second method. Therefore, the September and December instalments must be enough to reach this total.

The fourth method is to simply pay the amount specified for the quarter on the instalment reminder statement mailed to you twice a year by the CRA and Revenu Québec.

> Example
>
> Alexander is self-employed as a consultant and has no tax withheld at source. His 2015 tax payable (combined federal/provincial) was $20,000. His 2016 tax payable was $24,000. He expects his total 2017 tax bill to be $27,000.
>
> Alexander should pay quarterly instalments on March 15, June 15, September 15 and December 15, 2017, totalling $24,000, his tax payable for the previous year. If he wishes, he may pay four instalments of $6,000 each.
>
> The CRA will advise Alexander in February 2017, however, that his March and June payments should be $5,000 each—one-quarter of his 2015 tax payable, since his 2016 figures are not yet available. If he makes these payments, and then pays $7,000 on each of September 15 and December 15, he will have paid the required $24,000 and met his instalment obligations under the "third method".
>
> The $3,000 balance (assuming Alexander's estimate of income for 2017 turns out to be correct) will then be due on April 30, 2018. Because he is self-employed, however, his 2017 return need not be filed until June 15, 2018.

If instalments are made on time and in the correct amount as per any of the three methods or you follow the CRA reminder notices, no interest is payable. If instalments are not made when required or are deficient, interest is assessed at

> Consider prepaying instalments to reduce deficient instalment charges.

the CRA's and Revenu Québec's current high "prescribed rate" (see 9.3), compounded daily.

You cannot *earn* interest by paying instalments early, but you can earn "contra-interest" at the same rate as applies to late payments, to offset interest that would otherwise be assessed on late instalments. If you've fallen behind in your instalments, consider making an extra or early payment to offset the (non-deductible) interest that will otherwise be assessed.

Example

Alexander, from the above example, does not make any instalment payments for 2017 until June 15, 2017. On that day, he makes a single payment of $15,000. He then makes a $2,000 payment on September 15, 2017 and a $7,000 payment on December 15, 2017. At this time, he has paid his $24,000 tax instalment requirements equal to his 2016 tax payable.

Alexander should not owe much interest on instalments, assuming the prescribed interest rate stays constant through 2017. His June 15 payment can be thought of as three parts: $5,000 due in March, paid three months late; $5,000 paid on time; and $5,000 of the $7,000 not due until September, paid three months early. The payment that is early will generate "contra-interest" to offset the interest that Alexander would otherwise have to pay due to his being late with his March 2017 payment.

For federal purposes, if the interest owing on late instalments is greater than $1,000, you may be subject to an additional penalty of up to 50% of the interest.

### 9.2.3 Electronic tax payments and refunds

The federal government continues to promote the use of its "Direct Deposit" service whereby tax refunds, GST/HST credits and Canada Child Benefit payments will be deposited directly into your account at any financial institution in Canada.

To take advantage of the service, you can sign up online using the CRA's "My Account" service, by phone at 1-800-959-8281 or by mail by completing the CRA's "Direct Deposit Enrolment Form".

You may be able to pay your taxes electronically using the CRA's My Payment service and your financial institution's Internet banking services. Contact your financial institution for information about its electronic payment services.

You can use the CRA's My Account service to see your tax return and request changes to it. You can also get information about your tax refund or balance owing, RRSP and TFSA contribution room, carryforward amounts such as capital and non-capital losses, and a summary of your instalment payments, among other things. You can authorize a representative such as a family member or a tax professional to access your information on My Account as well.

## 9.3 Interest

Interest that you owe on late payments of tax and instalments and on refunds is calculated at a prescribed rate, which varies quarterly based on the average yield of Government of Canada 90-day treasury bills. The new rate for each quarter is announced by the CRA in a news release about three weeks before the quarter begins.

There are three different "prescribed" interest rates each quarter. The lowest rate, which is roughly the Bank of Canada rate for the previous quarter, applies for purposes of the attribution rules (see 5.2.2) and the employee and shareholder loan rules (see 10.3 and 14.2.6). The middle rate, which is two percentage points higher, applies to refunds paid by the CRA. The highest rate, which is a further two points higher, applies to late payments of tax and instalments owing by taxpayers.

> Be aware of the CRA's interest rates and compounding of interest.

Although the rate is expressed as an annual rate, it is in fact compounded daily, so the effective rate is somewhat higher than shown. A 5% interest rate, for example, is equivalent to a rate of about 5.13% in simple annual interest.

Interest that you owe on late payments runs from when the payment was due. Interest on refunds generally runs from 30 days after the due date for the return, or from the day on which you file your return, whichever is later. However, if you have a June 15 filing deadline because you have self-employment income (see 11.2.1), interest will not be paid until 30 days after April 30 or 30 days after the date that the return is actually filed, whichever is later.

Interest that you are required to pay to the CRA, such as on late payments of tax or instalments, is not tax-deductible.

Interest paid to you on a refund is taxable in the year in which you receive it. Thus, if you file your 2017 return when it is due in April 2018 and receive a refund in August 2018, you must report the interest from May 30, 2018 included in that payment on your 2018 return.

If you have tax owing at April 30 and you know interest will be charged because of late or deficient instalment payments, consider paying an estimate of the interest with your April 30 payment to stop any further interest from accruing.

> If you know you owe interest on late or deficient instalments, think about paying an estimate with your final payment.

The federal prescribed interest rates from April 2010 to the time of writing have remained stable at the following rates, except for the period from October 1, 2013 to December 31, 2013, when the low prescribed rate temporarily went up to 2%, resulting in a middle rate of 4% and a high rate of 6% for that quarter of 2013.

| Prescribed interest rates: | April 1, 2010–September 30, 2013 and January 1, 2014–June 30, 2017 |
|---|---|
| Low rate | 1% |
| Middle rate | 3% |
| High rate | 5% |

As noted, the high rate applies to late tax and instalment payments and the middle rate to refunds. The low rate applies for the purposes of the attribution rules and shareholder and employee loans.

For Quebec purposes, the low rate is the same as the federal rate and the middle rate is slightly lower (so less interest is paid to you on refunds). For late taxes, the Quebec high rate is higher than the federal rate, and 10% higher for late Quebec tax instalments.

## 9.4 Assessment, audit and reassessment

### 9.4.1 Initial assessment

When you file a conventional (paper) return, it is processed over a period of typically three to six weeks, after which you receive a "Notice of Assessment" and any refund owing to you. The processing includes a review of the numbers on your return to make sure they are consistent (for example, that your arithmetic is correct and that any numbers carried forward from prior years' tax returns are consistent with those in the CRA's systems).

Most EFILE and NETFILE users can expect their returns to be assessed in two to three weeks.

For a partnership, the tax authorities may issue a determination of the partnership's income or loss, which is effectively an assessment of each partner's portion of the income or loss (see 11.3.6).

### 9.4.2 Audit

Some time after the initial assessment, your return may be selected for audit. Most audits of individual taxpayers (as opposed to corporations) are "desk audits", in which the auditor will ask you to supply supporting material for claims you have made. Some audits are "field audits", in which the auditor will come to your place of business to look at your records.

If you file using one of the electronic options, you will not have to file any receipts with your return. However, the CRA or Revenu Québec may later "spot-check" your return to verify certain claims, such as donations, RRSP contributions or tuition fees. This is normally just a formality, designed to maintain the integrity of the electronic filing systems.

You should be aware of your rights on an audit. The auditor is not entitled to go on a "fishing expedition" through your books. He or she may request specific information, and you may ask why that information is needed. If you anticipate problems, you may want assistance from your professional advisers in dealing with the auditor.

If you and your family have a high net worth, the CRA may select your business and investment activities for audit as part of a project focusing on wealthy individuals. The CRA seems to be looking at individuals with complex affairs who may control or have broadly defined interests in a large number of entities such as corporations, trusts, partnerships and private foundations. If you are identified under this program, you may have a relatively short time to gather extensive information about your business and investment interests.

If you have a small or medium-sized business, the CRA may contact you as part of its recent Liaison Officer Initiative. Under this program, a Liaison Officer can visit taxpayers' businesses to provide general information and help them fulfill their tax obligations. The CRA says this service is not an audit but is designed to provide education and support.

### 9.4.3 Reassessment

If the audit (or an audit of another taxpayer) turns up an indication that your tax payable should be other than what was initially assessed, the CRA will issue a reassessment. If the reassessment results in more tax payable by you, this will not normally be done without you first being consulted and given an opportunity to explain your position.

A reassessment cannot normally be issued more than three years after the date of the original assessment. However, in cases of fraud, or misrepresentation attributable to "neglect, carelessness or wilful default", the reassessment may be issued at any time.

There are several other situations where the three-year limitation does not apply. The most important is where you have filed a waiver with the tax authorities. The waiver, which is usually directed to a specific issue that is in dispute, will allow the CRA to reassess you on that issue at any time. You can revoke a waiver on six months' notice to the CRA. A common way to limit the CRA's additional time is to sign both a waiver and its revocation, and to staple the revocation to the waiver itself. The revocation will take effect after six months from the date of signing.

Sign a waiver only if necessary.

If you are asked by a CRA auditor to sign a waiver, consider the request carefully and obtain professional advice before agreeing.

First, consider the auditor's alternative if you do not sign the waiver. You are under no obligation to file a waiver simply to make the auditor's life easier. If the three-year reassessment period is about to expire, and the auditor does not yet have enough information to justify a reassessment, it may be to your advantage not to sign the waiver. Bear in mind that a reassessment normally takes some time to work its way through the CRA's internal system, although it can be rushed through in a couple of days in extreme cases.

Second, make sure that the waiver is very specific and waives the normal three-year period only in respect of the specific issues that are under investigation or dispute.

Similar rules apply for Quebec tax purposes.

### 9.4.4 Requests for Taxpayer Relief

What happens if you cannot pay your taxes or make a tax filing on time because of a natural or human-made disaster, serious illness, accident or another valid reason? The *Income Tax Act*'s Taxpayer Relief rules give the CRA the discretion to waive penalties and interest on overdue taxes if you were unable to pay on time because of circumstances beyond your control. (In the case of large natural disasters such as floods, the CRA may extend tax-related deadlines for everyone in the affected area.)

Under these rules, the CRA may also issue tax refunds even where the return is filed after the late-filing deadline (that is, generally three years from the original due date) and accept late-filed elections, or allow you to amend or revoke an election after the applicable deadline.

Aside from natural disaster or personal misfortune, the Taxpayer Relief rules can apply if you could not make a tax payment or file an election on time for more mundane reasons such as incorrect information provided in writing by the CRA or service disruptions such as strikes. But if you were simply negligent or unaware of the rules, you will still have to pay the usual penalties and interest on your overdue taxes.

In weighing your request, the CRA may consider your previous compliance record and your promptness in bringing the matter to the CRA's attention.

### 9.4.5 Voluntary disclosures

If you've neglected to file returns, report income or make tax payments, consider making a voluntary disclosure to reduce penalties and interest.

If you have neglected to file your income tax return or other information returns and you have an outstanding tax liability or you may be subject to a penalty, consider using the CRA's Voluntary Disclosures Program. Under this program, you can make disclosures to correct inaccurate or incomplete information, or to disclose information not previously reported. Though you will still have to pay any taxes owing, you may not be charged any penalties, the interest charged may be reduced, and you may not be prosecuted.

To qualify for this relief, your disclosure must be complete, it must include information that is at least one year past due, and it must involve a penalty (if no penalty is involved, the CRA will simply process the new information as it would any other request for adjustment). Additionally, you must come forward before the CRA has started an audit, investigation or other enforcement action.

If you are unsure as to whether you want to make a voluntary disclosure, you or your representative can submit the facts of your situation to a CRA voluntary disclosures officer on a no-name basis.

Voluntary disclosures may also be made regarding deficiencies in meeting other tax requirements, such as source deduction remittances and GST/HST reporting and payment obligations.

In most cases, you are entitled to use the Voluntary Disclosures Program only once.

To qualify for relief for Quebec tax purposes, you must meet certain conditions as for federal tax purposes. However, for Quebec purposes, you must usually pay estimated taxes and interest up front when you file the voluntary disclosure form.

You may want to contact your professional adviser to help you determine whether a voluntary disclosure makes sense in your circumstances.

## 9.5    Objections and appeals

### 9.5.1    Notice of Objection

If you cannot come to an understanding with the auditor and a reassessment is issued, or if you disagree with the original assessment, you may file a Notice of Objection. This is done by writing to the Chief of Appeals of your local district taxation office, by using the My Account or My Business Account service, or by filing form T400A with the appropriate Appeals Intake Centre. This filing begins the formal administrative appeal process. The notice should set out the specific issue(s) that you are objecting to.

When you file a Notice of Objection, your objection is reviewed by an Appeals Officer within the CRA. The Appeals Officer is independent of the Audit Branch, and he or she should conduct the review impartially and objectively.

To be valid, a Notice of Objection must be filed either within 90 days of the date of the assessment or reassessment to which you are objecting, or within one year of the original due date for the return. For example, an objection to an assessment of your 2016 return would have to be filed by April 30, 2018 or 90 days after the (re)assessment you are objecting to, whichever is later if your tax return was due April 30, 2017. The same deadlines apply for Quebec purposes.

**File a Notice of Objection to preserve your right to appeal.** Filing your Notice of Objection before the deadline is vital—even if you are in the midst of discussions with the CRA authorities, and even if you have been assured that a reassessment in your favour will be issued. If you don't file a Notice of Objection, your legal right to appeal vanishes and any reassessment will be entirely up to the CRA.

Even if the period for objecting has expired, you may request a reassessment of your return. In this case, you have no legal right to force a reassessment, but in many cases the reassessment will be issued anyway. The CRA will allow a reassessment of a return for any of the preceding 10 years, if the request meets the guidelines issued under the government's Taxpayer Relief rules (see 9.4.4).

In some cases, you can also apply to the CRA or the Tax Court of Canada for extension of the time for filing a Notice of Objection.

**When your return is reopened on reassessment, consider requesting other adjustments.** If the CRA issues you a routine reassessment for some reason after your own right to force a reconsideration of your return has expired, bear in mind that the reassessment reopens your return for 90 days. If this happens and there are other issues that you want to contest or change, you can raise them within the 90-day period and file a Notice of Objection to preserve your rights of appeal. However, you cannot do this if the return was reopened for any of a number of special reasons (such as a carryback of losses from a later year).

If the CRA issues a reassessment, it will invalidate any Notice of Objection for that year and you will need to file another Notice of Objection to the new reassessment if your issue was not resolved.

Similar rules and deadlines apply for Quebec tax purposes.

You are not usually required to pay your tax assessment at the Notice of Objection stage but interest will continue to accumulate (see 9.5.4).

Please note that this book does not address the rules for objections and appeals related to GST/HST or other indirect taxes.

### 9.5.2 Appeal to the Tax Court

The Appeals Officer is normally your last level of appeal within the CRA. A further appeal is available to the Tax Court of Canada (or the applicable provincial court if provincial taxes are in dispute).

**Be sure you understand the legal issues when appealing.** You have a choice between the Court's "informal" and "general" procedures for making an appeal.

The general procedure normally requires you to retain a lawyer. It is similar to higher court proceedings in provincial courts. If the amount of tax in dispute for any one taxation year is more than $25,000 of federal tax (about $40,000 including provincial tax other than Quebec tax), you must follow the general procedure. In certain "test cases", the CRA may also force a case below the threshold into the general procedure, in which case the CRA will be required to reimburse you for most or all of your legal fees.

The informal procedure, as its name suggests, is much less complicated. You may appear on your own, or have someone else (such as a lawyer, accountant, consultant or friend) there to assist you. No specific form needs to be filed to launch the appeal. The formal rules of evidence that normally apply to court proceedings will not necessarily apply. Under the informal procedure, your case will normally be heard more quickly than under the formal procedure, and a judgment given within a year of when you first file the appeal. The decision given is not binding as a precedent for future cases, whether yours or another taxpayer's.

If you are taking an appeal to the Tax Court of Canada, make sure you understand the legal issues involved. Even if you wish to represent yourself or be represented by a friend or relative, consult with a qualified tax professional before the appeal. Many issues in tax law have answers on which all the advisers (and the judge!) will agree, yet which will not be obvious to the non-expert.

### 9.5.3 Appeal beyond the Tax Court

A decision of the Tax Court of Canada under its informal procedure can be appealed to the Federal Court of Appeal but the grounds for such an appeal are restricted. A decision under the general procedure can be appealed directly to the Federal Court of Appeal. In either case, you would need a lawyer for such an appeal, which would typically take about two years from time of filing until judgment is given. Provincial decisions may be appealed to the applicable provincial appeal court.

Once a decision is given by the federal or provincial appeals courts, either you or the tax authority may seek "leave to appeal" from the Supreme Court of Canada. Only if the Supreme Court grants the application for leave to appeal can an appeal be made. The Supreme Court rarely grants leave to appeal in tax cases; typically only three or four tax cases a year reach the Supreme Court.

### 9.5.4 Amounts in dispute—should you pay up?

Suppose you are contesting an amount of $20,000 of tax, but you are not sure whether you will win or not. Although you have filed a Notice of Objection or perhaps an appeal, you are receiving notices from the CRA

Collections asking you to pay even though the CRA cannot start collection action as long as you have an objection or appeal outstanding.

**Consider paying the amount owing even if you are filing an objection.**

Nonetheless, it may be a good idea to pay the balance anyway. The interest rate charged on late payments (see 9.3) is likely higher than the rate you would otherwise earn with your money, or higher than the rate at which you must borrow from the bank. If you ultimately succeed in your appeal, you will recover all the funds you paid, plus interest (at the middle rate shown in 9.3).

Note also that when you receive a statement from the CRA, you normally have 20 days to pay without further interest charges applying. If you are going to have to pay anyway, you may as well take advantage of this "interest-free" period and pay the balance on the 20th day.

Taxpayers sometimes think they should not pay an amount in dispute because "that would be an admission of guilt", or because the CRA would then have no incentive to settle the case. Such reasoning is misplaced. You cannot prejudice your case by paying the tax. The determination as to your legal rights is not affected by whether or not the tax has been paid.

The only circumstance where you are better not to have paid your account is where you are applying for a waiver of interest and penalty, at the CRA's discretion, on the grounds of "inability to pay". Once you have paid, it will be difficult to argue that you cannot find the money to pay your tax bill and require a waiver of interest to be able to meet the requested payments.

## 9.6 References

The following publications and more information, including forms and brochures, can be obtained on the CRA's website at *www.cra-arc.gc.ca* or by telephone request at 1-800-959-8281 for individual income tax and trust-related enquiries or 1-800-959-5525 for business and self-employed individual enquiries.

Information Circular 75-7R3, "Reassessment of a return of income"
Information Circular 00-1R5, "Voluntary disclosures program"
Information Circular 07-1, "Taxpayer relief provisions"
Pamphlet P148, "Resolving your dispute: Objection and appeal rights under the Income Tax Act"

Also, see the following selected topics on the CRA's website:

"About Auto-fill my return"
"NETFILE — Overview"
"Voluntary disclosures program"

# Chapter 10

## If you are employed

- Arrange to get non-taxable benefits (10.1.1)
- Ask to have your source withholdings reduced where possible (10.2)
- Pay interest owing on loans from employers by January 30 of the following year (10.3)
- Consider employees' profit-sharing plans for cash flow purposes (10.5.2)
- Transfer retiring allowances to an RRSP (10.6)
- Claim the employment tax credit to help cover your work-related expenses (10.7.1)
- Employed tradespeople—claim the deduction for the cost of new tools (10.8.8)
- Claim a rebate for GST/HST paid on expenses deductible from your employment income (10.9)

*As a general principle, all income (including tips) and benefits from or related to your employment are taxed, except where the federal or Quebec rules specifically provide otherwise. Also as a general principle, you cannot claim any deductions against employment income, except for those that are specifically allowed by the tax system. There are, however, many special rules, and we examine some of them in this chapter.*

## 10.1 Employment benefits

### 10.1.1 Non-taxable employment benefits

Certain employment benefits are not taxable, even though many of them are deductible expenses to the employer. The government is thus offering an incentive to employers to provide these benefits, since the after-tax returns are greater than straight salary. Non-taxable benefits include:

- Contributions to a registered pension plan (the pension is taxable when received—see 3.5.1)
- Contributions to a group sickness or accident insurance plan
- Contributions to a "private health services plan", such as those covering drugs, medical expenses and hospital charges not covered by public health insurance, and dental fees (except for Quebec purposes—see 17.10.2)

- All or a portion of the cost of free or subsidized school services for your children (for example, if the services are provided in a remote area)
- Contributions to a supplementary unemployment benefit plan
- Contributions to a deferred profit-sharing plan
- Non-accountable moving allowance of up to $650 (see 13.1.3)
- Reimbursement of certain moving expenses on work-related relocation (see 13.1.3; however, any reimbursement or compensation to help finance the new residence is excluded—see 13.1.4)
- Payment of club dues (e.g., at golf courses) if your membership in the club is principally to benefit the employer's business (however, these dues are normally not deductible to the employer)
- Employee discounts, where such discounts are commonly available to other employees (but not below the employer's cost)
- Non-cash gifts to an unrelated employee of up to $500 annually (combined for all gifts) intended to mark holidays, birthdays and other special occasions (the total value in excess of $500 is taxable)
- A separate non-cash award to an unrelated employee of up to $500 annually intended to mark length of service or an employment anniversary
- The value of customer loyalty points on personal credit cards offered by third parties where the points were earned on employer-reimbursed business trips or other expenses of the employer, as long as the points are not converted to cash and the plan is not a form of remuneration or tax avoidance scheme
- Home computer, as long as it primarily benefits your employer and such computers are made available to all employees (or employees within the same class)
- Tuition fees for courses taken to maintain or improve your skills in an area related to your current or future employment responsibilities
- Costs of other business-related courses such as stress management, employment equity and language skills
- Scholarships provided to your children for elementary, secondary or post-secondary education (the amount is included in the student's income)
- Counselling services related to mental or physical health, employment termination or retirement
- Subsidized meals, where you are required to pay a reasonable charge covering the cost of the food
- Uniforms or special clothing you need for your job
- Transportation to the job in certain circumstances, if provided directly by the employer
- Board and lodging at, and transportation to, a "special work site" where you work temporarily or a "remote work site" that is remote from any established community

- Use of your employer's recreational facilities
- Transportation passes given to bus, rail and airline employees, except for airline employees travelling on a space-confirmed basis
- Transportation and parking costs, whether paid directly by the employer or reimbursed to you, if you are blind or are disabled due to a mobility impairment
- The cost of an attendant to assist you at work if you are disabled
- Items of nominal value, such as coffee, T-shirts with your employer's logo, mugs, plaques and trophies.

Note that where your employer deducts its contributions to a sickness or accident insurance plan, disability insurance plan or income maintenance insurance plan, any benefits you receive from the insurance will be taxable (but reduced by your own premium payments to the plan).

Ask your employer to make use of the non-taxable benefits outlined above as much as possible. If you have an employment benefit package where you and the employer share the

Arrange to get non-taxable benefits.

costs, try to have the cost-sharing reallocated so your employer pays for all the non-taxable benefits and you pay for the benefits that are taxable if your employer pays them. In many cases, without changing the cost to your employer, you may be able to reduce your tax burden this way.

One non-taxable benefit that is often overlooked is that of board and lodging at a "special work site". Unlike a "remote work location", a special work site need not be far from an established community; as long as the duties you perform at that location are of a temporary nature, and you maintain another residence, the food and lodging paid by your employer are a non-taxable benefit. This could apply, for example, if you spend several months in another city working on a project for your employer.

The CRA does not treat employer-provided overtime meals or reasonable allowances for overtime meals as a taxable benefit if:

- the value of a meal or meal allowance is no more than $17 (including GST/HST)
- the employee works two or more hours of overtime directly before or after his or her scheduled hours of work
- the overtime is infrequent and occasional (usually less than three times a week but sometimes more if the work is needed to meet out-of-the-ordinary demands such as major repairs or periodic financial reporting).

If the overtime occurs frequently, the CRA considers overtime meal allowances to be a taxable benefit because they are akin to extra remuneration.

### 10.1.2 Taxable employment benefits

In general, employment benefits other than those listed above are taxed as though you had received an equivalent amount of income. Examples include:

- Tips (gratuities) that you receive from customers or suppliers
- Board, lodging and rent-free or low-rent housing (with some exceptions for remote or special work sites)
- Travelling expenses for personal travel, including expenses for your spouse to travel on a business trip of yours, unless your spouse was engaged primarily in business activities on behalf of the employer during the trip
- Personal use of employer's automobile (see 12.2)
- Gifts, except for non-cash gifts with a combined cost under $500 per year as noted above
- Allowing you and/or your family to use a vacation property
- Holiday trips, prizes and incentive awards
- Cost of employer-paid courses for personal interest or technical skills not related to your employer's business
- Payment of provincial (public) health insurance premiums (no longer charged by most provinces)
- Life insurance premiums
- Reimbursement for the cost of tools used in employment duties
- Loans to employees (see 10.3)
- Tax equalization payments to relocated employees to offset higher taxes in their new work location
- Stock option plans (see 10.4.1)
- Income tax return preparation and financial counselling (but not retirement or re-employment counselling).

In general, where the employer pays sales tax on goods or services, and then provides those goods or services to you as a taxable benefit, the calculation of the taxable benefit will require an additional 5% to account for the GST. This applies, for example, to automobiles. If you live in an HST province, your province's HST rate applies (see 11.2.5); for Quebec, the benefit is increased by the GST and QST.

## 10.2 Reductions of source withholdings

**Ask to have your source withholdings reduced where possible.**

As we saw in 9.2.1, your employer and others are required to withhold tax at source and remit it to the CRA. The same rules generally apply for Quebec purposes.

In any situation where you expect to receive a refund after filing your return (e.g., due to personal tax credits, RRSP contributions, medical expenses or charitable donations, alimony and maintenance payments), you should review the TD1 form (and MR-19.V in Quebec) you file with your employer and seek to have source withholdings reduced. You can ask your local CRA district office to permit your employer to reduce your source withholdings for deductions not normally provided for on the TD1 form, such as RRSP contributions and alimony and maintenance.

However, if your employer withholds from your remuneration RRSP contributions (up to your available RRSP contribution room—see 3.1.3), union and professional dues and alimony and maintenance payments for direct remittance to the intended recipient, the employer can take these withholdings into account in calculating your tax withheld at source without requesting permission from the CRA.

Your employer must withhold Canada Pension Plan (CPP) contributions from your income if you are between 18 and 70 years old. However, if you are between 65 and 70 and receive pension benefits under the CPP or Quebec Pension Plan, you can opt out of making contributions to these plans (see 20.3.1).

If you have a loan from your employer on which imputed interest is assessed as a taxable benefit (see 10.3 below), your source deductions of income tax will reflect that taxable benefit. If, however, you are using the funds for a purpose that allows you an offsetting deduction, you may write to the CRA, setting out that fact, and request that your employer be permitted to reduce the source withholding. An example of this is where you use the loan proceeds for investment purposes or use the funds to acquire shares of your employer.

Many people look forward to receiving a tax refund, but it's not good tax planning to get one. If you get a refund, that means the CRA has been holding your money and not paying you interest on it for many months. Although fiscal responsibility is needed to make sure you can pay your tax when it is due, it is better to be required to make a payment to the CRA at filing time, since it means that you have had use of the funds (for investment or other purposes) in the meantime. However, as we saw in 9.2.2, you must pay instalments if the difference between your tax payable and amounts withheld at source in both the current year and either of the two preceding years is more than $3,000 or, if you live in Quebec, $1,800 (see 17.1.3).

Note that interest is not paid on refunds for the first 30 days of processing after the filing deadline—that is, until after May 30 for most employees. If you have a June 15 filing deadline because you have self-employment income (see 9.1.1), interest will not be paid until 30 days after April 30 or 30 days after the date that the return is actually filed, whichever is later (see 9.1.1 and 9.3).

## 10.3 Loans to employees

If you receive a low-interest or interest-free loan from your employer (or past or future employer), you are considered to have received a benefit from employment. The benefit is set at the CRA's (and Revenu Québec's) current prescribed rate of interest, which varies quarterly, minus any interest you actually pay during the year or within 30 days after the end of the year. The prescribed rate is 4% lower (3% in Quebec) than the rate charged on late payments of tax (see 9.3). (There may be an offsetting deemed interest deduction, as we shall see.)

> **Example**
>
> Amélie receives a loan of $10,000 from her employer on January 1, 2017. She is required to pay it back one year later, without interest. Assume the prescribed rate throughout the entire year is 2%.
>
> Amélie is considered to have an employment benefit of $200, and will be required to include this amount in her employment income.
>
> But if, instead, the loan bore interest at 1%, and Amélie made an interest payment before January 30, 2018, her taxable benefit would be calculated as 1% (the prescribed rate of 2% minus her employer's 1% rate) of $10,000, or $100.

**Pay interest owing on loans from employers by January 30 of the following year.**

If you have received an interest-bearing loan from your employer, consider deferring the payment of interest on the loan until January 30 of the next calendar year. This will provide you with a cash flow advantage. Make sure you do pay the interest by that date, however.

### Exceptions

A home purchase loan is taxed on the same basis as other employee loans, but the rate applied in calculating the imputed interest for the first five years of the loan will not be greater than the prescribed rate in effect at the time the loan was made. At the end of the five-year period, it is considered a new loan, and the prescribed rate at that time will be the maximum for the next five years.

> Alex receives an interest-free loan from his employer to help him buy a house. (He is not relocating, just moving from an apartment to a house.) At the time, the prescribed interest rate is 3%. Two years later, interest rates have gone up, and the prescribed rate increases to 6%.
>
> Alex will still pay tax on the interest benefit calculated at only 3% of the amount of the loan. If the prescribed rate had gone below 3%, he would, however, pay tax on imputed interest at the lower rate as long as it stayed below 3%.

*Example*

If you relocate and receive a home purchase loan to acquire a residence at least 40 km closer to your new work location, then a special deduction in computing your taxable income is available to you for the first five years of the loan equal to the interest imputed on $25,000. You must still report the entire interest amount as a taxable benefit, and claim this special deduction as a separate item on your tax return. This deduction will no longer be available starting in 2018.

Where you use funds borrowed from your employer to purchase investments or to purchase an automobile (or aircraft) to be used for your employment, you can obtain an offsetting deduction. The amount of imputed interest that you include in your income as a taxable benefit is deemed to have been *interest paid by you*. As a result, if such interest would otherwise have been deductible, you can deduct it. (As we saw in 7.2.3, interest paid on loans to acquire investments is deductible, and as we'll see in 12.3.1, interest paid on loans to acquire a car is deductible if the car is required by your terms of employment.) The effect is to eliminate the tax cost of the taxable benefit.

If you are a shareholder of the company as well as an employee, or if a member of your family is a shareholder, you must be especially cautious. It is possible that the *entire* amount of the loan, rather than the imputed interest, will be included in your income for tax purposes, unless stringent conditions are met. In general, you can avoid this rule if the loan is made for certain specific purposes and with arrangements for repayment within a reasonable time, provided the loan was made because of your employment relationship. Alternatively, the entire loan must be repaid within one year and not be part of a series of loans and repayments (see 14.2.6).

## 10.4 Stock option plans

### 10.4.1 Regular stock option plans

A stock option plan is an arrangement whereby a corporation gives an employee the right (an option) to invest in its shares at a given price. The price may or may not be less than the market price at the time the option is granted. For example, suppose you work for a corporation whose stock trades at $20. In 2017, you are given an option to buy up to 1,000 shares at $20, good until 2019. If, in 2018, the stock is trading at $30, you can exercise the option, buy 1,000 shares for $20,000, and then, if you wish, turn around and sell the shares on the market for $30,000.

The general rule is that you are considered to receive a benefit from employment, not when the option is granted (the year 2017 in the above example) but when you exercise it (2018). The taxable benefit is the difference between the price you pay ($20,000) and the value of the shares when you exercise the option ($30,000). Your employer would, therefore, report a taxable benefit of $10,000 in your employment income for 2018. (The adjusted cost base of the shares you own will be $30,000, so you will not be double-taxed when you subsequently sell them.)

An offsetting partial deduction is available if certain requirements are met. The first requirement is that the shares be normal common shares (not preferred shares). Second, the exercise price must be no less than the fair market value of the shares at the time the option was granted. (Otherwise you could simply exercise the option the day you received it, so the benefit would be just like cash.) Third, you must deal at arm's length with the corporation (meaning essentially that you or members of your family do not control it). If these conditions are met, you can claim a deduction from income of one-half of the amount of the taxable benefit. The effect of this deduction is to tax the benefit at the same inclusion rate as a capital gain.

For Quebec purposes, the deduction is generally limited to one-quarter of the amount of the benefit relating to a stock option (see 17.10.3).

Stock options in Canadian-controlled private corporations receive preferential tax treatment (see 10.4.2).

You may wish to approach your employer about establishing a stock option plan as an employment benefit. It may cost your employer very little, and can even bring investment funds into the corporation. (The cost to your employer is the dilution of the existing shareholders' interests.)

## 10.4.2 Stock options in Canadian-controlled private corporations

If your employer is a Canadian-controlled private corporation (CCPC) with which you deal at arm's length, you report the taxable benefit related to stock options in your employer's company when you sell the shares, rather than when you exercise the option and acquire them. And, if you have held the shares for at least two years at the date of sale, you can claim a deduction when computing your taxable income for one-half of the benefit realized in the year the shares were sold, as long as you deal at arm's length with the corporation in your capacity as an employee. This exception is designed to stimulate employee participation in ownership of small businesses. It also recognizes that the valuation of shares in a private company at the time you exercise the option may be difficult.

Be cautious about relying on CCPC shares too much for your future retirement plans; shares in private corporations are generally not liquid, and they can drop in value should the corporation run into financial or business trouble.

If you receive shares in a CCPC through a stock option plan, consider contributing some of them to your RRSP or TFSA if the shares qualify for that purpose (see 3.1.6).

### 10.4.3 Stock option cash-out payments

The terms of some stock option plans may allow you to receive a cash payment equal to the value of the options instead of the shares. When you receive this form of payment, the same tax consequences may apply to the cash payment as would apply to the issuance of shares—the employment benefit is included in your income and the related one-half deduction is available if the required conditions are met. You can only claim the deduction of one-half of the employment benefit if your employer elects to forgo a deduction for the cash payment.

If your employer does not make this election, it will be entitled to a corporate tax deduction for the payment but you must pay tax on the full value of the employment benefit. This rule applies to all stock options that are cashed out regardless of when the options were issued.

If your employer decides to pay cash instead, the stock option rules would not apply and the cash payment would be taxable as regular employment income.

### 10.4.4 Stock purchase plans

A stock purchase plan is a possible alternative to a stock option plan. In a typical stock purchase plan arrangement, a defined group of employees (which could be all employees) may purchase a limited number of shares of the company at their fair market value or at a slight discount. The plan is usually administered by a trust. You contribute a portion of your salary to the trust and in many cases your employer will make matching contributions. The trustee then uses the funds to purchase the shares at their current fair market value.

Since you make your contribution from after-tax dollars, no additional tax arises. If your company does not contribute to the plan and your contributions are simply used to purchase the shares, there will be no tax consequences. However, if the shares are issued at a discount, you will be assessed a taxable benefit on the difference between the shares' purchase price and their fair market value.

If your company contributes to the plan, the tax consequences to you will depend on how the shares are purchased. If the shares are issued from treasury, the stock option rules will apply. If the shares are purchased on the open market, you will be assessed a taxable benefit equal to the value of the shares at the time they vest.

### 10.4.5 Stock bonus plans

Stock bonus plans reward employees with shares of the corporation instead of cash. In most cases, the same rules apply as those outlined in 10.4.1 for stock options.

### 10.4.6 Phantom stock plans

A phantom stock plan avoids the requirement that you acquire shares in the corporation, and thus may be more attractive to your employer's controlling shareholders. Under such a plan, you receive bonuses based on the increase in value of your employer's shares. Such bonuses are simply taxed as employment income when they are paid to you. If they are not paid to you on an ongoing basis, you will need to determine whether they constitute a salary deferral arrangement (see 10.5.1), in which case they will be taxed in your hands even if not received. This type of plan allows you to benefit from the potential appreciation in value of your company's shares without a cash outlay and with no risk of any loss in the value of the shares.

## 10.5 Deferred compensation

Various techniques have been tried over the years to defer paying tax on employment income by having some of it held back in one way or another. (In general, employment income is taxed when received.)

Registered pension plans and deferred profit-sharing plans were discussed in 3.5 and 3.6. They are accepted mechanisms for deferring employment income.

### 10.5.1 Salary deferral arrangements

The rules for salary deferral arrangements catch most arrangements for deferred compensation. For example, if you agree with your employer that your salary for 2017 will be $80,000, plus a further $20,000 to be paid in 2021, you will be taxed on the whole $100,000 in 2017. You can generally only escape this taxation if there is a substantial risk of forfeiting the future income.

The salary deferral arrangement rules allow certain exceptions. One is a self-funded leave of absence program, sometimes used by teachers, academics and others to fund sabbatical leaves. Provided you meet all of the conditions, you can arrange for your employer or a trustee to hold back a portion of your salary every year for up to six years, not recognize that portion as employment income each year, and receive it in the sabbatical year, paying tax on it then. Another exception is an arrangement whereby you have a right to receive a bonus to be paid within three years.

### 10.5.2 Employee profit-sharing plans

Employee profit-sharing plans do not defer the taxation of employment income. Rather, contributions are made by the employer, based on profits for the year. Although the contributions

> Consider employees' profit-sharing plans for cash flow purposes.

are paid to the plan, the amounts contributed are treated as income of the employees for tax purposes. Such plans can therefore operate as forced savings plans for bonuses. Income (such as interest income) earned within the plan must be allocated to specific employees, who pay tax on it as it is allocated (even if it is not paid to them).

Though these plans are not widely used, one of their tax advantages is that there is no source withholding on the amounts paid into the plan or on the amounts paid by the plan to you. Careful timing of the employer's contributions and the plan's disbursements can give you better cash flow than would a straight bonus payment.

If you receive payments from one of these plans and you or members of your family are significant shareholders in the company, you may be subject to a special tax if the company's contributions to the plan for you exceed 20% of your salary for the year.

### 10.5.3 Supplemental ("top-hat") retirement plans

Supplemental retirement plans are usually designed to provide retirement benefits similar to those offered under registered pension plans (see 3.5), but they are not subject to the same contribution limits. As a result, they are often used to enhance the retirement compensation packages of higher-income executives and employees (which is why they are also known as "top-hat plans"). Supplementary plans may be unfunded or funded. If they are funded, they will be treated as a retirement compensation arrangement (see 10.5.4).

Under the most common type of unfunded supplemental retirement plan, the employer simply makes a promise in a letter or more formal agreement to pay an additional amount to the employee on retirement. Because no funds are set aside, there is no immediate tax liability for either the employee or the employer. However, because the retirement benefits are not secured, their payment will ultimately depend on the employer's ability to pay on the employee's retirement.

If the payments from the supplementary retirement plan are arranged to qualify as retiring allowance payments (see 10.6), you may be able to transfer part or all the payments to your RRSP.

### 10.5.4 Retirement Compensation Arrangements

Retirement Compensation Arrangements (RCAs) are arrangements made outside the registered pension plan system, whereby a custodian will receive funds from an employer and make payments after the employee's retirement or termination. The employer receives a deduction for contributions to such plans, but a 50% refundable tax applies to the payments made to the custodian. The tax must be remitted to the CRA when the contribution is made and refunded when the payments are made to the employee. The employee does not report the income for tax purposes until he or she receives the payments from the custodian.

Restrictions may apply to RCA tax refunds when RCA property has lost value, effective for RCA tax on contributions made after March 28, 2012.

RCAs may also be funded through a letter of credit or through a life insurance policy. The letter of credit's terms usually allow it to be called upon if the employer does not fulfill its obligations under the RCA. The contribution to the RCA is equal to the amount charged by the financial institution for issuing the letter of credit. A letter of credit is often viewed as a compromise between an unsecured arrangement and a fully funded RCA.

In recent years, a variety of new methods have been developed for funding supplemental plans through exempt life insurance products (see 7.3.3).

If you're the beneficiary of an RCA and you or your family members own 10% or more of the company's shares, the RCA will no longer be permitted to invest in your company or other related ones. This rule applies to investments made after March 28, 2012 and may also apply to investments the RCA already owned on that date.

## 10.6 Retiring allowances, wrongful dismissal payments and severance pay

*Transfer retiring allowances to an RRSP.*

A "retiring allowance", as defined for tax purposes, includes what one would normally call severance pay or termination pay, as well as a court award or settlement for wrongful dismissal. It also includes, of course, a payment by an employer for long service on retirement.

A retiring allowance, like ordinary employment income, is included in your income in the year you receive it. If you receive your retiring allowance in a year after the year you terminated employment, you may ask the CRA to determine whether it is more advantageous to you to recalculate the tax on that income as if you received it in the prior year to which the payment relates. This option relieves the higher tax liability that would otherwise result if the entire lump-sum is taxed in the year of receipt, rather than year by year as a right to receive the income arose. Eligible payments must total at least $3,000 in the year and include superannuation or pension benefits (other than non-periodic benefits), wrongful dismissal and other employment-related payments arising from a court order or similar judgment, and certain other amounts.

Though damages awarded for wrongful dismissal are usually taxable as a retiring allowance, the amounts may not be taxable if the settlement includes damages related to mental anguish, humiliation, hurt feelings or loss of self-respect suffered on the job rather than as a result of losing the job. If you are suing for wrongful dismissal including damages for mental distress, ensure that any settlement contains a detailed breakdown of its components to show that it includes non-taxable general damages.

As we saw in 3.3.2, part or all of a retiring allowance can be transferred to an RRSP and thus sheltered from immediate tax. The amount that can be transferred is $2,000 for each calendar year (or part year) of service before 1996, plus $1,500 for each year (or part year) before 1989 for which employer contributions to your pension plan have not vested. (Vested pension rights are those that you can take with you on retirement or termination—see 3.5.1.)

Legal fees incurred in establishing your retiring allowance are deductible against the retiring allowance (see 10.8.5). Legal fees can be carried forward for up to seven years and deducted against the "retiring allowance" income. Note that you should probably not transfer the maximum amount to an RRSP if you have incurred legal fees in obtaining your award (even if the case was settled without going to court). If you transfer the entire retiring allowance into an RRSP, the legal fees will never become deductible. (When you take payments *out* of the RRSP, they are no longer considered a "retiring allowance".) However, if you intend to leave the funds to grow tax-free in the RRSP for many years, you may want to consider transferring the maximum anyway.

## 10.7  Tax credits for employees

### 10.7.1  Employment tax credit

Employees can claim a 15% non-refundable tax credit to help cover their work-related expenses. The credit is based on your employment income for the year, to a maximum of $1,177 for 2017. A Working Income Tax Benefit tax credit is also available for low-income employees. For Quebec tax purposes, employees may claim up to $1,040 as a deduction for 2017.

Claim the employment tax credit to help cover your work-related expenses.

### 10.7.2  Teachers' school supply tax credit

If you are a certified teacher or early childhood educator and you purchase school supplies for your classroom at your own expense, you may be able to claim a 15% refundable tax credit for up to $1,000 in eligible expenses per year (worth $150).

To qualify, you must certify that you purchased the supplies for the purpose of teaching or otherwise enhancing learning in a classroom or learning environment.

Eligible supplies include games, books, educational support software, items for science experiments, art supplies and stationery items.

### 10.7.3  Volunteer firefighters and search and rescue volunteers

If you are a volunteer firefighter, you may be able to claim a 15% tax credit based on an amount of $3,000 (worth $450). To be eligible, you must perform at least 200 hours of volunteer firefighting services in the year that consist primarily of responding to and being on call for firefighting and related emergency calls, and attending meetings and training.

If you are a ground, air or marine search and rescue volunteer, you may be able to claim a similar credit also based on an amount of $3,000 (worth $450). To claim the credit, you must perform at least 200 hours of service during the year.

If you perform at least 200 hours of combined eligible search and rescue and volunteer firefighting services in a year, you may claim either the credit for volunteer firefighters or search and rescue volunteers, but not both.

Alternatively, you may be eligible for a tax exemption of up to $1,000 if you received a payment from a government or municipality for carrying out your volunteer firefighter or search and rescue duties. If you choose to claim this exemption, you will not be eligible for the volunteer firefighters or search and rescue volunteers tax credit, so you should determine which is more beneficial.

## 10.8  Deductions from employment income

The only deductions allowed against employment income are those specifically provided for in the federal and Quebec tax rules. We look at some of them below.

### 10.8.1  Travelling expenses and allowances

If you are required by your employment to spend funds on employment-related travel, the amounts you pay will normally be deductible. Examples might include parking, taxis and train fares. You cannot deduct the costs of travelling between your home to your workplace. If you use your own automobile for employment-related travel, see 12.3.

If you travel for a transportation company (e.g., as a bus or truck driver or a flight attendant), you can also deduct costs of meals and lodging to the extent you are not entitled to be reimbursed. The deduction for meals will be further restricted to 50% of your cost (see 11.2.9). For eligible long-haul truck drivers, the meals deduction limit is 80%.

For non-employment related travel (such as commuting to and from work), you can claim the tax credit for the cost of eligible public transit passes (see 2.7.3). This credit is no longer available for public transit passes used after June 2017.

### 10.8.2 Commission sales person's expenses

If you are employed as a sales person under a contract that requires you to pay your own expenses, and you earn commissions, you may be able to deduct the costs of your employment-related expenditures—the same kinds of costs you could claim if you were self-employed (see 11.2.2). To do so, you must be required by your contract of employment to pay your own expenses, and you must be ordinarily required to carry on your duties of employment away from your employer's place of business. The total expenses you claim this way cannot exceed your total commission income.

### 10.8.3 Supplies, assistant's salary and home office

If you are required by your contract of employment to pay for any supplies or to pay for an assistant or substitute, you can deduct the cost of the supplies or the assistant's salary.

You can also deduct expenses relating to a home office, in limited circumstances. First, you must be required by your employment contract to maintain the office, and your employer must sign a certificate (federal Form T2200, which you must keep with your records and Quebec Form TP-64.3-V, which you must file with your Quebec tax return).

Second, either the home office must be the place where you "principally perform the duties of employment" or you must use it on a regular and continuous basis for *meeting* people (such as your employer's customers) in the ordinary course of your employment.

The second restriction is parallel to that which applies to self-employed people, as outlined in more detail in 11.2.10. The effect is that the deduction is rarely available to employed individuals. You will normally only be able to claim it if you spend more of your time working at home than at your employer's premises.

### 10.8.4 Union and professional dues

Union dues are deductible for federal tax purposes (see 17.10.4 if you live in Quebec). These are normally withheld at source and reported on the T4 and Quebec Relevé 1 you receive from your employer.

Dues required to maintain a legally recognized professional status are deductible, even if you do not need to maintain that status for your current job. Your status as a lawyer, engineer, accountant, physician, architect, nurse, dentist, etc., qualifies for this purpose. Dues to voluntary associations are not deductible, unless you are self-employed (see 11.2.2).

### 10.8.5 Legal fees

If you spend money on a lawyer to recover unpaid wages, you can deduct the legal fees.

Legal fees you incur to establish your right to a "retiring allowance" (which includes severance pay) or private pension plan benefits are deductible. You can only deduct the legal fees against the income from the retiring allowance or pension benefits in that year. To the extent you have not yet received that income, you can carry forward the expenses for up to seven years and claim them against such income in those later years. (See 10.6 if you transfer your retiring allowance to an RRSP.)

> **Example**
>
> Lewis was fired from his job in 2015. He retained a lawyer and sued for wrongful dismissal, spending $3,000 in 2015 and $5,000 in 2016 in legal fees. In 2017, the case is settled and his former employer pays him $50,000.
>
> Lewis can deduct his $8,000 in legal fees only in 2017 against his $50,000 "retiring allowance" income, thus recognizing only $42,000 as income in that year.
>
> Lewis could ask the CRA to recalculate his tax on the retiring allowance income as if it had been received in the year to which the payment relates (see 10.6).

See also 2.8.1 regarding the deductibility of legal fees that are not related to employment.

### 10.8.6 Musicians' instruments

If you are employed as a musician and required to supply your own instrument, you may deduct any maintenance, rental and insurance costs. If you have purchased the instrument, you may claim capital cost allowance (depreciation), at a rate of 10% for the first year and 20% of the remaining balance in each following year. All of these deductions can only be used to offset your income from employment as a musician, not against other income.

### 10.8.7 Artists' expenses

If you are employed as an artist (including a painter, sculptor, playwright, literary author, composer, actor, dancer, singer or musician), you may deduct up to $1,000 of your actual expenses incurred in order to earn income from such activities. This deduction is limited to 20% of your income from artistic employment, and the $1,000 limit is reduced by any amounts you claim as automobile expenses (see 12.3.1) and musical instrument costs (10.8.6). (No parallel deduction is allowed for Quebec tax purposes.)

Of course, if you earn income from your artistic activities that is not employment income, you are self-employed, in which case all your expenses are normally deductible (see 11.2.2).

### 10.8.8 Tradesperson's tools

If you are an employed tradesperson and you must use your own tools on the job, you can deduct the portion of the cost of new tools that exceeds $1,778 for 2017, up to a maximum of $500.

Employed tradespeople—claim the deduction for the cost of new tools.

You can also claim a rebate of the GST/HST (see 10.9) paid on the deductible portion of the purchase price of the new tools.

Your employer will have to certify that the tools you acquired are a condition of your employment. Computers, cell phones and other electronic communication devices and data processing equipment do not qualify for these purposes.

### 10.8.9 Northern employees

If your employer pays for you to take a vacation trip, with or without your family, the value of the taxable benefit is included in your income (see 10.1.2). If you live in northern Canada, a federal deduction is available to offset all or part of this benefit (a similar deduction is available for Quebec purposes). Provided you meet certain residency requirements, the deduction can eliminate the taxable benefit associated with up to two trips per year, based on the cost of airfare to the nearest large Canadian city. (There is no limit to the number of such trips if they are taken to obtain medical services not available locally.)

See also 2.8.2, regarding the special deduction for residents of northern Canada, and 10.1.1, regarding the non-taxability of benefits relating to a remote work site.

## 10.9 GST/HST rebate for employees

In general, where you can deduct expenses from your employment income, such as those discussed

Claim a rebate for GST/HST paid on expenses deductible from your employment income.

in 10.8, you may be entitled to claim a rebate of GST or HST paid on those expenses. A QST rebate is available for Quebec taxpayers. Documentation must be kept to support the claim for the rebate. The rebate claim is filed with your personal income tax return. That rebate will itself be considered income from employment in the year in which you receive it, except where it relates to capital cost allowance. If you drive your own car for employment-related travel, see 12.3.2.

## 10.10 References

The following publications and more information, including forms and brochures, can be obtained on the CRA's website at *www.cra-arc.gc.ca* or by telephone request at 1-800-959-8281 for individual income tax and trust-related enquiries or 1-800-959-5525 for business and self-employed individual enquiries.

Guide T4041, "Retirement Compensation Arrangements"
Guide T4130, "Employers' Guide—Taxable Benefits and Allowances"
Income Tax Folio S1-F2-C3, "Scholarships, Research Grants and Other Education Assistance"
Income Tax Folio S2-F1-C1, "Health and Welfare Trusts"
Income Tax Folio S2-F3-C1, "Payments from Employer to Employee"
Income Tax Folio S2-F3-C2, "Benefits and Allowances Received from Employment"
Interpretation Bulletin IT-63R5, Archived – "Benefits, including standby charge for an automobile, from the personal use of a motor vehicle supplied by an employer after 1992"
Interpretation Bulletin IT-113R4, Archived – "Benefits to employees— Stock options"
Interpretation Bulletin IT-148R3, Archived – "Recreational properties and club dues"
Interpretation Bulletin IT-158R2, Archived – "Employees' professional membership dues"
Interpretation Bulletin IT-337R4 Consolidated, Archived – "Retiring allowances"
Interpretation Bulletin IT-352R2, Archived – "Employees' expenses, including work space in home expenses"
Interpretation Bulletin IT-357R2, Archived – "Expenses of training"
Interpretation Bulletin IT-421R2, Archived – "Benefits to individuals, corporations and shareholders from loans or debt"
Interpretation Bulletin IT-508R, Archived – "Death benefits"
Interpretation Bulletin IT-518R, Archived – "Food, beverages and entertainment expenses"
Interpretation Bulletin IT-522R, Archived – "Vehicle, travel and sales expenses of employees"

Interpretation Bulletin IT-525R Consolidated, Archived – "Performing artists"

Interpretation Bulletin IT-529, Archived – "Flexible employee benefit programs"

Information Circular 73-21R9, "Claims for meals and lodging expenses of transport employees"

Information Circular 77-1R5, "Deferred profit sharing plans"

Pamphlet P119, "When You Retire"

Also, see the following selected topics on the CRA's website:

"Security options"

"Retiring allowances"

# Chapter 11

## If you are self-employed

- Arrange to be a consultant rather than an employee (11.1)
- Recover GST (or HST) that you've paid by claiming input tax credits for your business (11.2.4)
- If you're a residential landlord, account for sales tax costs when setting rents (11.2.4)
- Be aware of your obligations for sales to customers in HST provinces (11.2.5)
- Simplify your paperwork by using the "Quick Method" for GST/HST and QST reporting (11.2.6)
- Acquire depreciable assets before year-end (11.2.7)
- Consider claiming less CCA than the maximum (11.2.7)
- Deduct public transit fares, taxis and other business travel costs (11.2.8)
- Document and claim your business meals and entertainment expenses (11.2.9)
- Write off your eligible home office expenses (11.2.10)
- If you're a partner, claim sales tax rebates on your unreimbursed partnership expenses (11.3.7)
- Use your loss carryovers to maximum advantage (11.4.1)
- Keep detailed documentation to support your write-offs for losses from rental properties (11.4.2)
- Consider the potential benefits of incorporating your business (11.5)

*In this chapter, we highlight some of the major topics in the taxation of business income. If you are a professional, see Chapter 16 for additional information. If you are in a partnership, see also 16.2; if you are in Quebec, see also Chapter 17. Of course, anyone with a substantial amount of business income should obtain proper professional advice due to the many tax planning opportunities available.*

## 11.1 Employee or independent contractor?

As you will see in this chapter, people who are self-employed, carrying on business for themselves, generally have a wider scope for tax planning than do employees.

Carrying on a business has nothing to do with setting up a corporation (see 11.5 and Chapter 14). Anyone can carry on business. If you set up a second-hand clothing-for-cash exchange in your basement, you are carrying on business. If you decide to put a name to your business (say, "XYZ Second-Hand Clothing"), that is just you carrying on business under that name. You have not created a new entity. You simply have a proprietorship, which means you are the proprietor of a business.

The distinction between employee and independent contractor (i.e., self-employed) is not always clear in cases where you receive most or all of your "work" income from one source. If you provide services to an organization, you can be classed in either group, depending on the facts.

> Example
>
> Kathy is a technical writer. She develops software documentation under contract for ABC Corporation and is paid for each hour she works. She does a lot of her work at home, though she goes to ABC's offices for regular meetings.
>
> Is Kathy an employee of ABC, or an independent consultant who carries on business and whose major (or only) client is ABC?

In cases like this, one must look at all the facts to determine the person's status. There are no hard and fast rules. In general, you are more likely to be considered an employee if you:

- work a set number of hours per day
- have to account for your time to the company
- are told what to do each step of the way
- are a member of the company's group life, drug, dental and pension plans and receive other "benefits"
- use the company's computer equipment and supplies and have an office at the company.

By contrast, you would likely be considered an independent contractor carrying on your own business as a proprietor if you:

- agree to get the job done but don't make a commitment for any particular number of hours on any particular day
- work on your own with no supervision, and simply report back to the company periodically on progress
- issue invoices and receive payments (with no source deductions for income tax, EI or CPP/QPP) and receive no employee benefits
- use your own equipment and work at home, going to the company for planning meetings only
- provide services to more than one company.

These examples are fairly extreme. Between them is a large fuzzy area, where each case will depend on its facts. It doesn't matter very much what you and the company *call* your relationship; more specifically, calling it independent contracting doesn't make it independent contracting unless the facts support such a claim.

One case where the CRA has a clear administrative policy is that of real estate agents. You will be considered self-employed if you are entitled to the full amount of commissions, and either (a) you pay only a fixed amount to your broker for administrative operating costs, or (b) you pay a percentage of your gross commissions to your broker to cover such costs, and you set your own commission rate for sales on your listings.

If you are currently employed in a position where you maintain a fair amount of independence from your employer, investigate whether you can change your relationship so that you become an independent consultant rather than an employee. You will need to document the details of your relationship carefully, in case the CRA or Revenu Québec challenges you in the future.

> Arrange to be a consultant rather than an employee.

If you succeed in becoming independent, you will be able to take advantage of all of the planning tips throughout this chapter. You will lose certain advantages, however, including the right to Employment Insurance (EI) benefits, the employer's contribution to the Canada Pension Plan (CPP) for you, and possibly all of the employment benefits you now have (pension plan, drug plan, etc.). You may wish to negotiate to have your cash compensation increased in exchange for any employment benefits you are giving up.

The CRA has a questionnaire, Form CPT-1, through which your employer/ client can supply the details of its relationship with you and ask for a ruling as to whether you are an employee or not for CPP purposes (and, by extension, for income tax purposes). However, there is no requirement to apply for such a ruling, and you and your employer/client are not bound by the CRA's administrative decisions. If, after receiving professional advice, you believe that you are legally an independent contractor, then you are quite entitled to proceed on that basis. (Of course, if the CRA has expressed the view that you are an employee, your employer/client may not be willing to risk not withholding tax at source.)

## 11.2 Taxation of the business

In this section, we review how your business income is taxed. If you are a professional, see also Chapter 16.

### 11.2.1 Business year-end

Unlike corporations, all individuals, and all partnerships that have any individuals as members, generally have to use the calendar year for reporting their income.

### 11.2.2 Business income and expenses

As a general rule, business income for tax purposes is based on generally accepted accounting principles. (Among other things, this means operating on the accrual basis: you record your income when you have billed your clients, whether or not you have been paid.) However, there are many adjustments required for tax purposes. Some of them are discussed in the sections below.

When you earn business income, there is normally no withholding of tax at source. If you are providing services to a single organization and are able to classify your relationship as one of independent consultant rather than employee (see 11.1), you should submit invoices that will be paid in full, without tax (or EI premiums or CPP/QPP contributions) being taken off and remitted to the CRA. You may, however, be required to pay instalments of income tax. Instalments are discussed in 9.2.2.

In general, expenses are deductible if they are laid out to earn income from the business and are considered reasonable in the circumstances. There are certainly exceptions, as we shall see in the following sections. However, the underlying principle is the reverse of that for employees. *Employees can only deduct expenses that are specifically permitted under the federal* Income Tax Act *and the* Quebec Taxation Act. *Someone carrying on business can deduct any expenses that are not specifically prohibited by these statutes, provided such expenses relate to the earning of business income and are reasonable in the circumstances.*

### 11.2.3 EI, CPP and other payroll taxes

Employment insurance is available only to those who are employed. If you carry on business for yourself, you are neither required nor permitted to pay EI premiums. However, if your consulting contracts terminate and you are left without work, you cannot receive EI benefits.

Although you will not qualify for regular EI benefits, you can choose to voluntarily pay the employee's portion of EI premiums (up to $836 for 2017) to qualify for special EI benefits such as maternity, parental and adoptive, sickness and compassionate care benefits.

Canada and Quebec Pension Plan contributions are split equally between employees and their employers. If you are self-employed, you are required to pay the "employer's share" to make up what is not being paid for you, as well as your own share. Since you are not employed, no CPP/QPP contributions are withheld from your income. As a result, you will find yourself required to pay up to $5,128 for 2017 in mandatory CPP/QPP contributions when you file your personal tax return. You may then claim a deduction from taxable income for the portion of CPP/QPP contributions that represents the employer's share, up to $2,564 for 2017. You can also claim the non-refundable 15% federal tax credit for the employee's share of your CPP/QPP contributions (about $385, based on the credit amount of up to $2,564 for 2017—see 2.9.1). If it's any consolation, you'll be entitled to receive CPP/QPP retirement benefits after you turn 65, or optionally as early as age 60 at a reduced amount (see 20.3.1).

### 11.2.4 Recovering GST by claiming input tax credits

If you are self-employed, you can normally claim a refund ("input tax credit") of the Goods and Services Tax (GST) paid on most expenses incurred in your business. Please note that this book only addresses certain GST/HST topics.

The GST applies at a rate of 5% to taxable goods and services supplied in Canada. The Harmonized Sales Tax (HST), discussed in 11.2.5, is a blended federal/provincial sales tax that applies at various rates in Ontario, Nova Scotia, New Brunswick, Prince Edward Island and Newfoundland and Labrador. Generally, our comments throughout this book apply equally to the HST, with some exceptions.

To be eligible for input tax credits, you must register with the CRA. You are generally required to register if your total taxable revenues are more than $30,000 in the last four consecutive quarters or in a single quarter. If your revenues are below that threshold, you can still voluntarily register. Once you are registered, you must charge GST on all your taxable sales, even if your sales are less than $30,000.

While you can build the tax into your prices if you wish, you must advise your clients that the sale is subject to GST/HST (i.e., on invoices). You must generally provide your clients with documentation to support their own claims of input tax credits (see below). As is the case for income tax purposes, "personal or living expenses" are not eligible for input tax credits.

Make sure to keep accurate records so you can claim input tax credits where possible. Claims for input tax credits for GST paid must be supported by receipts or other documentation, not submitted with the GST return but held on file in case of audit. All documentation must show the vendor's name, the date (or, for a contract, the date the amounts are payable), and the total amount payable. Where the total (including all taxes) is $30 or over, the receipt must also show:

> Recover GST (or HST) that you've paid by claiming input tax credits for your business.

- the amount of GST, or a statement that the total includes GST, and a clear indication of which items are taxable, and
- the supplier's nine-digit GST registration number.

Where the total is $150 or over, the receipt must also show:

- the purchaser's name,
- the terms of payment, and
- a description sufficient to identify each item supplied.

Failure to have this documentation will normally lead to a reassessment of any input tax credit claim if the return is audited.

Input tax credits can only be claimed where the expenses were incurred in the course of providing "taxable supplies". A business engaged in providing supplies that are GST-exempt—such as a doctor, dentist, life insurance agent or financial institution—cannot claim input tax credits for GST paid on the costs of making those supplies.

**If you're a residential landlord, account for sales tax costs when setting rents.**

If you rent out residential real estate (whether a house or an apartment building), the rent will generally be exempt from GST. As a result, you cannot claim input tax credits to recover any of the GST that you pay on utilities, property management fees and other costs. You must set the rent high enough to cover your costs. (Rent for commercial real estate is subject to GST.)

In Quebec, similar rules apply for Quebec Sales Tax (QST) purposes.

### 11.2.5 Harmonized Sales Tax

**Be aware of your obligations for sales to customers in HST provinces.**

No matter where in Canada your business is located, you should be aware of your obligations under the HST, the blended federal/provincial sales tax that applies in Ontario, Nova Scotia, New Brunswick, Prince Edward Island and Newfoundland and Labrador.

The HST rates in these provinces are comprised of a 5% federal component and varying provincial components (see the table below). A major difference is that the HST applies at the provincial HST rate on goods and services supplied in the HST provinces, instead of the 5% GST and any other applicable sales taxes (e.g., QST) that apply in other provinces. As noted, in 11.2.4, our comments about the GST throughout this book apply equally to the HST, though there are some exceptions.

All GST registrants must collect HST on taxable supplies made in the HST provinces. If you are registered for the GST, you are also registered for the HST. Collection, reporting and remittance of the HST is done through the CRA in the same way as the GST, with a few exceptions.

The HST could complicate your recordkeeping and sales tax reporting if you make taxable sales to customers both inside and outside the HST provinces. Depending on the province to which the goods or services are delivered, you will have to determine whether you should charge GST or HST, QST or provincial sales tax (PST) and at what rate. Special rules apply to determine whether goods or services are supplied (i.e., delivered) in one of these provinces.

The table below shows indirect tax rates that apply across Canada as of July 1, 2017.

| Indirect Tax Rates in Effect as of July 1, 2017* | | |
|---|---|---|
| | GST or HST Rate | PST or QST Rate |
| British Columbia | 5% GST | 7% PST |
| Alberta | 5% GST | |
| Saskatchewan** | 5% GST | 6% PST |
| Manitoba | 5% GST | 8% PST |
| Ontario | 13% HST (5% federal and 8% provincial components) | |
| Quebec | 5% GST | 9.975% QST |
| New Brunswick | 15% HST (5% federal and 10% provincial components) | |
| Nova Scotia | 15% HST (5% federal and 10% provincial components) | |
| Prince Edward Island | 15% HST (5% federal and 10% provincial components) | |
| Newfoundland and Labrador | 15% HST (5% federal and 10% provincial components) | |

\* Other rates and other indirect taxes may apply.
\*\* Saskatchewan increased its PST rate to 6% (from 5%) as of March 23, 2017.

## 11.2.6 GST—the "Quick Method" and simplified accounting

Self-employed individuals and small businesses may elect to use the "Quick Method" to simplify recordkeeping for GST. Many businesses with annual sales (including tax) that do not exceed $400,000 (excluding financial services, real property, capital assets and certain other assets) can use this method. Annual sales include sales of associated businesses.

The Quick Method can be particularly useful for certain consultants. However, some businesses may not use this method, including businesses providing legal, accounting, actuarial, bookkeeping, financial consulting, tax consulting or tax return preparation services.

Simplify your paperwork by using the "Quick Method" for GST/HST and QST reporting.

Under the Quick Method, your business must still charge and collect the tax at the normal rates. However, instead of remitting total GST collected minus total GST paid as it would under the usual method, the business remits to the CRA a flat percentage of sales (including GST/HST). The percentages vary depending on whether your business operates exclusively outside of the HST provinces, exclusively in those provinces, or both in and out of those provinces. The rates also vary depending on whether your business primarily sells goods or services. Your business may have to use more than one rate, depending on its circumstances.

Some input tax credits are still available, including those on real property and other capital assets purchased for use in taxable activities. You must still remit the full amount of tax collected on supplies that are not eligible for the Quick Method calculation, such as real property and capital assets.

For businesses operating exclusively outside the HST provinces, where sales are mostly services rather than goods, the flat percentage for GST is 3.6%. For qualifying suppliers of goods whose costs, including GST/HST, of taxable personal property (other than basic groceries and other goods for which no tax is paid) purchased for resale are at least 40% of taxable sales (including GST/HST but excluding basic groceries and certain other items), the flat percentage is 1.8%. Input tax credits can only be claimed for capital purchases.

For businesses operating exclusively in HST provinces, the rate differs depending on the province.

For businesses operating both inside and outside the HST provinces, the rules are more complex—advice from a qualified sales tax professional is recommended.

Under the Quick Method, a business can generally claim a 1% credit on the first $30,000 (including GST/HST) of eligible supplies on which GST or HST has been collected in each fiscal year.

Example

John is a computer consultant who works exclusively in Alberta. In May 2017, he bills his clients $50,000 plus $2,500 GST. Because he is able to use his clients' equipment and facilities, his cost of doing business is very low. He pays a total of $50 GST on $1,000 of business expenses during the year.

Normally, John would remit his GST collected minus his GST paid to the CRA for the year. This would be $2,500 minus $50, or $2,450.

By electing to use the Quick Method, however, John will be required to remit $1,890 (a flat 3.6% of his sales of $52,500), minus a credit of $300 (1% × $30,000). He thus remits $1,590 instead of $2,450.

John will effectively be subject to income tax on the $860 difference ($2,450–$1,590).

As you can see, the Quick Method can be useful for eligible businesses that have few taxable expenses. If the business's taxable expenses are high, however, the loss of the ability to claim input tax credits may offset the benefit of the Quick Method's reduced remittance rate.

As an alternative to the Quick Method, the Simplified Method of accounting for input tax credits allows you to total up your GST-bearing purchases—including GST, provincial sales tax, late payment penalties and tips—and claim 5/105 of the total on purchases where 5% GST is paid for input tax credit purposes (different rebate rates apply to HST-bearing purchases). Among other conditions, your business's annual sales (including sales of associated businesses) generally must not exceed $1 million and taxable purchases must not exceed $4 million for you to use this method.

Not only does the Simplified Method make accounting for input tax credits simpler, it may also give you a slightly larger claim than you can make by totalling up individual amounts of GST paid.

For QST reporting in Quebec, you can use a similar "Quick Method" and simplified accounting (however, the rates under the QST system are somewhat different).

### 11.2.7 Capital cost allowance

The treatment of capital expenses is one of the major differences between business income based on accounting principles and income calculated for income tax purposes. In both cases, you cannot simply write off the cost of purchasing major capital assets (furniture, buildings, computers, automobiles, etc.). You must spread the cost over several years.

For accounting (not tax) purposes, the business owners, with professional assistance, will make a judgment call as to the appropriate depreciation to claim. Various methods of depreciation can be used.

For tax purposes, depreciation is subject to strict rules and limitations since it reduces your income (and thus the tax you pay). The income tax system of depreciation is called capital cost allowance (CCA); the rules are numerous and complex.

In general terms, your capital assets are grouped into classes, and capital cost allowance can be claimed annually against each class. The "declining balance" method is used for most classes; the maximum you can claim against each class is a fixed percentage of the "undepreciated capital cost". What you claim then reduces that balance for next year's claim.

| Some common CCA rates | |
|---|---|
| Automobiles (class 10 or 10.1) | 30% |
| Non-residential buildings: | |
| acquired after March 18, 2007 (class 1) | 6% |
| acquired after March 18, 2007 and used in manufacturing and processing (class 1) | 10% |
| acquired after 1987 and before March 19, 2007 (class 1) | 4% |
| Computer hardware (class 50) | 55% |
| Most computer software (class 12) | 100% |
| Furniture and fixtures (class 8) | 20% |
| Eligible tools costing less than $500 acquired after May 1, 2006 (class 12) | 100% |

**Acquire depreciable assets before year-end.**

For most acquisitions, only one-half of the CCA you could otherwise claim for the asset will be allowed in the year of acquisition. As a result, acquiring an asset just before your year-end will accelerate the timing of your tax write-off, while acquiring the asset at the beginning of the year will delay your CCA claim. Assets are normally required to be available for use in the business and not simply "on the books" to be eligible for CCA, unless you have owned them for at least two years. (The term "available for use" has a specific and complex definition, and professional advice should be sought if you are unsure as to how it applies in your case.)

Note that you are never required to claim the maximum CCA. You may in any year choose to claim less than the maximum, or nothing at all, for any given class of assets. The undepreciated capital cost for that class will remain intact, so you can make claims in later years based on that carried-forward balance.

**Consider claiming less CCA than the maximum.**

In some circumstances, you may wish to claim less CCA than you are entitled to. For example, if you have prior-year non-capital losses or investment tax credits that would otherwise expire, you are better off not to claim

CCA, use up the losses or credits, and save your "undepreciated capital cost" balances for CCA claims in future years.

You might also choose not to claim CCA if you are in a low-income year and expect your income to be much higher (and thus taxed at higher marginal rates) in later years. Such a decision should only be made after careful analysis of the present value of the future tax savings, including the impact on your ability to make an RRSP contribution in the subsequent year.

### 11.2.8 Transportation expenses

If you rely on modes of travel other than an automobile for your business travel, you can generally deduct the related expenses. Keep records of all such business trips, and deduct the appropriate costs of public transit, taxis and so on. (If you use your own car, see 12.3.)

> Deduct public transit fares, taxis and other business travel costs.

You cannot consider transportation from your home to your own office as a business expense. However, if you have an office in your home and you travel from there to your major client (who might happen to provide you with an office on its premises), you are engaging in business travel.

For non-business-related travel (such as commuting to and from your office), you can claim the tax credit for the cost of eligible public transit passes for the period January 1 to June 30, 2017. This tax credit is not available for transit expenses after this date (see 2.7.3).

### 11.2.9 Meals and entertainment

If you treat a client or potential client (or a group of such people) to a meal, you can normally consider the cost of the meal as a business expense. The tax rules restrict the amount you can claim to 50% of the amount paid; the restriction is designed to deny a deduction for some of the personal benefit you receive (since you would need to eat anyway). The same 50% limitation applies to entertainment expenses, such as taking a client to a sports event. (If you pay Quebec tax, see 17.10.5.)

> Document and claim your business meals and entertainment expenses.

Similarly, if you are registered for GST purposes, you can only claim input tax credits for half of the GST paid on such expenses (see 11.2.4).

Make sure you claim all lunches and dinners that you can justifiably relate to your business. For audit purposes, you should make a notation on your receipt of the individual(s) entertained and the reason for the meeting.

### 11.2.10 Home office expenses

If you have an office in your home, you can claim a portion of your ongoing home expenses as

> Write off your eligible home office expenses.

business expenses, subject to the restrictions discussed below. The portion is normally based on the fraction of the home that is used for your office (you should usually exclude common areas, such as hallways, kitchen and washrooms, when making the calculation).

> Mary is a software developer and works as a consultant to various companies. She works in her home, where her office is a room that is 200 square feet (18.5 square metres). The total area of the rooms in her house (bedrooms, living room, dining room and the office) is 2,000 square feet (186 square metres).
>
> Provided her home office qualifies (see below), Mary can claim 10% of her costs such as mortgage interest, property taxes, house insurance and utilities as expenses for tax purposes.

The expenses you can claim include:

- rent, if you are a tenant
- mortgage interest (but not the principal portion of blended mortgage payments)
- property taxes
- utilities, such as electricity, heat, water, gas
- telephone (if you have a separate business telephone which is fully deductible, consider whether you also use your personal phone for business calls)
- home insurance.

Also make sure to claim your business portion of some of the less obvious expenses, such as garden service, driveway snowplowing, and minor repairs. You will need to keep receipts on file; do not simply estimate your expenses.

You may also claim capital cost allowance on the appropriate fraction of your home, but this is often not advisable. If you claim CCA, the CRA will take the position that that fraction of your home is not part of your principal residence and disallow your claim for the principal residence exemption (see 6.5.2) for that portion of the home. Any CCA you claimed can also be "recaptured" into income when you sell your home. (If you bought your home at the top of the housing market and do not expect to recover your costs when you sell, claiming CCA may be a good idea, however.)

Home office expenses are subject to restrictions. First, you can only claim the expenses against your income from the business. You therefore cannot use home office expenses to produce an overall business loss that is applied against other income. However, losses disallowed because of this rule can be carried forward and used in any later year against income generated from the same business.

Second, the home office will only be allowed if:

- your home is your principal place of business—that is, you do not have an office elsewhere (if you have one major client and that client provides you with an office on its premises, it is still the client's premises and it will not disentitle you to your claim for a home office), or
- the home office is used exclusively for your business and used "on a regular and continuous basis for meeting clients, customers or patients".

> **Example**
>
> Les is an optometrist and has an office outside his home. He also has an office in his basement, where he does a lot of his business's paperwork and occasionally sees patients (usually neighbours who come over for treatment in the evening).
>
> Les cannot claim any expenses for his home office unless he can show that he uses it "on a regular and continuous basis" to see patients.

Of course, supplies that relate exclusively to your home office are fully deductible and not subject to the above restrictions. Fully deductible expenses normally include a separate business phone line, printer paper, printer ink, photocopier toner cartridges, computer repairs (assuming your computer is used only for your business) and so on.

If you pay Quebec tax, see also 17.10.6.

### 11.2.11 Health and dental premiums

Self-employed individuals whose primary source of income is business income may write-off premiums paid for supplementary health care coverage as a business expense. For the premiums to be deductible, your coverage must be no greater than the benefits provided to your arm's length employees. If you have no such employees, your deductible premiums are limited to $1,500 for yourself, $1,500 for your spouse and $750 for each child.

### 11.2.12 Convention expenses

The CRA allows you to deduct the costs of attending two conventions a year in connection with your business or profession. A portion of your expenses may be subject to the limitation on the deductibility of meals and entertainment expenses discussed at 11.2.9.

For the expenses to be deductible, the convention must be held at a location that can reasonably be considered to be within the scope of the host organization. For example, if the convention's sponsor is a business or professional body that is provincial in scope, the convention must be held in that province. Under the Canada-U.S. tax treaty, expenses to attend a Canadian-sponsored convention in the U.S. are deductible, but only if the Canadian organization is a national one. (The CRA does not allow you to deduct any costs for attending a convention held during an ocean cruise, no matter who sponsors it.)

### 11.2.13 Capital gains

Any capital gains that you realize are accounted for directly, through the capital gains system discussed in Chapter 6. They are not counted within the business's income.

### 11.2.14 Investment tax credits

Federal investment tax credits (ITCs) are available for investment in certain regions of the country (for example, parts of the Maritimes) and for investment in scientific research and experimental development.

ITCs are claimed in the return for the calendar year in which they are generated. Unused ITCs can be carried back three years or carried forward for up to 20 years.

## 11.3 Partnerships

> *Caution: The tax planning ideas discussed in this section may be affected by the federal government's proposed new tax regime for private companies, as outlined in the Department of Finance's July 2017 consultation paper and draft legislation. See Appendix I for details.*

If you join together to carry on business with one or more other people—which could include your spouse—you will be in partnership. You are still, for tax purposes, carrying on business. (As well as the discussion below, see 16.2, where we discuss some special rules applying to professional partnerships.)

### 11.3.1 How partnership income is taxed

Partnerships do not pay tax. Partnerships are required to file "information returns" with the CRA to report partnership income, but these are not tax returns. Some partnerships are exempt from this filing, based on a financial activity test and type of partnership.

The individual partners must each report their share of the partnership's income (or loss) as their own, *whether or not they have taken any of the profits out of the partnership.* The partnership is generally required to report income on a December 31 year-end basis. (Resource allowances and certain other resource-related expenses are claimed by the individual partner rather than at the partnership level.)

Note that a partnership cannot pay a "salary" to a partner. Even if you, as a partner, receive something called a "salary", it is really partnership drawings (withdrawal of profits or capital from the partnership). You are *not* taxed on your partnership drawings, but on your share of the partnership's income, which may be very different.

If the partnership suffers losses, you can normally claim your share of those losses against your other sources of income. (This may not be the case where the partnership is a limited partnership.)

### 11.3.2 Adjustment of partnership allocation

The allocation of partnership income (or losses) among the partners is normally left up to the partners to resolve. If you set up an unreasonable allocation for income-splitting purposes (see Chapter 5), however, the CRA may disallow your allocation and substitute a reasonable one.

For example, if you and your spouse are in partnership together and you supply all of the capital and do almost all of the work in your business, while your spouse does almost nothing, the CRA could disallow a 50/50 allocation of the business's income between the two of you.

### 11.3.3 Capital gains

Capital gains or losses realized by a partnership are allocated to the individual partners at the end of the partnership's taxation year.

### 11.3.4 Allocation of investment tax credits

Investment tax credits (see 11.2.14) earned by a partnership are allocated to the individual partners and claimed in the year in which the partnership's year ends.

### 11.3.5 Gain or loss on partnership interest

When you are a member of a partnership you own a "partnership interest", which has an adjusted cost base for capital gains calculation purposes (see 6.2.1). If you sell your interest in the partnership (or are deemed to dispose of it at fair market value on death or emigration—see 6.5.4 and 13.3.2), the adjusted cost base determines whether you have a capital gain or capital loss.

Your initial cost base of your partnership interest is the capital you put into the partnership. Each year, when you report your share of the partnership's income, that amount is added to your cost base (since you have already been taxed on it, it should not be taxed again if you sell your interest without withdrawing the profits). When you withdraw profits from the partnership (see 11.3.1), the amount you withdraw reduces your adjusted cost base. Thus, in simplified terms, your adjusted cost base of your partnership interest is your contributions, plus all partnership profits, minus all partnership losses and your withdrawals. (The details are much more complicated and there are many special rules, but that is the essence of it.)

### 11.3.6 Assessment of partnership

The CRA is able to issue a "determination" of a partnership's income or loss. This determination is much like an assessment of a taxpayer's tax (see 9.4.1), in that it is binding on the partners unless a Notice of Objection is filed. One partner would have to be designated by the partnership to file any such Notice of Objection, and the other partners would not be able to object directly to the determination.

### 11.3.7 Partners' sales tax rebates

If you're a partner, claim sales tax rebates on your unreimbursed partnership expenses.

Like employees, partners who are not registered themselves for GST purposes and who have unreimbursed expenses, such as automobile expenses that are deductible for income tax purposes, can generally claim a rebate for the GST, HST or QST paid on those expenses (see 12.3.2 for an example).

Make sure to keep records through the year and obtain invoices that indicate the amount of tax paid. The rebate is claimed with your individual income tax return.

## 11.4 Losses

### 11.4.1 Business losses

If your business expenses claimed for tax purposes exceed the revenues from the business, you have a loss. You also have a loss for tax purposes if you share in a portion of a partnership's loss.

You can only claim a business loss or loss arising from a partnership against other income if your business activity is clearly commercial and undertaken in pursuit of profit. If the activity has a personal element or has the aspect of a hobby, such as breeding race horses, the venture is considered to be in pursuit of profit if it is undertaken in a sufficiently commercial manner.

A business loss must first be used in the year in which it arises, to offset income from other businesses and other types of income, such as employment income, interest, (grossed-up) dividends and taxable capital gains. You do not have any choice in this matter; even if, for example, the tax on your dividend income could be offset by the dividend tax credit anyway, you must apply your business losses against any income you have in that year.

Use your loss carryovers to maximum advantage.

Business losses not deductible in the year they arise can be applied to other years' income. These "non-capital losses" can be carried back for up to three years or carried forward for up to 20 years. They can be applied against any source of income in those years. All such claims are optional.

<table>
<tr><td rowspan="1">Example</td><td>

Judy had no income in 2014, and she earned $40,000 in 2015 and $50,000 in 2016 as an employee. In 2017, she went into business for herself, and, for her 2017 business year, she suffered a loss for tax purposes of $100,000.

Judy can file a form requesting that her non-capital loss from 2017 be applied against any amount of her 2015 and 2016 income. She will then receive a refund for the tax she paid in those years. If she wipes out all of her 2015 and 2016 income, she will still have a $10,000 non-capital loss, which can be carried forward to future years.

Judy should not, however, use up $90,000 of her loss. She only needs to use enough to bring her 2015 and 2016 income so low that she pays no tax at all (about $11,327 for 2015 and $11,474 for 2016). If she wishes, she may choose to use even less, and leave some of the 2015 and 2016 income taxed at relatively low rates.

</td></tr>
</table>

This example shows the need to use any non-capital losses carefully. When using non-capital losses against income for any given year, consider whether you want to keep some of the income taxed at a low rate. For example, if you have a loss in 2017 and are carrying it back to 2016, bear in mind that taxable income below $45,300 in 2016 was taxed at only about 25%. If you (confidently) expect to have a large income within the next few years, so that you can apply the loss against income that would otherwise be taxed at approximately 50%, you may be better off not bringing your 2016 taxable income below $45,300.

Of course, you should never use loss carryovers to reduce your taxable income below the level where no tax is payable anyway ($11,474 for 2016, or more depending on the credits you can claim—see Chapter 2).

### 11.4.2  Losses from rental properties

If you are a residential landlord, your losses from your rental property are deductible in the same way as other business losses as long as your rental business meets the general tax law requirements for business deductions. The CRA is quite aggressive in targeting rental loss deductions, so you should be sure to have adequate supporting documentation on hand to support your rental loss deductions.

The CRA is likely to question your rental losses if your ownership of the property has a personal-use element, for example, if you or one of your relatives live there rent-free or you plan to live

> Keep detailed documentation to support your write-offs for losses from rental properties.

there in the future. The CRA may ask for detailed documentation such as a
floor plan of the building showing which areas you use, rent out and share
with your tenants. You should also be prepared to show which of your
expenses relate to the whole property as opposed to the rental portion only.
If you rent to a relative, your losses may be disallowed if you charge a lower
rent than you would charge an unrelated tenant.

You should be prepared to prove the commercial nature of your rental
activities. Where possible, keep complete records to show that you did
thorough research on rental properties before you chose one to buy and
complete records of the information that led you to believe your rental
property would be a profitable investment. The tax courts have ruled that
rental businesses may take several years—up to eight years in one case—to
turn a profit. An explanation for your losses and description of steps taken to
increase revenue or reduce expenses would also help support your case.

The Supreme Court has ruled that the tax system should not penalize
taxpayers for lack of business acumen. Even if you do not have detailed
profit projections and market research on hand, you should seek professional
tax advice if the CRA seeks to deny your rental losses.

## 11.5  Should you incorporate your small business?

> *Caution: The tax planning ideas discussed in this section may be affected by
> the federal government's proposed new tax regime for private companies,
> as outlined in the Department of Finance's July 2017 consultation paper and
> draft legislation. See Appendix I for details.*

If you have an unincorporated business, you may be considering
incorporation to save on taxes. But whether you and your business would
gain a tax benefit from incorporation depends on your personal cash flow
needs, the personal and corporate tax rates in your province and the status of
your business. (If you are considering setting up a corporation for the sole
purpose of holding your investments, see 14.6.)

If you rely on all of your business's profits to support your personal cash
flow needs, incorporation may not be a good idea—the cost of setting up
and maintaining the corporation could outweigh the tax benefits. But if
you can leave some of your profits in the corporation to be reinvested,
incorporation could result in significant tax savings.

The taxation of corporations is discussed in 14.1. Generally, if you earn
income through a corporation, the income is taxed at the corporation level
and then again at the personal level when the corporation distributes its
after-tax income to you as a shareholder in the form of a dividend. In theory,
the total corporate and personal income tax incurred by using a corporation

to earn income should be the same as the personal tax that would result if the income were earned directly by an individual who was taxable at the top marginal rate. In practice, this is not always the case. Before you incorporate your business, ask a professional tax adviser to help you compare the total amount of tax you would pay if you earn your business income directly or through a corporation. Some advantages of incorporating your business include the following:

*Asset protection*—Incorporation can limit your liability by keeping your personal and corporate assets separate. But since banks often ask small business owners for personal guarantees before they'll provide financing, incorporation may not protect you from all creditors.

Consider the potential benefits of incorporating your business.

*Deferring expenses*—You may be able to defer certain expenses if you incorporate. For example, if you report a bonus paid to an employee for tax purposes, you do not have to pay out the money until six months later.

*Fiscal year flexibility*—As we saw in 11.2.1, an unincorporated business must use the calendar year to report income for tax purposes. An incorporated business can choose a non-calendar fiscal year, which may work better for your business cycle. If the fiscal year-end is in the later part of the calendar year, the payment of a bonus six months after the end of the year would put the payment into the next calendar year.

*Access to the small business deduction*—With a corporation, you may be able to take advantage of the special lower tax rates for the first $500,000 of active business income of small "Canadian-controlled private corporations" (see 14.1).

*Income splitting*—If your spouse and adult children are shareholders in the corporation, any dividends they receive will be taxed in their hands. Your corporation can also employ your family members as long as the amount paid is reasonable for the work performed (see 5.3.2). Also bear in mind the income splitting tax on certain income received by minor children (see 5.2.4).

*Capital gains exemption*—If your corporation is a qualifying small business corporation, the lifetime capital gains exemption discussed in 6.4.1 is available to shelter your gain and the gains of each of your family members that will arise when the shares of the corporation are sold or transferred through a will.

*Group insurance and retirement benefits*—Once you incorporate, you can create a registered pension plan and obtain tax-deductible group health and life insurance for yourself and your employees, which could include family members. (Unincorporated businesses can also deduct group health insurance premiums if certain conditions are met and within certain limits—see 11.2.11.)

Against these potential advantages, you need to weigh the legal and administrative costs of setting up and maintaining the corporation, keeping separate books and filing federal and provincial corporate tax returns. Also bear in mind that once you incorporate you can no longer deduct business and capital losses of the corporation against your other sources of income. Your decision about whether and when you should incorporate your business should be made with appropriate professional advice.

## 11.6  References

The following publications and more information, including forms and brochures, can be obtained on the CRA's website at *www.cra-arc.gc.ca* or by telephone request at 1-800-959-8281 for individual income tax and trust-related enquiries or 1-800-959-5525 for business and self-employed individual enquiries.

Guide RC4022, "General Information for GST/HST Registrants"
Guide RC4058, "Quick Method of Accounting for GST/HST"
Guide RC4070, "Information for Canadian Small Businesses"
Guide RC4110, "Employee or Self-Employed?"
Guide T4002, "Business and Professional Income"
Guide T4036, "Rental Income"
Income Tax Folio S2-F1-C1, "Health and Welfare Trusts"
Income Tax Folio S3-F4-C1, "General Discussion of Capital Cost Allowance"
Income Tax Folio S3-F6-C1, "Interest Deductibility"
Income Tax Folio S4-F2-C2, "Business Use of Home Expenses"
Income Tax Folio S4-F16-C1, "What is a Partnership?"
Interpretation Bulletin IT-79R3, Archived – "Capital cost allowance—Buildings or other structures"
Interpretation Bulletin IT-131R2, Archived – "Convention expenses"
Interpretation Bulletin IT-232R3, Archived – "Losses—Their deductibility in the loss year or in other years"
Interpretation Bulletin IT-364, Archived – "Commencement of business operations"
Interpretation Bulletin IT-518R, Archived – "Food, beverages and entertainment expenses"
Interpretation Bulletin IT-521R, Archived – "Motor vehicle expenses claimed by self-employed individuals"
Interpretation Bulletin IT-525R, Archived – "Performing artists"

# Chapter 12

## If you use an automobile for business

- Keep track of—and maximize—business use of your car (12.1, 12.2.1, 12.3.1)
- Check to see if you qualify for a reduced standby charge benefit (12.2.1)
- Reduce the amount of time your company car is available for personal use (12.2.1)
- Avoid employer-owned vehicles costing over $30,000 (12.2.1)
- Take steps to reduce the taxable benefit from car operating costs (12.2.2)
- Claim a rebate for GST/HST paid on expenses deductible from your employment income (12.3.2)

*If your employer provides you with an automobile, you may be assessed a taxable benefit for your personal use of the car. If you drive your own car in the course of your job or your business, you may be able to write off your work-related automobile costs against your employment or business income. In this chapter, we map out the complex rules that the CRA uses to arrive at your automobile-related taxable benefit or deduction. Along the way, we also point out some tax-saving opportunities.*

## 12.1 Keeping a log

Whether you drive your employer's car or your own in the course of your work, keep careful track of the distance you drive for work-related purposes to verify your automobile-related tax claims with the CRA. You may wish to keep a log book on the dashboard, or record your business driving in your daily appointment calendar. The log must show the total number of kilometres driven and total business kilometres for the year. It should also include the date, destination and distance driven for each business trip.

> Keep track of—and maximize—business use of your car.

If you're a business owner, you may use a simplified log book for reporting your business travel to the CRA. After you have kept a full log book for one complete year to establish a base year, you can then choose to use a three-month sample log book to extrapolate business use for the entire year, as long as the results are within 10 percent of the use in the base year. You must be able to show that the vehicle's use in the base year remains representative of normal use.

Quebec employees using employer-provided automobiles are required to provide their employers with a copy of such a log book within 10 days of either the end of the year or the end of the period the automobile was available to them, or they will face a $200 penalty.

## 12.2 Using a company automobile

Special rules apply for determining the taxable benefit when your employer provides you with an automobile. (If you use your own car for employment purposes, see 12.3.1.)

There are two elements to the benefit that must be reported for tax purposes: a standby charge, and a benefit for operating costs. These will normally be reported together on your T4 slip (and Quebec Relevé 1) from your employer as a single amount, and included in your total "income from employment" for tax purposes.

### 12.2.1 Standby charge

The standby charge is, essentially, 2% of the original cost of the car for each month that it is available to you—that is, 24% per year. (For automobile sales persons, it can instead be 1.5% per month of the average cost of the dealer's cars acquired in the year.)

You can have your standby charge reduced if you can show both that:

- your business use of the car is more than 50% of the kilometres driven, and
- your personal use of the car is less than 1,667 km per month, or 20,000 km in total during the year.

*Check to see if you qualify for a reduced standby charge benefit.*

If you meet these conditions, your employer can reduce your reported standby charge to a percentage equal to the number of personal-use kilometres driven divided by 20,000 (assuming the car was available to you for a full 12 months). For example, if you drive an employer-owned car 25,000 km for business purposes and 15,000 km for personal purposes, your standby charge can be reduced to 75% (15,000 ÷ 20,000) of the regular standby charge.

Note that driving between your home and your place of employment is normally *not* considered business use (unless you meet certain conditions—see 12.2.4). It can thus be very difficult to satisfy the above tests for a reduction in the standby charge.

When the car is leased, the standby charge is two-thirds of the monthly leasing cost instead of 2% of the purchase price. Up-front, lump-sum leasing charges (or "balloon" payments) are prorated over the term of the lease for purposes of the calculation.

Lease termination charges are normally considered a lease payment in the year paid. If you and your employer agree, a lease termination payment may be retroactively spread over the term of the lease for purposes of the standby charge, as long as the years are not statute-barred and your employer issues amended T4 slips (Relevé 1 for Quebec) for those years. This option will generally be advantageous if your income in the year that the lease is terminated is taxed at a higher rate than in previous years, although you will need to factor in the non-deductible interest that will be payable on the increase in your taxes for the earlier years.

The standby charge is based on the number of 30-day periods in the year that a company car is "made available" to you or a member of your family. However, the actual calculation is based on the number of *days* during which the car is

> Reduce the amount of time your company car is available for personal use.

available. This number is divided by 30 and rounded to the nearest whole number, and rounded down if it is exactly in the middle.

If you can get the number of "available days" down to 345, which is 11.5 30-day periods, the standby charge will be reduced to only 11 times 2% of the automobile cost instead of 12 times 2%.

If you take three weeks or more of vacations or business trips during the year, leave the car at the company's premises during those times. If the car cost $30,000 new in 2017, you can thus reduce your taxable income for the year by $600 (and save about $300 in tax if you are in the highest tax bracket) by getting the number of "available days" down to 345. Note, however, that the CRA holds the view that the car is still made available to you during this time unless you are *required* to return the car and control over its use to your employer. You might wish to arrange for your employer to impose this requirement on you.

As we will see in 12.3.1, there is a ceiling on the capital cost of cars for capital cost allowance purposes that creates an element of double taxation. For example, if you drive a company car

> Avoid employer-owned vehicles costing over $30,000.

that was purchased in 2017 and cost say $50,000 (plus GST/HST and PST), your taxable standby charge benefit is 2% per month of the actual cost of the car. However, only $30,000 (plus GST/HST and PST) can be written off (over time) as capital cost allowance by your employer. In this situation, it may be more economical for you to purchase the car yourself and arrange for an appropriate increase in remuneration from your employer.

## 12.2.2 Operating cost benefit

Car operating costs include items such as gasoline and oil, maintenance, repairs, licences and insurance. Operating costs do not include interest, capital cost allowance for a car you own, lease costs for a leased car, parking costs, highway or bridge tolls.

The taxable benefit for operating costs is 25¢/km of personal use for 2017. If your employer pays any operating costs during the year for your personal use of an employer-provided car (and you don't fully reimburse your employer by the following February 14), the 25¢/km rate applies. If you are employed principally in selling or leasing automobiles, this rate is 22¢/km.

An alternative calculation is available for the operating expenses where your business use of the car exceeds 50%. If you notify your employer in writing *by December 31* that you wish this option, the operating costs benefit will be a flat 50% of the standby charge.

If you qualify for a standby charge reduction (see 12.2.1), you should look into whether you could also benefit from the alternative operating cost benefit calculation. A benefit of one-half of the standby charge will also be to your advantage where the cost of the car is relatively low (for a small car, or a car that was purchased used) and the number of personal kilometres is relatively high even though it is used for personal purposes less than 50% of the time.

**Take steps to reduce the taxable benefit from car operating costs.**

If your employer pays only part of the operating costs of an employer-owned car that you use, the taxable benefit from operating costs can cost you more than the amount the employer pays. Sometimes the employer pays only the insurance and the employee pays for all gas and repairs, or the employer does not pay most operating expenses but might cover an occasional major repair bill.

For example, suppose you put 20,000 km on your company car over the year, all of which is personal use (including driving to work and back). Your employer pays the insurance ($800 per year) and you pay the rest of the operating expenses. Your taxable benefit for operating costs will be 25¢ per personal-use kilometre, or $5,000, which will cost you about $2,500 in tax if you are in the top tax bracket. So having the employer pay for the insurance is very disadvantageous.

In such a case, you should repay the $800 to the employer *by February 14* of the following year, so that the "25¢ per kilometre" rule does not apply. Of course, your employer can pay you sufficient additional salary so that the after-tax amount will be enough to offset your repayment of the insurance costs.

### 12.2.3 Allowances and advances for automobile expenses

If you receive a reasonable allowance for automobile expenses, the allowance is not included in your income if it is based solely on the number of kilometres driven in performing your employment duties. If it is a flat amount not calculated in terms of your employment-related driving, it will be taxable (though you may be able to claim offsetting automobile expenses—see 12.3.1).

The CRA will agree to consider a flat periodic amount to be an accountable advance (rather than a taxable allowance) if you and your employer agree at the beginning of the year that you will receive a reasonable stated amount for each employment-related kilometre driven and you and your employer settle up at the end of the year regarding the difference between your actual business-related kilometres and the stated amount.

For 2017, the CRA and Revenu Québec accept as a "reasonable allowance" 54¢/km for the first 5,000 km and 48¢/km for each additional kilometre driven (4¢ more in the territories). In some cases, you may be able to justify a higher amount as "reasonable".

If you receive an allowance from your employer that is a combination of flat-rate and reasonable per-kilometre allowances that covers the same use for the vehicle, the total combined allowance is taxable as an employee benefit.

### 12.2.4 Employer-provided vehicles taken home at night

As noted, travel between home and work in a motor vehicle provided by an employer is generally considered personal use of the vehicle. However, in special cases, your employer may require you to take the vehicle home with you overnight, for example, if you are on-call to respond to emergencies or if there are security concerns over tools and equipment being left at a worksite or overnight at your employer's premises.

While the travel between work and home is still considered a taxable benefit in these cases, the benefit is reduced for employer-provided vehicles (except regular automobiles) that are specially designed or suited for the employer's business or trade and that are essential for carrying out the employee's duties. Examples include taxis, ambulances, hearses, and trucks and vans modified to carry or store tools, equipment or goods.

For these vehicles, the benefit is the operating benefit rate of 25¢/km for 2017 as long as the vehicle has not been used for any other personal use other than commuting between home and work and the employer has genuine business reasons for requiring the employee to take the motor vehicle home at night. In these cases, the benefit does not include a standby charge.

The use of these vehicles is considered business use if the employee drives directly from home to a point of call (e.g., an emergency scene) or vice versa.

## 12.3 Using your own automobile for business purposes

### 12.3.1 Automobile expense deductions for employees

If you are required by the terms of your employment to use your own automobile and are not receiving a (non-taxable) reasonable allowance based on the number of kilometres you drive for employment purposes (see 12.2.3), you can deduct a portion of your automobile expenses from your employment income. (Your employer must certify that you were required to use your own vehicle on federal Form T2200, which you must keep on file, and Quebec Form TP-64.3-V, which you must file with your Quebec tax return.)

You can deduct operating costs, such as gas, repairs and car washes, to the extent they relate to your employment. As noted in 12.1, you need to keep a detailed log of your driving to track your employment-related use as opposed to your personal use.

You can also deduct capital cost allowance (depreciation), or your monthly lease payments for the proportion of employment-related use. The allowable rate of capital cost allowance is 15% in the year of acquisition of the car, followed by 30% *on the remaining balance* in each subsequent year. However, there is a cap on the cost of the car for this purpose:

| Year car purchased | Limit |
|---|---|
| 2001–2017 | $30,000* |

*plus GST/HST and PST on this amount

Example

Michelle buys a new car in Ontario in July 2017 for $35,000 plus 13% HST. She is required to drive 10,000 km for employment-related purposes during the year. She also drives 10,000 km on personal trips.

Since half of her driving is employment-related, Michelle can claim half of the capital cost allowance normally allowed for a car. Although she spent $35,000, the cost is capped at $30,000, plus $3,900 HST (total of $33,900), for tax purposes. The maximum capital cost allowance for the year of acquisition is 15%. Fifteen percent of $33,900 is $5,085. Michelle can therefore claim half of this amount, or $2,543, as a deduction against her employment income for 2017.

Further, because she uses her car partly for business, Michelle can claim an HST rebate for 2017 from the CRA equal to 13/113 of her capital cost allowance claim—see 12.3.2.

You can also deduct interest on any loan you have taken out to purchase the car (including financing on the purchase itself, where you make monthly payments that combine interest and capital). Your monthly interest is limited to $300 for 2001–2017.

> **Example**
>
> James bought a new car in January 2017 for $60,000, and pays $1,100 per month on his car loan. He paid $5,000 down and the loan interest rate is 7%. One-half of his driving relates to his employment.
>
> Calculations show that James pays $320 per month in interest for the first month, and slightly less over the following months. His interest for tax purposes over the year is limited to $300 per month, or $3,600. Of this, he can deduct half, or $1,800, to reflect the proportion of his driving that was employment-related.

If you lease the car, your deduction for the lease payments is restricted to parallel the dollar limit on purchases:

| Year lease entered into | Limit |
|---|---|
| 2001–2017 | $800* |

*plus GST/HST and PST on this amount

Your maximum deductible monthly lease charge is the lesser of the maximum lease limit set out above and an amount determined through a complex formula that takes into account your leasing charges and cumulative payments, the manufacturer's suggested list price, the prescribed purchase limit for CCA purposes and refundable deposits.

If you lease the car and you make an up-front lump-sum payment (or "balloon" payment), the CRA normally considers the amount to be part of your normal lease charge in the year paid and your deduction may be restricted by the lease deduction limit. However, the full balloon payment amount may be deductible if the sum of:

- the amount of the balloon payment divided by the number of months in the term of the lease, plus
- your monthly lease payment

does not exceed your maximum monthly lease deduction limit.

If you are reimbursed by your employer for employment-related use of your automobile, the reimbursement payments are not taxed. Of course, you cannot deduct your own expenses to the extent you have been reimbursed for them.

Driving between home and work is normally considered personal use. If you travel from your home to a business call (to visit a client or supplier, for example), that will constitute business use. You can maximize your employment-related travel by making all of your business calls at the beginning and end of your day, before you go to work and after you leave work. You can thus make your entire trip from home to work count as travel for employment purposes.

### 12.3.2 GST/HST rebate for employees' auto expenses

Claim a rebate for GST/HST paid on expenses deductible from your employment income.

Where you can deduct expenses from your employment income, you can also generally claim a rebate of GST or HST paid on those expenses (see 10.9). If you have auto expenses you're deducting from your employment income, you may be entitled to a GST or HST rebate, as the following example shows.

**Example**

Continuing our first example in 12.3.1, Michelle is required to drive 10,000 km for employment-related purposes during the year. She also drives 10,000 km on personal trips. Over the year, she spends $2,260 (including 13% HST) on gas and repairs for her car and does not receive any reimbursement from her employer. All the expenses are paid in Ontario.

Since one-half of Michelle's expenses are required by her employment, she can claim $1,130 as a deduction from employment income. That figure, however, already includes $130 in HST that applied to the gas and repairs. Michelle can claim a rebate of the $130 on a form filed with her income tax return. The $130 rebate is taxable in the year she receives it.

Further, because she uses her car partly for business, Michelle can claim an HST rebate in 2017 from the CRA equal to 13/113 of her capital cost allowance claim. That is, Michelle can claim a refund of 13/113 of the $2,543 she can deduct as capital cost allowance, or $293. This $293 is deducted from the undepreciated capital cost of the car at the beginning of 2018.

In the above example, we assume that Michelle's employer is a GST registrant and not a financial institution. If she were employed by a financial institution or non-GST registrant, she would not be entitled to the employee GST/HST rebate.

We have also assumed that Michelle did not receive a per kilometre allowance from her employer. If she had, she would not be able to claim a GST/HST rebate on any of her automobile expenses unless her employer certified on her Form GST370 that the allowance was "unreasonable" and that her employer would not be claiming a GST/HST input tax credit for her allowance. However, in the unlikely case that Michelle's employer certifies that her per kilometre allowance is unreasonable, the amount would be included in her income and her employer must withhold income tax and other source deductions on the amount.

A rebate is only available if GST/HST was paid on the purchase. Michelle cannot receive a rebate for the deductible portion of her car insurance, since insurance is not subject to GST/HST. Similarly, there would be no GST/HST rebate if Michelle purchased gas in the United States because no GST/HST would be included in its price.

Finally, note also that the 13/113 rebate rate is only used in a province that imposes HST at the 13% rate (in this example, Ontario). Had Michelle's expenses been incurred in a province with 5% GST only or in a province with a different HST rate, the rebate she generally would be entitled to claim for 2017 would be calculated using the rate imposed by that province. For example, if Michelle paid 5% GST on an expense incurred in Alberta or paid 15% HST on an expense in Nova Scotia, the rebate rate would be 5/105 of the GST-included price or 15/115 of the HST-included price respectively. See 11.2.5 for GST/HST rates in each province. (GST or HST rebates are also available to members of partnerships—see 11.3.7.)

### 12.3.3 Automobile expense deductions for the self-employed

If you're self-employed, you can generally deduct the proportion of your automobile expenses that represents your business use of the vehicle, normally based on kilometres driven.

If half of your driving is done for your business (excluding driving from your home to your own place of business) and half is personal use, you can deduct one-half of the expenses of the car for that year. The expenses would include gas, car washes, repairs, insurance, interest on financing the vehicle, leasing costs if the car is leased and capital cost allowance if you own it.

However, there are limits to how expensive a vehicle you can write off. Your claims for CCA and leasing costs will be based on a maximum cost:

| Year car purchased | Purchase limit | Lease limit |
|---|---|---|
| 2001–2017 | $30,000* | $800* |

*plus GST/HST and PST on this amount (to the extent they are not recoverable)

If you have financed the purchase of a car, your monthly interest expense before determining the business portion will be limited to $300 for cars purchased in 2001–2017.

The CRA counts lease termination payments as normal lease payments in the year paid, and their deductibility is also subject to your lease limit for the year. However, the CRA will make the adjustment at your request over the term of the lease (instead of just in the year of sale), provided none of the years to be adjusted are statute-barred.

The $30,000 purchase limit also applies for purposes of calculating GST/HST input tax credits (see 11.2.4) and QST input tax refunds.

See the planning tips suggested for employees in 12.3.1—the same techniques can help maximize your deductions for business-related use of your own car.

## 12.4 References

The following publications and more information, including forms and brochures, can be obtained on the CRA's website at *www.cra-arc.gc.ca* or by telephone request at 1-800-959-8281 for individual income tax and trust-related enquiries or 1-800-959-5525 for business and self-employed individual enquiries.

Guide T4002, "Business and Professional Income"
Guide T4044, "Employment Expenses"
Guide T4130, "Employer's Guide—Taxable Benefits and Allowances"
Interpretation Bulletin IT-63R5, Archived – "Benefits, including standby charge for an automobile, from the personal use of a motor vehicle supplied by an employer after 1992"
Interpretation Bulletin IT-521R, Archived – "Motor vehicle expenses claimed by self-employed individuals"
Interpretation Bulletin IT-522R, Archived – "Vehicle, travel and sales expenses of employees"

# Chapter 13

## If you are moving

- If you're planning to move, arrange to meet the tests for deducting your moving expenses where practical (13.1.1)
- Arrange to avoid a taxable benefit on your employer-paid moving expenses where possible (13.1.3)
- Take steps to cease Canadian residency if you are moving abroad (13.3.1)
- Beware of Canadian departure tax on emigration (13.3.2)
- Obtain a certificate of compliance from the CRA if you sell your Canadian home after you emigrate (13.3.5)
- If you wish to wind up your RRSP, consider waiting until after you become non-resident (13.3.6)
- Repay Home Buyers' Plan and Lifelong Learning Plan withdrawals within 60 days of becoming non-resident (13.3.6)

*Moving expenses are often overlooked as a deduction. Depending on your circumstances, many of your expenses may be tax-deductible if you're moving within Canada to start a new job or business or attend school. If you're immigrating to or emigrating from Canada, there are complex tax rules that you'll need to consider before and after your move. In this chapter, we discuss the tax treatment of moving expenses and other tax rules related to moving, including some planning opportunities to help make your move as tax-efficient as possible.*

## 13.1 Moving within Canada

### 13.1.1 Work-related moving expenses

If you start working at a new location of employment, or start a new business, and you move to a home that is 40 km closer to your new work location than your old home was, you can deduct moving expenses for tax purposes. The 40-km distance is measured by the shortest normal route of travel, including roads, bridges and ferries, rather than "as the crow flies".

Expenses incurred in moving from another country to Canada, or from Canada to another country, are not deductible for Canadian tax purposes unless you are either a student receiving scholarship or grant income (see 13.1.2) or a deemed resident of Canada. (If your employer reimburses you for expenses of moving to or from Canada, the benefit is not taxable as long as the reimbursed expenses are included in the list of moving expenses in 13.1.3.)

Except to the extent you are reimbursed by your employer, you can deduct the following for moves within Canada:

- Reasonable travelling costs, including meals and lodging, to move you and the members of your household
- The moving costs for your household effects, including storage charges
- The cost of meals and lodging near either the old or the new home for up to 15 days
- Lease cancellation costs
- The costs of revising legal documents to reflect your new address, replacing driver's licences and automobile permits, and connecting and disconnecting utilities
- Selling costs for your old home, including real estate commissions
- Where you are selling your old home, the legal fees and land transfer tax payable when you buy a new home (but not GST/HST and QST)
- Mortgage interest, property taxes, insurance premiums and utility costs related to your old residence (provided it remains unoccupied), to a maximum of the actual costs during a period when reasonable efforts were made to sell the home, or $5,000, whichever is less.

The real estate commissions alone can easily run into many thousands of dollars.

*If you're planning to move, arrange to meet the tests for deducting your moving expenses where practical.*

So when considering a move, ensure if possible that your move coincides with a new employment location or a new place of business, and that your move meets the 40-km test.

As an alternative to providing detailed receipts for your actual moving costs for meals and vehicle expenses, you may use a simplified method of determining these moving costs. You can also use this option to calculate vehicle expenses if you used your own vehicle to transport household effects between your old and new residences. If you use the simplified method, supporting receipts are not required.

In the case of meals, you can claim a flat rate per meal under the simplified method of $17 per meal, to a maximum of $51 per day (at the time of writing).

For vehicle expenses, you must keep a record of the number of kilometres driven during the move. The amount you can claim for vehicle expenses is determined by multiplying the number of kilometres travelled while moving by a flat per kilometre rate ranging from 43.5¢ to 59¢ per kilometre (at the time of writing), depending on the province or territory in which you begin travelling.

Current rates per meal and per kilometre are available from the CRA's Tax Information Phone Service at 1-800-267-6999, or on the CRA's website at *www.cra-arc.gc.ca/travelcosts/*.

### 13.1.2 Students' moving expenses

If you are a student, you can claim moving expenses if you move when you begin a job (including a summer job) or start a business. If you are moving to attend full-time post-secondary education (in Canada or abroad), you can deduct the expenses but only to the extent you have scholarship or research grant income.

### 13.1.3 Moving allowances and reimbursements paid by your employer

If your employer is paying your moving expenses, you may be assessed a taxable benefit for the payments, depending on how they are structured. Generally, if your employer pays you an allowance related to relocation expenses without asking you to account for the use of the money, the CRA considers it to be a taxable benefit. However, you may be able to deduct your actual qualifying expenses incurred (as listed in 13.1.1) if you move within Canada. If your employer reimburses you for your documented expenses or pays you an accountable advance, the payment is usually not considered a taxable benefit. Your employer can reimburse you for certain moving expenses for you and your family without conferring a taxable benefit, including:

- The cost of house-hunting trips to the new location, including child care and pet care expenses while you are away
- Travelling costs, including meals and lodging, while you and members of your household are moving from old to new homes
- The cost of transporting or storing your household effects and other personal property such as cars and boats while moving from old to new homes
- The costs of revising legal documents to reflect your new address, replacing driver's licences and automobile permits, and connecting and disconnecting utilities
- Selling costs of the old residence (advertising, legal fees, real estate commissions and mortgage prepayment or discharge fees)
- Where the old residence has been sold, legal fees to purchase the new residence and any taxes on the transfer or registration of title on the new residence
- Mortgage interest, property taxes, insurance premiums and utility costs related to the former residence (provided it remains unoccupied), to a maximum of the actual costs during a period when reasonable efforts were made to sell the home or $5,000, whichever is less.

If your employer pays a non-accountable moving expenses allowance of up to $650, it is not a taxable benefit as long as you certify in writing that you used the allowance for moving expenses. Any amount over $650 paid as a non-accountable moving allowance is considered a taxable benefit and you may be able to deduct your actual moving expenses.

Arrange to avoid a taxable benefit on your employer-paid moving expenses where possible.

Where possible, you should try to avoid being assessed a taxable benefit by arranging for your employer to reimburse you for your moving costs or pay you an accountable advance or a non-accountable moving allowance of up to $650, rather than paying you a non-accountable allowance over $650.

Moving allowances are treated differently for Quebec tax purposes. If you are relocated by your employer and receive a moving allowance, you do not have to include in your Quebec income an amount equal to two weeks' worth of your salary (based on your new salary after your relocation).

If you relocate and receive a home purchase loan from your employer, a special deduction is available for the imputed interest on the loan (see 10.3).

### 13.1.4 Other relocation payments

Your employer may make certain types of relocation payments to help you defray higher home financing costs in your new location. Most direct or indirect financing support payments are considered taxable benefits. These payments include:

- Mortgage interest differential payments made by your employer to compensate you where the interest rate on your new mortgage is higher than the interest rate on the old one
- Mortgage subsidy payments to offset the larger mortgage interest payments created by a higher mortgage principal amount due to higher housing prices in the new location for homes of the same size as your previous one
- One-half of the excess of reimbursements over $15,000 for a loss on the sale of a former residence, calculated as the difference between the employee's cost of the home and the selling price, or the difference between the selling price of the home and its fair market value as determined by an independent appraisal
- Tax equalization payments and cost-of-living payments made to compensate you for higher taxes and higher living costs in your new location.

## 13.2 Moving to Canada

When you immigrate to Canada, most property you own is deemed to be acquired by you at its fair market value as of your date of immigration (not including Canadian real estate, pension plans, stock options and certain other property). Thus Canada will tax only the capital gain that accrues while you are resident in Canada.

If you are moving to Canada to settle permanently for the first time or coming to Canada for temporary employment for three or more years, you can bring your personal and household effects free of duties and taxes if you owned and used these goods before arriving in Canada (leased goods are subject to regular duties). But if you sell or give the goods away within the first year, duty and tax will apply.

If you are moving to Canada, you should obtain professional advice regarding ways to help minimize your tax burden. There may be steps you should take before you arrive in Canada.

## 13.3 Moving from Canada

### 13.3.1 Ceasing Canadian residence
Generally, Canada imposes tax on the worldwide income of its residents but only on the Canadian-source income of non-residents. So whether you are considered resident in Canada can make a significant difference to your potential Canadian tax liability after you move.

If you move to another country, you may still be considered a Canadian resident for tax purposes if you keep certain ties with Canada, such as maintaining a home, club memberships, credit cards or medical plan, or if your spouse or dependants remain in Canada. If you're moving to another country permanently or for an extended period, you may want to take steps to cease Canadian residency.

The *Income Tax Act* does not include rules for determining residency. The CRA assesses each situation on its own merits. Generally, you are considered a non-resident of Canada if your stay abroad has a degree of permanence, you sever your residential ties to Canada and establish new ties elsewhere, you are considered a resident of another country, and your visits to Canada after your departure are occasional and sporadic.

Take steps to cease Canadian residency if you are moving abroad.

Starting at the time of your departure, you should spend significantly less than 183 days in Canada per year. Days during any portion of which you are physically present in Canada count as full days.

Other steps that show you have ceased Canadian residency include:

- Selling your home in Canada or renting it to an arm's-length party on a long-term lease

- Selling your personal property such as furniture or cars or taking them with you to your new country
- Cancelling or suspending club memberships
- Cancelling your Canadian driver's licence and plate (you may want to obtain a driver's licence in your new country before giving up your Canadian licence)
- Closing your Canadian bank accounts or putting them on non-resident status
- Cancelling credit cards issued in Canada and having them re-issued in your new country
- Changing your mailing address for all correspondence
- Cancelling your Canadian medical plans and taking out new ones in your new country
- Situating your primary place of business outside Canada.

If you move to a country that has signed a tax treaty with Canada, the treaty may apply to resolve your residency in cases where the above items are not determinative.

As a non-resident of Canada, you are still subject to Canadian tax if at any time during a calendar year you:

- Are employed or perform services in Canada
- Carry on business in Canada
- Dispose of property not subject to Canadian departure tax (see 13.3.2), such as Canadian rental real estate
- Dispose of shares of private companies or interests in certain partnerships that derive their value from Canadian real estate
- Receive income from Canadian trusts
- Receive Canadian-source pension or dividend income, or
- Receive rental income from rental properties in Canada.

A tax treaty between Canada and your new country may reduce or eliminate your Canadian tax liability in many circumstances.

### 13.3.2 Canadian departure tax

If you leave Canada and become non-resident, you are deemed to have sold most of your assets at fair market value and have to recognize any resulting capital gains in the tax year that you depart. The range of assets treated as having been sold for fair market value on emigration includes *all* property, with certain exceptions such as:

- Canadian real estate
- Property that you already owned when you became resident in Canada or inherited while in Canada, if your residence in Canada totaled no more than five years out of the last 10
- Pension entitlements, including RRSPs or RRIFs
- Property used in a business in Canada

- Certain stock options and other types of equity compensation
- Certain interests in Canadian trusts
- Tax deferred accounts including RESPs, TFSAs, RDSPs and DPSPs.

For other property, the deemed disposition may result in an immediate tax liability on the resulting gains, although the CRA allows you to defer paying the tax on gains as long as you post acceptable security. Acceptable security could be a letter of credit, a mortgage or a bank guarantee. You do not have to post security for departure tax on the first $100,000 of capital gains. The tax is still due on gains for which you posted security or which qualified for the $100,000 exemption, but not until the assets are sold or gifted or on your death (whichever occurs first).

> Beware of Canadian departure tax on emigration.

If you post the security, interest is not charged for the period up to the actual disposition of the property or death of the owner (whichever occurs first). If the security subsequently becomes deficient (e.g., due to a decline in value of the assets posted), you will have 90 days after you're notified by the CRA to make up the deficiency.

If you return to Canada at any time and you still own the assets for which you posted security, you can unwind the deemed disposition and treat it as though it did not occur. Thus, using the deemed security on $100,000 of capital gains can be beneficial if you plan to return to Canada before you sell the assets.

Gains accruing while you are non-resident on certain property known as "taxable Canadian property" continue to be taxable in Canada when you sell it. Taxable Canadian property includes, among others, shares of private Canadian corporations that derive 50% or more of their value from Canadian real estate, Canadian resource property or timber resource property. If less than 50% of the shares' value is derived from these types of property, keep in mind that these shares may still be taxable Canadian property unless they meet this "less than 50% of their value" test for the five-year period immediately before you sell them.

Gains accruing while you are non-resident on certain other property, such as marketable securities, are not taxable in Canada, even if you return; however, you cannot claim losses accruing on such property while you are non-resident for Canadian tax purposes. When you return to Canada, the assets' cost base will be adjusted to ensure any pre-departure gain is captured later and any loss during the non-resident period is not available to offset the gain.

You must report all of your property subject to the deemed disposition on Form T1243, "Deemed Disposition of Property by an Emigrant of Canada" and file it with your tax return for the year you cease to be a resident of Canada. If you are an active or retired partner of a professional partnership and you are leaving Canada, see 16.2.5.

*Security for private Canadian company shares*

If you're a private Canadian company shareholder and you give up your Canadian residency status but retain your shares, the rules may create valuation and financing problems if your shares have significantly appreciated in value. For example, determining the fair market value of your shares generally requires professional assistance, resulting in valuation costs. If you don't have your shares valued, the CRA will fix the value. Financing your tax liability may also pose a problem if it is not advisable or possible to use the business's banking facilities and you do not have other liquid resources available to satisfy the debt.

In the past, the CRA has not normally accepted non-liquid assets, such as shares of private corporations, as security for future tax liabilities. The CRA prefers a letter of credit to other security; however, recognizing the dilemma many taxpayers will face, CRA officials say that they may accept such shares as security for the debt. The CRA will act as any other commercial lender and expect the normal representations, warranties and covenants to ensure that the shares retain their value. To satisfy the CRA, you may have to change existing collateral arrangements and shareholder agreements.

If you plan on posting private corporation shares as security, your discussions with the CRA should begin well before the deadline for filing your departure-year tax return.

### 13.3.3 Capital gains exemption on emigration

Once you are non-resident, you cannot use the lifetime capital gains exemption discussed in 6.4. So if you still have some exemption room available and you own qualifying farm or fishing property (which includes Canadian real estate), you may wish to take steps to "crystallize" your gain before you emigrate. That way, you will trigger a gain that is absorbed by the exemption that would not otherwise be available after you have emigrated, and only the increase from the current fair market value will be taxed in Canada when you, as a non-resident, eventually dispose of the property.

Alternatively, if you realize gains on the deemed disposition of certain qualified farm or fishing property or shares in a qualified small business corporation, you would want to apply any of your remaining exemption against these gains.

### 13.3.4 Reporting rules for emigrants with property worth over $25,000

If you emigrate from Canada and you own property with a total value of $25,000 or more, you are required to file an information form (T1161) listing all your significant assets with your final Canadian tax return for the year of emigration. In determining whether your property exceeds the $25,000 reporting threshold, the following assets are not included:

- Cash, including bank deposits
- RRSPs, TFSAs, RESPs, RDSPs, private company pension plans (RPPs), RRIFs, retirement compensation arrangements (RCA), employee benefit plans and deferred profit sharing plans (DPSPs)
- Items for personal use (such as household effects, clothing, cars, collectibles) whose fair market value is less than $10,000
- Property you owned at the time you last became a resident of Canada or property you inherited after you last became a resident of Canada if you were a resident of Canada for 60 months or less during the 10 years before you emigrated.

There are significant penalties for failure to file this form on time even if you are not otherwise required to file a tax return (e.g., if you keep your house in Canada and have no other assets).

### 13.3.5 If you rent or sell your Canadian home after emigration

Real property that you own in Canada is not subject to the deemed disposition rules discussed above when you emigrate. If you decide to rent your property, the tenant will generally have to withhold and remit to the CRA a 25% non-resident withholding tax on your gross rental income. If you will incur expenses to earn your rental income, you can file Form NR6 before your first non-resident tax payment is due and the withholding tax will be assessed on your net rental income. If you file the form, you will need to appoint a Canadian resident agent.

You must file Form NR4 and the related summary by the end of March each year to report rental income and taxes withheld, and you will have to file an annual rental income tax return by June 30 of each following year. Filing this income tax return late will result in assessment of the 25% withholding tax on gross rental income.

Generally, there is no Canadian income tax levied on the gain from selling a principal residence (see 6.5.2). If you sell your former principal residence while you are a non-resident of Canada, you must notify the CRA (and Revenu Québec if the property is in Quebec) of the disposition and request a certificate of compliance. If you don't obtain a certificate of compliance before the disposition, the purchaser must withhold and remit 25% of the gross proceeds to the CRA and a further 12.875% to Revenu Québec, where applicable. You should file the CRA's Form T2062 reporting the disposition before the closing date of the sale or within 10 days of the sale to obtain

> Obtain a certificate of compliance from the CRA if you sell your Canadian home after you emigrate.

the certificate of compliance. (You must also file Revenu Québec Form TP-1097-V if the property is located in Quebec.)

If you sell your former principal residence after the end of the year following the year of your move, only a portion of the gain would be exempt under the principal residence exemption (see 6.5.2). The principal residence exemption calculation is based on the fraction of one plus the number of taxation years ending after 1971 for which the property was a principal residence and during which you are a resident of Canada over the total number of years (after 1971) it was owned by you. The "one plus" part of the calculation does not apply if you were not resident in Canada in the year the property was acquired. For each additional year that you do not sell your principal residence after you cease Canadian residency, the denominator increases while the numerator stays constant and a smaller portion of the gain is exempt from Canadian tax.

Beginning with the 2016 tax year, if you sell your principal residence, you are required to report certain basic information on Schedule 3 of your T1 income tax and benefit return. This information includes the address of the property, the date you acquired it, and the amount of the disposition proceeds.

If you plan to rent out your former principal residence, the property's use will change from personal to income-producing and will be subject to a deemed disposition at fair market value at that time. Any gain accruing up to the date of the change in use will be taxable but the principal residence exemption may reduce or eliminate the tax. Future increases in value will be taxable as capital gains since you can no longer shelter these gains from tax by claiming the principal residence exemption (see 6.5.2).

You may be able to make an election not to deem a change in use of the property. You cannot claim depreciation on the property while the election is in effect. However, the election could be beneficial if you expect the property to increase significantly in value since you would be able to shelter some of the resulting capital gain with the principal residence exemption because of the proration calculation.

### 13.3.6 If you have RRSPs, TFSAs or RESPs

As noted in 13.3.2, your RRSPs are not subject to the deemed disposition rules when you leave Canada. For Canadian tax purposes, you can continue to make deductible contributions to your RRSP as long as you have contribution room available. Of course, if you have no income subject to Canadian tax, you would not realize any current tax savings from making contributions.

If you need to collapse your RRSP, you may want to wait until you are a non-resident of Canada to do so. As a non-resident, you will be subject to a 25% withholding tax on the proceeds received from the plan. Many tax treaties reduce the Canadian withholding tax rate if the payments are periodic rather than lump-sum. If you collapse the plan while you're a resident of Canada, the proceeds will be taxed at your marginal tax rate, which will be about 50% if you are in the top tax bracket, depending on the province you live in.

> If you wish to wind up your RRSP, consider waiting until after you become non-resident.

If you withdrew funds from your RRSP under the Home Buyers' Plan (see 3.3.6) or Lifelong Learning Plan (see 3.3.7) and you become a non-resident, you should repay the entire withdrawal within 60 days of becoming non-resident. To the extent you do not make the repayment within 60 days, the unpaid balance will be included in your income on your Canadian income tax return for the year of your departure.

> Repay Home Buyers' Plan and Lifelong Learning Plan withdrawals within 60 days of becoming non-resident.

If you have a TFSA when you become non-resident (see 4.1.4), you can maintain your existing TFSA and your investment income and withdrawals will remain exempt from Canadian tax. You should not contribute to your TFSA after the date you become a non-resident because significant penalties apply to contributions made as a non-resident of Canada. No new contribution room will accrue for any year in which you are a non-resident for the entire year. You must also consider foreign tax implications of TFSA income and withdrawals, if they apply.

If you have RESPs (see 4.3), remember that contributions should only be made by residents of Canada, the beneficiary must be resident in Canada, and both the contributor and the beneficiary must have Social Insurance Numbers. Original contributions to the plan may be paid to the beneficiary without Canadian tax consequences. However, if the beneficiary is a non-resident of Canada when withdrawals are made from an RESP, any CESGs paid to the plan must be repaid to the federal government. Investment income earned by the plan may be paid to a non-resident beneficiary if he or she attends a post-secondary institution, but non-resident withholding tax may apply to the payments.

## 13.4 References

The following publications and more information, including forms and brochures, can be obtained on the CRA's website at *www.cra-arc.gc.ca* or by telephone request at 1-800-959-8281 for individual income tax and trust-related enquiries or 1-800-959-5525 for business and self-employed individual enquiries.

Guide T4058, "Non-Residents and Income Tax"
Income Tax Folio S1-F3-C2 "Principal Residence"
Income Tax Folio S1-F3-C4, "Moving Expenses"
Income Tax Folio S5-F1-C1 "Determining an Individual's Residence
    Status"
Pamphlet T4055, "Newcomers to Canada"

# Chapter 14

## If you have your own corporation

- Keep the corporation a small business corporation at all times (14.1)
- Consider crystallizing your lifetime capital gains exemption (14.1)
- Multiply your access to the capital gains exemption (14.1)
- Defer income to the next calendar year by accruing bonuses (14.2.2)
- Maximize capital dividend payments (14.2.4)
- Consider a tax-free repayment of capital (14.2.5)
- Crunch the numbers to calculate your optimum salary/dividend mix (14.2.9)
- Consider the tax benefits of setting up a holding corporation (14.3)
- Look into the potential advantages of a corporate partnership (14.3.1)
- Weigh the potential advantages of incorporating your investments (14.6)
- Be cautious about having investment income in your corporation that carries on an active business (14.6)

*In this chapter, we suggest some tax planning strategies that may be available if you are an owner/manager—that is, you carry on your business through a corporation. We do not discuss tax planning for the corporation itself, except in relation to how to most effectively get its profits into your hands. If you are thinking about setting up a corporation for running your business, see 11.5 for a discussion of some of the pros and cons. The tax rules in this area are substantially the same for both federal and Quebec tax purposes.*

---

*Caution: The tax planning ideas discussed in this chapter may be affected by the federal government's proposed new tax regime for private companies, as outlined in the Department of Finance's July 2017 consultation paper and draft legislation. See Appendix I for details.*

---

## 14.1 Taxation of the corporation

A corporation is a distinct legal entity, and if you have an incorporated business, the corporation's profits are not yours simply to take. You, as a director of the corporation (even if you are the sole director), act in a different capacity from yourself as a shareholder of the corporation. Legally, as a shareholder your only right is to elect the board of directors, who then cause the corporation to take specific actions.

To extract funds from the corporation you must follow one of the "correct" methods we discuss in 14.2 below. If you do not, the tax system will penalize you.

For tax purposes, the corporation's business and investment income will be calculated in much the same way as your own. (See 11.2 regarding the calculation of business income.) As with individuals, certain deductions (such as loss carryforwards) are available in computing taxable income. The corporation then pays federal and provincial tax on its taxable income.

For 2017, the federal general corporate tax rate is 15% for active business income and income from manufacturing and processing.

For small "Canadian-controlled private corporations", for 2017, the federal rate is 10.5% on the first $500,000 of active business income. (A Canadian-controlled private corporation is a corporation that is resident in Canada and is not controlled in any manner by any combination of non-residents or public corporations.) The general 15% corporate tax rate applies on active business income over the $500,000 threshold. For 2017, investment income of a Canadian-controlled private corporation is taxed at a federal rate of 38.7% (see 14.6).

The federal small business rate is not available for large corporations. It begins to be phased out once the capital of the corporation and its associated group exceeds $10 million.

The general provincial corporate tax rate ranges from 11% to 16%. For 2017, all provinces have reduced rates for the first $450,000–$500,000 of "small business income", depending on the province. The combined federal and provincial tax burden ranges from about 10.5% to 18.5% of income under the small business income thresholds. The remainder is taxed at combined rates ranging from about 26% to 31%.

**Keep the corporation a small business corporation at all times.** If possible, ensure that your corporation remains a "small business corporation" (see 6.2.3) and that your shares are "qualified small business corporation shares" (see 6.4.1) at all times. This will preserve, respectively, your ability to claim allowable business investment losses in respect of any loss on the corporation's shares (see 6.2.3), and the lifetime capital gains exemption on any gain (see 6.4).

Note that you cannot always predict when the sale of the shares will be triggered for tax purposes. On the death of any shareholder, there will be a deemed disposition of that shareholder's shares at their fair market value unless the shares are transferred to a spouse or a qualifying "spousal trust" (see 21.5.2).

As an alternative, you may wish to "crystallize"
your capital gains exemption. "Crystallizing"
means triggering a capital gain on your shares
of a qualified small business corporation,

> Consider crystallizing
> your lifetime capital
> gains exemption.

while continuing to own (or at least control) the corporation. This may
permanently increase your adjusted cost base of the shares and possibly
eliminate the need for the corporation to retain its qualified small business
corporation status. Several possible alternatives (such as selling shares to a
family member or exchanging existing shares for a new class of shares) can
be used to crystallize an exemption; professional advice should be sought.

To protect your assets, you could arrange to have a family trust hold the
interest in the corporation rather than having your spouse and children own
the shares of the corporation directly. The family trust may be set up so that
you and your family members (or others) are the beneficiaries and you are a
trustee (possibly with other trustees). This structure allows you to maintain
control of the shares held by the family trust while offering the flexibility of
income splitting with your family members (see 21.5).

If you arrange for your spouse to invest in
common shares of your corporation, you can
possibly double the available exemption of
$835,716 for 2017 by each claiming it. Your

> Multiply your access
> to the capital gains
> exemption.

spouse's own funds must be used for the investment, to avoid the attribution
rules discussed in 5.2.2. You may also be able to multiply the exemption
by transferring shares to your adult children or by using a family trust as
described above. (The income splitting tax may apply if minor children are
involved, see 5.2.4.)

On death, it is possible to double the available capital gains exemption by
leaving shares to your spouse or to a trust for your spouse (see 22.2.3 and
21.5.2).

## 14.2 Ways of extracting funds from the corporation

Since the corporation is legally a separate "person", you must follow one of
the methods described below to get your hands on the corporation's income.

### 14.2.1 Dividends

Dividends are the distribution of a corporation's profits to its shareholders.
They are not deductible to the corporation.

Generally, the Canadian taxation of dividends is based on the theory of
"integration": If a corporation earns income, pays tax on it and pays what is
left to you as a dividend, the combined effect of the corporation's tax and

your personal tax should be about the same as if you had earned the income directly.

To attain integration, dividend income is "grossed up" (increased). You then claim an offsetting federal dividend tax credit. Similar credits are available at the provincial level (see 7.1.2). As a result of this gross-up and credit system, in theory, you and the corporation should pay the same combined amount of tax that you would pay if you had earned the income directly.

There are two types of dividends, and they require different gross-up and dividend tax credit calculations. This difference is intended to recognize that some active business income may be taxed at the lower corporate rate due to the "small business deduction" while other active business income may be taxed at the higher general corporate tax rate (see 7.1.2).

At the corporate level, cumulative income taxed at the high general corporate tax rate is tracked in the "general rate income pool" (GRIP) account. Dividends paid from the GRIP account attract lower personal taxes because corporate income tax has already been paid on the underlying income at a higher rate. To benefit from the lower personal taxes on dividends paid from the GRIP account (called "eligible dividends"), the source of the dividend should be properly documented at the time the dividend is paid.

> **Example**
>
> Jac owns all the shares of Jac Ltd., which is a Canadian controlled private corporation. All of the income of Jac Ltd. is eligible for the small business income tax rate. In 2017, Jac Ltd. earns $100,000 in small business income, which is taxed at a combined federal/provincial rate of 15%. Jac Ltd. then pays the remaining $85,000 as a dividend to Jac.
>
> Jac will "gross up" the $85,000 dividend by 17%, or about $14,450, and will pay tax on about $99,450, which conceptually represents the corporation's original income. Jac will then in theory receive a combined federal/provincial dividend tax credit worth about $15,000, equal to the amount of tax the corporation paid. So Jac and the corporation will together be effectively taxed as if Jac had earned the $100,000 as salary income.

The above treatment applies to dividends paid by Canadian controlled private corporations in 2017 from income eligible for the small business income tax rate. Dividends from public companies and Canadian controlled private corporations that have been paid out of income taxed at the high general corporate tax rate are treated differently—see 7.1.2 for details of the treatment of both types of dividends.

Due to ongoing changes in federal and provincial tax rates, the goal of integration is rarely achieved in full. As a result, the actual combined federal and provincial corporate and personal tax rates that apply to the income should be taken into account when determining how much income to extract from your corporation in the form of dividends (see 14.2.9).

## 14.2.2 Salary

When the corporation pays you a salary, the amount paid is deductible to the corporation and taxable to you as employment income. If the corporation pays all of its profits to you as salary, you are therefore in much the same position as you would be if you earned the income directly, without having a corporation.

Although your salary may become quite high in such situations, the CRA's general policy is not to consider it an unreasonable deduction (for the corporation) where you are the owner/manager of the corporation. It is usually acceptable to consider that the corporation's income is due to your efforts, and therefore a salary equal to that income is a reasonable one. Of course, you are paying tax on the salary anyway.

You may decide on a base salary followed by a bonus, to be paid to you after the corporation has calculated its income at the end of the year. In general, you are taxed on employment income

> Defer income to the next calendar year by accruing bonuses.

only when you receive it, while the corporation can accrue salary or bonus, counting it as deductible in the year even though it is paid after its taxation year-end.

However, any salary or bonus that is deducted by the corporation must actually be *paid* to you no later than 179 days after the end of the corporation's fiscal year. Otherwise, it is deductible by the corporation only in the taxation year in which it is actually paid.

If the corporation's year-end occurs after early July, it can declare a bonus to you as of its year-end but pay the bonus within 180 days, which will be after December 31. The corporation can thus get a deduction from its income, but you do not have to recognize the income personally for tax purposes until the next calendar year. Keep in mind that employee (and employer) source deductions are payable to the CRA as part of the corporation's payroll remittance requirements at the time the bonus is paid.

## 14.2.3 Payments on loans from shareholders

If you lend funds to the corporation (or if you did so when originally setting up the business), the corporation can repay any amount of the loan without tax consequences. Such a repayment is neither deductible to the corporation nor taxable to you.

You could arrange to have the corporation pay you interest on your loan. The interest paid would normally be taxable to you as investment income.

The tax effect would be about the same as if the corporation paid you that amount in salary. However, if your loan to the corporation does not *require* that interest be paid or there is no formal loan document, there is a danger that the interest would not be deductible to the corporation since it has not been paid pursuant to a legal obligation to pay interest. (Conversely, if you arrange for documentation requiring that interest be paid, the annual interest accrual rule discussed in 7.2.1 may require you to include interest in your income even in years when it is not paid!)

### 14.2.4 Capital dividends

*Maximize capital dividend payments.*

We mentioned capital dividends in 5.3.8 and 7.1.4. As you will recall from Chapter 6, only one-half of capital gains are taxed. When a "private" (i.e., non-public) corporation realizes a capital gain, the untaxed portion is added to its "capital dividend account". Similarly, one-half of capital losses reduce the capital dividend account.

Any amount in the corporation's capital dividend account may be paid out entirely tax-free to its shareholders. This preserves the non-taxability of the appropriate fraction of the capital gain. So if the corporation has realized any capital gains (net of realized losses), you should cause it to pay out capital dividends as your first choice for extracting funds.

> **Example**
>
> Tod owns all the shares of Todcorp Inc. In March 2017, Todcorp Inc. sells some land for a capital gain of $120,000, one-half of which is brought into Todcorp's income and taxed as a taxable capital gain.
>
> Todcorp can pay a tax-free dividend of up to $60,000 (one-half of the capital gain) to Tod in 2017 or any later year, provided he elects beforehand to make the dividend a "capital dividend" and provided Todcorp does not realize capital losses that would reduce the capital dividend account. The capital dividend will then be completely tax-free to Tod. (Of course, because it is a dividend, it is not deductible to Todcorp.)

For the dividend payment to qualify for tax-free distribution, the appropriate tax election forms and directors' resolutions must be filed with the CRA before the dividends are declared payable from the corporation. If you do not file the tax elections in advance, two types of penalties could apply:

- a penalty of 1% of the capital dividend amount if the election and directors' resolutions are filed late
- a penalty of 60% of the excess of the actual dividend paid over the capital dividend account balance.

The latter penalty can be avoided by electing to treat the excess dividend as a taxable dividend. In light of these potential penalties, you should seek professional advice before making capital dividend payments.

Note also that if you allow a capital dividend account to build up in the corporation without paying capital dividends, the account can be reduced or wiped out by future capital losses. Once you have paid out capital dividends, however, they are safely out of the corporation, and subsequent capital losses will have no effect on them.

### 14.2.5 Repayment of capital

Any amount that is less than the corporation's "paid-up capital" may be paid out to the shareholders as a repayment of capital, generally with no tax consequences, if the paid-up capital is reduced by that amount.

> Consider a tax-free repayment of capital.

Paid-up capital (PUC) is essentially the amount of capital contributed to the corporation in exchange for its shares. However, the figure can be adjusted in various ways for tax purposes, as a result of transactions involving the corporation. As such, the legal PUC can often differ from the tax PUC.

If the corporation was originally funded with a substantial amount of capital, consider extracting funds by a reduction of the paid-up capital of the corporation. Make sure the corporation remains sufficiently capitalized to satisfy any requirements of its creditors or bankers.

> **Example**
>
> ABC Corp., a Canadian corporation, was capitalized with $500,000, the amount that the original shareholders contributed when subscribing for 1,000 common shares.
>
> If the directors of ABC approve a reduction in paid-up capital to $200,000 and a simultaneous repayment of $300,000 in capital to the shareholders, there will be no adverse tax consequences for either ABC or its shareholders. The $300,000 simply comes out tax-free. ABC then has 1,000 common shares issued with a paid-up capital of $200,000 and an adjusted cost base to its shareholders of $200,000.

### 14.2.6 Loan to shareholder

All of the mechanisms we have looked at so far—dividend, salary, repayment of a shareholder loan, capital dividend and repayment of capital—are legitimate ways to get your hands on the corporation's income or funds. We now turn to some of the rules designed to prevent you from doing so without following the normal routes.

Suppose the corporation simply lends you its funds. If you do not fit within certain exceptions, the entire amount of the loan will simply be included in your income. This is a very serious penalty, because the corporation receives no deduction for the loan, and you do not benefit from the dividend tax credit. The same rule applies if you become indebted to the corporation in some other way (e.g., you buy property from it but pay for the property with a promissory note rather than cash). However, where a loan has been included in your income and you subsequently repay it, you are allowed a deduction from your income.

To avoid the income inclusion, bona fide repayment arrangements must be made at the time the loan is made and the loan must fall into one of the following exceptions:

- a loan to an employee who (along with family members) does not own 10% or more of the shares of any class of the corporation, where the reason for the loan is the individual's employment rather than the shareholding
- a loan to an employee, where the reason for the loan is the individual's employment rather than the shareholding, to help the employee purchase a home, shares in the employer or a related corporation, or a car to be used in employment duties (the rules do not specify a threshold for the percentage interest owned in the corporation for purposes of determining the reason for the loan)
- a loan that is repaid within one year of the end of the corporation's taxation year in which the loan was made and that is not part of a series of loans and repayments.

If the loan falls into one of the above exceptions but is made at a low or no rate of interest, you would be considered to have received a taxable benefit from the corporation based on the difference between the CRA's current low prescribed rate of interest (see 9.3) and the rate you are paying. This rule is exactly the same as for loans to employees, which we saw in 10.3. As in the case of employees, you may be allowed an offsetting deduction as a notional interest expense (which affects your entitlement to the capital gains exemption—see 6.4.3) if such expense would otherwise meet the rules concerning the deductibility of interest.

### 14.2.7 Deemed dividends

Certain types of actions that involve changes to a corporation's capital structure deem you to have received a dividend from the corporation. Generally, this happens when the corporation takes actions that would otherwise allow you to extract profits as a repayment of capital.

For example, if the corporation redeems shares that you own, any amount paid by the corporation exceeding the paid-up capital of the shares is deemed to be a dividend (and not part of your proceeds of disposition for capital gains purposes). The return of the paid-up capital on the redemption is generally tax-free.

### 14.2.8  Shareholder appropriations

We have covered all of the "proper" mechanisms for extracting funds from a corporation. Suppose you don't follow any of the legalities, and you simply take the corporation's funds or property and use them as your own. If you are the sole shareholder, there would be no one to object to you doing this.

In such cases, the *Income Tax Act* deems that any benefit the corporation confers on you is income for tax purposes. So, for example, if you simply take $10,000 out of the corporation's bank account without declaring a dividend, that $10,000 is added to your income (without you benefiting from the dividend tax credit).

Since the $10,000 is taxable in your hands and the corporation is unable to deduct this amount, the $10,000 is taxed at both the corporate and personal levels. Clearly, it is to your advantage to follow the proper mechanisms for extracting funds. In the next section, we explore some of the considerations that will affect your decision as to the appropriate mix between salary, dividend and other forms of remuneration for yourself.

### 14.2.9  Determining your salary/dividend mix

Careful analysis is needed to calculate the best mix of salary and dividends for your case. It depends on your cash flow needs, your income level, the corporation's income level, payroll

> Crunch the numbers to calculate your optimum salary/dividend mix.

taxes on the salary, the corporation's status for tax purposes, and many other factors. Computer spreadsheets and planning tools are available to assist in this task. Due to significant changes to the taxation of dividends in recent years (see 7.1.2), you should also consider engaging a qualified tax professional to assist in your analysis.

You may want to pay yourself enough salary to allow the maximum possible contribution to an RRSP (see 3.1.3). The same goes for any family members you've employed (see 5.3.2). Salaries paid to non-active shareholders must be reasonable for the CRA to allow the corporation to deduct the salary amounts. If the CRA determines the salary to be unreasonable, the deduction to the corporation will be disallowed but the shareholder will still be subject to tax and so double taxation will result. To avoid this result, be sure to keep documentation on hand to support the reasonableness of the salaries.

If you are in a business that can suffer a downturn, paying out a large salary can prevent you from carrying back a later year's loss. Suppose, for example, your business earns $1 million in 2017, and you pay out $500,000 to yourself as a salary, leaving $500,000 as the business's income. If the business loses $1 million in 2018, you would have no way of carrying back the loss against your personal income. If you had left the funds as business income and paid out dividends, you would be able to carry back the 2018 loss to 2017, retroactively wiping out the business's 2017 corporate tax, and obtain a refund of that tax from the CRA.

## 14.3 Effect of having a holding company

You may choose to interpose a holding company between yourself and your corporation for various reasons. One reason for doing this is to pay out dividends from the operating business to help protect the funds from the risks associated with the operating business, while keeping the income subject to a lower level of taxation than would apply if it were paid out to you personally.

Consider the tax benefits of setting up a holding corporation.

For example, you own 100% of the shares of ABC Holdings Ltd., which owns 100% of the shares of ABC Manufacturing Ltd. Dividends may be paid from the manufacturing company to the holding company without any tax effects, providing certain conditions are met. Consult your tax adviser whenever you're paying dividends from one corporation to another.

If your children do not have any ownership in the business, you can consider bringing them in as shareholders at the time you set up the holding corporation. (See the estate planning example in 21.6.2 for one way of bringing in children as shareholders.) Doing so may be desirable for several reasons, including income splitting and planning for your succession. However, if your children are under 18 you must be particularly careful about the attribution rules and income splitting tax (see 5.2.3 and 5.2.4).

When family members such as your spouse or minor children are shareholders, care should be taken to avoid running afoul of the attribution rules discussed in Chapter 5. Some of these attribution rules do not apply if the corporation is a "small business corporation" (see 6.2.3). In this case, it could be advantageous to set up a structure in which a holding company, your spouse and your minor children are shareholders of the operating company. Excess cash or investments can then be paid as dividends to the holding company, thereby ensuring that the operating company maintains its small business corporation status. This arrangement would allow you to avoid the attribution rules and may allow the shares held by your family members to qualify for the lifetime capital gains exemption.

A holding company is often appropriate where you have family members involved in your business and there are other shareholders not related to you. If you and your family members own shares in the holding corporation and the holding corporation owns all of your family's interest in the operating company, the other shareholders of the operating company need not be concerned with your internal family arrangements.

### 14.3.1 Corporate partnerships

An alternative to the use of holding companies is a corporate partnership. This is a partnership between your corporation and one or more other corporations (owned by other people).

Advantages to this form of corporate structure include increased flexibility to allocate income and expenses between the partners and the ability to flow through income and losses and other attributes to the partners.

> Look into the potential advantages of a corporate partnership.

Professional advice should be obtained to determine whether a corporate partnership structure is appropriate.

## 14.4 Shareholders' agreements

When you share the ownership of a private corporation, it is usually wise to have a shareholders' agreement. Such an agreement can set out rights and obligations of the shareholders that go beyond the basic ownership of shares.

Typically, a shareholders' agreement provides for the orderly termination of the relationship between the shareholders if there is a future disagreement, or death or disability of one of the shareholders.

> **Example**
>
> Euan and Jonathan start a small manufacturing business together. Each owns 50% of the shares of the corporation. Over the years, the business becomes very successful, but Euan and Jonathan cannot get along and decide that one of them must leave.
>
> Euan and Jonathan signed a shareholders' agreement that contains a "shotgun" clause. Euan now offers Jonathan $1 million for Jonathan's shares in the corporation. If Jonathan refuses to sell, the agreement provides that Jonathan must buy Euan's shares for the price Euan is offering ($1 million).

The "shotgun" clause is just one example of a provision that can resolve (or prevent) major disputes between key shareholders. Typical provisions in a shareholders' agreement deal with:

- desire of a shareholder to sell his or her shares
- dissension among shareholders
- death or disability of a shareholder
- agreement as to who the directors and/or officers of the corporation will be
- agreement to vote the shares in a particular way on certain issues
- what will happen if the corporation's shares are awarded to a key shareholder's spouse on separation or divorce.

Tax considerations play a major part of planning for shareholder agreements. The tax treatment of life insurance payments, the availability of the lifetime capital gains exemption, the valuation of shares, and many other issues must be considered. Clearly, shareholder agreements should always be drafted with professional advice to properly address legal, business and tax issues.

## 14.5 Pension plans for small business owners

Registered pension plans were discussed in 3.5.1. Both money-purchase and defined-benefit pension plans can be used to accrue benefits for major shareholders who are employees. As an alternative to saving for retirement exclusively through an RRSP, consider having your company establish an individual pension plan, which we discussed in 3.5.2. This is a complex area; professional advice is essential.

If you are a small business owner and you don't want the trouble of administering a pension plan, you may simply want to set up an RRSP for yourself and ensure that you have sufficient "earned income" (i.e., salary from the corporation) to be able to make adequate contributions (see 3.1.3).

## 14.6 Investment income earned in a corporation

The Canadian tax system is designed so that income earned in a corporation and distributed to a shareholder as a dividend should attract the same amount of net income tax, both corporate and personal, as if the income was earned directly by an individual. However, this regime, known as "integration", does not always work perfectly in every province. In general, a tax cost arises in all provinces for individuals who earn investment income in a corporation rather than holding the investments personally.

An important part of the integration system is a federal refundable tax of 10-2/3% (6-2/3% before 2016) that applies to interest and other investment income earned by a Canadian-controlled private corporation. Most dividends received by a private corporation from public companies are also subject to a 38-1/3% refundable tax (Part IV tax) for 2016 and later years (33-1/3% for 2015 and earlier years). These refundable taxes are paid back to the corporation only when it has paid out sufficient taxable dividends (resulting in tax being paid by the shareholders). Combined federal and provincial corporate tax rates for investment income range from 49.7% to 54.7%, depending on the province.

Changes to provincial personal tax rates can also affect the way integration works. In some provinces, you may get a modest tax deferral advantage or you may have to effectively prepay tax if you earn investment income in a corporation. The precise calculation depends on your province of residence, your level of personal income, the extent to which you extract the funds from the corporation, and how you extract those funds.

Looking beyond the potential for tax deferral or prepayment, you may benefit in other ways from holding investments in a corporation. For example, incorporating your investments can help you shield your investments from creditors, reduce probate fees on your death (see 21.4) and protect your assets from U.S. estate tax (see 19.4).

> Weigh the potential advantages of incorporating your investments.

Incorporation also gives you control over the timing of dividend payments and thus the timing of income receipts in your own hands, allowing you to:

- maximize Old Age Security (OAS) benefits (if your income from sources other than investments for 2017 is less than $74,789 (see 20.3.2)
- reduce your exposure to alternative minimum tax (see 7.6)
- manage the timing of dividend payments in order to manage your cumulative net investment loss (CNIL) account balance (see 6.4.3)
- increase your earned income and thus your RRSP contribution room (see 3.1.3) through the payment of directors' fees and/or salaries.

Against the potential benefits, you also need to weigh the incremental costs of forming and maintaining the corporation, including substantial startup and ongoing legal and administrative costs.

Be particularly wary of moving investments into a corporation carrying on an active business. You may jeopardize the eligibility of the corporation's shares for the lifetime capital gains exemption (see 6.4.1 and 14.1). In addition, the creditors of the active business will have access to the investments.

> Be cautious about having investment income in your corporation that carries on an active business.

## 14.7 Selling the business

If you decide to sell your incorporated business, there are two general approaches that can be taken. One is for the corporation to sell the assets of the business. The other is for you to sell the shares of the corporation.

If your shares are "qualified small business corporation shares" (see 6.4.1), you may be able to claim an exemption for up to $835,716 of your gain on the sale in 2017. No capital gains exemption is available to the corporation if it sells the assets. From your point of view, you may be better off selling the shares.

The buyer of your business, however, would likely prefer to purchase the assets. One reason is that this will normally allow the buyer to claim higher capital cost allowance on the cost of depreciable assets (see 11.2.7).

No GST or other sales tax applies on a sale of shares. On a sale of assets, GST (or HST) and QST usually applies but may be recovered by the purchaser through an input tax credit if the purchaser meets certain conditions (see 11.2.4). Alternatively, in many cases on the sale of part or all of a business, an election can be made to have no GST (or HST) or QST apply to the sale. Keep in mind that many conditions apply to this election. Provincial sales tax generally applies to the sale of tangible assets other than qualifying manufacturing equipment, but the rules vary depending on the province.

To help maximize the value of your business and reduce taxes on its sale, consider making a "change in ownership" plan at least two years before you anticipate any actual sale or transfer of the business.

Needless to say, any purchase and sale of a business must be done with detailed professional advice.

If your business goes public without you selling the shares, you can make a special election to "crystallize" part or all of your accrued capital gain and get the capital gains exemption as if you had sold the shares (see 6.4).

## 14.8 References

The following publications and more information, including forms and brochures, can be obtained on the CRA's website at *www.cra-arc.gc.ca* or by telephone request at 1-800-959-8281 for individual income tax and trust-related enquiries or 1-800-959-5525 for business and self-employed individual enquiries.

Guide T4012, "T2 Corporation Income Tax"
Income Tax Folio S3-F2-C1, "Capital Dividends"
Income Tax Folio S4-F16-C1, "What is a Partnership?"
Interpretation Bulletin IT-119R4, Archived – "Debts of shareholders and certain persons connected with shareholders"
Interpretation Bulletin IT-432R2, Archived – "Benefits conferred on shareholders"

# Chapter 15

## Farming

- Establish that your farming business is undertaken solely in pursuit of profit (15.1)
- Classify farming as your chief source of income (15.1)
- Claim deductions available for the self-employed (15.2)
- Consider using the "cash method" of accounting to defer taxes (15.2.1)
- Make the most of the lifetime capital gains exemption for qualified farm or fishing property (15.4.1)
- Take advantage of the intergenerational transfer rules (15.4.2)

*The income tax system has special rules to deal with farming. We outline some of them in this chapter.*

### 15.1 Farming—a business or not?

No matter what kind of activity you undertake, you are only allowed to write off losses for tax purposes if you are engaged in a business that is clearly undertaken in pursuit of profit (see 11.4.1). This issue comes up repeatedly in the case of part-time farmers.

"Farming", for tax purposes, includes a number of activities ranging from growing crops to raising livestock, fur farming, fruit growing, keeping bees and training horses for racing. The *Income Tax Act* classifies individuals engaged in farming into three groups. The principal difference among the groups is the extent to which they can deduct expenses relating to their farming activities.

At one extreme are the full-time farmers, for whom farming is **a chief source of income**. These people are allowed to treat their farming business like any other business, and can therefore claim losses against other income for tax purposes if they suffer losses in any given year (see 15.3.1).

> Establish that your farming business is undertaken solely in pursuit of profit.

At the other extreme are people whose farming activity is a personal pursuit. These people are sometimes called "hobby farmers", as farming is considered to be their hobby rather than something they are doing in order to make money. Hobby farmers may not deduct any losses from their farming activity.

In the middle are the people who undertake farming activities in pursuit of profit, but whose "chief source of income is neither farming nor a combination of farming and some other source of income that is a subordinate source of income". These people are allowed only **"restricted farm losses"**, limited to certain dollar amounts (see 15.3.2).

**Example 1**

Darryl lives on his farm and raises dairy cattle. Almost all his income comes from selling the cows' milk. In 2017, Darryl's dairy business has a bad year and he loses $30,000.

Darryl can deduct his $30,000 against any other income he has (such as investment income) and carry it forward or back to be used in other years (see 15.3.1). His farming loss is very much like a loss from any other kind of business, such as manufacturing or retailing.

**Example 2**

Bob is a dentist who lives and works in Toronto. He spends his weekends on his ranch, where he keeps a stable of racehorses. In past years, Bob's horses have won a fair amount of prize money. In 2017, Bob has a bad year and spends $50,000 on maintaining his horses without winning any prize money at all.

Bob's loss is likely to be considered a "restricted farm loss", and only a portion of it (see 15.3.2) is deductible against his dental practice income. Although his horse-racing business (which for income tax purposes is considered farming) is clearly a commercial venture, it is not a chief source of income to him and therefore falls into the "restricted" category.

| Classify farming as your chief source of income. |

You need to keep records that establish on an objective basis that your farming business is carried on in a sufficiently commercial nature. If your activities never actually turn a profit over many years, a claim that your activity is clearly commercial may be hard to sustain in court.

Many court cases have considered the question of whether farming, or farming in combination with some other subordinate source of income, constitutes a taxpayer's "chief source of income".

You may wish to consult a tax professional to determine how to best establish a claim that will entitle you to a full deduction for farm losses, rather than the more limited deduction for "restricted farm losses".

## 15.2 Computing farming income

If you are engaged in a farming business—
whether or not your losses will be "restricted" as
we saw in 15.1—you may take advantage of a
number of special rules when calculating income
for tax purposes.

> Claim deductions
> available for the self-
> employed.

In addition to the specific rules for farmers discussed in this chapter, see
11.2 for deductions that can be claimed by the self-employed. If you
successfully establish that your farming business is a commercial venture,
such deductions will be available to you.

### 15.2.1 The cash method

Businesses are generally required to follow the
accrual method of accounting for income. That is,

> Consider using the "cash
> method" of accounting to
> defer taxes.

you take your sales for the year into income, even though you may not have
been paid for some of those sales until after your business year-end. You
claim expenses the same way (see 11.2.2).

For a farming business, you may choose to use the **"cash method"** instead.
In general, this means you count payments received, rather than your sales—
and only deduct amounts that you have paid, and not unpaid expenses that
you have incurred. This usually provides a certain amount of deferral of
income, and may result in lower tax payable. Once you have chosen the cash
method, you are normally required to continue to use that method for the
farming business for all subsequent years.

When you are using the cash method, you may, if you wish, include in
income any amount up to the fair market value of your inventories on hand
at year-end (subject to the mandatory inventory adjustment discussed in
15.2.2). The amount you include is then deductible in the following year.
You might wish to do this for 2017, for example, if you had very low
income in 2017 and can see by the spring of 2018 (when you file your
return) that your 2018 income would increase enough to put you into a
higher tax bracket.

### 15.2.2 Purchases of inventory and prepaid expenses

If you are using the cash method of accounting, it is clearly possible to
generate a loss for tax purposes by purchasing large amounts of inventory.
Special rules have been introduced to deal with this possibility and to limit
the loss you can claim.

> Darryl, from our example in 15.1, purchased dairy cows for $5,000 just before his year-end on December 31, 2017. This purchase was included as an expense in arriving at his farming loss of $30,000. He had no other purchased inventory on hand at the end of the year. For income tax purposes, he is required to include $5,000 as a mandatory inventory adjustment to his 2017 income, reducing his farm loss to $25,000. In 2018, this $5,000 mandatory inventory will be treated as a farm expense.

In general, you are denied the portion of a loss that is attributable to purchases of inventory. However, for horses and certain registered bovine animals, you can deduct a portion of the loss. Professional advice should be obtained when dealing with these complex rules.

Claims for prepaid expenses are also restricted if the expenses relate to a year that is two or more years after the year of payment.

### 15.2.3  Cost of improving land for farming

Normally, when calculating income from a business, the cost of work done to improve land is considered a capital expense and is not deductible. However, for a farming business, amounts paid for clearing land, levelling land or installing a land drainage system are deductible.

### 15.2.4  Sales of livestock in a drought region

If you are farming in a region designated for the year as a "drought region", special relief is available if you sold a significant portion of your breeding herd. This rule is designed to allow you to defer paying tax if you are forced to sell off part or all of your herd because of drought.

The rule only applies if, by the end of the year, you have sold off (and not replaced) at least 15% of your "breeding herd". When it applies, some or all of your sales of the breeding animals are not counted into your income, but are deferred until a later year when your area is no longer designated as a drought region.

### 15.2.5  Business risk management programs

The federal government provides a group of business risk management programs for the agriculture, agri-food and agri-based products industry. The programs include:

- AgriInvest, a savings account in which producers can deposit a percentage of annual net sales, which the government will match

- The AgriStability program, which provides benefits based on a decline in current-year program margins as compared to reference years

- AgriRecovery, a rapid response program for disasters
- AgriInsurance, a crop insurance program that has been expanded to include additional commodities.

## 15.3 Farming losses

### 15.3.1 Ordinary farm losses

As we saw in 15.1, if your chief source of income is farming, or your chief source of income is "a combination of farming and some other source of income that is a subordinate source of income", you may deduct your farm losses as though they were ordinary business losses.

The carryforward available for such losses is 20 years. Farm losses can also be carried back and used against income of the past three years.

### 15.3.2 Restricted farm losses

As noted in 15.1, a loss from farming cannot *all* be used if you do not meet the "chief source of income" test. In this case, the loss you claim is limited to the first $2,500, plus one-half of the next $30,000 (that is, up to an additional $15,000).

> **Example**
>
> Bob, the dentist, who we met in 15.1, loses $50,000 on his racehorses in 2017.
>
> Bob's "restricted farm loss" is $2,500, plus one-half of the next $30,000. Since his total loss is more than $32,500, he reaches the maximum and he can only deduct $17,500 against the income from his dental practice for 2017.

Any amount of loss that cannot be used because of the "restricted farm loss" rules can be carried back for three years and forward for 20 years, but can be used only against farming income. So, in our example, Bob has $32,500 that can be used to offset income from his horse operations during the years 2014 to 2016 and 2018 to 2037.

## 15.4 Transfers of farming assets

> **Caution: The tax planning ideas discussed in this section may be affected by the federal government's proposed new tax regime for private companies, as outlined in the Department of Finance's July 2017 consultation paper and draft legislation. See Appendix I for details.**

A number of special rules, as outlined below, are available to alleviate the tax burden of selling or transferring a farm and the assets of a farming business.

### 15.4.1 The lifetime capital gains exemption

Make the most of the lifetime capital gains exemption for qualified farm or fishing property.

As discussed in 6.4.2, a $1 million exemption from capital gains is available on the disposition of qualified farm or fishing property. If you are disposing of farm or fishing property, investigate whether it qualifies for the exemption. In general terms, farm land and buildings, shares of farm companies and interests in farming partnerships may qualify for the exemption if they meet certain tests; equipment, inventory and most other assets do not qualify.

In some circumstances, you may be able to take action, such as delaying the sale, so you can gain time to reorganize your affairs to take advantage of the exemption. You also may be able to take steps to increase the cost base of your qualifying farm property to reduce the tax liability that will arise in the future on the property's sale. The tax rules in this area are complex so you should seek professional tax advice if you own farm property that qualifies for the exemption.

### 15.4.2 Transferring farm or fishing property to your children or grandchildren

Normally, if you sell or give property to members of your family other than your spouse, you are deemed to have sold the property for its "fair market value", and thus have to recognize as a capital gain or income the difference between your original cost and the property's current value.

Take advantage of the intergenerational transfer rules.

If you transfer property used in a farming or fishing business to a child, grandchild or great-grandchild (including a spouse of your child, a child of your spouse, etc., where "spouse" includes a common-law or same-sex spouse as outlined in 2.2.1), you may not be subject to this rule. If you simply give the property, it is deemed to be transferred at your cost (adjusted cost base [see 6.2.1] for capital property, or undepreciated capital cost [see 11.2.7] for depreciable property). Any gain on the property will thus be deferred.

For this "rollover" rule to apply, you or your spouse or one of your children must have used the property "principally" in a farming or fishing business in which you, your spouse, your parent or your children were actively engaged on a regular and continuous basis.

When the rollover applies, the recipient (your child, grandchild, etc.) are deemed to have acquired the farm or fishing property for the amount at which you are deemed to have sold it, so the gain will eventually be taxed when the child sells the property at some later time. If your child sells the property within three years after the date of transfer, the gain on the sale could be taxed in your hands.

> **Example**
>
> Florence operates a grain farm in Saskatchewan. In 2017, Florence decides to retire and gives the farm to her grandson Daniel. The farmland cost her $10,000 in 1980 and is now worth $950,000.
>
> Florence is deemed to receive $10,000 for the land, and so has no capital gain. Daniel is deemed to have acquired the land for $10,000; if he ever sells the land, the $10,000 figure would be used as his cost for capital gains calculation purposes. (Of course, if Daniel transfers the farm one day to his child, a further rollover would be available, assuming the rules have not changed.)

If you are transferring farm or fishing property to a child, grandchild, etc., you may wish to realize a partial capital gain in order to use up your $1 million capital gains exemption and give your child a higher cost base on the property. If you sell the property for something in between your cost and the current market value, that amount would be accepted for tax purposes. Where land is being transferred, do not forget to consider the possible cost of provincial land transfer tax. GST, HST or QST may apply, depending on the circumstances. The transfer could also trigger alternative minimum tax (see 7.6) or a clawback of Old Age Security benefits (see 20.3.2).

Note that the tax rules do not let you transfer farm inventory to a child on a tax-free basis. Gifting farm inventory results in the same income inclusion as a sale of farm inventory at fair market value.

### 15.4.3 Capital gains reserve on sale of farm or fishing business to your child

We discussed capital gains reserves briefly in 6.5.1. It was noted there that the capital gain must be recognized at a cumulative rate of one-fifth each year, so that no reserve can last for more than four years after the year of sale.

Where you sell property used in a farming or fishing business (including land) to your child, grandchild or great-grandchild, the allowable reserve is 10 years rather than five. As with the rules discussed in 15.4.2, a spouse of your child, grandchild or great-grandchild, and a child, grandchild or great-grandchild of your spouse also qualify. (For this purpose, "spouse" includes a common-law or same-sex spouse as outlined in 2.2.1.)

### 15.4.4 Farming partnerships

A partnership structure is common in farming businesses. In certain situations, taxpayers (usually spouses) may decide to split income by converting to a partnership structure from a proprietorship. Without proper planning, a disposition of the farming assets at fair market value may occur, resulting in capital gains, income and recaptured depreciation. This outcome can be avoided by filing appropriate election forms to defer taxable income.

Farming as a family partnership also provides an opportunity to transfer the interest in the partnership to a corporation and use the lifetime capital gains exemption as described in 15.4.1.

## 15.5  References

The following publications and more information, including forms and brochures, can be obtained on the CRA's website at *www.cra-arc.gc.ca* or by telephone request at 1-800-959-8281 for individual income tax and trust-related enquiries or 1-800-959-5525 for business and self-employed individual enquiries.

Guide T4003, "Farming Income"
Interpretation Bulletin IT-232R3, Archived – "Losses—Their deductibility in the loss year or in other years"
Interpretation Bulletin IT-268R4, Archived – "*Inter vivos* transfer of farm property to a child"
Interpretation Bulletin IT-322R, Archived – "Farm losses"
Interpretation Bulletin IT-349R3, Archived – "Intergenerational transfers of farm property on death"
Interpretation Bulletin IT-373R2 Consolidated, Archived – "Woodlots"
Interpretation Bulletin IT-425, Archived – "Miscellaneous farm income"
Interpretation Bulletin IT-427R, Archived – "Livestock of farmers"
Interpretation Bulletin IT-433R, Archived – "Farming or fishing—Use of cash method"
Interpretation Bulletin IT-485, Archived – "Cost of clearing or levelling land"
Interpretation Bulletin IT-526, Archived – "Farming—Cash method inventory adjustments"

# Chapter 16

## If you practise a profession

- Consider using a professional corporation to split income with family members (16.1.2)
- Maximize your deductible interest (16.2.1)
- Pay retiring partners income or capital as appropriate (16.2.2)
- Consider paying club dues at the partnership level (16.2.3)

*Most of income tax planning for professionals is the same as that for other self-employed people (see Chapter 11). Self-employed professionals are, after all, carrying on business. However, a number of special rules exist that we consider in 16.1. Since many professionals carry on their practice in partnership, we also look at some rules that apply to partnerships in 16.2.*

> **Caution: The tax planning ideas discussed in this chapter may be affected by the federal government's proposed new tax regime for private companies, as outlined in the Department of Finance's July 2017 consultation paper and draft legislation. See Appendix I for details.**

## 16.1 Specific rules for professionals

### 16.1.1 The modified accrual method of accounting for income

As we noted in 11.2.2 and 15.2.1, businesses other than farming businesses are generally required to report income on the accrual basis. That is, you take your sales into income even though you may not be paid until after your year-end.

Most businesses must also account for work in progress—work that has been done but not yet billed. Until recently, there was an exception for designated professionals, that is, accountants, dentists, lawyers, medical doctors, veterinarians and chiropractors. As a designated professional, you could have elected to exclude work in progress from your income. However, the federal government recently eliminated this election, so it can no longer be made for taxation years that begin on or after March 22, 2017.

This method of accounting is sometimes called the "modified accrual" method or "billed-basis accounting" method. It is not the cash method, since once an amount has been billed, it must be reported as income even if not yet paid. But excluding work in progress is a step away from the full accrual method, and making the election could have resulted in a substantial deferral of tax.

Designated professionals are required to include the lesser of the cost or the fair market value of work in progress in computing their business income, like other taxpayers, for tax years that begin after March 21, 2017.

If you made the election before then, transitional relief is available for your first taxation year that begins after March 22, 2017. In that year, you may still exclude 50% of the lesser of the cost and the fair market value of the work in progress from your income. After that, you must include all of the value of your work in progress in your income.

> **Example**
>
> Dianne is a lawyer who is in sole practice. She spends almost the entire month of December 2017 preparing for a major trial to defend her client Michael. The trial takes place in January. She does not bill Michael until the conclusion of the trial, in January 2018.
>
> If Dianne elects to exclude work in progress from her income for 2017 she would not have to recognize as income any amount from her work in preparing for the trial until her business year ending December 31, 2018. For Dianne's business year ending December 31, 2018, she must include 50% of the lesser of the cost and the fair market value of her work in progress in income. For December 31, 2019, Dianne must include the entire value of her work in progress.

On retirement or withdrawal from the business, the remaining work in progress is brought into your income. Such income is normally considered to be "earned income" for RRSP contribution limit purposes (see 3.1.3).

### 16.1.2 Professional corporations

Most provinces allow certain professionals to incorporate their professional practices. Provincial law governs professional corporations and so the applicable rules can vary depending on the province. You should seek professional advice to determine the rules that apply in your province and the most appropriate corporate structure for your professional practice.

Income splitting opportunities can arise in provinces that allow your family members to be shareholders of your professional corporation. As shareholders, your spouse or children can earn dividends that may be taxed at lower rates than the rate that would apply if you earned the income directly. However, proper planning is needed to avoid the attribution rules (see 5.2.3) and the income splitting tax on certain income earned by minor children (see 5.2.4).

For tax purposes, a professional corporation is generally treated like any other small business corporation (see Chapter 14). If you are considering incorporating your practice, see 11.5 for a discussion of some of the pros and cons.

> Consider using a professional corporation to split income with family members.

Professional corporations that are members of partnerships must use a December 31 business year-end (see 11.2.1). Other professional corporations may use an off-calendar year-end.

## 16.2 Specific rules that apply to partnerships

In 11.3, we discussed the taxation of partnerships in general. In this section, we look at some rules for partnerships that are particularly relevant to professionals.

### 16.2.1 Deductibility of interest paid by the partnership

As we saw in 7.2.3, interest paid is normally deductible as long as the funds borrowed are used to earn income from business or property. Where a partnership borrows funds for working capital, the interest is therefore clearly deductible.

As a member of a partnership, consider whether you can accelerate your drawings or have the partnership repay a portion of your capital contribution. You could then use the funds to pay

> Maximize your deductible interest.

off non-deductible debt (such as a home mortgage), while the partnership can borrow funds to replace the lost working capital. The interest expense on the partnership's new borrowing would then become deductible to the partnership. Alternatively, you could borrow funds to inject back into the partnership. However, the CRA could challenge such an arrangement under the general anti-avoidance rule (discussed in 5.2.6) if it considers this type of refinancing technique to be a misuse or abuse of the *Income Tax Act*.

If the partnership borrows funds in order to make a distribution of profits and/or capital to the partners, the interest paid on such borrowings is normally deductible but only up to the amount of the partnership's "net equity" as determined under generally accepted accounting principles.

### 16.2.2 Income payments to retired partners

Normally, if you withdraw from a partnership and you receive a payment to compensate for your interest in the partnership, the payment is considered capital. That is, any excess over your adjusted cost base in the partnership is a capital gain and taxed as discussed in Chapter 6. (Your adjusted cost base is essentially the amount you contributed to the partnership, plus your share of the profits on which you have been taxed, minus your drawings—see 11.3.5.)

Another option is available, however. If your partners agree to pay you a share of the income from the partnership and treat it explicitly as an income payment, you would be considered as still being a partner for tax purposes. You would therefore be taxed on that income, but your former partners would effectively pay less tax, since part of their partnership income and the related tax liability would be allocated to you.

**Pay retiring partners income or capital as appropriate.**

When you (or a partner of yours) decide to withdraw from a partnership, you need to calculate the best way of paying out the retiring partner's interest.

To avoid confusion or dispute, ensure your partnership agreement specifically addresses the tax treatment of payments to retired partners.

> *Example*
>
> Joel, an accountant, retires from his firm at the beginning of 2017. There are three other partners, who share equally in profits. The firm's income for 2017 is $600,000. The partners agree to pay Joel $120,000 on his retirement, and declare the $120,000 to be a share of the income from the partnership (rather than as a repayment of his capital interest).
>
> Joel will be required to report the $120,000 as income for 2017. However, each of the partners will effectively get a deduction of $40,000, since after Joel's allocation, there is only $480,000 left to be divided three ways. Each partner will thus report $160,000 in income instead of $200,000 for 2017.

### 16.2.3 Club dues

Most club dues are not allowed as business expenses. Many professional partnership agreements provide that such dues should be paid by the partners personally (since they are not deductible from the partnership's income anyway).

**Consider paying club dues at the partnership level.**

There may be an advantage to having the partnership pay these dues even though they are not deductible. The individual partners' adjusted cost bases in the partnership are not reduced by such disallowed expenses, even though the assets of the partnership are reduced by making the payments. (As noted above, your adjusted cost base is essentially the amount you contributed to the partnership, plus your share of your after-tax profits, minus your drawings—see 11.3.5.) As a result, having the partnership pay the club dues can effectively reduce the capital gain (or increase the capital loss) on an eventual sale of the partnership interest.

### 16.2.4 RRSP contribution limit

As discussed in 3.1.3, the amount you can contribute to an RRSP is generally limited to 18% of your "earned income" for the previous year or $26,010 for 2017, whichever is less (minus your pension adjustment, if any). Whether partnership income is considered earned income depends on whether the partner is active in the partnership during the year.

Partnership income of active partners is included in earned income for purposes of calculating their RRSP contribution limit.

Continuing income payments to retired partners are not included in earned income. Retiring partners are deemed to be active for the entire calendar year in which they withdraw from the partnership, but any allocation of partnership income in following years is not eligible for RRSP purposes.

For example, if you withdraw from a partnership in September 2017, your partnership income reported on your 2017 tax return is included in earned income for purposes of computing your 2018 RRSP contribution limit. However, partnership income reported in 2018 and later years will not create new RRSP contribution room.

### 16.2.5 Emigration of a partner

If you emigrate from Canada, as either an active or a retired partner, any income allocated to you from the partnership will continue to be taxable in Canada. If the income is also taxable in your new home country, you should be able to claim a foreign tax credit (see 18.2.2) for any taxes paid in Canada to fully or partially offset taxes paid in the foreign jurisdiction.

As we saw in 13.3.2, when you become a non-resident of Canada, you are deemed to have sold most of your assets at fair market value at the time of emigration. You then have to pay tax on any resulting income or capital gains or post acceptable security for the tax with the CRA. If you are a retired partner and you retain a right to continue receiving partnership income, this right may also be considered an asset. On emigration, the right would be deemed to be sold and Canadian departure tax would apply on the present value of your future income entitlements.

If you hold your partnership interest through a professional corporation (see 16.1.2), the shares of the corporation will be deemed sold when you emigrate, and the value of the shares will have to be determined to compute your Canadian departure tax liability. If the shares are qualifying small business corporation shares, you can apply your lifetime capital gains exemption against the gain on the deemed sale of the shares (see 13.3.3). Note that if your professional corporation retains a right to continuing partnership income, the CRA takes the position that this right is not active income, and thus may deny your claim for the lifetime capital gains exemption on the shares.

If you are an active or retired partner emigrating from Canada, it is strongly recommended that you review your situation with a tax professional before you leave Canada, both to plan for the tax consequences of your departure and to determine the tax consequences to you in the foreign country.

### 16.2.6 Death of a partner

When an active or retired partner dies, the partner is subject to the tax rules that generally apply on death. As we will see in 22.2.3, capital assets, such as stocks and real estate, are deemed for tax purposes to have been sold at fair market value on the date of death. Any accrued gains or losses on the assets are realized at that time, unless the assets are left to the deceased's spouse or to a spousal trust. In this case, the assets transfer at your tax cost (unless you elect otherwise—see 22.2.3) and your spouse or the trust inherits the accrued tax liability.

A deceased partner's capital interest in the partnership is such a capital asset if the full amount of the partner's capital contribution has not been paid out to the partner before death. However, continuing income payments of retired partners and other income rights of partners are not capital assets. Various options are available for reporting these items for tax purposes.

A deceased partner's share of partnership income can be included in the partner's terminal return or possibly in a second, separate tax return (also known as a "rights or things" return—see 22.2.4). The advantage of claiming this income in a separate tax return is that the income may be subject to lower marginal tax rates and some of the same personal tax credits can be claimed as on the deceased's terminal return.

Similarly, continuing income payments of retired partners can be reported on the deceased's terminal return or on a separate return, or they can be included in the income of the partner's estate or beneficiary as they receive these amounts.

In light of the various choices for reporting income entitlements of deceased partners, you should ensure your will gives your executors sufficient discretion to file whatever tax elections and separate returns are necessary to take full advantage of any tax saving opportunities in settling your estate. (For a general discussion of tax-oriented will planning, see 21.2.3.)

## 16.3 References

The following publications and more information, including forms and brochures, can be obtained on the CRA's website at *www.cra-arc.gc.ca* or by telephone request at 1-800-959-8281 for individual income tax and trust-related enquiries or 1-800-959-5525 for business and self-employed individual enquiries.

Guide T4002, "Business and Professional Income"

Income Tax Folio S4-F16-C1, "What is a Partnership?"

Interpretation Bulletin IT-242R, Archived – "Retired partners"

Interpretation Bulletin IT-278R2, Archived – "Death of a partner or retired partner"

Interpretation Bulletin IT-457R, Archived – "Election by professionals to exclude work in progress from income"

# Chapter 17

## If you live in Quebec

- Be aware of differences between the federal and Quebec tax systems (17.1.4)
- Ask Revenu Québec to pay your refundable child care expense credit in advance in monthly instalments (17.3.2)
- Claim the refundable tax credit for youth activities (17.3.3)
- Claim a refundable credit if you adopt a child or have infertility treatment (17.3.4)
- Claim the refundable tax credit for seniors' activities (17.5.2)
- Claim the refundable tax credit for caregivers of related adults (17.6)
- Boost your Quebec business entertainment expense deduction by subscribing to eligible Quebec cultural performances (17.10.5)
- Defray the cost of a new environment-friendly car through Quebec's green vehicle rebate program (17.13.2)
- Claim the temporary RénoVert tax credit (17.13.3)
- Claim the temporary residential waste water treatment systems tax credit (17.13.4)

*Unlike the other provinces, Quebec administers its own tax system and Quebec residents must file a separate provincial tax return. The* Quebec Taxation Act (Loi sur les impôts) *is largely modelled on the federal* Income Tax Act, *but, as we will see in this chapter, there are a number of differences.*

## 17.1 Quebec income tax

### 17.1.1 2017 Quebec tax rates

Quebec's 2017 provincial income tax rates are listed in Appendix II.

Quebec residents are allowed a refundable Quebec abatement on their federal tax return, which reduces their federal tax by 16.5% of basic federal tax. As a result, Quebec residents earn federal non-refundable tax credits at a rate of about 12.5%, instead of the 15% rate earned in the other provinces. Quebec non-refundable tax credits are usually earned at a 16% rate, so an amount that is eligible for federal and Quebec credits is generally worth about 28.5% of the related amount.

### 17.1.2 Dividends

For Quebec tax purposes, "eligible" Canadian dividends from public companies and Canadian controlled private corporations that have been paid out of income taxed at the high corporate tax rate (see 7.1.2) are grossed up by 38% for 2017. The offsetting Quebec credit for 2017 is 11.9% of the grossed-up dividend. As a result, the top marginal tax rate (combined federal and Quebec) is 39.8% for eligible dividends in 2017.

"Non-eligible" Canadian dividends are grossed-up by 17% and the Quebec credit is 7.05% of the grossed-up dividend. As such, the top marginal tax rate (combined federal and Quebec) is 43.8% for non-eligible dividends in 2017.

### 17.1.3 Instalments

Quebec instalment requirements parallel those for federal tax described in 9.2.2, with some minor differences.

The penalty for late or insufficient instalments is an extra 10% in addition to the normal interest rate. This penalty is substantially higher than the federal penalty, so if you can only pay part of your instalments, you are better off to pay your Quebec instalments on time.

The determination of who has to pay instalments is the same as under the federal system, as outlined in 9.2.2. Quarterly instalments are required where your balance of Quebec tax owing at the end of the year exceeds $1,800 for both the current year and either of the previous two years.

For Quebec residents, quarterly *federal* tax instalments are payable if you have federal taxes owing of $1,800 in the current year and either of the previous two years. Since Quebec tax can be higher or lower than federal tax for any individual (depending on many factors including those outlined throughout this chapter), there can be cases where you must remit federal instalments but not Quebec instalments, or vice versa.

### 17.1.4 Differences from federal tax

In the following sections, we highlight the principal differences between Quebec and federal tax law that affect personal tax.

Be aware of differences between the federal and Quebec tax systems.

If you live in Quebec, you should review the differences between the federal and the Quebec income tax systems, as highlighted below.

## 17.2 Basic personal and family credits

The federal basic credit is discussed in 2.2. Quebec offers a 16% personal tax credit of $14,890. The value of this credit for 2017 is $2,382 (i.e., 16% of the credit amount of $14,890).

Instead of a spousal tax credit, Quebec allows for the transfer of the unused portion of non-refundable tax credits between spouses. Under this measure, you may only claim the deduction resulting from the transfer after deducting all other non-refundable credits from your Quebec tax otherwise payable. This transfer mechanism also applies on the main tax return for the year of death of one of the spouses.

Students enrolled in full-time studies in vocational training at the secondary level and for full-time studies at the post-secondary level can transfer to either parent an amount, known as the recognized parental contribution, relating to the unused portion of the student's basic personal credit amount for the year.

Quebec allows a refundable tax credit for contributions to an RESP (see 4.3), known as the Quebec Education Savings Incentive (QESI). Each year, an RESP may receive a credit of 10% of the net contributions paid during the year, up to $250, and up to $250 of any rights accumulated during previous years can be added to the basic amount. Lower income families can add up to $50 more each year, depending on their family income. The credit is added to the plan rather than refunded to the contributor. The cumulative amount of the credit cannot exceed $3,600 per beneficiary.

Instead of the eligible dependant credit offered at the federal level (see 2.2.1), Quebec allows a credit for "other dependants" who are related by blood, marriage or adoption. To claim the credit, the dependant must be age 18 or over during the year, dependent on you, and ordinarily live with you, and you must not have benefited from a transfer of the recognized parental contribution from this dependant. For 2017, the credit amount is $3,907, which is worth up to $625.

Quebec also allows a non-refundable tax credit worth $273 for a "person living alone". To qualify, you must have lived by yourself for the entire calendar year in a self-contained home with no person other than a minor or an adult child enrolled in post-secondary studies who is eligible for the tax credit transfer mechanism (see above). If you live with an adult child, you may be able to add a non-refundable single-parent family tax credit of $337 to your person-living-alone credit.

If you are separated but you support your spouse, you cannot claim this credit; however, if you pay only spousal support payments that you deduct on your tax return, you and your spouse can both claim the credit. The credit is reduced by 18.75% of Quebec family net income over $33,755, so the credit is fully eliminated if your family net income is $42,855 or more in that year.

The family net income test is used to reduce the tax credit for persons living alone, the Quebec age credit and the Quebec pension income credit (see 17.5). For 2017, your amounts eligible for claiming all three of these credits are added together and then reduced by 18.75% of your family net income over $33,755.

## 17.3 Children

### 17.3.1 Child assistance payments

Instead of tax credits for dependent minor children, Quebec provides a non-taxable child assistance payment, payable in quarterly instalments. For 2017, the maximum annual payments for each eligible dependent child under 18 are $2,410 for the first child; $1,204 for the second and third children; and $1,806 for each additional child. An additional maximum annual payment of $845 is granted to single-parent families. The payments begin to be phased out for two-parent families with income over $47,868 ($34,824 for single-parent families). Families with a child with a disability receive an additional monthly allowance of $190.

### 17.3.2 Child care expenses

The Quebec tax rules for child care expenses are quite different from the federal rules discussed in 2.3.1. Child care expenses give rise to a refundable credit in Quebec instead of a deduction. (See 2.1.2 for a discussion of refundable credits and the difference between a deduction and a credit.) The credit is on a sliding scale, worth 75% of the expenses of low-income families, down to 26% for families with Quebec family net income over $156,255. Thus, the Quebec credit for child care expenses is more valuable to lower-income families, such as where both parents are attending school full-time.

> Ask Revenu Québec to pay your refundable child care expense credit in advance in monthly instalments.

You may ask Revenu Québec to pay you the refundable credit for child care expenses in advance, in monthly instalments, if your estimated tax credit for the year is over $1,000 or if you are entitled to a work premium of over $500 for the year. (You can make the request by filing Form TPZ-1029.8.F.)

Unlike the federal child care expense deduction, child care expenses eligible for the Quebec credit are not limited by either parents' earned income. Eligible expenses include child care costs incurred during a period in which you or your spouse received Employment Insurance or Quebec Parental Insurance Plan benefits.

To be eligible, the child must be, at any time in the year, either:

- age 16 or under and your child or your spouse's child
- age 16 or under and dependent on you or your spouse, and have income of no more than $9,582, or

- infirm and dependent on you or your spouse, and have income of no more than $9,582.

For 2017, Quebec child care expense claims are capped at $9,000 per child under age seven; at $5,000 per child age seven to 16; and at $11,000 where a child, at any age, has a severe and prolonged mental or physical impairment for which the disability credit can be claimed (see 2.3.1).

Example

Nicole and Daniel have two pre-school children. In 2017, Daniel earns $130,000, and Nicole earns $27,000 working part-time. They pay $5,500 in day care, required to enable them both to work.

For federal purposes, Nicole can claim the least of (a) the amount paid—$5,500; (b) $8,000 per child—$16,000; and (c) two-thirds of her earned income—$18,000. She can thus deduct $5,500 from income.

For Quebec purposes, Nicole's credit is based on the least of (a) the amount paid—$5,500; and (b) $9,000 per child—$18,000. Since Nicole and Daniel's Quebec family net income is more than $156,245, the credit is 26% of $5,500, or $1,430.

Child care expenses paid to a boarding school or camp are subject to weekly limits of $175 per child under age seven; $250 per child of any age suffering from an impairment; and $100 per child age seven to 16.

The contribution payable by parents of children attending the province's early childhood centres is not eligible for purposes of the Quebec child care expense credit.

### 17.3.3 Youth activities

If your child participates in fitness or arts activities, you may be able to claim the youth activities tax credit. This credit equals 20% of amounts up to $500 paid in 2017 (up to $1,000 if your child is disabled) for eligible programs.

You may be able to claim this credit if your child is at least five but not yet 16 years old at the beginning of 2017 (or not yet 18 if he or she is disabled) and your household income for 2017 does not exceed $135,085.

Claim the refundable tax credit for youth activities.

Eligible children's physical programs involve activities that contribute significantly to your child's strength, endurance, flexibility and balance.

Soccer, hockey and other programs involving significant physical activity, such as dance lessons, are eligible. These programs must last at least eight weeks with at least one session per week. Children's camps can also qualify if they last at least five consecutive days and devote more than 50% of the children's time to physical activity.

Eligible children's art programs involve activities that are artistic, cultural, recreational or developmental.

These programs must last at least eight weeks with at least one session per week. Children's camps can also qualify if they last at least five consecutive days and devote more than 50% of the children's time to eligible activities.

### 17.3.4 Adoption and infertility treatment expenses

The federal credit for adoption expenses is discussed at 2.3.3. Quebec also offers a refundable credit for adoption expenses to help finance the expenses associated with adopting children from overseas and is available for local adoptions. The credit is 50% of up to $20,000 in expenses paid by you, or by you and your spouse, to a maximum credit of $10,000 per child. Qualifying expenses include court fees, legal fees, travelling and translation expenses (for adoptions from other countries), and fees charged by approved agencies.

Claim a refundable credit if you adopt a child or have infertility treatment.

Since the credit is refundable, it is available even if you have no tax to pay for the year. You must keep records of your expenses and claim only those that qualify.

If you're being treated for infertility, you may be able to claim a refundable credit for the costs associated with *in vitro* fertilization paid by you or your spouse, provided these treatments are not covered by Quebec's health insurance plan and they meet certain conditions. The tax credit rate ranges from 20% to 80% of up to $20,000 in eligible expenses, depending on your family's income. As such, the maximum annual credit ranges from $4,000 to $16,000.

## 17.4 Students

### 17.4.1 Tuition fees

Tuition fees qualify for an 8% non-refundable credit for Quebec tax purposes. Quebec allows the transfer of undeducted tuition fees to one of the student's parents or grandparents. Students can carry forward unused tuition fees indefinitely and claim them as a credit in later years.

Quebec does not have a credit to parallel the federal education amount. Instead, Quebec offers a non-refundable 16% tax credit for children under 18 and engaged in full-time (part-time if infirm) professional training or post-secondary education. For 2017, the credit is based on an amount of $2,682 for each term completed, for up to two terms per year.

### 17.4.2  Interest on student loans

A non-refundable tax credit is available for 20% of interest paid in the year on a student loan that you received under a federal or Quebec student loan program. You can carry forward any unused portion of the credit to a later year. To claim the credit, you must include a receipt from your financial institution showing the amount of interest paid.

## 17.5  Seniors

Quebec offers a 16% non-refundable tax credit similar to the federal credit for persons who are 65 and older (20.3.4) and for pension income (see 20.3.5). For 2017, the Quebec age credit is worth up to $501 and the Quebec pension credit is worth up to $445.

The amounts available for claiming each of these credits and the credit for persons living alone are added together and then reduced by 18.75% of your Quebec family net income for 2017 over $33,755 (see 17.2).

### 17.5.1  Home support, rehabilitation and safety equipment for seniors

Quebec allows a refundable tax credit for the home support of persons age 70 or older. For seniors who are not recognized as dependent, the tax credit is 35% of up to $19,500 of eligible expenses, for a maximum refundable credit of $6,825. For dependent seniors, the credit is 35% of up to $25,500 of eligible expenses, for a maximum refundable credit of $8,925. If you and your spouse are both eligible for the credit, only one of you can claim it. The credit is reduced by your family income over $56,935 for 2017.

You cannot claim the same amount for this credit and for the medical expense credit described in 17.8, so be sure to do the math to see which credit provides the most benefit.

Another refundable tax credit for individuals aged 70 or older is equal to 20% of costs incurred for a qualifying stay in a private or public rehabilitation centre, up to a maximum of 60 days.

A refundable tax credit is also available for the purchase or rental of qualifying equipment used in the principal residence of a person aged 70 or older to improve his or her safety and security. This credit is equal to 20% of the amount paid over $500.

### 17.5.2  Seniors' activities

If you are 70 or older in 2017, your income for the year is $41,165 or less and you participate in fitness or arts activities, you may be able to claim the seniors' activities tax credit.

Claim the refundable tax credit for seniors' activities

This refundable credit equals 20% of amounts up to $200 paid for eligible physical activities and artistic, cultural and recreational activities similar to those eligible for the Quebec refundable tax credit for youth activities (see 17.3.3).

### 17.5.3 Seniors' assistance program to partially offset a municipal tax increase

If you are 65 or older in 2017 and your 2016 family taxable income does not exceed $50,400, an assistance program permits you to partially offset a municipal tax increase pursuant to a new 2016 assessment roll.

If you are a long-time homeowner, you may receive a grant to partially offset the municipal taxes payable on your residence following an increase in its value, if the increase significantly exceeds the average increase for certain residential properties and certain other conditions are met.

## 17.6 Caregivers of related adults

**Claim the refundable tax credit for caregivers of related adults.**

You may be able to claim the refundable tax credit for caregivers of related adults if you are in one of three situations:

- you house an eligible relative in your home who is 70 years of age or older or is an adult who has a severe and prolonged mental or physical impairment
- you live in the home of an eligible relative who is unable to live alone due to a severe and prolonged mental or physical impairment
- you live in your own home (other than a seniors' residence) with a spouse who is 70 years of age or older or who has a severe and prolonged mental or physical impairment.

For 2017, this credit of up to $1,176 per eligible relative includes a basic amount of $647, plus a supplement of $529. The credit is reduced by 16% of the eligible relative's income over $23,505. Caregivers of an elderly spouse are not entitled to the supplement but may claim an increased basic amount of $1,007 for 2017.

Eligible relatives include a child, grandchild, brother, sister, nephew, niece, uncle and aunt, among others.

Another refundable tax credit is available for caregivers equalling 30% of total expenses of up to $5,200 paid in the year for specialized respite services for the care and supervision of an eligible person. The maximum credit amount of $1,560 is reduced by 3% of the caregiver's family income over $56,935 for 2017. If you are claiming the expense for another credit, you cannot also claim the expense for this credit.

## 17.7 Donations

### 17.7.1 Charitable donations

In addition to the federal credit for charitable donations discussed in 8.1, in 2017 you can claim a Quebec non-refundable credit of 20% for the first $200 of charitable donations, and of 24% for amounts over $200. To the extent your income exceeds $103,915, you can claim a 25.75% donation tax credit.

> Lionel earns $200,000 in 2017, and he donates $30,000 to a registered charity. His provincial tax credit for his donation is $7,714, which is the total of:
>
> * $40, which is 20% on the first $200
>
> * $7,674, which is 25.75% of the lesser of:
>
>   * $29,800, the amount of the gift exceeding $200, or
>
>   * $96,085, the amount by which his $200,000 income exceeds the highest income tax threshold of $103,915
>
> * $0, which is 24% of the amount of the gift less the two credit amounts used above ($30,000 – $200 – $29,800 = $0).
>
> Instead, suppose Lionel earns $100,000 In 2017 and donates the same $30,000 amount. Now Lionel's provincial tax credit is $7,192, which is the total of:
>
> * $40, which is 20% on the first $200
>
> * $0, which is 25.75% of the lesser of:
>
>   * $29,800, the amount of the gift exceeding $200, or
>
>   * $0, the amount by which his $100,000 income exceeds $103,915
>
> * $7,152, which is 24% of the amount of the gift less the two credit amounts used above ($30,000 – $200 – $0 = $29,800).

As of 2016, there is no income-related limit for the purpose of calculating the tax credits for gifts.

Capital gains arising from your gifts of publicly traded securities and other appreciable property are not included in your income for tax purposes.

Quebec's rules include a special restriction on the credit for gifts of works of art. The valuation of the gift is limited to the price the charity receives when it sells the art plus 25% of that amount. You can only claim the credit if the charity sells the art within five years of accepting the donation. This rule does not apply to donations to certain museums and galleries, recognized artistic organizations, governments or municipalities.

### 17.7.2 Political contributions

As noted in 2.7.2, many provinces provide credits for contributions to provincial political parties, riding associations and election candidates. In Quebec, only municipal electoral contributions are eligible. You can claim a non-refundable credit for municipal contributions of up to $155.

## 17.8 Medical expenses

For Quebec purposes, the non-refundable tax credit for medical expenses is reduced by 3% of Quebec family income, which is the combined net income of both spouses. Unlike the 3% federal reduction, the Quebec reduction is not capped, so many Quebec residents are not entitled to this credit.

The list of allowable expenses is similar to the federal list. Expenses for services provided for cosmetic purposes (such as liposuction, facelifts, botox injections and teeth whitening) are not eligible for Quebec purposes. Also, the amount you can claim for eyeglass frames is limited to $200 each for you, your spouse and any other person for whom you or your spouse purchased frames.

Quebec also offers a 25% refundable tax credit for certain medical expenses. The maximum amount for 2017 is $1,175, reduced by 5% of family income exceeding $22,725.

Also, as noted in 17.10.2 below, the taxable benefit for employer-paid private health insurance premiums qualifies as a medical expense for Quebec purposes.

## 17.9 People with disabilities

Quebec offers a non-refundable tax credit for persons with severe and prolonged physical or mental impairment. The Quebec credit is similar to the federal credit discussed at 2.5.1 and you must meet essentially the same criteria to be eligible. The supplementary credit for a child with a disability is not available in Quebec.

To claim the Quebec credit for the first time, you must file Form TP-752.0.14-V with your Quebec tax return for that year. For 2017, the maximum amount available for the credit is $3,307, which means it may be worth up to $529 to you.

## 17.10 Employment and self-employment

### 17.10.1 Parental Insurance Plan premiums

The Quebec Parental Insurance Plan (QPIP) provides benefits to any eligible worker who takes a maternity, paternity, adoption or parental leave.

Employers, employees and self-employed workers have to pay mandatory premiums up to a maximum of $397 for employees, $556 per employee for employers and $705 for self-employed individuals for 2017.

An employee's premiums factor into the calculation of his or her non-refundable personal tax credit, along with QPP, employment insurance and Health Services Fund contributions. Employer premiums are deductible, while self-employed worker premiums are partially deductible.

Benefits paid under the plan are taxable in the year received, and are subject to source deductions.

### 17.10.2 Employer-paid private health insurance

As we saw in 10.1.1, employer contributions to a private health services plan are non-taxable employee benefits for federal purposes. These contributions are, however, taxable for Quebec tax purposes. Thus, if your employer pays for your group sickness, drug or dental plan, the value of the benefit is included in your employment income on your Relevé 1 and must be reported on your Quebec tax return, even though it does not appear on your T4 slip for federal income tax purposes.

As a result, employer health plan contributions will normally make your employment income for Quebec tax purposes higher than it is for federal purposes. You (or your spouse) can claim the taxable benefit as a medical expense on your Quebec tax return (see 17.8).

### 17.10.3 Employee stock options

Quebec's tax treatment of employee stock options is similar to the federal treatment (see 10.4), except that the amount you are allowed to deduct from your taxable benefit may be less for Quebec tax purposes.

As we saw in 10.4.1, you may be able to claim a deduction for federal purposes of 50% of the taxable benefit arising from exercising employee stock options or from selling stock option shares in a Canadian controlled private corporation (see 10.4.2). For Quebec purposes, your deduction is generally limited to 25% of the amount of the benefit.

If you received your stock options from a small or medium-sized business engaged in innovative activities in Quebec, you may be able to claim a deduction of 50% of your taxable benefit. To qualify, the corporation must carry on business in Quebec and have an establishment there, and its assets and those of associated corporations must be less than $50 million in the taxation year ending in the calendar year before the options were granted. Also, the corporation must have claimed a Quebec tax credit for scientific research and experimental development in the taxation year ending in the calendar year that the options were granted or in one of its three previous taxation years.

You may also be able to claim a 50% deduction on a stock option benefit for Quebec tax purposes if you donate stock option shares to charity.

### 17.10.4 Union and professional dues

Union and professional dues (excluding professional insurance), which are deductible for federal tax purposes (see 10.8.4), are not deductible on your Quebec tax return. Instead, they entitle you to a 10% non-refundable tax credit. This rule applies to employees and self-employed individuals alike. The cost of professional insurance is deductible for Quebec tax purposes.

### 17.10.5 Meals and entertainment expenses

As under the federal rules (see 11.2.9), if you are self-employed and you take a client or business contact out for a meal or entertainment event, your deduction for your costs as a business expense is limited to 50% of the amount paid for Quebec tax purposes.

For Quebec purposes, entertainment expenses are further limited to:

- 2% of total sales, if your total sales are $32,500 or less
- $650, if your total sales are between $32,500 and $52,000
- 1.25% of total sales, if your total sales are $52,000 or more.

Relief from these limits is available for certain sectors, such as businesses requiring frequent travel and sales agencies.

Boost your Quebec business entertainment expense deduction by subscribing to eligible Quebec cultural performances.

Some business entertainment expenses for cultural events held in Quebec are 100% deductible for Quebec tax purposes. These include the cost of a subscription to a symphony orchestra, classical or jazz ensemble, and opera, dance, theatre and vocal performances. To qualify for this special deduction, the subscription must be for at least three performances in eligible artistic disciplines.

### 17.10.6 Home office expenses

The federal tax rules governing deductions for home office expenses are discussed in 10.8.3 and 11.2.10. For Quebec tax purposes, the deduction for self-employed individuals is limited to 50% if the expenditures relate to the cost of maintaining a residence (e.g., maintenance and repair costs, rent, mortgage interest, property and school taxes, insurance premiums and depreciation). The home office expense claims of employees are not subject to this restriction.

### 17.10.7 Self-employed QPP/CPP and QPIP deduction

Self-employed individuals are eligible to deduct 50% of their QPP/CPP contributions on pensionable self-employed earnings and a portion of their QPIP premiums in calculating their net income. The remainder of these contributions and premiums is eligible for a non-refundable pension tax credit. This deduction also applies when calculating the income used to determine the 1% contribution to the Health Services Fund (see 17.12.2).

### 17.10.8 Experienced workers tax credit

If you are 63 or older in 2017 and have more than $5,000 in eligible work income, you may be able to claim a tax credit for experienced workers. The maximum amount of work income eligible for the credit varies based on your age. For 2017, depending if you are 63, 64 or 65 or older, the credit applies to $4,000, $6,000 or $8,000 in income that exceeds the $5,000 threshold. Eligible work income includes salary and business income. The age eligibility for this tax credit will be lowered to 62 in 2018.

## 17.11 Investments

### 17.11.1 Limit on deductibility of investment expenses

For Quebec purposes, your ability to deduct expenses incurred to earn income from property is limited to your income from such investments earned in the year. Investment expenses that cannot be used in the current year can be carried back to offset investment income earned in the three preceding tax years and they can be carried forward indefinitely, as long as the investment income in that year exceeds the investment expenses.

### 17.11.2 Rental expenses—documentation

If you use a building located in Quebec to earn rental or business income and you claim any expenses for renovation, improvement, maintenance or repair of the property, you must include with your Quebec income tax return Form TP-1086.R.23.12-V. On this form, you must disclose the contractor's name, address, social insurance number (if an individual) and QST registration number (if available), as well as the amount paid for the work carried out. This measure is designed to combat tax evasion in the contracting and renovation sectors.

### 17.11.3 Cumulative net investment loss

As we saw in 6.4.3, investment expenses and tax shelter write-offs create a cumulative net investment loss (CNIL), which reduces your ability to claim the lifetime capital gains exemption.

For Quebec tax purposes, certain special Quebec investment incentives are not included in your CNIL calculation. That is, they do not affect your ability to claim the capital gains exemption on your Quebec tax return.

## 17.12 Health Services Fund contributions

### 17.12.1 Health Services Fund contribution

Your income from all sources (other than employment income) is subject to a contribution to the Health Services Fund. The income taxed is generally the total shown on your income tax return, including business income, investment income, pension or retirement income and taxable capital gains but not employment income, Old Age Security or alimony.

Certain deductions are permitted to arrive at the base amount for the contribution, and a further $14,545 exemption is allowed for 2017. If your 2017 income is between $14,550 and $50,570, your Health Services Fund contribution is 1% of income over $14,545, to a maximum of $150. If your income is over $50,570, your contribution is $150 plus 1% of your income over $50,570, to a maximum of $1,000. Your contribution is then indirectly offset by the non-refundable personal tax credit of 16% (see 17.2).

If you are required to pay income tax instalments (see 17.1.3), you must also pay quarterly instalments on your Health Services Fund contribution.

## 17.13 Other Quebec credits and deductions

### 17.13.1 Legal fees for establishing support payments

Under the federal system, you may deduct legal costs to establish or enforce a right to child or spousal support or to obtain an increase in child or spousal support amounts (see 2.6). For Quebec purposes, fees paid due to a court application to increase the level of support are deductible.

You can also deduct judicial and extrajudicial expenses paid regarding an initial right to receive or obligation to pay an amount for support, as long as the expenses are not reimbursed and you did not deduct them from income in a previous year.

### 17.13.2 Rebate for purchase or lease of green vehicles

Defray the cost of a new environment-friendly car through Quebec's green vehicle rebate program.

You may be eligible for a rebate if you purchase or lease a green vehicle. The rebate program mainly focuses on hybrid vehicles, rechargeable hybrid electric vehicles and vehicles that are exclusively electric. The rebate ranges between $500 and $8,000 for 2017 and is based on battery capacity in kilowatt-hours.

### 17.13.3 RénoVert tax credit

Claim the temporary RénoVert tax credit.

You can claim the temporary RénoVert refundable tax credit if you have recognized eco-friendly home renovation work done to an eligible dwelling you own or co-own that is your principal residence or a winterized cottage that you normally occupy.

The initial construction of the dwelling must have been completed before January 1, 2016, and the dwelling must be one of the following:

- a single-family home
- a permanently installed prefabricated house or mobile home
- an apartment in a building held in divided co-ownership (i.e., condominium)
- a dwelling in a residential duplex or triplex
- a winterized cottage that you normally occupy.

The renovation work must be done by a qualified contractor under a contract entered into after March 17, 2016 and before April 1, 2018. The home renovation work must have a positive environmental impact or must improve the dwelling's energy efficiency. To qualify for the credit in 2016, you must have paid the eligible expenses after March 17, 2016 and before January 1, 2017. To qualify for 2017, you must pay the eligible expenses after December 31, 2016 and before December 31, 2018. If you wish to claim the credit for 2018, you must pay the eligible expenses after December 31, 2017 and before December 31, 2019.

The maximum amount you can claim for the tax credit over the three-year period is 20% of the portion of your eligible expenses that exceed $2,500, up to a maximum tax credit of $10,000.

### 17.13.4 Residential waste water treatment systems tax credit

You can claim a new temporary refundable tax credit for upgrading the residential waste water treatment systems of your principal residence or cottage. The credit applies to the costs of constructing, renovating, modifying or rebuilding a system for discharging, collecting and disposing of waste water, toilet effluents or grey water.

> Claim the temporary residential waste water treatment systems tax credit.

To be eligible for the credit, the work must be carried out by a qualified contractor under a service agreement entered into after March 31, 2017 and before April 1, 2022.

The tax credit you can claim is capped at $5,500 per eligible dwelling, and it is based on 20% of the portion, of qualified expenditures you paid in the year that exceed $2,500.

### 17.13.5 Solidarity tax credit

Quebec's solidarity tax credit replaces the Quebec sales tax (QST) credit, the property tax refund and the tax credit for people who live in northern villages.

If you are eligible for this credit, it will be paid to you monthly. You must be registered for direct deposit to your bank account.

## 17.14 References

Revenu Québec produces a number of publications to assist taxpayers, the most notable of which is the *Guide to the Income Tax Return* that accompanies the provincial income tax return. Quebec tax forms and guides are also available in French and English from the Quebec government's website at *www.revenu.gouv.qc.ca.*

# Chapter 18

## If you are a U.S. citizen in Canada

- Consider claiming the foreign earned income exclusion (18.2.1)
- Claim the maximum foreign tax credit (18.2.2)
- Keep records of expenses deductible on your U.S. return (18.3.1)
- Beware of differences between Canadian and U.S. rules governing retirement income (18.3.3)
- Defer U.S. taxation of income accruing in your RRSP and other Canadian retirement plans (18.3.3)
- Beware of non-qualified deferred compensation plans (18.3.3)
- Watch out for ownership of Canadian corporations and funds earning passive income (18.3.5)
- Be cautious of using the Canadian lifetime capital gains exemption (18.4.3)
- Review income splitting arrangements to prevent double taxation (18.6.2)
- If you're married, file a joint U.S. return where appropriate (18.7.1)
- Consider using the annual US$14,000 U.S. gift tax exclusion to transfer wealth to children and grandchildren (18.8.2)
- Beware of U.S. gift and foreign trust reporting rules (18.8.4)
- Consider expatriating from the U.S. to protect your Canadian assets from U.S. tax and simplify your tax filing obligations (18.9)

*In this chapter, we address the difficult and complicated tax problems of the United States citizen who lives in Canada. We can only scratch the surface, due to the interaction of two highly complex tax systems that are both subject to continual change. You should seek professional advice if you are a U.S. citizen living in Canada.*

## 18.1 Two systems of taxation

The income tax systems of the United States and Canada are similar in some general ways, but very different in their details. A U.S. citizen resident in Canada must deal with both systems.

The United States is one of the few countries in the world that taxes its citizens on their worldwide income, whether or not they are physically in the United States. Canada taxes only Canadian residents on their worldwide income; non-residents (including Canadian citizens) are taxed by Canada only on certain income from Canadian sources.

The result is that U.S. citizens living in Canada must file returns under both systems, and they often must pay tax to both governments. Safeguards exist to prevent double taxation: clearly, you could not afford to pay a large percentage of your income to each country. But the safeguards, which are outlined in 18.2 below, are not perfect. Much of this chapter deals with the taxation issues that arise due to differences between the two systems' ways of calculating income and tax.

In general, you will find that U.S. taxation is lower than Canadian. U.S. federal tax currently reaches a maximum rate of 39.6%. Canadian federal tax reaches 33%, but as a resident of Canada you also have a provincial tax liability, which raises the top rate to about 50%, depending on your province of residence. As a U.S. citizen not resident or domiciled in any state, you have no liability for any U.S. state tax except, perhaps, to the extent you have income arising in a state.

The 2017 U.S. income tax rates for single persons with no dependants and for married couples filing joint returns (see 18.7.1) are:

| Single (see 18.7.1) | |
| --- | --- |
| Taxable income | Federal tax |
| $0–9,325 | 10% |
| $9,325–37,950 | $932.50 + 15% of the amount over $9,325 |
| $37,950–91,900 | $5,226.25 + 25% of the amount over $37,950 |
| $91,900–191,650 | $18,713.75 + 28% of the amount over $91,900 |
| $191,650–416,700 | $46,643.75 + 33% of the amount over $191,650 |
| $416,700–418,400 | $120,910.25 + 35% of the amount over $416,700 |
| $418,400 and up | $121,505.25 + 39.6% of the amount over $418,400 |

| Married filing joint income tax returns (see 18.7.1) | |
| --- | --- |
| Taxable income | Federal tax |
| $0–18,650 | 10% |
| $18,650–75,900 | $1,865 + 15% of the amount over $18,650 |
| $75,900–153,100 | $10,452.50 + 25% of the amount over $75,900 |
| $153,100–233,350 | $29,752.50 + 28% of the amount over $153,100 |
| $233,350–416,700 | $52,222.50 + 33% of the amount over $233,350 |
| $416,700–470,700 | $112,728 + 35% of the amount over $416,700 |
| $470,700 and up | $131,628 + 39.6% of the amount over $470,700 |

The rates for other types of taxpayers are different; see 18.7.1 for a discussion of the types of filers.

The highest effective federal marginal rate is 39.6% for most taxpayers. The 39.6% marginal rate applies to taxable income over US$470,700 for married taxpayers filing jointly. Married individuals filing separately (see 18.7.1) become subject to the highest rate at taxable income exceeding US$235,350.

### 18.1.1 Net investment income tax

If you have investment income, you may be subject to a net investment income tax in addition to regular income tax. A tax rate of 3.8% is applied to the lower of two amounts: net investment income for the year or modified adjusted gross income over a threshold amount. Net investment income includes interest, dividends, capital gains, certain annuities, royalties, rents and passive income from partnerships and "S corporations".

The thresholds for modified adjusted gross income are US$250,000 for married individuals filing jointly, US$200,000 for single filers and US$125,000 for married individuals filing separately.

This tax should be creditable in Canada (subject to the regular limitations) if the investment income is U.S. source income. The U.S. does not allow the net investment income tax to be offset with foreign tax credits. As a result, many U.S. citizens with significant investment income will pay U.S. net investment income tax.

## 18.2 Basic mechanisms for avoiding double taxation

There are three mechanisms in place to help you avoid paying tax twice on the same income.

### 18.2.1 Foreign earned income exclusion (U.S. tax law)

The simplest way to avoid double taxation is the U.S. "foreign earned income exclusion". On your U.S. tax return, you may exclude from your income up to US$102,100 of "earned income" (employment or services income) earned from services provided outside the United States.

Example

Cathy is a U.S. citizen who lives in Calgary. She works at a company as an accountant and earns Cdn$100,000 in 2017. (Assume the Canadian and U.S. dollars are trading at par through 2017.) She has no other income.

On her U.S. tax return, Cathy reports her income of approximately US$100,000. She then elects to use the foreign earned income exclusion and deduct the same $100,000, for total income of $0. As a result, she pays no tax to the United States. Her Canadian tax return is not affected by her U.S. citizenship.

If you do not have any income other than your employment or professional services income and your annual income is under US$102,100, this exclusion is all you need to escape U.S. tax entirely. You must still file a U.S. return (see 18.7.2 below) and claim the exclusion.

If you file as "married filing jointly" (see 18.7.1 below), you and your spouse can each claim up to US$102,100 for purposes of the exclusion against your respective earned incomes. This can be done even if your spouse is not a U.S. citizen.

The foreign earned income exclusion is first deducted and then added back to taxable income to calculate a tentative tax liability. Tax is then calculated on the amount of the foreign income exclusion as though it was the taxable income for the year. The excess of the first amount over the second amount is the amount of tax payable. As a result of this calculation, tax is paid at higher graduated rates on the amount of taxable income that exceeds the foreign earned income exclusion amount.

*Consider claiming the foreign earned income exclusion.* The regulations make it possible to elect the foreign earned income exclusion on late-filed returns in a number of cases. If you are eligible for the foreign earned income exclusion, you should normally claim it. However, in some circumstances (mostly involving carryovers of foreign tax credits—see 18.2.2), claiming a foreign tax credit can be more beneficial than claiming the exclusion. If you claim the exclusion and then, in a later year, elect not to claim it, you cannot normally claim it again for five years.

### 18.2.2 Foreign tax credit (both U.S. and Canadian law)

The foreign tax credit is a unilateral mechanism provided by many countries to prevent double taxation. Both the U.S. and Canada provide foreign tax credits. While the details differ, the concept is basically the same for both.

*Claim the maximum foreign tax credit.* Consider the U.S. foreign tax credit as an example. If you are subject to U.S. taxation (because you are a citizen) but you have paid tax to Canada on Canadian-source income, you can, in general, claim a foreign tax credit to offset your U.S. tax on that income. Your credit cannot be greater than the Canadian tax you paid.

Example

Dave is a U.S. citizen who lives and works in Toronto. He earns Cdn$1,000 (equivalent to US$1,000) in interest on his Toronto bank account in 2017. He also receives a salary in Canada and income from investments in the United States.

Dave is required to include the US$1,000 in his income for U.S. tax purposes. (Because it is investment income and not earned income, it is not eligible for the foreign earned income exclusion.) Assume that he is in the 33% U.S. bracket (i.e., his taxable income is less than US$416,700 and he is single), so his additional U.S. tax is US$330. If he is in a 50% tax bracket in Canada, so that he has paid the equivalent of US$500 to Canada (and Ontario) on the income, he can receive a foreign tax credit for the full US$330 on his U.S. return. By contrast, if his Canadian tax rate were lower and he paid only US$250 to Canada (and Ontario), he could only claim US$250 as his foreign tax credit.

The above example is highly simplified, but it demonstrates the basic effect of the credit. When you total up the tax to both countries (including provincial and state tax) and the foreign tax credits of each, you should end up paying an amount that is equal to the higher of the two countries' rates of tax.

The Canadian foreign tax credit follows essentially the same principles. Since Canada taxes Canadian residents on their worldwide income, Dave, in our example has to report his U.S.-source investment income on his Canadian tax return. He is then eligible for a foreign tax credit for U.S. taxes paid on his U.S.-source investment income to offset the Canadian tax that applies but only up to the amount of U.S. tax he would have paid if he was not a U.S. citizen. Canada only allows foreign tax credits for the amount of U.S. tax that would have been payable by non-U.S. citizens.

The U.S. then allows an additional credit under the Canada-U.S. tax treaty (see 18.2.3), which many taxpayers neglect to claim. (Note that each country's foreign tax credit generally applies only to foreign taxes on income from sources outside that country.)

The details of the foreign tax credit rules are very complicated. If you receive income for personal services performed in both the U.S. and Canada, it is a good idea to keep a diary to record U.S. and Canadian work days.

For U.S. foreign tax credit purposes, excess (non-creditable) foreign tax can be carried back one year and forward 10 years. For Canadian foreign tax credit purposes, certain excess foreign tax can be deducted from income in the current year. If the excess foreign tax relates to business income, the excess generally can be carried back three years and forward 10 years. Foreign taxes on investment income and employment income that are not used as a credit or deduction in the year can't be carried back or forward in Canada.

If you have various sources of income and need to claim a foreign tax credit under one or both systems, you should consult a professional adviser.

### 18.2.3 Canada-U.S. tax treaty

The third safeguard against double taxation is the Canada-U.S. tax treaty (also known as a tax convention). Both Canada and the U.S. have such treaties with many countries. The purpose of a tax treaty is twofold: to prevent double taxation and to reduce tax evasion by allowing exchange of taxpayer information between the two governments.

The Canada-U.S. treaty, for the most part, does not apply to limit the U.S. tax liability of U.S. citizens resident in Canada except in specific circumstances.

For example, the treaty allows a U.S. citizen resident in Canada to defer U.S. taxation of income in RRSPs and other pension plans, which are not qualifying deferral plans under U.S. rules. Absent this provision, U.S. tax could apply to the accruing funds, which are specifically exempt from Canadian tax (see 3.1.5 and 18.3.3).

If you are using the treaty to reduce your U.S. tax liability, you are generally required to disclose the specific details of the treaty benefits you are claiming on your U.S. tax return. If you do not, the treaty benefits can be denied. However, deferring RRSP income no longer requires disclosure with your U.S. tax return (see 18.3.3).

Under the treaty, if you are a Canadian resident and you receive U.S. social security benefits, you are not subject to U.S. tax on these amounts. However, 85% of the amount received is subject to tax in Canada.

## 18.3 Differences in calculating income

In theory, the foreign tax credit mechanism prevents you from paying tax twice on the same income. However, there are many differences between U.S. and Canadian calculations of income for tax purposes. These differences can lead to unexpected tax liabilities.

### 18.3.1 Deductions available in the U.S. but not in Canada

While you can normally deduct home mortgage interest and property taxes on your U.S. tax return, they are not deductible in Canada, except to the extent you can claim an office in your home (see 7.2.3 and 11.2.10).

State taxes, which may be imposed to the extent you reside in or have income arising in a U.S. state, are generally deductible for U.S. income tax purposes, while provincial income taxes are not deductible in Canada.

Itemized deductions allowed are limited to the extent adjusted gross income exceeds certain thresholds. In 2017, the thresholds are US$313,800 for a joint return, US$261,500 for a single filer and US$156,900 for married individuals filing separately.

Certain employment-related expenses that are not deductible in Canada can be deducted on your U.S. return. If you are claiming deductions on your U.S. return that are not allowable in Canada, make sure to keep records sufficient to establish your claim.

> Keep records of expenses deductible on your U.S. return.

### 18.3.2 Deductions available in Canada but not in the U.S.

As we saw in 7.2.3, interest paid may be deducted for Canadian tax purposes where the funds were borrowed for the purpose of earning income from investments. The amount of interest expense that can be deducted is generally not limited by investment income.

For U.S. tax purposes, your investment interest expense deduction is limited to your investment income. You cannot write off interest expense against other income such as employment or business income. This principle extends, under a separate set of complex rules, beyond interest expenses to all deductions relating to "passive" activities, including limited partnerships and most rental losses. Amounts not allowed as deductions in one year can be carried forward and may be deducted in future years.

Other expenses and deductions that are permitted for Canadian purposes, such as RRSP contributions, one-half of the stock option benefit (see 10.4.2) and the capital gains exemption (see 6.4), are not allowed on your U.S. return.

### 18.3.3 Retirement and profit-sharing plans

RRSPs, TFSAs, RESPs, RPPs, RDSPs and DPSPs (see Chapters 3 and 4) can cause problems for U.S. citizens because they are not given any special status in the U.S. Internal Revenue Code.

Employer contributions to a registered pension plan or a deferred profit-sharing plan are exempt from immediate Canadian tax (see 10.1.1). As we saw in 3.5.1, you are taxed on the funds only when you receive them (usually on retirement).

> Beware of differences between Canadian and U.S. rules governing retirement income.

For U.S. tax purposes, there is no such exemption. The amount contributed by your employer is treated as an employment benefit and is taxed once the contributions have vested (that is, you are entitled to them even if you leave your employment). Furthermore, these amounts are explicitly excluded from the definition of "foreign earned income" under U.S. tax law, so you cannot make use of the foreign earned income exclusion (see 18.2.1). You may have to pay U.S. tax on these contributions, depending on the circumstances and the amount of your unused foreign tax credit carryover. When you later withdraw the funds, they should not be taxable in the U.S.

Your own contributions to an RRSP or RPP, which are deductible on your Canadian return, are not deductible for U.S. tax purposes unless the treaty specifically allows a deduction.

Defer U.S. taxation of income accruing in your RRSP and other Canadian retirement plans.

Income accruing in your RRSP, RRIF and other Canadian retirement plans (see Chapter 3) would normally be taxable in the U.S. As noted in 18.2.3, the Canada-U.S. tax treaty allows you to elect each year to defer the taxation of the accruing income until you actually receive the funds from the plan. This allows you to report the income in the same year for Canadian and U.S. purposes.

Previously, the election to defer income from an RRSP/RRIF was made on Form 8891. In 2014, the Internal Revenue Services announced that Form 8891 was no longer required as part of the income tax return and that the election to defer income from an RRSP/RRIF would be automatic.

Income earned in your TFSA and RESP is taxable in the U.S. because these plans have no special status in the U.S. Internal Revenue Code or the Canada-U.S. tax treaty. These plans are likely to be considered foreign trusts for U.S. purposes, which require additional annual reporting of contributions, distributions and earnings (see 18.7.4). U.S. citizens should consider the onerous filing requirements before deciding to invest in these plans. If you have existing plans with only modest amounts invested, you may want to consider collapsing the plans to avoid the additional annual filing requirements.

If you contribute to a regular IRA (U.S. Individual Retirement Account), your contributions are not deductible for Canadian tax purposes. Income accruing in an IRA is not taxed by Canada. When you withdraw funds from an IRA, Canada generally taxes the same amount that you would have had to include in your income under U.S. laws if you were a resident of the U.S. at the time of withdrawal. While you may be able to transfer lump sum payments received from an IRA into an RRSP free of Canadian tax, the amount transferred would be subject to U.S. tax. Foreign tax credits may alleviate double taxation.

Contributions to a U.S. deferred income plan by a U.S. employer may be taxable in Canada as an employment benefit or "retirement compensation arrangement" (see 10.5.4).

The Canada-U.S. tax treaty now allows deductions in one country for certain contributions to pension plans in the other country. These rules generally apply to cross-border commuters, employees on temporary assignment and U.S. citizens in Canada.

Employees temporarily transferred from Canada to the U.S. (for no more than 60 months in the 120 preceding months) can continue to contribute to their Canadian qualified plan and claim a deduction on their U.S. tax return, provided they were resident in Canada and participating in the Canadian plan before they began performing services in the U.S. Similar rules apply for U.S. residents who are temporarily transferred to Canada.

Cross-border commuters can contribute to a qualified plan in the country where they work and claim a deduction in the country where they are resident. U.S. citizens resident in Canada who work in Canada and contribute to a Canadian qualified plan can claim a deduction on their U.S. tax returns.

The use of non-qualified deferred compensation plans in the U.S. is discouraged by the related tax implications. Deferred compensation arises when an individual is entitled to receive an amount in a year that is not paid until a later year. These rules affect certain deferred stock unit plans, bonuses and other deferred compensation; stock option and stock appreciation rights plans that are not issued at a discount are exempt.

**Beware of non-qualified deferred compensation plans.**

Under these rules, only deferred compensation plans that meet specific distribution criteria allow recognition of income to be deferred. Additionally, the employee/director may need to make an election before the year in which the services are being performed if there is any employee discretion in the timing of the payments. If the plan does not meet the distribution requirements, the "deferred" compensation is fully taxable and a 20% U.S. penalty tax and interest charges apply.

If the amount is subject to substantial risk of forfeiture, it should not be included in current income until this substantial risk of forfeiture no longer exists (usually on the vesting date).

U.S. citizens with Canadian employers should tread with extra care in this area as their employers may not be designing their deferred compensation plans with the U.S. tax rules in mind.

### 18.3.4 Dividends
As we saw in 7.1.2, Canada taxes dividends from Canadian corporations using the "gross-up and credit" system, which results in less tax being levied than on other kinds of income. For U.S. purposes, most dividends are taxed at a lower rate (up to a maximum of 20% in 2017). The actual amount that

you receive, rather than the grossed-up amount, is included in income for U.S. purposes.

### 18.3.5 Canadian corporations earning passive income

Owning an interest in a Canadian corporation that earns passive income can result in an unexpected U.S. tax liability. Under U.S. law, if you invest in a non-U.S. corporation that earns a substantial part of its income from investments (a "passive foreign investment corporation") and then sell the stock or receive an "excess" distribution, there may be a theoretical deferral of U.S. tax (which would have applied if you had earned the investment income directly). In such a case, an interest charge on this "deferred tax" may be imposed under U.S. tax law.

Watch out for ownership of Canadian corporations and funds earning passive income.

There is no minimum U.S. ownership required in a Canadian corporation to be subject to these rules. Capital gains would be treated as ordinary income for U.S. purposes, resulting in higher U.S. tax. Dividends from passive foreign investment corporations are not eligible for the lower U.S. tax rate.

There are ways to avoid the interest charge, however. One way is to elect to include your *pro rata* share of the corporation's earnings in your U.S. income on a current basis each year (which may result in a mismatching of income and foreign tax credits for Canadian and U.S. purposes).

Different rules apply if the investment income is earned in a Canadian corporation of which more than 50% of the votes or value is owned by U.S. shareholders who each own more than 10% of the votes. In these cases, the controlled foreign corporation rules require an annual income inclusion by the U.S. shareholders if the corporation earns passive income.

The passive foreign investment corporation rules and the controlled foreign corporation rules both impose onerous filing requirements on U.S. shareholders, and significant penalties may apply if you fail to file the forms on time. Annual planning is needed to avoid double taxation.

### 18.3.6 U.S. taxation of Canadian income fund investments

Most Canadian fund investments should be considered foreign corporations for U.S. purposes. The earnings distributed (including capital gains distributions) would be taxable as ordinary income for U.S. purposes. Capital distributions (i.e., return of capital) should not be taxable for U.S. purposes, provided all of the earnings have been distributed. (The Canadian taxation of income fund investments is discussed at 7.3.2.)

If you invest in Canadian funds, including mutual funds, unit trusts and exchange traded funds, consider the impact of the passive foreign investment company rules on your tax liability and filing requirements in the U.S., including annual reporting requirements for investments in foreign corporations.

### 18.3.7 Charitable donations

As discussed in 8.1, charitable donations of up to 75% of your net income entitle you to a credit for Canadian federal tax purposes (see 17.7.1 if you live in Quebec).

For Canadian tax purposes, charitable donations must normally be made to a Canadian charity to qualify (subject to certain specific exceptions). The Canada-U.S. tax treaty, however, provides that donations to U.S. charities will qualify, up to a limit of 75% of your U.S.-source net income. You need to obtain receipts from the U.S. charities to support your claim.

Similarly, charitable donations are normally deductible in the U.S., subject to a limit of 50% of income for donations to public charities or 30% of income for donations to private foundations. However, donations to Canadian charities may only be deducted for U.S. tax purposes to the extent of 50% or 30% of your *Canadian-source* "adjusted gross income".

### 18.3.8 Moving expenses

Moving expenses paid by your employer are not taxable benefits for Canadian purposes (see 13.1.3). For U.S. purposes, no taxable benefit arises if your employer pays for the cost of moving your household goods and for transporting you and your family. If your employer pays additional amounts for you, such as real estate commission on the sale of your home, this amount is included in your taxable employment income for U.S. tax purposes. This could cause an additional U.S. tax liability which, in many cases, your employer would reimburse to you. Such reimbursements are also taxable benefits.

## 18.4 Differences in taxation of capital gains

### 18.4.1 Basic calculation

The field of capital gains is where you find the most glaring differences between the Canadian and U.S. tax systems. Not only are many details different, but the basic scheme of taxation of capital gains is itself fundamentally different, which creates problems for U.S. citizens resident in Canada.

For Canadian tax purposes, only one-half of capital gains are taxed (see 6.2.1).

For U.S. tax purposes, short-term capital gains from property held for one year or less are normally taxed like other income, at your marginal rate (see table in 18.1 above). However, the rate for long-term capital gains (generally from property held more than 12 months) is limited to 20%, 15%, or even 0%, depending on your tax bracket. Certain gains and depreciation recapture are subject to a maximum rate of 25%. Keep in mind that the foreign exchange rate can significantly affect your total tax liability.

> **Example**
>
> Jeff purchases 100 shares of XYZ Corporation on the Toronto Stock Exchange when the Canadian dollar is at US70¢. He pays $20 per share including commission, or Cdn$2,000 (US$1,400). He sells the shares several years later, when the Canadian and U.S. dollars are at par, for $19 each (after commission), or Cdn$1,900 (US$1,900).
>
> For Canadian tax purposes, Jeff has a $100 capital loss, one-half of which can be deducted against taxable capital gains. For U.S. tax purposes, however, Jeff has a $500 capital gain, which is taxed. Since he does not pay any Canadian tax on the gain, no foreign tax credit is available to offset his tax (maximum 20%) on US$500.

### 18.4.2 Use of capital losses

For Canadian purposes, allowable capital losses (one-half of your capital losses) can only be used to offset taxable capital gains, though they can be carried back three years and forward indefinitely against such gains (see 6.2.2). An exception exists for allowable business investment losses (on shares or debt of small business corporations), which can be used against any income (see 6.2.3).

For U.S. purposes, capital losses can only be used against capital gains. In addition, US$3,000 of capital losses can be written off against other income (US$1,500 for a married person filing separately). Unused capital losses can be carried forward (but not back) to be applied against capital gains or against US$3,000 (or US$1,500) per year of other income in any future year. Keep in mind that carrying back capital losses in Canada reduces the Canadian tax that is available as a foreign tax credit on the U.S. return for the carryback year.

### 18.4.3 The Canadian capital gains exemption

A lifetime capital gains exemption is available in Canada for certain small business shares and farm and fishing property (see 6.4.1 and 6.4.2). No such exemption exists for U.S. tax purposes.

*Be cautious of using the Canadian lifetime capital gains exemption.*

If you sell small business corporation shares or farm property, the Canadian lifetime capital gains exemption won't protect you from U.S. tax on the gain, even if you are not subject to Canadian tax. Generally, you should steer clear of the options discussed in 14.1 to "crystallize" your gains and use up your exemption.

### 18.4.4 Foreign exchange gains or losses

When you sell Canadian property, you must calculate your gain for U.S. tax purposes using the U.S. dollar equivalent of your cost, as of the date you purchased the property. The proceeds are converted at the exchange rate in effect at the date of sale. This treatment can lead to a foreign exchange gain or loss that is independent of your (Canadian-dollar) gain or loss on the property.

Similarly, when you sell U.S. property, your gain for Canadian purposes must be calculated in Canadian dollars.

### 18.4.5 Pre-1972 holdings

As noted in 6.5.4, Canada taxes only capital gains accrued since 1972. The U.S. does not have any such rule. If you are a U.S. citizen and have owned property since before 1972, your gain for U.S. tax purposes could be substantially higher than your gain for Canadian tax purposes.

### 18.4.6 Principal residence

As we saw in 6.5.2, a gain on a "principal residence" is normally completely exempt from tax in Canada. The U.S. rules related to sales of a principal residence are very different from the Canadian rules and are more restrictive.

Under the U.S. rules, you may claim an exclusion of up to US$250,000 of gain on a principal residence. The exclusion is increased up to US$500,000 for spouses filing jointly.

Certain requirements must be met to claim the exclusion; for example, you and your spouse must have actually occupied the home for at least two of the past five years, and neither you nor your spouse must have claimed this exclusion in the past two years. Exceptions from the holding period requirement may apply in the event of a relocation for employment, health problems or unforeseen circumstances.

If you and your spouse file jointly but do not share a principal residence, the US$250,000 exclusion is available on the sale of one of the principal residences. Similarly, you can claim the US$250,000 exclusion if you marry someone who has used the exclusion in the past two years.

Be careful if you and your spouse sell more than one home during the two-year period. You would have to pay tax on the entire gain arising on one of the homes.

A further difference between Canadian and U.S. exemptions for a principal residence lies in the definition of the term. As we saw in 6.5.2, a vacation property such as a cottage generally qualifies for Canadian tax purposes, although you can only designate one principal residence for each year. For U.S. purposes, a home only qualifies if it is the place where you "regularly reside".

The U.S. rules provide that the gain will not be excluded if you put the property to a non-qualified use (e.g., you did not use it as a principal residence) after December 31, 2008, with certain exceptions for temporary absences.

### 18.4.7 Other capital gains differences

Canada and the U.S. have very different rules with respect to the transfer of capital property to corporations or partnerships, corporate reorganizations, estate freezes, mergers, windups, recapitalizations, debt forgiveness, etc. Investments in U.S. limited liability companies and "S corporations" also result in a mismatching of income recognition between Canada and the U.S. and higher effective tax rates. If you are involved in such transactions, professional advice is essential, especially since both systems continuously change.

## 18.5 Minimum tax

Canada's minimum tax was discussed in 7.6. The U.S. alternative minimum tax (AMT) has the same general structure, but there are some important differences.

First, the U.S. AMT exemption for 2017 is US$84,500 for married taxpayers filing jointly (or a surviving spouse) and US$54,300 for a single taxpayer. The U.S. exemption is phased out for those with adjusted minimum taxable income over US$160,900 if married filing jointly (US$120,700 if filing as a single taxpayer).

Second, the U.S. AMT rate is calculated under a two-tier graduated rate schedule. A 26% rate applies to the first US$187,800 of alternative minimum taxable income over the AMT exemption amount, and a 28% rate applies to alternative minimum taxable income over US$187,800. The 28% rate comes into effect for alternative minimum taxable income over US$93,900 for married individuals filing separate returns. For long-term capital gains, the AMT rate is reduced to a maximum of 20%.

Third, the list of "AMT adjustments"—items added back to income for AMT purposes—is, of course, different between the two countries. For U.S. tax purposes, the list includes the standard deduction, itemized property and state taxes paid, oil and gas drilling costs, mining exploration and development costs, a portion of accelerated depreciation, certain stock option benefits and various other specific deductions.

Married U.S. citizens who file separately and have significant itemized deductions often owe AMT on their U.S. tax returns because the AMT calculation for married couples filing separately requires a "phantom" addition to AMT income if AMT income exceeds certain thresholds.

## 18.6  Income earned by children

### 18.6.1  Effects on dependent deduction

If you claim a deduction for a dependent child (US$4,050) on your U.S. return, that child may not claim the regular personal exemption on his or her own tax return. The effect is that any income the child earns is taxed.

### 18.6.2  Attribution rules

> **Caution: The Canadian tax planning ideas discussed in this section may be affected by the federal government's proposed new tax regime for private companies, as outlined in the Department of Finance's July 2017 consultation paper and draft legislation. See Appendix I for details.**

We discussed the Canadian attribution rules for minor children in 5.2.3. The basic rule is that if you give or lend funds to your child, the income from those funds (but not the capital gains) are taxed in your hands, rather than the child's, until the year your child turns 18.

The U.S. tax system accomplishes the same general anti-income-splitting objective in a very different way. The income of the child is taxed in the child's hands but may in part be taxed at the parent's marginal tax rate.

*Review income splitting arrangements to prevent double taxation.*

The first US$1,000 of unearned income (roughly equivalent in meaning to Canadian "income from property") of a child under 18 is not taxed. The next US$1,000 is taxed as the child's income. Beyond US$2,000, if the child has no *earned* income (compensation for services rendered), any further unearned income is taxed at the rate of the parent with the greater taxable income. So, beyond the US$2,000 level, little is usually gained from a tax point of view by having a child under 18 earn investment income.

This U.S. "income splitting tax" also applies to children aged 18 to 23 who are full-time students and whose earned income is less than half of their annual support.

If certain requirements are met, the parent whose taxable income is used for calculating the child's tax rate may elect to include the child's income directly. Doing so eliminates the need to file a tax return for the child and leads to a better matching of incomes between the Canadian and U.S. tax systems.

Income splitting arrangements that are set up for Canadian income tax purposes can result in double taxation if you are not careful. For example, suppose you and your 13-year-old son are both U.S. citizens, your son has no income, and you lend funds to him with the intention of building up "secondary" income over time that will not be attributed back to you (see 5.3.5). The income on the funds you have lent would be taxed in your hands under Canadian law but in your son's hands (albeit at your marginal rate while the child is under 18) under U.S. law. Because different taxpayers are paying the tax, no foreign tax credit would be available and you may end up being taxed twice on the same income.

In this example, you may be able to elect to include his unearned income on your return for U.S. tax purposes. That should solve the double taxation problem, since the income would be taxed in your hands under both systems. However, there are limits on the availability of this election.

Bear in mind that attribution problems may arise in certain cases if you and your spouse do not file a joint U.S. return (see 18.7.1). For example, if you give your spouse Cdn$100,000 to invest and the investment earns Cdn$10,000 in Canadian-source dividend income, you would pay Canadian tax on the income and your spouse will pay the U.S. tax. If you and your spouse file a joint U.S. return, all Canadian taxes would be combined for foreign tax credit purposes. But if you and your spouse do not file jointly, no foreign tax credit would be available because different taxpayers are taxable on the income.

In addition, if the income earned by your spouse is U.S.-source income, your spouse would be taxable on the income for U.S. purposes and you would be taxable on the income for Canadian purposes. Canada would not provide you with a foreign tax credit for U.S. tax paid by your spouse, resulting in double tax.

## 18.7 U.S. filing requirements

### 18.7.1 Joint return or not?

For federal Canadian tax purposes, every taxpayer is distinct and must file separately. Combining the income of two spouses is only considered for certain specific purposes, such as eligibility for the GST/HST credit (see 2.9.3).

For U.S. tax purposes, you have the option of filing a joint return with your spouse. If one spouse has little or no income, this usually results in less tax than if you file as "married filing separately".

For U.S. purposes, a joint return is mandatory (if you are married) if you wish to claim certain deductions and credits. The child care credit is one example. Another is the US$25,000 loss allowance for an owner who actively participates in rental real estate.

If you do not have a spouse, your filing status is "single", "head of household" or "surviving spouse", all of which have different implications for your U.S. tax return.

> If you're married, file a joint U.S. return where appropriate.

If your spouse is a U.S. citizen, the decision as to whether to file jointly can be made annually. If your spouse is not a U.S. citizen, the decision to file jointly can only be made once.

If your spouse is not a U.S. citizen, has no U.S.-source income and thus is not subject to U.S. tax, consider filing a "married filing separate" return. As a "non-resident alien", your spouse's Canadian income is not relevant for U.S. tax purposes. By contrast, if your spouse has little income from any source but you are paying tax to the U.S., you may elect to include the spouse's income on your joint return. In this case, filing a joint return can be beneficial, as it gives you larger exclusions and wider tax brackets at the lower rates.

If you elect to file jointly with a non-resident alien spouse, you must always file jointly unless the election is revoked; however, once revoked, the decision can never be made again (unless you have a new spouse).

You should also keep in mind that the Canadian election to split pension income (see 20.3.6) is not relevant for U.S. tax purposes. The individual who earns the pension is required to report it for U.S. tax purposes.

### 18.7.2 Time requirements for filing

The requirements for filing Canadian tax returns are discussed in 9.1.

U.S. tax returns must normally be postmarked by April 15 each year.

If you are a U.S. citizen whose "tax home" (place of employment) and "abode" (place of residence) are *both* outside the U.S., your filing deadline is automatically extended to June 15 each year. You must attach a statement to your return identifying that you are eligible for this extension.

If you are unable to meet your U.S. filing deadline, you may file for an extension of the deadline to October 15. The extension will be granted automatically.

Even though you are permitted to file your return in June or October, you must pay your balance owing by April 15. Interest on any balance of taxes owing will accrue from April 15.

### 18.7.3 Estimated taxes

We discussed the Canadian tax instalment requirements in 9.2.2. The U.S. has parallel requirements, which are called payments of "estimated taxes".

Estimated tax payments are due quarterly, on April 15, June 15, September 15 and the following January 15. As with the Canadian system, you can generally choose either last year's tax or this year's tax as the basis for your quarterly estimated tax payments.

If you base your payments on the current year's tax, you need only pay 90% of the year's tax liability (regular tax or AMT) in estimated tax payments—22.5% each quarter. If you use last year's tax, you must normally pay 25% of that amount each quarter (or 27.5% each quarter if your prior-year adjusted gross income exceeded US$150,000). In order to use last year's tax, you must have filed a return in the previous year and the year must have been a 12-month period.

In either case, any balance still owing is due with your tax return. No estimated tax payments are required if your total tax for the year is less than US$1,000.

If you do not make your estimated tax payments on time, non-deductible late payment penalties will apply.

### 18.7.4 Disclosure requirements

As well as filing a tax return, you must disclose a substantial amount of financial information under U.S. law.

First, you must disclose holdings in any non-U.S. corporations that you and certain family members control directly or indirectly, or in which you have increased or decreased your interest. You must provide this information for each foreign corporation by filing a separate Form 5471, "Information Return of U.S. Persons with Respect to Certain Foreign Corporations". The IRS uses this information, among other things, to help determine your liability for tax on any undistributed income of closely held non-U.S. corporations that earn passive income.

Similar reporting rules are now in place for investments in foreign partnerships and foreign disregarded entities. This information is disclosed by filing Form 8865, "Return of U.S. Persons with Respect to Certain Foreign Partnerships", and Form 8858, "Information Return of U.S. Persons with Respect to Foreign Disregarded Entities".

In some cases, a Canadian corporation's reporting year must be the calendar year for U.S. reporting purposes.

Second, you are required to file a "Report of Foreign Bank and Financial Accounts" form annually with the U.S. Department of the Treasury if the total value of your foreign (non-U.S.) bank accounts, brokerage accounts, RRSPs, etc. exceeds US$10,000 at any time in the year. You must report:

- accounts where you have signing authority but no financial interests

- accounts of any entity in which you own directly or indirectly more than 50% of the voting power, equity, assets or profits
- accounts of trusts in which you have a greater than 50% beneficial interest in assets or income.

For tax years beginning on or after January 1, 2016, the due date for this form is automatically extended to October 15. This form must be filed electronically. A penalty of up to US$10,000 applies for non-willful violations of the disclosure rules. For willful violations, the penalty can be as high as US$100,000.

Third, if you hold foreign financial assets that exceed a specific dollar threshold, you are required to report certain information about these assets on Form 8938, "Statement of Foreign Financial Assets". The dollar threshold, which depends on your filing status and where you live, can be as low as US$50,000 of foreign financial assets. A higher threshold applies for taxpayers living outside the U.S.—US$200,000 for unmarried or married filing separately and US$400,000 for married filing jointly.

Specified foreign financial assets include bank accounts, investment accounts, RRSPs, RRIFs, registered pensions, equity compensation plans (for example, stock options), shares of private corporations, interests in partnerships, and certain non-U.S. life insurance policies.

If you meet the filing requirements for the "Statement of Foreign Financial Assets" and "Report of Foreign Bank and Financial Accounts", you have to file both even though some of the information may be the same.

Fourth, if you have interests in certain Canadian corporations that earn investment income and certain types of funds, you are required to file Form 8621, "Information Return by a Shareholder of a Passive Foreign Investment Company or Qualified Electing Fund" for each passive foreign investment company in which you have an interest. Canadian corporations that earn investment income and are not controlled by U.S. persons, as well as most Canadian mutual funds and exchange traded funds, are considered passive foreign investment companies.

Finally, as discussed in 18.8.4, reporting rules also apply for certain gifts and bequests over US$100,000 received in one year. Any transfers to and from foreign trusts (including loans) must also be reported by filing Form 3520, "Annual Return to Report Transactions with Foreign Trusts and Receipt of Certain Foreign Gifts". If you are treated as the owner of a foreign grantor trust (such as an alter ego or joint partner trust), you must report annually on Form 3520A. Form 3520 is due at the same time as your U.S. personal tax return. Form 3520A is due on March 15 (i.e., before your U.S. personal tax return). An extension of the filing date for Form 3520A is available, but you must file your application for the extension by March 15.

Canadian TFSAs and RESPs are generally considered foreign trusts for U.S. tax purposes. If you have a TFSA or have contributed to an RESP, you should file Form 3520 and Form 3520A each year. In addition to the U.S. reporting requirements for foreign trusts, the income in your TFSA and RESP is taxable on your U.S. tax return each year (see 18.3.3).

Severe penalties apply under U.S. law for not complying with these reporting requirements.

## 18.8 U.S. gift and estate taxes

U.S. gift and estate taxes are part of a complex tax system for property transfers that has no equivalent in Canada. The transfer tax applies to transfers made during your lifetime (gift tax) and at death (estate tax).

In 2017, estate taxes is levied on a graduated scale based on the cumulative value of all gifts made during your lifetime and at death, ranging from 18% to 40%. The 40% rate applies to cumulative transfers over US$1 million.

In this section, we discuss how the gift and estate tax rules apply to U.S. citizens residing in Canada. If you are a non-U.S. citizen who owns U.S. property, see 19.4.

### 18.8.1 Lifetime gift and estate tax credit

U.S. citizens are permitted a lifetime estate tax credit to offset the transfer tax on US$5.49 million for 2017.

U.S. citizens are also permitted a lifetime gift tax exemption, which is set at US$5.49 million in 2017. Any exemption amount used for gifts reduces the amount available on death.

### 18.8.2 Gift tax

Canada does not have a gift tax, although the giver of a gift (except to a spouse) is deemed to have sold the property at its current fair market value, possibly leading to income tax on a resulting taxable capital gain (see 6.5.4).

The U.S. does have a gift tax, which applies only to those who make very substantial gifts. The *giver* is liable for the tax. Where the giver and recipient are spouses who are both U.S. citizens, no gift tax applies at all. Otherwise, if only the giver is a U.S. citizen, gift tax may apply.

The gift tax generally does not apply to gifts to charities, U.S. political parties, and amounts given directly to institutions to pay for another person's tuition or medical expenses.

Up to US$14,000 may be given tax-free each year to any number of donees and up to US$149,000 to a spouse who is not a U.S. citizen.

A common estate planning strategy is to use the US$14,000 annual gift tax exclusion to transfer wealth to children and grandchildren. For the gift to be eligible for the exclusion, the recipient must have the right to use the gift without restriction. In these cases, steps should be taken to ensure that an adult retains control over the assets while the child remains a minor, such as opening a *Uniform Gift to Minors Act* account in the U.S. or establishing a formal trust (with certain powers for the child to ensure that the exclusion will apply).

> Consider using the annual US$14,000 U.S. gift tax exclusion to transfer wealth to children and grandchildren.

The Canadian tax (if any) that applies on a gift is an income tax, while the U.S. tax is not. As a result, no foreign tax credit applies in either system for taxes of the other system. Caution must therefore be exercised if you are making large gifts. A further problem with gifts is that, for U.S. purposes, your cost base of property (plus a portion of the gift tax paid) carries through to the recipient of a gift, whereas on death, any property left to your beneficiaries is treated as acquired by them at its fair market value. In Canada, the cost base to the recipient is increased to fair market value at the time of the gift or death (except for transfers to spouses).

You must also watch out for the Canadian attribution rules, as outlined in Chapter 5.

The Canada-U.S. tax treaty does not provide any relief for U.S. gift tax, although you can elect to have a deemed disposition for U.S. purposes in order to match income recognition in the U.S. and Canada. Making this election would allow you to increase the property's cost base to its fair market value at the time the gift is made. However, making the election does not reduce any gift tax payable or allow you to claim foreign tax credits for income tax against gift tax or vice versa.

As discussed below in 18.8.4, U.S. recipients of gifts from foreign individuals must also report gifts received if they exceed US$100,000 in a calendar year.

## 18.8.3  Estate tax

The U.S. imposes estate tax on death of U.S. citizens based on the fair market value of the deceased's gross estate, which includes all worldwide assets owned at death, regardless of whether the assets pass outside the will.

If the gross estate exceeds US$5.49 million in 2017, an estate tax return must be filed within nine months after the date of death, even if no estate tax is payable. Under the U.S. rules, the executor of the estate is personally liable for any taxes and penalties owed by the estate until official clearance is granted by the IRS.

The taxable estate is determined by deducting debts of the deceased (including the Canadian tax liability) and funeral and certain other death-related expenses from the value of the estate. The taxable estate is subject to graduated rates that reach 40% estate tax on amounts over US$1 million.

An unlimited marital deduction is provided for any amounts left to your spouse on death, if your spouse is a U.S. citizen. As a result, leaving all of your estate to your U.S. citizen spouse will result in no estate tax applying on your death.

Changes to U.S. law introduced "portability" for U.S. citizen spouses for deaths after 2010. Any amount of the US$5.49 million exemption amount not used by the first spouse to die is available to the surviving spouse. However, you should still consider taking steps so that the increase in value after the death of the first spouse to die is not subject to U.S. estate tax.

To use the portability provisions, a U.S. estate tax return must be filed for the first spouse to die in order to calculate the exemption amount available to the surviving spouse even if the estate value is less than US$5.49 million.

Generally, a marital deduction for a transfer to a U.S. citizen spouse is only permitted for property passing to the spouse outright with no restrictions on its use. But you may intend for the assets to be used by your spouse and pass to your children or others on your spouse's death, even if, for example, your spouse remarries. Such property may be treated as "qualified terminal interest property", which is eligible for the marital deduction if an election is made on the estate tax return and certain other requirements are met.

If you hold property jointly with a non-U.S. citizen spouse or other individual, the value of the property's inclusion in your gross estate would be based on the proportionate initial contribution to purchase the property. As such, it is important to save receipts or other documentation relating to property purchased jointly with others.

Life insurance proceeds are subject to U.S. estate tax if the insured had a beneficial interest in the policy, such as a right to change beneficiaries, borrow against the policy or cancel the policy. Certain options are available to minimize the estate tax burden on life insurance proceeds, including the use of life insurance trusts and gifting plans. To use these options, advice from an estate planning professional is essential.

Some items in an individual's estate are subject to both U.S. income and estate taxes. These items include accrued compensation or commissions for personal services received after death, investment income, instalment sales, employment survivor benefits and retirement plans such as IRAs. Planning options may be available to reduce the resulting double taxation. For example, you could gift income-producing assets to individuals or trusts during your lifetime or bequeath specific assets to charities. Professional advice on implementing these options is recommended.

### 18.8.4 U.S. reporting rules for gifts and foreign trusts

As a U.S. citizen, you must file an annual gift tax return if your gifts to one individual made in the calendar year exceed the annual US$14,000 exclusion (or US$149,000 to a non-U.S. citizen spouse), if you elect to split gifts with your U.S.-citizen spouse, or if any gifts are in trust. The return is due at the same time as your regular U.S. personal income tax return.

If you are a U.S. citizen and you transfer money or property to a foreign trust or receive a distribution from one, you must report the transfer to the IRS. The penalty for not complying with these reporting rules is 35% of the gross value of the money or property transferred, and additional penalties for continued failure can run up to 100% of the transferred amount.

> Beware of U.S. gift and foreign trust reporting rules.

U.S. citizens must also report each gift or bequest received in a year if the total of all gifts and bequests received from any foreign person or foreign estate in that year is more than US$100,000. Penalties for non-compliance are substantial.

If you are treated as the owner of a foreign grantor trust (e.g., alter ego trust, RESP or TFSA), you must file Form 3520A, "Annual Information Return for Foreign Trust with a U.S. Owner", each year by March 15 of the following year or apply for an extension by that date.

### 18.8.5 Generation-skipping transfer tax

The U.S. imposes a special tax to ensure gifts and bequests made to grandchildren do not skip a level of transfer taxation as a result of bypassing the intermediate generation. The generation-skipping transfer tax adds an additional tax on transfers from grandparents to their grandchildren or great-grandchildren that results in the same net gift that would have resulted had the gift passed from grandparent to parent to grandchild or great-grandchild.

A lifetime exemption of US$5.49 million is available to offset the generation-skipping tax in 2017. This exemption is separate from the lifetime exemption for estate and gift taxes discussed in 18.8.1. Making the election to use this exemption is extremely complex and should not be done without professional advice. Additionally, transfers to trusts having direct or contingent beneficiaries who are significantly younger than you should be made in consultation with a qualified tax adviser.

## 18.9 If you expatriate from the U.S.

**Consider expatriating from the U.S. to protect your Canadian assets from U.S. tax and simplify your tax filing obligations.**

If you are a U.S. citizen or green card holder living in Canada, you may wish to expatriate from the U.S. by renouncing your U.S. citizenship or surrendering your green card to protect your Canadian income from U.S. income tax and your Canadian assets from U.S. estate, gift and generation-skipping transfer taxes (see 18.8).

If you are considering expatriating, professional advice is recommended. You may be subject to tax consequences if:

- your average annual U.S. income tax liability exceeded US$162,000 in the five years before expatriation
- your net worth exceeds US$2 million at the time of expatriation, or
- you cannot certify that you have complied with all U.S. federal tax obligations for the five years preceding expatriation.

If you meet one of the above conditions, you are considered a "covered expatriate" and you might be treated as if you had sold all your property for its fair market value on the day before you expatriate and you would owe tax on any capital gain over US$699,000 for 2017. You can defer paying the tax until the property is sold but you will be charged interest on the deferred tax. You will not be able to claim a foreign tax credit to offset any foreign tax that may apply when you sell the property in a future year. Special income recognition rules apply in the year of expatriation to certain assets, including retirement plans (e.g., IRAs, RRSPs), tax-deferred accounts and interests in certain types of trusts. Before expatriating, planning should be undertaken to reduce the exposure to tax to the U.S. citizen at the time of expatriation and to U.S. citizen beneficiaries of estates or gifts.

Once you have expatriated, any U.S. citizen or resident (except for your spouse or a charity) who receives a gift or bequest from you at any time in the future may be required to pay tax on the transfer at the highest applicable rate of gift or estate tax (40% for 2017). This tax does not apply if you are subject to U.S. gift tax or estate tax (for example, if the property transferred is U.S. real estate). No credits would be allowed in Canada for gift or estate tax paid by the U.S. recipient.

If you were both a Canadian and U.S. citizen from the time of your birth, you have not resided in the U.S. for more than 10 of the 15 years before expatriation, and you reside in Canada at the time of expatriation, then you only need to meet the third test above (i.e., five years of tax compliance) in order to not be considered a "covered expatriate".

If you expatriated before June 17, 2008, different rules apply.

"Long-term" green card holders who surrender their green cards are subject to the same taxation rules as U.S. citizens. You are considered a long-term green card holder if you have held a green card in eight out of the last 15 years. Part of a year counts as a year for these purposes. For example, if you obtained a green card on December 28, 2010, you must count 2010 as one year and you would be considered a long-term green card holder starting on January 1, 2017.

Even if your green card is no longer valid for immigration purposes, you are considered a green card holder for tax purposes until you officially surrender your green card at a border crossing or U.S. consulate.

You should seek professional advice before renouncing your U.S. citizenship or surrendering your green card. You should also be aware that your green card can be taken from you if you are not residing in the U.S. and the expatriation rules above would apply at that time.

## 18.10 References

The following publications and more information, including forms and brochures, can be obtained on the CRA's website at *www.cra-arc.gc.ca* or by telephone request at 1-800-959-8281 for individual income tax and trust-related enquiries or 1-800-959-5525 for business and self-employed individual enquiries.

> Income Tax Folio S5-F1-C1, "Determining an Individual's Residence Status"
> Income Tax Folio S5-F2-C1, "Foreign Tax Credit"
> Interpretation Bulletin IT-506, Archived – "Foreign income taxes as a deduction from income"

The following technical publications may be obtained from any office of the Internal Revenue Service, and are generally available at U.S. embassy and consular offices, or from the IRS's website at *www.irs.gov.*

> Publication 17, "Your Federal Income Tax"
> Publication 54, "Tax Guide for U.S. Citizens and Resident Aliens Abroad"
> Publication 514, "Foreign Tax Credit for Individuals"
> Publication 519, "U.S. Tax Guide for Aliens"
> Publication 521, "Moving Expenses"
> Publication 523, "Selling Your Home"

# Chapter 19

## If you visit, work or own property in the U.S.

- Avoid becoming a U.S. resident while visiting (19.1.1)
- If you own rental real estate in the U.S., elect the net rental income method (19.2.3)
- Beware of high effective tax rates when considering an investment in a U.S. limited liability corporation (19.2.5)
- Ensure a U.S. tax return is filed for every disposition of U.S. real property (19.3.1)
- Consider applying for a U.S. "withholding certificate" on the sale of real estate (19.3.1)
- Be cautious when acquiring shares in U.S. corporations due to potential U.S. estate tax (19.4.1)
- Leave U.S. property to your spouse or a qualified trust (19.4.5)
- Mortgage property (non-recourse) to reduce the value of your U.S. real estate (19.4.5)
- Acquire property jointly with your spouse or another person (19.4.5)
- Split your worldwide assets with your spouse (19.4.5)
- Consider a split interest purchase with your child (19.4.5)
- Hold your U.S. property through a Canadian corporation (19.4.5)
- Hold your U.S. assets through a properly structured trust or a Canadian partnership that elects to be treated as a corporation in the U.S. (19.4.5)
- Sell U.S. property before death (19.4.5)
- Consider taking out life insurance to cover U.S. estate taxes (19.4.5)

*In this chapter, we discuss the United States taxes that apply to Canadian residents who are not U.S. citizens and who acquire U.S. investments such as stocks and real estate. (Taxation of U.S. citizens resident in Canada is covered in Chapter 18.) Such investments are taxed in four ways: on the income they generate; on their sale; on gift; and on death of the owner. We also discuss the "snowbird" rules that can make you resident in the U.S. for tax purposes.*

*The interaction between the U.S. and Canadian tax systems can be highly complex. Cross-border transactions should be undertaken only with qualified professional tax advice.*

## 19.1 U.S. residency rules for Canadians

As a Canadian, you can become resident in the U.S. for tax purposes if you spend a significant amount of time in the U.S. or if you hold a green card.

### 19.1.1 Snowbirds

If you spend a substantial portion of the year in the U.S., you may become a U.S. resident for tax purposes. If this happens you may be required to file tax returns and additional reporting forms in the U.S., even if you are deemed resident in Canada under the Canada-U.S. tax treaty's "tie-breaker" rules described below. If you become a U.S. resident for tax purposes, the cost of complying with filing requirements can be substantial.

*Avoid becoming a U.S. resident while visiting.*

If you are physically present in the U.S. for a significant number of days (183 days or more in a three-year period, as calculated below), you may meet the substantial presence test, causing you to be deemed a U.S. resident for tax purposes. For this calculation, you must sum up the total number of days spent in the U.S. in the current year, 1/3 of the days in the preceding year, and 1/6 of the days in the second preceding year. Any part of a day spent in the U.S. counts as a full day unless you are travelling between two points outside the U.S. and you are in the U.S. for less than 24 hours. For example, if you arrive in the U.S. at 11:00 pm, that counts as a day. If you cross the border to go golfing or shopping for the day, that counts as a day. The U.S. immigration rules for counting days are not necessarily the same as the U.S. income tax rules.

*Example*

Simone spends the winter each year in Miami and the fall, spring and summer in Montreal. For 2015, 2016 and 2017, she is physically in the U.S. for 150, 90 and 140 days respectively.

For 2017, Simone's "physical presence" calculation is $140 + (1/3 \times 90) + (1/6 \times 150)$, or 195. Since this figure exceeds 183, she is considered resident in the U.S. for 2017 (subject to the "closer connection" rule described below).

If you are deemed a U.S. resident under the substantial presence test but the number of days you spent in the U.S. in the *current* year is less than 183, you can be treated as non-resident for purposes of U.S. tax if you can establish that you have a "closer connection" to Canada than to the U.S. To make this determination, the IRS looks at factors such as where your family, automobile and personal belongings are located, where your driver's licence was issued, where you are registered to vote, where you derived the majority of your income for the year, and whether you are covered by provincial health insurance in Canada. This information is reported on Form 8840, which is due by June 15 of the following year.

If your current year's days in the U.S. equal or exceed 183 days, you can gain a measure of protection from the Canada-U.S. tax treaty if you can establish that under the treaty you are resident in Canada and not the U.S. (This protection is not as broad as being treated as a non-resident under the "closer connection" rule above.)

For this purpose, you need to show that you have a permanent home in Canada and not in the U.S. If you have a permanent home available at all times in both countries, you must then prove that your personal and economic relations are closer to Canada. You have to file information with the IRS within certain time limits to be entitled to this treaty "tie-breaker" protection.

Although you may not be subject to U.S. income tax on your Canadian income, you are still required to follow the regular U.S. reporting rules, including reporting ownership of non-U.S. corporations and partnerships, reporting transfers to and distributions from non-U.S. trusts, and reporting receipts of foreign gifts and bequests. You must also file a Report of Foreign Bank and Financial Accounts (see 18.7.4).

If possible, plan to spend 182 days or fewer in the U.S. each year to minimize your U.S. filing obligations.

## 19.1.2 Green card holders

If you have a green card (also known as a permanent resident card), you are considered a U.S. resident for U.S. federal income tax purposes, regardless of where you live. You are required to file U.S. income tax returns annually to report your worldwide income, just like a U.S. citizen (see 18.7.1). You must also file the Report of Foreign Bank and Financial Accounts form annually (see 18.7.4).

Even if your green card has expired and is no longer valid for immigration purposes, you are still considered a U.S. resident for income tax purposes. If you have a commuter green card (which, unlike a regular green card, does not require that you live in the U.S.), you also have the status of a U.S. resident for income tax purposes.

As a green card holder, you cannot use the closer connection exception described above in 19.1.1 but it is possible to use the Canada-U.S. tax treaty to be considered resident in Canada for U.S. tax purposes, provided you have more ties to Canada than the U.S. and are a resident of Canada. This "tie-breaking" to Canada results in your worldwide income being taxable only in Canada and only your U.S. source income being taxable in the U.S. However, you are still required to file a U.S. tax return (as a non-resident) and all the U.S. reporting forms that a U.S. resident would otherwise be required to file.

If you're considering tie-breaking to Canada, keep in mind that doing so could jeopardize your green card status because a green card holder is generally required to reside in the United States.

Green card holders also need to consider U.S. estate tax. Residing in the U.S. with a green card is generally an indication that you are domiciled in the U.S. and thus may be subject to U.S. estate tax on the value of your worldwide assets (see 18.8.3).

If you live in Canada with a green card, you may want to consider surrendering it to minimize your exposure to U.S. tax and U.S. filing requirements.

To cease being considered a U.S. resident, you need to formally surrender your green card at a U.S. border crossing or U.S. consulate and complete Form I-407, "Abandonment of Lawful Permanent Residence". You may face U.S. tax consequences if you surrender your green card or have it revoked after holding it in eight or more of the preceding 15 years (see 18.9).

Before applying for or surrendering a green card, you should seek advice about your U.S. tax obligations. Careful planning can often help minimize adverse U.S. tax consequences.

## 19.2  Income from U.S. sources

Certain U.S.-source income is subject to U.S. income tax or U.S. tax withholding or disclosure requirements even if you are not resident in the U.S.

### 19.2.1  Obtaining a U.S. Individual Taxpayer Identification Number (ITIN)

If you invest or perform services in the U.S., you may be asked to provide an Individual Taxpayer Identification Number (ITIN) for tax reporting and withholding purposes. The IRS issues ITINs to individuals who are required to have a U.S. taxpayer identification number but who do not have a U.S. Social Security Number and are not eligible to obtain one.

You can obtain an ITIN by filing Form W-7 "Application for IRS Individual Taxpayer Identification Number". If you plan to invest or perform services in the U.S., consider seeking help from a professional tax adviser in navigating the ITIN application process.

If you have or are applying for a visa that entitles you to work in the U.S., then you should apply for a U.S. Social Security Number (Form SS-5).

### 19.2.2 If you work in the U.S.

If you live and have a job in Canada and your employer sends you to work temporarily in the U.S., you will face U.S. federal and state tax and reporting requirements.

Canadians are generally subject to U.S. tax on their income from U.S. sources. Income from employment is considered to come from the location where the services were performed. If you physically work in the U.S., your income from the work is U.S.-source income and subject to U.S. tax under U.S. domestic law.

Your U.S. tax bill is generally determined by allocating your total salary between your workdays in Canada and the U.S. in the year. Depending on the state you work in, you may also be liable for state income tax on your income earned in that state.

> **Example**
>
> Margot earns $100,000 in 2017 working as an analyst for a Canadian software company. She works a total of 240 days in 2017 and works 60 of these days in the company's U.S. location. The amount of Margot's U.S.-source income subject to U.S. federal tax for 2017 is 25% (60 ÷ 240) of $100,000, or $25,000.

The Canada-U.S. treaty offers some relief from U.S. tax on U.S.-source income, though this relief usually does not extend to U.S. state income tax (most states do not follow the treaty). As a Canadian resident employee, you are not subject to U.S. tax based on the treaty if:

- you earn less than US$10,000 of U.S.-source income, or
- you spend less than 183 days in any 12-month period beginning or ending in the relevant fiscal year (including work and non-work days) in the U.S. *and* you are not paid directly or indirectly by a U.S. resident or "permanent establishment", which generally means a "fixed place of business".

The second exception generally should not apply if the U.S. entity reimburses your Canadian employer for your wages.

Thus, Margot in our example above would possibly escape U.S. federal tax on her U.S.-source income if she only spent 60 days in the U.S. and her Canadian employer paid her salary.

If your U.S.-source employment income qualifies for relief from U.S. tax under the treaty, your employer must ask you to complete Form 8233 (and include your ITIN—see 19.2.1), after which your employer must certify it and file it with the IRS. If you do not qualify for the treaty exception, your employer may have to withhold U.S. tax from your wages and report the wages and related withholding to the IRS.

If you are self-employed, your U.S.-source income may be exempt from U.S. tax. Under a separate treaty provision, independent contractors are exempt from U.S. tax as long as they do not have a "permanent establishment" in the U.S.

Whether or not you qualify for an exemption under the treaty, you must file a U.S. income tax return (Form 1040NR) if you have U.S.-source income. You may also need to file a U.S. state return to report income earned in a state. Canada generally provides a foreign tax credit for any U.S. federal and state tax owing to offset Canadian tax on your U.S. income.

If you are a U.S. citizen or green card holder, you are subject to tax on your worldwide income (see 18.1) and certain treaty exemptions discussed above generally do not apply.

### 19.2.3 Rent from U.S. real estate

A withholding tax of 30% normally applies to the gross amount of any rent paid to a resident of Canada on real estate located in the United States. (Unlike withholding taxes on interest and dividends, this tax is not reduced by the Canada-U.S. tax treaty.)

> **Example**
>
> Leanne lives in Canada and owns a condominium in Arizona. She rents out the condominium for the entire year, receiving US$20,000 in rent. Her mortgage interest, maintenance costs, property taxes and depreciation total US$16,000.
>
> Over the year, 30% of the rent paid to Leanne, or US$6,000, should be withheld by her tenant and remitted to the IRS.
>
> At the end of the year, Leanne may elect to file a U.S. tax return and calculate U.S. tax on her net rental income, which would be only US$4,000 rather than US$20,000. She can then receive a refund for the withholding tax, to the extent it exceeds the tax payable on her U.S. return. However, note that state tax (and possibly a small amount of city or county tax) may be payable on the rental income.

If you own rental real estate in the U.S., elect the net rental income method.

If you have any expenses related to your U.S. rental property (mortgage interest, maintenance, insurance, property management, property taxes, etc.), you would almost always want to elect the "net rental income" method. The amount subject to tax at your marginal rate would be substantially lower than the amount subject to 30% withholding.

Once you've elected to file on a net basis, the election is permanent and you will be taxed on the net basis in future years. If you make the election, it applies to all of your U.S. rental real estate. Make sure you take into account the fact that the election can only be revoked in limited circumstances.

If you make the election, you can provide Form W8-ECI to your tenant or agent, and 30% of the rent would not need to be withheld.

Depreciation must be claimed for U.S. income tax purposes if the property is not solely for personal use. Unlike Canada's capital cost allowance system (see 11.2.7), depreciation is not a discretionary deduction in the U.S. Any allowable amount, regardless of whether you claim it, reduces the property's cost base and increases the gain on its disposition.

### 19.2.4 Dividends and interest from U.S. corporations

Like rental payments, payments of dividends and interest by U.S. persons and corporations to residents of Canada are subject to U.S. withholding tax. The Canada-U.S. tax treaty limits the tax to 15% for dividends and nil for interest in most cases.

You do not file a U.S. income tax return in respect of dividend income on which the correct tax has been withheld or for interest that is exempt from U.S. income tax.

### 19.2.5 Income from U.S. limited liability corporations

U.S. limited liability corporations (LLCs) are created under state law and are generally treated as partnerships for U.S. tax purposes. As a result, the LLC's income flows through to the members and is taxable in their hands for U.S. tax purposes. The LLC itself does not pay tax in the U.S. unless it has elected to be treated as a corporation.

However, Canada treats the LLC as a corporation for Canadian tax purposes and taxes only distributions from the LLC.

The different tax treatments in Canada and the U.S. result in a combined Canadian and U.S. effective tax rate of 60% or more on income from U.S. LLCs, compared to a maximum tax rate of 50% on income earned through a U.S. partnership. If you are considering an investment in a U.S. LLC, keep this high effective tax rate in mind.

> Beware of high effective tax rates when considering an investment in a U.S. limited liability corporation.

## 19.3 Sale of U.S. properties

### 19.3.1 Withholding tax (FIRPTA) on sale of real estate

If you sell real estate located in the U.S., a federal withholding tax is normally payable on the proceeds under FIRPTA (the Foreign Investment in Real Property Tax Act of 1980). Where proceeds are not more than US$300,000 and the buyer is an individual who will use the property as a residence, withholding may not be required.

The tax withheld can be offset against the U.S. income tax payable on any gain you realize on the sale, and refunded if it exceeds your U.S. tax liability when you file your U.S. tax return to report the disposition.

**Ensure a U.S. tax return is filed for every disposition of U.S. real property.**

A U.S. tax return must be filed for every disposition of U.S. real property.

You may be able to reduce the FIRPTA withholding by applying to the IRS before the sale closes for a "withholding certificate" on the basis that your expected U.S. tax liability will be less than 15% of the sale price. The certificate will indicate what amount of U.S. tax should be withheld by the purchaser. You must file the application before the sale's closing date. You must have or apply for an Individual Taxpayer Identification Number (see 19.2.1) to apply for a withholding certificate.

**Apply for a U.S. "withholding certificate" on the sale of real estate.**

Be sure to apply for a withholding certificate if you are making an instalment sale—otherwise, the 15% withholding is required on the entire sale price up front.

Some states such as California and Hawaii have state withholding tax provisions that parallel FIRPTA.

### 19.3.2 Income tax on the sale of U.S. real estate

For income tax purposes, you must file a U.S. tax return to report the disposition of U.S. real estate. You can offset any U.S. tax liability with the FIRPTA tax withheld. The maximum federal U.S. tax rate on capital gains for assets held for more than 12 months is 20% in 2017. Regular graduated U.S. rates apply for assets held for less than one year. The effective highest Canadian rate is about 25% because Canada only taxes one-half of the gain (see 6.2.1). However, 100% of the gain is taxed for U.S. purposes. State tax should also be considered. You will need an Individual Taxpayer Identification Number (see 19.2.1) to file your U.S. tax return.

The U.S.-Canadian exchange rate affects the amount of the gain taxable in Canada because the cost of the property is converted to Canadian dollars at the exchange rate at the time of purchase and the proceeds are converted at the exchange rate at the time of the sale. Any improvements added to the cost should be converted to Canadian dollars at the exchange rate at the time they were made.

If you have owned U.S. non-business real property and have been resident in Canada since before September 27, 1980, you can likely take advantage of the Canada-U.S. tax treaty (see 18.2.3) to reduce the amount of your gain that is taxable in the U.S. In this case, only your gain accruing since January 1, 1985 will be taxed.

Example

Roxanne bought a cottage in the U.S. for personal use in 1978 for US$10,000. On January 1, 1985, it was worth US$30,000. In 2017, Roxanne sold the cottage for US$60,000.

The U.S. taxes only US$30,000 of Roxanne's gain, which is the increase in value of the property since the beginning of 1985. State income tax may be based on a gain of either US$30,000 or US$50,000, depending on whether the state adheres to the Canada-U.S. tax treaty.

If you cannot establish a January 1, 1985 valuation, the gain accrued to that date is determined by assuming that the entire gain accrued equally over each month in the holding period.

To claim the benefit under the treaty, you need to make the claim on your U.S. return and include a statement containing certain specific information about the transaction.

U.S. tax on the sale of U.S. property generates foreign tax that can be used to reduce the Canadian tax on the sale. (See 18.2.2 for an explanation of the operation of foreign tax credits.) If the property qualifies, you can shelter the amount of the gain taxed in Canada by claiming the Canadian principal residence exemption (see 6.5.2). However, using the exemption proportionately reduces the foreign tax credit available to you for Canadian tax purposes and may not be advisable if you have a home in Canada that would qualify as your principal residence.

### 19.3.3 Sales of U.S. stocks and bonds

If you are not a resident or citizen of the U.S., U.S. tax does not normally apply to sales of shares in U.S. corporations, whether public or private, regardless of where they are traded.

However, if the majority of the corporation's assets are U.S. real estate, the corporation may be considered a "U.S. real property holding corporation" (unless it is a publicly traded company and you own less than 5% of the shares). In such a case, any gain on the sale of the shares of the corporation would be taxed by the U.S. in a manner similar to the sale of real property.

## 19.4 U.S. gift and estate taxes for Canadians

U.S. gift and estate taxes can impose a serious burden on the death of Canadians and other non-U.S. citizens who own U.S. stocks and real estate.

In this section, we discuss only federal gift and estate taxes. Some states impose estate taxes that you should also consider.

The rules discussed here only apply in situations where both the deceased and the surviving spouse are Canadian citizens and residents. If either spouse is a U.S. citizen or resident, the planning alternatives outlined in this section may not be appropriate.

### 19.4.1 Property subject to estate tax

U.S. estate tax applies to the property of Canadians that is "situated within the United States". This includes:

- real property located in the U.S.
- certain tangible personal property located in the U.S.
- shares of U.S. corporations, regardless of the location of the share certificates and regardless of where the shares are traded
- debts of U.S. persons, including the U.S. government (with specific exceptions)
- U.S. pension plan and annuity amounts (including IRAs).

U.S. estate tax could apply to any of your personal assets that are located in the U.S. at the time of your death. U.S. case law has established that the assets must be located in the U.S. with a degree of permanence, so the tax probably would not apply to jewellery or other items you might take with you on vacation. However, furniture and artwork in your Florida condominium, for example, may be subject to U.S. estate tax.

For RRSPs and RRIFs, you consider the underlying property held in the account.

Be cautious when acquiring shares in U.S. corporations due to potential U.S. estate tax.

Assets normally excluded from the definition of property situated within the U.S. include: shares of a foreign (non-U.S.) corporation, regardless of where the corporation's assets are situated; U.S. bank deposits; certain U.S. corporate bonds that are publicly traded outside the U.S.; and certain debt obligations.

The "taxable estate" for estate tax purposes is the gross value of all of the deceased's property situated in the U.S., minus certain allowable deductions. The most significant deductions are:

- amounts left to the deceased's spouse if the spouse is a U.S. citizen
- amounts transferred to a "qualified domestic trust" (see 19.4.5)
- a deduction for a non-recourse mortgage (see 19.4.5) encumbering U.S. property
- a deduction for a share of the deceased's liabilities at time of death— including Canadian income taxes payable.

Once the "taxable estate" has been determined, U.S. federal estate tax applies on the cumulative value of all taxable gifts made during your lifetime and at death, at graduated rates ranging from 18% to 40% in 2017. An applicable credit amount then reduces this tax (see 19.4.2).

If you're considering whether to gift U.S. property to a beneficiary during your lifetime or leave the property to that individual in your will, keep in mind that the U.S. tax treatment of gifted property for beneficiaries is different from the treatment of bequests.

For property inherited on death, the beneficiary's cost base of property is adjusted to the fair market value on the date of death for U.S. tax purposes. For Canadian tax purposes, the cost base of property inherited on death is also adjusted to the fair market value on the date of death, except where the transfer is to a spouse and no election to recognize a gain has been made (see 22.2.3).

For U.S. purposes, transfers by gift result in the cost basis of the property being carried over from the gift giver to the gift recipient. The cost basis is not adjusted to fair market value on the date of the gift. When the recipient disposes of the property, he or she has to pay the tax on any capital gain that has accrued since the original acquisition of the property. In Canada, the treatment of a gift is the same as for a bequest—a gift to anyone other than a spouse results in an adjustment of the recipient's cost base to fair market value on the date of the gift.

Since the Canada-U.S. treaty provides relief for estate tax and not for gift tax (see 18.8.2 and 19.4.2) and since a beneficiary's cost base in a property is adjusted on death but not on a gift, it is rarely beneficial for tax purposes to gift property during life if that property would be subject to U.S. income or estate tax.

### 19.4.2 Lifetime estate tax credit

Under U.S. domestic law, non-residents of the U.S. who are not U.S. citizens can apply a credit amount of US$13,000 against the estate tax (for U.S. citizens, see 18.8.1). This credit amount effectively exempts US$60,000 of the estate from taxation.

The Canada-U.S. tax treaty increases the U.S. credit amount for residents and citizens of Canada from the US$13,000 allowed under U.S. law to US$2,141,800 in 2017, sheltering US$5.49 million of taxable estate. This credit must be prorated by the value of the Canadian deceased's U.S. estate over the value of the deceased's worldwide estate (as determined under U.S. rules).

The proration of the credit means that Canadians are not subject to U.S. estate tax in 2017 if the value of their worldwide gross estate does not exceed US$5.49 million. It also means that wealthy Canadians who hold a relatively small proportion of their total estate in the United States are still subject to substantial U.S. estate tax. These Canadians should consider the planning options discussed in 19.4.5.

Your estate must file a U.S. estate tax return if your property within the United States is worth more than US$60,000 at the time of your death, even if no tax is payable. To access the treaty benefits, your estate must disclose all of your worldwide assets to the IRS on this return. The return is due nine months after the date of death.

### 19.4.3  Marital credit

A "marital credit" is available under the Canada-U.S. tax treaty if an estate tax marital deduction would have been available had the surviving spouse been a U.S. citizen. However, this credit is capped at the lesser of the applicable credit amount allowed to the deceased's estate and the U.S. estate tax payable after other credits. This effectively allows a minimum US$26,000 credit (i.e., 2 × US$13,000) where U.S. property is transferred to a spouse on death. Effectively, the marital credit almost doubles the exemption available when the deceased transfers his or her assets to a surviving spouse.

The executor of the estate must elect to take advantage of this provision and must irrevocably waive the benefit of any estate tax marital deduction that may have otherwise been allowable. In effect, the executor must either claim the treaty marital credit or create a qualified domestic trust (but not both). The deadline for the election and waiver is usually nine months after the date of death.

### 19.4.4  Canadian credit for U.S. estate taxes

On death, Canada normally taxes the accrued capital gains in the deceased's estate (see 22.2.3). A foreign tax credit is available in Canada to offset foreign income taxes paid on foreign-source income. However, U.S. estate taxes are not income taxes. As a result, no foreign tax credit is available under Canadian domestic law to offset taxes on death.

Under the treaty, Canada permits U.S. estate tax on U.S. assets to be deducted from a Canadian resident's Canadian tax otherwise payable for the year of death. The credit is limited to the Canadian tax attributable to the deceased's U.S.-source income for the year of death. U.S.-source income includes gains on U.S. real estate, U.S. dividends and rental income. For this purpose, the definition of U.S.-source income is expanded to include gains on deemed dispositions of U.S. securities. The CRA takes the position that the U.S. estate tax can only be credited against the Canadian federal tax and not the provincial tax.

### 19.4.5  Ways to reduce your exposure to U.S. estate tax

Leave U.S. property to your spouse or a qualified trust.

Once you have determined which of your assets are subject to U.S. estate tax and estimated your potential exposure, you may want to consider some strategies to reduce or eliminate your estate's potential U.S. estate tax liability.

When property is left to a surviving spouse who is a U.S. citizen, or to a qualified domestic trust (QDOT), the U.S. estate tax can be deferred until the death of the surviving spouse.

To qualify as a QDOT, the trust instrument must provide that at least one trustee be a U.S. citizen or U.S. corporation, and that no distribution of capital may be made from the trust without the U.S. trustee being able to withhold U.S. estate tax. Any capital paid out of a QDOT then becomes subject to estate tax. More stringent rules apply to QDOTs with assets exceeding US$2 million in value. A properly structured QDOT may be considered a "qualified spousal trust" for Canadian tax purposes (see 21.5.2). The deceased can use either a QDOT or the treaty marital credit but not both. Since the treaty marital credit produces tax savings of up to US$2,141,800 in 2017 and the QDOT only provides a deferral of estate taxes, there are few situations where establishing a QDOT is beneficial.

Another alternative is to transfer the property to a spousal trust in which the surviving spouse does not have a general power of appointment. This would not avoid estate tax on the death of the first spouse, but it would ensure that the assets in the trust are not included in the surviving spouse's estate for U.S. estate tax purposes.

A "non-recourse" mortgage is one that entitles the lender to have recourse only against the property mortgaged. That is, if you default on payment, the mortgagee can seize the mortgaged property but cannot sue you for the balance if the property is not worth enough to pay off the debt. A non-recourse mortgage outstanding on your U.S. real estate reduces your equity in the property and thus reduces the value of your taxable estate. The current lending environment generally limits the loan-to-value ratio to 60% with a non-recourse mortgage. As you repay the loan, the estate tax exposure increases.

> Mortgage property (non-recourse) to reduce the value of your U.S. real estate.

Another way you can reduce your estate tax exposure is by acquiring U.S. assets jointly with your spouse (or another person). For this approach to work, you and your spouse each have to supply your own funds; you cannot simply give half of the interest in the property to your spouse or give your spouse the funds to invest, or you could be subject to U.S. gift tax. Where assets are jointly held and it can be proven that each joint tenant paid for their interest with their own money, on the death of the first joint tenant, each tenant is deemed to own their share of the property. If it cannot be proven that each spouse paid for their own

> Acquire property jointly with your spouse or another person.

interest, the first joint tenant to die is deemed to own 100% of the property for purposes of determining the value of the taxable estate for U.S. purposes.

For example, suppose you and your spouse each invested your own funds into a condominium worth US$400,000. On your death, only US$200,000 of that value would be included in your estate.

You can also acquire the property as tenants-in-common, but beware of potential gift tax if you transfer funds to your spouse for the purchase of the property. You also need to consider the Canadian attribution rules (see 5.2.2).

**Split your worldwide assets with your spouse.**
If your spouse's assets have a lower value than yours, consider having your spouse acquire full ownership of one or more of your U.S. assets, such as a vacation property. Seek professional tax advice before doing so, however, since the transfer could trigger the attribution rules or gift tax if your spouse does not use his or her own funds.

**Consider a split interest purchase with your child.**
In some situations, it may be beneficial for U.S. estate tax purposes for you to split your interest in an asset with your child. In this strategy, you would acquire a life interest in the property and your child would acquire a remainder interest with his or her own funds. The rules in this area are extremely complex—if you want to pursue this strategy, professional advice is a must.

**Hold your U.S. property through a Canadian corporation.**
A more obvious solution to U.S. estate tax is to hold any U.S. stocks and real estate in a Canadian corporation rather than personally. When you die, your corporation does not, and U.S. estate tax does not apply to holdings in a Canadian corporation. You have effectively converted the "location" of your assets from the U.S. to Canada. While this solution is often useful, it is fraught with pitfalls, and qualified professional advice should be obtained. Some possible problems that should be addressed include:

- Beyond the initial setup costs, there are ongoing costs to maintaining a corporation, including legal and accounting fees.
- The acquisition of the U.S. assets by the corporation must be legally complete, and all corporate formalities must be observed. If it is determined that the corporation was only acting as an agent or title holder for you, estate tax can still apply to the property on your death.
- Any income earned by the corporation on its U.S. assets (such as interest, dividends, rent) is subject to tax both when originally earned and when paid out to you in the form of dividends. The combined effect of the taxes is higher than the tax you would pay if you held the assets directly.

- If you or members of your family will be using the real estate for personal purposes, you will be taxed in Canada as having received a taxable shareholder benefit from the corporation equal to the rental value of the property for all days it was available for your use.
- If the property is sold after death and the funds distributed, the total income tax cost may be higher than the potential estate tax cost in certain cases.

In 2004, the CRA changed its administrative policy of not assessing a taxable benefit to a shareholder of a "single purpose corporation", which is generally a Canadian corporation established for the sole purpose of holding residential real property in the U.S. for the shareholder's personal use and enjoyment. Single purpose corporations that existed before 2005 are exempt from this policy change until the property is sold or the shares of the corporation are transferred to someone other than a spouse or common-law partner. Because of this change, no new single purpose corporations should be established.

Instead of using a Canadian corporation, you might consider establishing a Canadian limited partnership (with a Canadian corporation as the other partner) to hold your U.S. assets and have the partnership elect to be treated as a corporation for U.S. tax purposes. On your death, your partnership interest and the underlying assets

> Hold your U.S. assets through a properly structured trust or a Canadian partnership that elects to be treated as a corporation in the U.S.

can be transferred directly to your beneficiaries. Since the U.S. will treat the partnership as a corporation, the assets held by it should bypass your estate entirely for U.S. estate tax purposes. And since Canada will treat the entity as a partnership, you can avoid some of the negative Canadian tax implications discussed above of holding U.S. property through a Canadian corporation. This strategy is complex and should not be pursued without professional tax advice.

A properly structured trust where the settlor uses cash to settle the trust and has no retained interest or any right to the trust property may also be used to acquire U.S. assets. The trust must be established for as long as possible before an offer is made on any property to minimize gift tax exposure. Again, professional tax advice is essential.

You could plan to sell your U.S. assets (say, to a family member) before your death, and receive in exchange assets that are not "located in the U.S." (e.g., cash or a promissory note situated in

> Sell U.S. property before death.

Canada). Thus, you would have no U.S. assets left to form a taxable estate.

This step may be useful when death is anticipated within a short time. For example, property could be sold to a child to whom you intend to leave the property anyway, in exchange for a bona fide promissory note. The note might then be left to your spouse or to another family member. If the note were left to the child (and effectively forgiven), the sale may be treated as a gift and subject to U.S. gift tax.

On a sale of U.S. real estate, U.S. and Canadian income tax apply to any gain (the Canadian tax applying to one-half of the capital gain—see 6.2.1). A foreign tax credit is normally available in Canada to offset part or all of the tax paid. Canadian tax, rather than U.S. tax, applies to any gain on securities sold or gifted before death.

Be aware of the possible application of the Canadian attribution rules (see Chapter 5) where you have transferred property to your spouse or to a family member who is under 18. Also, make sure you do not take back debt (such as a promissory note) from someone resident in the United States, since certain debts of U.S. residents are considered to be property located in the U.S. Before undertaking any transaction, be sure to compare the tax consequences that would arise on death to the tax consequences that would arise on a transfer before death.

Consider taking out life insurance to cover U.S. estate taxes.

If you anticipate that substantial estate tax will apply on your death, consider taking out life insurance as a way of funding the payment of the tax without requiring the sale of your U.S. assets. Life insurance proceeds would not form part of your estate on death, even if provided by a U.S. insurer (although they would be included in your worldwide assets for purposes of determining the applicable credit amount discussed in 19.4.2). Bear in mind that premiums paid on a life insurance policy are not deductible for either Canadian or U.S. income tax purposes. Also, if the policy is with a U.S. insurer, have your professional adviser review the Canadian income tax implications of holding the policy.

If your will provides that your U.S. assets are to be transferred to a U.S. charity on your death, then you should not be subject to U.S. estate tax on those assets.

### 19.4.6 U.S. gift tax on real estate for Canadians

U.S. gift tax applies to the donor of gifts of U.S. real estate made by Canadians. The highest gift tax rate is 40% in 2017. The tax does not apply to gifts of U.S. securities by Canadians, even though U.S. estate tax applies to their value on death.

Gifts valued up to US$14,000 annually (US$149,000 for gifts to a spouse who is not a U.S. citizen) are exempt from U.S. gift tax. Gifts to a spouse who is a U.S. citizen are exempt. The Canada-U.S. tax treaty offers no additional relief. For U.S. tax purposes, the cost basis of the gifted property is transferred from the donor to the donee.

In Canada, gifts attract income tax if the gifted property has an accrued gain. As we saw in 5.2, attribution rules apply to gifts to spouses and children under age 18. No foreign tax credits are allowed in Canada for U.S. gift tax.

> Henry owns a home in California that he bought for US$200,000. The home is now worth $500,000. Henry decides to give the home to his son James.
>
> In Canada, Henry pays income tax on one-half of the US$300,000 capital gain. He also has to pay U.S. gift tax on the value of the home, less his US$14,000 annual gift tax exemption, or US$486,000. No foreign tax credit is available for the U.S. gift tax.
>
> The cost base of the property to James for Canadian tax purposes is $500,000, while his basis for U.S. federal and California purposes is US$200,000 (plus a portion of the gift tax). When James sells the property, he will have to pay U.S. federal and state tax on any proceeds over this amount. Henry's total tax would be much lower if he kept the property and transferred it to James on death because of the significant treaty benefits available for estate tax purposes. No treaty benefits are available for gift tax purposes.

As you can see, due to the different tax treatment of gifts in Canada and the U.S. and the double tax problems that may arise, gifting U.S. real estate is rarely advisable.

## 19.5  References

The CRA publishes information for Canadians who spend part of the year in the U.S. under the title "Canadian Residents Going Down South", available from the CRA's website at *www.cra-arc.gc.ca*.

The following technical publications may be obtained by telephoning or writing to any office of the Internal Revenue Service (IRS). They may also be available at United States embassy and consular offices, or from the IRS website at *www.irs.gov*.

> Publication 515, "Withholding of Tax on Non-resident Aliens and Foreign Entities"
> Publication 519, "U.S. Tax Guide for Aliens"

# Chapter 20

## Planning for your retirement

- Start planning and saving for retirement at least 15 years before you plan to retire (20.1)

- Consider topping up your RRSP and using the tax refund to pay down your mortgage (20.1)

- Prepare detailed cash flow forecasts to project changes in your expenses and sources of income as you get older (20.2.1)

- Reconsider your investment strategy as you near retirement (20.2.2)

- Split income by assigning CPP/QPP benefits to the lower-income spouse (20.3.1)

- Delay or defer income until 2017 where possible to minimize the OAS clawback (20.3.2)

- Aim for at least $2,000 of pension income annually for each spouse (20.3.5)

- File a joint election to split pension income with your spouse (20.3.6)

- Top up your RRSP before the end of the year in which you turn 71 (20.4.1)

- Convert your RRSP to a RRIF or annuity at the end of the year in which you turn 71 (20.4.6)

- Contribute excess after-tax RRIF or annuity income to your TFSA (20.4.7)

*This chapter discusses financial planning issues to consider as you plan your retirement. The decisions you make when planning your retirement can greatly affect your quality of life throughout your retirement and the financial resources you can make available to your heirs. We strongly recommend that you seek professional financial and tax planning advice. Since retirement planning and the estate planning issues discussed in Chapter 21 are closely related, you should consider developing your retirement and estate planning strategies at the same time.*

## 20.1 Saving for your retirement

Most people can live comfortably in retirement on 70% to 80% of their pre-retirement income (adjusted for inflation). Meeting this target requires dedicated long-term planning. Generally, the principal sources of retirement income for Canadians are employer-sponsored pension plans, government pension plans, Tax-Free Savings Accounts (TFSA), registered retirement savings plans (RRSP) and other savings.

If you are a member of an employer-sponsored pension plan, you should consider this as one potential source of retirement income, not as your total retirement fund. Similarly, you should not plan to rely too heavily on Old Age Security (OAS) or the Canada and Quebec Pension Plans (CPP/QPP) since these government programs will not provide much more than subsistence level income.

Beyond these types of income, you'll probably have to develop resources on your own through other savings and investment strategies. If you don't start at least 15 years before you reach retirement age, you'll probably find yourself working longer than you had intended and/or unable to afford the retirement lifestyle you expect.

*Start planning and saving for retirement at least 15 years before you plan to retire.*

By your mid- to late-forties, depending on your circumstances, you should generally find it easier to put larger amounts of funds toward your retirement nest egg: you will be entering your peak income-earning years, your children may be nearing independence and most of your major lifestyle acquisitions (except maybe your home) will probably be bought and paid for. But don't wait until then—due to the exponential growth of your retirement investments through compounding, the earlier you can start saving for retirement, the better off you will be.

Your RRSP is one of the best available retirement savings vehicles. It allows you to set aside money and to defer the taxes you would otherwise pay on it. Try to contribute as much as possible, and do so early in the year so your contribution can earn tax-sheltered income for the entire year. In Chapter 3, we discussed the tax rules governing RRSPs and strategies for maximizing your RRSP's growth, along with registered pension plans (RPPs) and other deferred income plans.

Your TFSA can allow you to earn a significant amount of tax-free investment income for your retirement or other financial goals. Though your contributions to this type of tax-assisted savings account are not tax-deductible, the investment income and capital gains earned on investments in the account are tax-free. You can withdraw this income and your contributions to your TFSA at any time without tax consequences. See 4.1 for a detailed discussion of TFSAs and related planning ideas. TFSAs can continue to shelter your after-tax savings after you wind up your RRSP at age 71 (see 20.4.7).

*Consider topping up your RRSP and using the tax refund to pay down your mortgage.*

Building funds in your RRSP and TFSA and building equity in your home should be key components of your retirement savings plan. A commonly asked question is whether you would be further ahead in the long run to maximize your RRSP or TFSA contributions or to put the same funds toward paying down your mortgage (see 1.2.3). Since you gain no deduction for your TFSA contributions, it probably makes more sense in most cases to reduce your non-deductible mortgage interest as soon as possible. Regarding RRSPs, however, the answer depends on a variety of factors, including your mortgage's interest rate and remaining amortization period, your RRSP balances and types of investments, your marginal tax rate, the number of income-earning years you have left until you plan to retire, and the availability of other pension plan funds. To hedge your bets, consider making maximum annual RRSP contributions and using the resulting tax refund to make lump-sum mortgage payments.

## 20.2 Getting ready to retire

### 20.2.1 Assessing your financial situation

As you get closer to retirement, you will need to update your net worth statement (see 1.1.2) to get a clear picture of your potential retirement income resources. You will also need to prepare new cash flow forecasts to reflect the upcoming changes in your financial situation and to determine your monthly disposable income. As in preparing a budget (see 1.1.3), your cash flow forecasts should list the amounts you expect to receive and pay out monthly.

You should prepare several cash flow statements to take into account changes in your expenses and sources of income as you get older. For example, preparing a statement at retirement will show cash flow changes resulting from your loss of employment income and your receipt of pension income; it should also reflect reduced employment-related expenses for items such as clothes and commuting to work and perhaps increased expenses for items such as travel and medical bills. Cash flow statements at ages 60 and 65 will reflect the impact of your CPP/QPP and Old Age Security benefits (see 20.3) on your finances. A further cash flow statement at age 71 or when you mature your RRSP should forecast TFSA, RRIF or annuity income you will receive.

> Prepare detailed cash flow forecasts to project changes in your expenses and sources of income as you get older.

These detailed forecasts will show whether your resources will be enough or whether you will need to reduce your planned spending or sell assets to help meet your cash flow needs (see 20.2.3). The projections will also give you the information you need to make decisions such as when you should apply to receive CPP/QPP benefits (see 20.3.1), when and how much to withdraw from RRSPs or TFSAs and whether you should opt for an integrated pension (see 20.3.7).

You should review your retirement projections every one or two years to take into account any changes in your personal circumstances or goals, tax or pension law amendments, economic events and changes to any other assumptions on which your plan is based.

### 20.2.2 Reconsidering your investment strategy

In 1.1.4, we discussed the importance of determining your objectives and risk tolerance in developing your investment strategy. As you enter retirement, your investment objectives will likely change: instead of building your asset base, your aim will be to preserve or draw on your capital gradually so it will provide a steady and dependable source of income throughout your own and your spouse's lifetimes.

Reconsider your investment strategy as you near retirement.

The closer you get to retirement, the less able you will be to replace substantial investment losses and the less risk you should tolerate. Consider changing your investment mix in the years leading up to your retirement so that a greater proportion of your wealth is invested in more secure, fixed income assets such as government or other high quality bonds, preferred shares and guaranteed investment certificates (GICs). Since your retirement could last 30 years or more, you will probably need to have some proportion of your portfolio invested in growth equities such as shares or other equities. (For a discussion of asset allocation, see 1.1.4.)

### 20.2.3 Planning for the sale of assets

> **Caution: The tax planning ideas discussed in this section may be affected by the federal government's proposed new tax regime for private companies, as outlined in the Department of Finance's July 2017 consultation paper and draft legislation. See Appendix I for details.**

On reaching retirement, you may need to reorganize your finances to meet your cash flow needs. This could involve selling some of your assets, withdrawing funds from your RRSP or selling your home. Before doing so, watch out for unintended tax consequences.

If you own (or previously owned) a business, you may have funds in an investment holding company. The best timing and method of withdrawing these funds should also be considered when you reach retirement. Although these funds generally will be taxable when you withdraw them, you may wish to seek professional advice in this area to determine whether tax-effective ways for extracting the funds may be available.

Many tax incentives and social programs are based on your net income for tax purposes (essentially your total income less certain deductions—see 2.1.1). The capital gains arising from asset sales or the income inclusion resulting from your RRSP withdrawals could significantly increase your net income and your tax bill for the year. If your net income is too high, some tax and social benefits will be reduced or eliminated. These include the federal age credit (see 20.3.4) and the Quebec age and pension income credits (see 17.5). You could also wind up having to pay back some of your Old Age Security benefits for the current year and receiving reduced OAS payments in July through June of the next year (see 20.3.2). A liability for minimum tax could also arise (see 7.6). Withdrawals from your TFSA do not have these adverse effects.

Before you sell your investments or dip into your RRSP funds, consider the following strategies for avoiding an unnecessary income inclusion:

- Consider using resources that do not affect your income for tax purposes first. For example, withdraw from your savings account (without using your emergency fund; see 1.3.1), TFSA (see 4.1) or certain fixed income investments before withdrawing from your RRSP.
- Spread your sales of assets such as shares and RRSP withdrawals over several years to avoid creating a large income inclusion in any one year.
- Instead of receiving your sales proceeds in one payment, consider making it part of the terms of sale that the proceeds are to be paid to you in equal instalments over five years. This will enable you to spread the income inclusion over the five years by claiming a capital gains reserve (see 6.5.1). Of course, you'll want to consider your cash flow needs and the risk of default of payment.
- Remember that selling your home or cottage will not affect your income for tax purposes if the property is eligible for the principal residence exemption (see 6.5.2).
- Instead of selling your home, consider a reverse mortgage whereby the lender pays you a fixed amount of money each month toward a mortgage that the lender holds on your property. When your home is ultimately sold, the lender will get back the total amount of its payments plus interest and you or your estate will be entitled to the remainder of the sale proceeds. Since a reverse mortgage is not a beneficial strategy for everyone, be sure to consult an independent financial planning professional before entering such an arrangement.
- Borrow against a life insurance policy, but only after assessing your life insurance needs.

### 20.2.4 Insurance coverage and other post-retirement benefits

As a retiree, your life insurance needs are somewhat different from those discussed in 1.3.2. While you will still want to be sure that funds will be available to cover your estate's tax liability arising on your death and to provide for your spouse and other dependants, you will likely have fewer debts to service and no need for coverage for loss of employment or self-employment income.

In reviewing your insurance needs, be sure to investigate the existing death benefit and survivor's benefits available on your death. Many employers provide life insurance to their pensioners, although the amount may decrease over time. Some employers also pay a death benefit (see 22.3), which may help your spouse financially.

You should also review your spouse's medical insurance coverage under your post-retirement benefits in the event of your death. Many survivors lose their entitlement to medical insurance coverage on their spouse's death, and you should consider alternate arrangements in advance to ensure your spouse will have coverage after your death.

Since life insurance fills many important roles in estate planning, your review of your coverage on retirement should take place in the wider context of the issues discussed in 21.7. For example, you may wish to consider purchasing life insurance to fund capital gains tax or other tax liabilities that may arise on your death.

### 20.2.5 Survivor's benefits

When you retire, if you are a member of a company pension plan, it will normally provide you with several choices regarding the payment of your pension after your death. These options may include a life-only benefit, a specified guarantee period, a surviving spouse benefit at amounts ranging from 50% to 100%, or a combination of these options.

If you choose a specified guaranteed payment period of, say, five, 10 or 20 years, your company guarantees it will pay your pension for that period. If you die before the period is over, your pension amounts will be paid to your estate until the period expires.

If you choose a 100% joint and last survivor guarantee, the company will pay you a pension until you die and continue to pay the same pension to your spouse until your spouse dies.

Under a 50% spousal benefit, your spouse will receive half of your pension on your death. Most provinces require that the surviving spouse receive 50% (60% in some cases) of your pension amount on your death, unless your spouse specifically renounces this entitlement in writing when you choose your pension option.

When you are assessing the various options, bear in mind that the longer the potential payout period, the lower the pension payment. For example, the monthly pension payment for a five-year guarantee period is usually much higher than payments under a surviving spouse benefit option.

### 20.2.6 Phased retirement under defined benefit pension plans

Employees in most provinces can receive pension benefits under defined benefit pension plans (see 3.6.1) while accruing further benefits at the same time under the same or another plan.

The rules are designed to allow older workers to continue working while at the same time receiving a partial pension and accruing further pension benefits for their part-time work. Employers can offer phased retirement programs that allow employees to reduce their work schedules and receive a proportionate mix of pension and salary income.

Employers can offer employees up to 60% of their accrued defined benefit pension, while incurring additional pension benefits. To qualify, employees must be at least age 55 and otherwise eligible to receive a pension under the plan. There is no requirement related to whether the employee continues to work full- or part-time.

This phased retirement option is not available to designated plans (generally, one-person plans or small plans for groups of executives) or to employees connected with their employer (generally, employees who do not deal at arm's length with their employer or who own 10% or more of the shares of the employer or a related corporation).

## 20.3 Government assistance for retirees

### 20.3.1 Canada Pension Plan/Quebec Pension Plan benefits

Between the ages of 60 and 70, you can apply to begin receiving your monthly pension benefits under the Canada Pension Plan or Quebec Pension Plan. You can receive benefits as early as age 60 without stopping work or reducing your hours.

The amount of your CPP/QPP payments will depend on how many years you have contributed to the plan, the amount of your contributions and the age at which you decide to start receiving your pension. CPP/QPP benefits are adjusted annually for inflation; the maximum monthly retirement benefit at age 65 is $1,114.17 for 2017. These benefits are taxable as income.

Although you can apply to receive pension amounts as early as age 60, you will have to pay a penalty in the form of reduced benefits for receiving these amounts early. In 2017, the penalty is 0.6% of your benefits otherwise payable at age 65 for every month (or 7.2% a year) before your 65th birthday that you collect CPP/QPP benefits and will apply to reduce your benefits for life.

Example

Vanessa accepts an early retirement package from her company in 2017 and decides that she wants to start receiving her CPP/QPP benefits later in the year when she turns 62. Since she will begin receiving her pension benefits 36 months before her 65th birthday, she estimates her monthly CPP/QPP pension benefits at $1,114.17 less $240.66 ($1,114.17 × 36 × 0.6%), for a total monthly pre-tax pension amount of $873.51.

If you decide to wait and receive benefits after age 65, your CPP benefits will increase by 0.70% per month or 8.4% per year. As such, if you start receiving your benefits at age 70, you will receive 42% more than you would if you had taken your benefits at age 65.

To estimate your benefits, you may request a Statement of Contributions from Service Canada or the Régie des rentes du Québec.

Many factors will influence your decision about when to apply for your benefits. If you expect your expenses to be higher during the early part of your retirement, perhaps because you wish to travel, you may appreciate receiving benefits before age 65. By contrast, if you do not need the funds to pay your living or other expenses, you may be better off delaying your application since the benefits will be included in your taxable income. Your life expectancy should also be considered—if you are expected to reach your late seventies and early eighties, you may benefit from starting to collect your CPP/QPP benefits at age 65 or later.

You will need to apply for your CPP/QPP benefits at least six months before you wish to begin receiving them. CPP applications are filed with Human Resources Development or over the Internet with Service Canada (see 20.6); QPP applications are filed with the Régie des rentes du Québec.

### Working beneficiaries

If you are retired and receiving CPP pension benefits and you go back to work, you are not required to restart your CPP contributions as a working beneficiary, though you and your employer must still make CPP contributions if you are a working beneficiary under age 65.

If you are a working beneficiary age 65 or over, you can choose to make CPP contributions to build your pension. Contributions that you make after your 65th birthday will increase your retirement benefits. Additional benefits would be earned at a rate of 2.5% of the maximum pension amount ($13,370 in 2017) per year of additional contributions. As a result, your pension could be higher than the maximum monthly benefit.

If you change your mind about making these contributions, you can opt out of making them by completing an election form. If you are considering opting out, you should weigh the benefit of your future CPP benefits against the cost of your current CPP withholdings. The election form can be submitted only once in a calendar year. If, for example, you elect to stop making CPP contributions and you give a copy of this completed form to your employer in 2017, you would have to wait until 2018 to file a new form to restart CPP contributions.

### Death benefit and survivor's benefit

The CPP/QPP also pays a death benefit equal to six months of regular CPP/QPP benefits to a maximum of $2,500; this amount is taxable to the estate or the survivor in the year received. The surviving spouse may also apply for a survivor's benefit under the CPP/QPP, which is a percentage of the deceased's benefits based on the survivor's age and other factors. For example, if the surviving spouse is 65 and not receiving other CPP benefits, the survivor's benefit is generally 60% of the deceased's CPP/QPP benefits.

### Splitting CPP benefits between spouses

To help you save taxes through income splitting, you may direct that up to 50% of your CPP benefits be paid to your spouse, provided both of you are over age 60. If either of you does this, a portion of the other spouse's CPP is assigned automatically back to the first spouse.

*Split income by assigning CPP/QPP benefits to the lower-income spouse.*

If both spouses are eligible for maximum CPP benefits, assignment would not change anything, since each would assign half of the maximum to the other. But if one has high CPP benefits and the other has low benefits or none, the assignment can effectively transfer up to half of the CPP income to the lower-income spouse. The amount that can be split is equal to the retirement pensions you both earned while together, to a maximum of 50%.

The attribution rules discussed in Chapter 5 specifically do not apply to an assignment of CPP benefits. If you and your spouse are both over 60, and you have higher CPP benefits and are in a higher tax bracket, you should consider such an assignment in addition to the pension income splitting rules that allow certain other qualifying pension income to be split between spouses (see 20.3.6). Be sure to consider the effect of assigning CPP benefits on your spousal tax credit claim (see 2.2.1).

CPP benefits can be assigned by completing a form available from Service Canada; QPP benefits can be assigned by completing a form available from Régie des rentes du Québec.

If you are resident in the U.S. and you receive CPP/QPP benefits, see 20.3.3.

### 20.3.2 Old Age Security benefits and the OAS clawback
OAS benefits are a taxable pension available at age 65. Unlike CPP/QPP payments, which are based on prior contributions, your entitlement to the

OAS benefit is based on your age and how long you have lived in Canada. To receive the maximum pension, you must have lived in Canada for 40 years or more after turning 18. Partial pension may be available if you lived in Canada for 10 or more years after turning 18. A social security agreement between Canada and another country may allow you to add your period of residence in the other country to your period of Canadian residence for purposes of determining your OAS entitlement.

OAS benefits are paid monthly and benefit rates are indexed quarterly for inflation. At the time of writing, the maximum OAS payment is about $580 per month. For high-income taxpayers, these payments are completely taxed back through a special tax, known informally as the "clawback". The tax reduces benefits for taxpayers whose net income (after most deductions such as RRSP contributions) is over $74,788. If your net income exceeds about $121,071, the clawback will apply to 100% of your OAS benefits. Spouses' incomes are not combined for purposes of the clawback; each taxpayer's income is considered separately.

The clawback tax on OAS benefits is deducted from your monthly benefits. The amount withheld is based on your income in the prior two years. For example, for the first six months of 2017, your tax withheld is based on your 2015 income while your tax withheld for the last half of 2017 is based on your 2016 income. If too much tax is withheld, the excess will be applied to reduce your income taxes otherwise owing or refunded to you after you file your return for the year. If the tax withheld falls short of your liability, you will have to repay the difference.

*Delay or defer income until 2017 where possible to minimize the OAS clawback.*

To minimize the clawback's potential effect, try to delay or defer recognition of income until the following year where possible. For example, if you are thinking about selling investments that have appreciated in value in 2017, consider waiting until 2018 to cash them in—preserving your OAS benefits may well outweigh the returns you'll forgo by waiting a few months for the proceeds from your appreciated investments (provided their value does not decline in the meantime).

To start receiving your OAS benefits as quickly as possible after turning 65, you should file your application with Service Canada at least six months before your 65th birthday. If you make your application after turning 65, it may be approved retroactively for up to one year.

If you are resident in the U.S. and you receive OAS benefits, see 20.3.3.

### 20.3.3 Cross-border payments of CPP/QPP, OAS and U.S. social security benefits

Under the Canada-U.S. tax treaty (see 18.2.3), U.S. residents who receive CPP/QPP or OAS benefits are not liable for Canadian withholding tax on these amounts. These benefits received by U.S. residents are taxable only in the U.S.

Similarly, if you are a resident of Canada and you receive U.S. social security benefits, no U.S. withholding tax applies on these amounts; 85% of the benefits are subject to Canadian tax.

### 20.3.4 Age credit

If you are 65 or older by the end of the year, you get an additional federal tax credit of up to $7,225 (worth $1,084) for 2017. This credit is linked to your income and is phased out by 15% of your net income over $36,430. Thus, the credit completely disappears once your net income reaches $84,597. (Your spouse's net income does not affect this calculation.) The Quebec age credit is discussed at 17.5.

### 20.3.5 Pension income credit

You are entitled to a federal tax credit of 15% for 2017 of your qualifying pension income, up to $2,000 of pension income for the year. A similar credit is available in Quebec for up to $2,782 of pension income in 2017 (see 17.5).

Qualifying pension income does not include Canada Pension Plan, Old Age Security or Guaranteed Income Supplement payments. It basically means private pension income received through a life annuity. If you are 65 and over or are receiving payments as a result of your spouse's death, it also includes annuities out of an RRSP or deferred profit-sharing plan, payments from a RRIF (see 20.4.4) and the income portion of a regular annuity.

To make the most of this credit, you should aim to have at least $2,000 of qualifying pension income annually, plus another $2,000 for your spouse if possible.

> Aim for at least $2,000 of pension income annually for each spouse.

### 20.3.6 Pension income splitting

In Chapter 5, we described the potential tax savings you can achieve by splitting income with other family members so that the income is taxed at lower marginal tax rates (see 5.1). You may be able to split some of your pension income by transferring up to 50% of your income eligible for the pension income credit (see 20.3.5) to your spouse or common-law partner.

> File a joint election to split pension income with your spouse.

You and your spouse must jointly agree to the income splitting arrangement by each filing a joint election on or before the due date of your income tax return.

The amount of split pension income that will produce the most tax savings varies greatly among couples, depending on the income of each spouse. Be sure to consider the impact that the split pension income would have on the various personal tax credits such as the spousal, age and medical expense credits as well as the impact on each spouse's OAS clawback (see 20.3.2) and instalment requirements (see 9.2.2). You may want to consult a tax professional to help determine the split that is most advantageous for you.

### 20.3.7  Integrating government assistance with your pension benefits

Many pension plans offer the choice of an integrated or normal pension. An integrated pension takes into account the approximate amount of government assistance payments you will receive over the course of your retirement, providing higher payments in the early retiring years and lower payments when you become entitled to receive CPP/QPP payments (see 20.3.1) and/or OAS payments (see 20.3.2).

If you choose the integrated pension, you would normally have the same monthly income before and after age 65 (unless you decide to apply for CPP/QPP before then). Maintaining a consistent level of income before and after you start receiving your OAS and CPP/QPP benefits can help keep your income in a lower tax bracket and avoid having your government payments taxed back or reduced.

## 20.4  Maturing your RRSP

In Chapter 3, we discussed the tax rules and some planning ideas regarding RRSPs. This section discusses your options for maturing your RRSP. There are basically four routes for getting your money out of an RRSP—you must use one of the options described below by the end of the year in which you turn 71. Note that life income funds discussed in 20.4.5 are only available for locked-in retirement accounts.

### 20.4.1  RRSP contributions at age 71 and after

If you turn 71 and must wind up your RRSP in 2017, remember that you only have until December 31, 2017 (and not March 1, 2018) to contribute to your RRSP for 2017. You can continue making deductible contributions to a spousal RRSP until the end of the year in which your spouse turns 71, as long as you have earned income in the previous year or unused RRSP contribution room carried forward from prior years.

*Top up your RRSP before the end of the year in which you turn 71.* If you have earned income (generally salary and wages—see 3.1.3) in 2017, this will create new RRSP contribution room for 2018. But if you turn 71 in 2017, you must contribute both your 2017 and 2018 amounts before you wind up your RRSP at the end of 2017. If you have contributed your maximum amount for 2017 and your $2,000 penalty-free overcontribution, your additional contribution would attract a penalty tax of 1% per month. The penalty would only apply for the period between the date of the overcontribution and January 1, 2018—after that, your 2018 deduction room would be available.

### 20.4.2 RRSP maturity option #1—Withdraw the funds and pay the tax

The first, and easiest, way to cash out your RRSP is simply to withdraw the funds in a lump sum. The amount withdrawn from the RRSP is included in your income for the year in which you do so. It is taxed as ordinary income, just as if it were salary, even if some of the value of the RRSP represents capital gains (which outside an RRSP are normally only partially taxed and, in some cases, could be entirely exempt). A percentage to cover income tax is withheld at source by the financial institution and remitted to the CRA (and Revenu Québec if appropriate) on your behalf (see 3.2). You then report the income and the amount of tax withheld on your annual income tax return and either receive a refund or, if not enough tax was withheld, pay the difference.

### 20.4.3 RRSP maturity option #2—Purchase an annuity

The second method is to purchase an annuity, which will provide you with a steady income stream over the life of the annuity. The RRSP proceeds are not taxed immediately; annuity payments are taxed as you receive them. (As discussed in 20.3.5, up to $2,000 per year of the income may be effectively exempted through the pension income tax credit.)

There are three general kinds of annuities, each of which can be tailored through a variety of options to suit your needs: "term-certain", payable to you or your estate for a fixed number of years; "single life", payable to you as long as you are alive; and "joint and last survivor life", payable as long as either you or your spouse is alive. Other features may include a guaranteed term as part of a life annuity, indexing for inflation, reduction of payment on the death of your spouse, reduction of payment when Old Age Security payments begin, and so on. Unless you purchase a life annuity with a guaranteed period or a survivor option, your annuity dies with you and no residual balance is left to your heirs.

If you are interested in converting your RRSP to an annuity, you should discuss the available options, and their effect on the monthly annuity payment you receive, with your life insurance agent or trust company. Prevailing interest rates must also be considered to determine whether annuities alone, or a combination of annuities and RRIFs, might provide greater flexibility and returns.

### 20.4.4 RRSP maturity option #3—Convert your RRSP to RRIF

The third option for maturing your RRSP is to convert it into a Registered Retirement Income Fund, or RRIF. A RRIF is somewhat like an RRSP, in that you can have it invested in various kinds of securities. However, you must withdraw at least a "minimum amount" from the RRIF each year and report what you withdraw for tax purposes. (Again, currently up to $2,000 per year of such income may be effectively exempted through the pension income tax credit, as explained in 20.3.5.)

The amount that must be withdrawn from the RRIF is a fraction of the value of the RRIF at the beginning of the year that increases gradually each year based on your age, starting at 5.28% at age 71 and levelling out at 20% once you turn 95. You may use your spouse's age for the calculation of your RRIF minimum withdrawal amounts instead of your own. Doing so may allow you to extend the tax deferral on the funds in the plan if your spouse is younger than you are.

### 20.4.5 RRSP maturity option #4—Convert locked-in RRSP to LIF or LRIF

A life income fund (LIF) provides an alternative to a life annuity when certain individuals, who were formerly members of a registered pension plan, terminate employment or plan membership. The LIF is an option for individuals who have previously transferred pension funds to a locked-in retirement account (see 3.3.2).

A LIF is a RRIF for tax purposes (see 20.4.4) with additional restrictions. Generally, LIFs are available for pension and locked-in funds, subject to federal and provincial pension laws. Like any other RRIF, a minimum amount must be withdrawn each year. As well, under a LIF there is a maximum amount that can be withdrawn each year. In some provinces, the remaining balance of funds in the LIF must be used to purchase a life annuity by December 31 of the year in which the individual turns 80.

You may also want to consider a life retirement income fund (LRIF), now available in many provinces. If you hold a LRIF, you are usually not required to purchase an annuity at age 80, and the maximum amount available for withdrawal typically has some reference to the investment earnings remaining in the fund.

A LIF or LRIF can offer an attractive alternative to a life annuity option. The alternatives for accessing pension money and locked-in funds are evolving and changing in jurisdictions across the country. Contact your financial adviser to determine which options are available to you.

### 20.4.6 What's the best option?

By the end of the year in which you turn 71, you have to decide what to do with your RRSP. While your personal cash flow needs should be your primary concern, your decision should take into account your overall investment and estate planning goals. A straight withdrawal is rarely the best option, since you would be taxed on the total income in the current year— and none of it would be eligible for the pension tax credit (see 20.3.5).

Instead, if you wish to retain some control over the investment of your RRSP funds, you should purchase a RRIF (see 20.4.4). If you prefer simply to have a steady monthly income that you don't have to worry about, you could contact your life insurance agent and purchase an annuity (see 20.4.3).

> Convert your RRSP to a RRIF or annuity at the end of the year in which you turn 71.

A RRIF gives you more flexibility than an annuity in establishing the amount withdrawn each month, although you must still withdraw a monthly minimum. LIFs also offer flexibility within a range of minimum and maximum monthly withdrawals.

If you are maturing your RRSP, consider the effect of the tax brackets on your income. Your main goal, of course, is to ensure that you have enough income each month to meet your needs. If you can satisfy those needs with a longer-term payout that keeps your income below the high-tax brackets, you may be financially better off.

### 20.4.7  Using TFSAs in retirement

Tax-Free Savings Accounts (TFSA) are discussed at 4.1 and, together with your RRSPs, registered pension plan and other retirement investments, your TFSAs should be an integral component of your retirement plan. Although these plans are relatively new, the amount of retirement savings that you can contribute to your TFSAs will increase substantially over time and, unlike your RRSP, you can maintain your TFSA for your entire lifetime.

Once you are over 71 and you have wound up your RRSP, a TFSA can still offer a tax benefit if you want to save any of the income you receive once you are required to start drawing down your retirement savings. For example, excess after-tax funds received from an annuity or RRIF can be invested in a TFSA, subject to your available contribution room.

> Contribute excess after-tax RRIF or annuity income to your TFSA.

If you have enough contribution room, consider transferring non-registered investments to your TFSA. Whatever your age, new contribution room will be created each year. You can make even more room for your most highly taxed investments with high growth potential by removing some of your existing TFSA investments that may attract less tax. If you wish to transfer investments with accrued gains or losses to your TFSA, you should seek professional advice beforehand as the transfer would trigger tax on the unrealized gains while unrealized losses would be denied (similar to the treatment of investments transferred to RRSPs discussed at 3.1.6).

Income earned in your TFSA does not affect your eligibility for federal income-tested benefits and credits such as Old Age Security (see 20.3.2), the Age credit (see 20.3.4), or the Guaranteed Income Supplement and GST credit (see 2.9.3).

## 20.5 Cross-border retirement planning

If you have lived and worked in Canada and the U.S. (or in another country) and you are considering which country you want to live in after you retire, your retirement planning will be quite complex. In addition to two sets of income tax rules, you have to consider differences in your health care coverage, government-assisted investment vehicles and how your assets will be taxed at death. Beyond your lifestyle goals, the taxation of your investment and pension income in Canada and the U.S. should be a key factor in your decision about where to retire.

If you have lived and worked in both countries, you may have built up retirement assets on both sides of the border. These assets can include RRSPs (see Chapter 3), U.S. Individual Retirement Accounts (IRAs) (see 18.3.3), Canadian company pensions (see 3.5), U.S. company pension plans (also known as 401(k) plans) and a variety of other types of plans. You may have paid into both the Canada/Quebec Pension Plan and "FICA", the U.S. social security plan.

Retirement planning in cross-border situations involves the same retirement planning steps discussed in 20.1: you need to assess your net worth, outline your goals and objectives, review your cash flow requirements now and in retirement and determine your sources of retirement income. You also need to consider the usual areas of risk management (including disability and life insurance), taxation, investment strategies and estate planning. Due to differences between the laws of the two countries, planning opportunities may be available to minimize your overall tax liability and maximize your retirement assets and cash flow. But without proper advice, double taxation can result, especially on death.

As we saw in 20.2, retirement planning typically involves the preparation of financial projections to incorporate outside sources of retirement income, such as government and employer pensions, and to determine which assets should be accessed and in what order to maximize your retirement income. Before these projections can be prepared, you need to review the rules for withdrawal of funds from the various Canadian and U.S. tax-sheltered plans. The tax treatment of withdrawals from these funds varies depending on their status under the tax laws of Canada and the U.S. The same income may be taxable in both countries and, in certain cases, a foreign tax credit is available to minimize or even eliminate double taxation (see 18.2.2).

When you are deciding whether to retire in the U.S. or in Canada and developing your retirement plan, you should address the following questions. The answers depend on your particular situation; professional advice is strongly recommended.

- What is your tax status in each country and how are you taxed as a result? Is this the best result from a tax perspective? Do you have any choices?
- How would your RRSP be taxed as a non-resident of Canada? Can you still contribute to your RRSP if you do not live in Canada? If you do not return to Canada, should you withdraw your RRSP in a lump-sum?
- Would your expenses be higher in Canada or in the U.S.?
- How would you pay for your health care coverage? How does your provincial health care coverage compare to your U.S. coverage, if any?
- How would your U.S. tax-deferred plans be treated for Canadian tax purposes if you are resident here?
- Can you transfer the funds in your U.S. plans to an RRSP? Would this be beneficial?
- How do the CPP and the U.S. social security pensions interact in your situation? Could you collect two separate pensions and when should you start collecting them?
- Would it be more advantageous to hold U.S. or Canadian-denominated investments? Should you adopt a different investment strategy depending on the country of retirement?

In creating your estate plan for the distribution of your assets on death, you need to review the laws of both Canada and the U.S. in detail. From a tax perspective, residing in the U.S. at death or simply holding U.S. property can be costly. For a detailed discussion of U.S. estate taxes on death, see 19.4.

## 20.6 References

Old Age Security and Canada Pension Plan application kits are available (in person or by telephone request) from Service Canada. You can apply for CPP online at *www.servicecanada.gc.ca*. At this website, you can also find several booklets and fact sheets about the Old Age Security program, the Canada Pension Plan and the retirement income system.

You can apply for the Quebec Pension Plan and find related information online on Retraite Québec's website at *www.rrq.gouv.qc.ca*.

The following publications and more information, including forms and brochures, can be obtained on the CRA's website at *www.cra-arc.gc.ca* or by telephone request at 1-800-959-8281 for individual income tax and trust-related enquiries or 1-800-959-5525 for business and self-employed individual enquiries.

Fact Sheet RC4177, "Death of an RRSP Annuitant or a PRPP Member"

Fact Sheet RC4178, "Death of a RRIF Annuitant"

Guide RC4466, "Tax-Free Savings Account (TFSA), Guide for Individuals"

Guide T4040, "RRSPs and Other Registered Plans for Retirement"

Income Tax Folio S3-F10-C1, "Qualified Investments—RRSPs, RESPs, RRIFs, RDSPs and TFSAs"

Income Tax Folio S3-F10-C2, "Prohibited Investments—RRSPs, RRIFs and TFSAs"

Interpretation Bulletin IT-307R4, Archived – "Spousal and common-law partner Registered Retirement Savings Plans"

Interpretation Bulletin IT-500R, Archived – "Registered Retirement Savings Plans—Death of an annuitant"

Information Circular 72-22R9, "Registered Retirement Savings Plans"

Information Circular 78-18R6, "Registered Retirement Income Funds"

# Chapter 21

## Estate planning

- Make a will, or review your existing will (21.2)
- Take steps to minimize probate fees (21.4)
- Take action before the 21st anniversary of a trust's creation to manage the impact of a deemed disposition of all of a trust's capital property (21.5.3)
- Consider the advantages of establishing one or more family trusts (21.5.4)
- If you are 65 or older, consider setting up an "alter ego" or "joint partner" trust (21.5.5)
- Look into the potential benefits of an estate freeze (21.6.2)
- Make sure you have sufficient life insurance (21.7)
- Plan for the succession of your business (21.8)
- Consider a pre-paid plan to finance your funeral and cemetery arrangements (21.10)

*Careful estate planning can help you manage the taxes arising on death and leave as much as possible to your beneficiaries. In this chapter, we provide some estate planning strategies that you may want to consider. Keep in mind that estate planning can be extremely complicated and depends very much on your personal situation and goals. It should be undertaken in conjunction with the development of your retirement plan, as discussed in Chapter 20. Professional advice is highly recommended. If you or your spouse is not a Canadian resident, much of our commentary in this chapter does not apply to your situation; if you or your spouse are a U.S. citizen, see Chapter 18.*

> *Caution: The tax planning ideas discussed in this chapter may be affected by the federal government's proposed new tax regime for private companies, as outlined in the Department of Finance's July 2017 consultation paper and draft legislation. See Appendix I for details.*

## 21.1 What is estate planning?

The goal of estate planning is to achieve the state of financial affairs you desire, either at your death or later in your life when you wish to transfer family property to others. Like your financial plan (see Chapter 1), your estate plan should not be something you do once, then file away. Rather, it is a continual process that should evolve to meet changing family circumstances and wishes concerning who inherits your estate. You should give serious consideration to your estate plan at least every five years and more often if the law in this area or your family situation changes significantly.

Estate planning may involve more than merely creating or changing the terms and features of a will. For example, you should also consider the way you hold assets. Whether you own your assets personally, through a trust or through a holding company has important estate planning implications. Like other aspects of estate planning that evolve with changing circumstances, you may wish to periodically consider whether the structure of your asset holdings remains appropriate for your estate planning goals.

## 21.2  The will

### 21.2.1  Purpose of a will

Make a will, or review your existing will.

The will is a key element of estate planning. It allows you to provide for an orderly distribution of your assets in accordance with your desires and in a way that minimizes the tax burden on your estate and your beneficiaries. Depending on your circumstances, having more than one will may be advantageous—for example, multiple wills may help reduce probate fees (see 21.4) or facilitate the administration of your estate if you have assets in different countries.

Your will's primary function is to specify to whom and when your assets are to be distributed. You may want to leave specific properties (e.g., jewellery, furniture or shares in your business) to specific beneficiaries. You may want to leave a stated sum of money to certain people or to named charities (make sure you get the correct legal name of the charity). You also want to specify a "residual" beneficiary, who will get everything left in the estate after your specific bequests are satisfied.

The way you choose to direct assets to beneficiaries is influenced by several factors. For example, you may wish to simply leave everything directly to your spouse (including a common-law or same-sex spouse—see 2.2.1). Alternatively, you may want to use a "spousal trust" that, as we'll see in 21.5.2, can offer certain tax advantages and a measure of protection from potential creditors without any loss in flexibility for your surviving spouse. As discussed in 22.2.3, there will be no tax on the accrued capital gains on your property when the property is transferred to your spouse or a spousal trust, provided your spouse or spousal trust obtains ownership and unfettered rights to the property.

If you do not make a will, provincial law will determine how your assets are distributed. The result can vary significantly, depending on where you reside at the time of death. In Ontario, for example, the law provides that a surviving spouse gets the first $200,000 of an estate and divides any additional amounts with the deceased's children under a formula. However, in Alberta, the surviving spouse is entitled to all of the estate, unless the deceased had children from more than one relationship. In that case, the estate is divided among the surviving spouse and the deceased's children under a formula.

In some provinces, family law can effectively override the instructions in your will. In Ontario, for example, your spouse can elect to ignore the will and take the amount of money due to him or her under the "net family property" rules (see 21.3). If this is done, your estate may lose the benefit of the capital gains rollover described in 22.2.3.

If you have specific desires as to who should have custody of or guardianship over your children after your death and while they are under 18, you can put these desires into your will for consideration by the courts. However, in some provinces, this designation is not binding.

While in some provinces an entirely handwritten will may be valid, it is strongly advisable to have your will prepared or reviewed with the assistance of a lawyer, or a notary in Quebec, and a tax adviser to ensure it meets your wishes and takes tax and family law considerations into account.

Periodic reviews of your will are necessary to ensure that your estate plan is consistent with changes in the tax law, which occur regularly, as well as any changes in provincial family law and succession law.

Changes in your own personal circumstances such as the birth of a child or a change in marital status could also necessitate a change to your will. For example, in many jurisdictions, a will becomes void if you marry after making the will, unless it was made in contemplation of the marriage. By contrast, a will may not become void after a divorce.

If you do not make a will or if your will is invalid, the process of obtaining court approval for distribution of your assets may be cumbersome and expensive. Your representative or heirs must apply to the court to appoint an administrator (also called an "estate trustee") to administer and distribute the estate in accordance with a formula set out in legislation.

As discussed in 1.3.4, consider also executing powers of attorney in the event you become unable to act by reason of disability or mental incompetence—one for decisions related to your finances and one for decisions related to your personal care. If, for example, you become mentally disabled, the continuing powers of attorney would enable the named "attorney" to act in your stead. (In Quebec, you can designate such a person in a document called a "mandate in case of incapacity".) You may wish to give the powers of attorney to the same person you name as your executor, such as your spouse.

### 21.2.2 Choosing your executor and estate trustee

In your will, you should designate one or more persons as your executor(s) (also called estate trustee(s)). The person should be someone you can trust to take charge of your affairs and distribute your assets in accordance with your desires as set out in your will. The executor and estate trustee will normally apply to the court for "letters probate" (see 21.4), which will give court approval for the executor to take over your property, manage it and distribute it to your beneficiaries.

The responsibilities of your executor and estate trustee include determining the assets and liabilities of the estate, filing all income tax returns for you and the estate (including any foreign succession duty or tax returns) and paying the debts (including all taxes) outstanding at the date of your death.

Ideally, you should choose an executor and estate trustee who is familiar with your personal situation. Often the executor would be your principal beneficiary (such as your spouse). Sometimes this may not be appropriate, however, because of a possible conflict of interest with other beneficiaries.

You should consider naming an alternate executor and estate trustee in case your executor dies before you do. Otherwise your estate may be handled by the executor of your executor's estate. Naming an alternate executor and estate trustee is also important in case the named executor is either unable to or chooses not to act. This can avoid costly court proceedings.

If you are an executor and estate trustee yourself, see Chapter 22 for a discussion of your role and responsibilities.

### 21.2.3 Will planning to manage your estate's tax liability

There are many tax-oriented clauses that can be included in a will to help manage a tax liability at death. The will should include a provision granting executors and estate trustees broad authority to make or join in any election, designation or allocation under tax legislation. This will ensure that your executor can use benefits such as the principal residence designation and capital gains exemption. The following clauses should also be considered:

- forgiveness of certain loans made to family members
- a discretionary power permitting trustees to determine which assets are to form the trust property of spousal or other trusts
- a reminder to your executors that if you have not made your maximum RRSP contribution at the time of your death, one should be made by your estate to your spouse's RRSP before the required deadline.

In your will, you can name the beneficiary of your RRSP, RRIF, TFSA, deferred profit-sharing plan, death benefits and life insurance proceeds. Alternatively, these plans and policies usually allow for naming a beneficiary directly within the plan documents. While designating beneficiaries directly in the plan documents may reduce probate costs, there may also be implications for spousal rights under family law. You should also consider confirming these designations in your will and providing for the proceeds to form part of your estate if the designated beneficiary dies before you and no contingent beneficiary is named.

Note that your estate may have to pay tax on the full value of your RRSP or RRIF on your death if you designate as the beneficiary someone other than your spouse or, under a special election, your financially dependent children (see 22.4.1).

If you plan to make a charitable gift through your will, instead of donating cash, consider donating publicly traded securities, mutual funds or segregated funds of a life insurance company in order to help reduce taxes payable at death (see 8.2 and 8.3.2).

## 21.3  Family law

Provincial family law can have a significant impact on your estate planning. Every province has legislation to protect the interests of spouses on marriage breakdown. This legislation may apply on death as well. We'll use Ontario family law for purposes of this discussion. The laws of each province are different, however, and professional advice should be obtained.

On marriage breakdown, Ontario's *Family Law Act* provides for an equal division of "net family property", which includes almost all property acquired during the marriage and the increase in the value of property owned at the time of the marriage. Business assets, shares in a privately held or public corporation and investments are typically all included in "net family property". Each spouse's assets are totalled and an equalizing payment is required, so that each spouse ends up with half of the value of the net family property.

The above provisions apply on death as well. The surviving spouse may elect to take an equalizing payment for one-half of the difference in net family property rather than whatever has been left to him or her under the deceased's will. Clearly, such rules can interfere with estate planning, and they should be considered when making a will.

Spouses can agree to have these provisions of the *Family Law Act* not apply, or only apply to specific assets, by signing a "domestic contract". Separate independent legal advice for each spouse is required before signing such a contract.

## 21.4 Probate fees

Probate fees are charged by the courts in each province (except Quebec) to grant letters probate, which confirm that the deceased's will is valid and the executor has the authority to administer the estate.

The probate charge generally applies to the total value of the deceased's assets at the time of death, without any deduction for debts other than those encumbering real property. In some cases, the assets can be distributed and the estate wound up without probate but probate is generally required before third parties such as financial institutions (e.g., banks, investment dealers) will release property to the executor or estate trustee. If there is no will, probate is still required because the court has to confirm that an executor has been appointed to distribute the deceased's property as required by law.

Probate fees are highest in Ontario and British Columbia, where they are 1.5% and 1.4%, respectively, of the value of the estate over $50,000 (with lower rates applying to the value below $50,000). In Nova Scotia, the top rate is 1.695% of the value of the estate over $100,000 (with progressive flat rates applying to values below $100,000). In other provinces, the top rates are typically 0.4% to 0.7% of the value of the estate. Quebec levies a nominal flat fee that is not based on the estate's value. Alberta has progressive flat rates based on the estate's value to a maximum of $525. The probate fees for large estates in other provinces can be substantial as there is no maximum.

Property held by two people as "joint tenants" with right of survivorship (rather than as "tenants in common") is not subject to probate, since on the death of one joint tenant the property does not form part of the estate but simply becomes wholly owned by the other. Property is commonly held by spouses in this manner.

You may also hold property in joint tenancy with your adult children to reduce probate fee exposure (known as a "Pecore" joint tenancy arrangement, after the court case confirming the acceptability of this technique). In this case, your adult child holds the assets as bare trustee for you during your lifetime and, on your adult child's death, is expected to transfer the assets to the beneficiaries under the will. Provided the will does not otherwise require probate, the value of the property is not subject to probate fees.

Example

Jonah, who lives in Ontario, dies in 2017. His estate consists of a house worth $1 million, with a $700,000 mortgage on it, $100,000 in personal effects, and the shares of his business, worth $1 million. He also owes $80,000 on a personal line of credit to the bank at the time of his death.

The value of Jonah's estate for probate purposes is $1.4 million. The house is counted as $300,000 (i.e., minus the mortgage), and his other assets are $1.1 million. The $80,000 debt is not deducted. The fee for probating Jonah's will is $20,500 (calculated as 0.5% of the first $50,000, plus 1.5% of the balance of $1.35 million).

The following options can reduce the cost of probating your estate. Note, however, that any planning to reduce probate fees must take numerous other issues (such as family law, income tax effects, land transfer tax, GST/HST and other sales taxes) into account—professional advice is strongly recommended.

- If you are leaving property outright to your spouse (or another person), consider holding the property as joint tenants with your spouse (or that other person) with a right of survivorship. On your death, the property will pass automatically to the other joint tenant and not form part of your estate. Note that there may be immediate adverse tax consequences if you transfer the property to a joint tenant who is someone other than your spouse. Also, there are some situations where a joint tenancy will be severed on death by provincial legislation.
- If you are leaving property to a person subject to a Pecore joint tenancy arrangement (discussed above), properly documenting the arrangement is critical to ensure no immediate tax consequences arise.
- Try to keep certain assets out of the estate. This is quite practical in the case of life insurance, RRSPs, RRIFs and TFSAs, where beneficiaries (other than the estate) can be designated in the RRSP, RRIF or TFSA plan documents or in the life insurance policy. Also consider transferring property during your lifetime, either directly to your intended beneficiaries or to a trust for their benefit. Again, take care that this does not trigger premature recognition of accrued capital gains.
- If you own real estate with no mortgage and you also owe money (perhaps on a personal line of credit or on a debt secured by other assets), consider having the debt converted to a mortgage or charge on the real estate. Doing so may reduce the value of the real estate for probate purposes.

- If you have certain assets that can pass to beneficiaries without probate, such as shares in a private company, you may be able to reduce probate fees by making a secondary will that only includes these assets. Your executor would then apply for probate on the primary will but not the secondary one. This type of planning has become common in many jurisdictions and can be an effective way of reducing probate costs.
- If you are age 65 or over, two types of trusts—"alter ego" and "joint partner" trusts—can help you keep assets out of your estate and reduce its value for probate purposes without giving up your right to those assets during your lifetime (see 21.5.5).

## 21.5 Trusts

### 21.5.1 What is a trust?

A trust is an arrangement whereby one or more persons (the trustees) hold legal title to property (the trust property) for the benefit of other persons (the beneficiaries). The person who creates the trust and puts ("settles") property into it is called the settlor.

> **Example**
>
> Brian is leaving the country to work in Africa for several years. He gives Paul $120,000 to hold in trust for Brian's two teenagers, Dianne and Darryl. Brian draws up a trust agreement that allows Paul to use the trust funds to pay for Brian's children's education, to invest the funds not yet used, and to pay half of the capital of the trust to each child when they turn 23.
>
> In this example, Brian is the settlor, Paul is the trustee and Dianne and Darryl are the beneficiaries. Paul has legal ownership of the $120,000, but he is required to use it only for Dianne's and Darryl's benefit and not for his personal use. If the trust document permits, he can pay himself a fee for his services as trustee.

There is no legal requirement that the settlor and the trustee be different people. (In the example above, Brian could simply declare and document that he is holding funds in trust for his children, and a trust would be created.) Similarly, the settlor and the beneficiary can be the same person. (This is what happens when you put funds into a self-directed RRSP, for example. You are the settlor and beneficiary, and a trust company is the trustee of your assets—see 3.1.6.) However, the choice of settlor, trustee and beneficiaries affects the taxation of the trust and its beneficiaries. For example, a number of attribution rules apply to trusts, including those outlined in Chapter 5. Careful planning is required.

Note that the mechanics and terminology of trusts are somewhat different in Quebec, which is governed by the province's *Civil Code* rather than by the common law that governs the rest of Canada.

Court cases involving trusts' legal constitution and residency highlight the importance of ensuring that trust arrangements are properly made, especially when the trust and its beneficiaries reside in different jurisdictions. Trustees should properly maintain the trust's accounting records and promptly document their decisions in trust minutes.

### 21.5.2 What kinds of trusts are there?

A trust can be set up during the settlor's lifetime (as in the example above). Such a trust is called an *inter vivos* (Latin for "among the living") trust.

A trust can also be created by the settlor's will, in which case it is called a testamentary trust.

A trust for the settlor's spouse that meets certain conditions is a "spousal trust". The principal conditions are that all of the income of the trust must be payable to the spouse during the spouse's lifetime and that none of the capital can be distributed to anyone other than the spouse during the spouse's lifetime. (After the spouse's death, however, the income and capital can be distributed to someone else, such as the settlor's children.) Such a trust can be either testamentary or *inter vivos*. A transfer of property from the settlor to a spousal trust does not trigger tax on any accrued capital gain; instead the property passes at the settlor's tax cost, and any capital gain is taxed only when the trust eventually disposes of the property or the spouse dies (see 22.2.3).

If your will creates a trust, that trust would be separate from your estate. The estate would be taxed as a trust for as long as it takes to wind up your affairs and distribute your assets. A trust set up in your will, on the other hand, could be designed to continue for many years beyond your death.

Many types of trusts are in use today. Each meets a purpose or addresses an aspect of tax or common law. For a discussion of two kinds of trusts called "alter ego" and "joint partner" trusts, see 21.5.5.

### 21.5.3 How is a trust taxed?

A trust is a separate person for income tax purposes. The trustee(s) must file a T3 trust tax return (and a TP-646 Quebec trust return in some cases) and pay tax on the trust's income. A trust is generally taxed as an individual but is not eligible for the personal credits (see Chapter 2). *Inter vivos* trusts pay tax at a flat rate—the top rate of combined federal and provincial tax for individuals (about 50%). Testamentary trusts paid tax at the same marginal rates as individuals (see 5.1) until December 31, 2015. Beginning in 2016, testamentary trusts (except certain estates, see 22.2.2, and qualified disability trusts, see below) also pay tax at the top rate.

A trust's income includes its income from carrying on business (see Chapter 11), from taxable capital gains (see Chapter 6) and from investments (interest, dividends, rent, etc.—see Chapter 7), calculated as if the trust were a living individual. Amounts that are payable or paid to beneficiaries are deducted from the trust income, and the beneficiaries report such income on their tax returns, subject to the attribution rules discussed in Chapter 5.

Certain kinds of income, such as capital gains and dividends, preserve their character when flowed through to a beneficiary. Thus, such income can be treated as capital gains (see Chapter 6) or as dividends (see 7.1.2) on the beneficiary's tax return. Other income loses its character as it flows through a trust.

A special election called the "preferred beneficiary election" may be available where a beneficiary is disabled (as defined for tax purposes in 2.5.1). This election allows the trust and the beneficiary to agree that the trust's income will be taxed in the beneficiary's hands so that, in a later year, the income can be paid out by the trust to the beneficiary free of tax.

Other special tax rules allow income and capital gains to be taxed in the trust even if these amounts have been paid out to the beneficiary during the year. For these rules to apply in 2016 and later years, the taxable income of the trust must be nil. As such, these rules only apply if the trust has unused losses from other years that can offset this income.

If your will currently provides a separate testamentary trust for each beneficiary to allow each trust to benefit from lower graduated rates of tax for the income retained in such a trust, you may want to reconsider this arrangement because testamentary trusts are no longer entitled to graduated rates of tax in 2016 and later years.

However, if your will creates a testamentary trust for a disabled beneficiary, the trust may still be able to pay tax at graduated rates after 2015 rather than at the top rate. To qualify for graduated rates, one or more of the trust's beneficiaries must have a disability tax credit certificate (see 2.5.1). Further, the capital of such a qualified disability trust that was taxed at graduated rates must be paid to a disabled beneficiary. If such trust capital is paid to a non-disabled beneficiary, the tax savings previously realized must be repaid.

Take action before the 21st anniversary of a trust's creation to manage the impact of a deemed disposition of all of a trust's capital property.

Every 21 years a trust (other than a spousal, alter ego or joint partner trust—see 21.5.2 and 21.5.5) is deemed to dispose of all of its property, so that accrued capital gains are taxed as if the assets have been sold. Before the end of each 21-year period, consult a professional adviser to determine whether steps can be taken to manage the impact of this deemed disposition.

### 21.5.4 The benefits of setting up a family trust

A trust offers tremendous flexibility in structuring your affairs and controlling the future use of your property. The powers of the trustees can be strictly limited and defined; or they can be given full discretion as to when and whether to pay income or distribute capital to the beneficiaries, how to manage the trust property and when to wind up the trust.

Setting up the trust while you are alive can provide several advantages:

- by making yourself a trustee, you can keep control of the trust assets (such as shares of your business)
- by getting the assets out of your estate, you can reduce probate fees (see 21.4)
- because the assets will not be in your estate, they will not form part of the public record that anyone can examine in the court office
- income splitting may be possible, depending on the application of the attribution rules (see Chapter 5).

A trust can also be useful as part of an estate freeze (see 21.6). In many cases, you may not know at the time you set up the freeze how you want the growth allocated among your children.

> Consider the advantages of establishing one or more family trusts.

You may not want to give them direct ownership in the business yet. In such an event you should consider setting up a family trust and having the trust subscribe for the "growth" common shares (or have them gifted to the trust). If you are the trustee and have discretion as to how to allocate the income and capital of the trust, you can decide several years later (or even in your will) which of your children should inherit the business. This may also provide some flexibility for your children when dealing with family law legislation (see 21.3). If you have already established such a plan, ensure that its benefits will not be neutralized by the income-splitting tax on certain income received by minors (see 5.2.4).

An *inter vivos* trust can offer benefits over a power of attorney or applying to the court to appoint a guardian in the event of incapacity. As we saw in 1.3.4, a power of attorney allows you to designate a person who would take control of your financial affairs if you become incapacitated due to illness or injury. Potential advantages of trusts over powers of attorney include the following:

- Unlike a power of attorney, the trust agreement is a comprehensive document that sets out the trustee's specific duties and powers.
- A higher standard of fiduciary duty applies to a trustee than to a power of attorney.

- The trust survives death but a power of attorney does not.
- Property held under the trust agreement can be managed by the trustees in the event of incapacity without the settlor's involvement, thereby offering protection against third-party abuse, since the settlor does not have independent control of his or her assets.
- A power of attorney may not be adequate to manage assets outside of your own province—each province and state in North America has different legislation. The authority of a trustee acting on behalf of a trust would be more readily recognized by a foreign bank or other institution.

### 21.5.5 Alter ego and joint partner trusts

Two types of trusts, called "alter ego" and "joint partner" trusts, may be useful as substitutes for wills and powers of attorney and can produce significant benefits in terms of avoiding probate fees and reducing difficulties for your survivors or your business while your estate is being settled.

If you are 65 or older, consider setting up an "alter ego" or "joint partner" trust.

If you are 65 or over, an alter ego trust can help you keep assets out of your estate without giving up your right to those assets during your lifetime. Under the terms of such a trust, all of the income and capital of the trust property would be held and used for your benefit alone. No income tax is triggered when you put the property into the trust. Income and capital gains generated by the trust property would be taxable in your hands, as they would if you continued to own the assets personally. On your death, the alter ego trust document performs the same function as a will would have by setting out how the trust assets should be distributed.

A joint partner trust works the same way except that the assets are held for the benefit of you and your spouse. Spouses (provided they are also over 65) can also transfer assets to the trust without triggering any income tax, except that they would be taxed on all of the income and capital gains of the property they transferred during their lifetime.

If you plan to transfer qualified small business corporation shares or qualified farm or fishing property to an alter ego or joint partner trust, keep in mind that it may not be possible to use the lifetime capital gains exemption (see 6.4) for these types of property while you are alive.

On the death of the settlor of an alter ego trust or the second partner of a joint partner trust, the trust is deemed to have disposed of its assets at fair market value, and any capital gains are taxed in the trust's hands.

It is not possible to claim any unused lifetime capital gains exemption of the settlor or surviving partner to offset these deemed gains. As a result, you may want to elect out of the rollover provisions so you can trigger a capital gain and claim the capital gains exemption at the time the property is transferred to the alter ego or joint partner trust.

For alter ego and joint partner trusts, the deemed realization at fair market value discussed in 21.5.3 does not occur every 21 years; rather, as noted above, it occurs on the day on which the settlor or surviving partner dies. If the trust continues to exist, a deemed disposition will occur every 21 years after the death of the settlor (for alter ego trusts) or surviving partner (for joint partner trusts).

However, since alter ego and joint partner trusts are *inter vivos* trusts, they pay tax at the highest marginal rate for individuals. As such, trust income does not benefit from graduated rates of tax and any capital gain that arises on the deemed disposition resulting from the settlor or surviving partner's death may bear more income tax in the trust than it would if taxed in the deceased's hands.

## 21.6 Estate freezing

### 21.6.1 What is an estate freeze?

"Estate freezing" is the term used to describe steps taken to fix the value of your estate (or some particular asset) at its present value, so that future growth will accrue to the benefit of others, such as your children (or a trust for your children) and not be taxed on your death. Several provisions of the *Income Tax Act* are designed to facilitate this type of planning.

Estate freezing is most often used when you own a business that your family will continue to own after your death and that you expect will increase in value in future years. Your children may be involved in running the business. Even if they are not, you may want them to own it after your death.

### 21.6.2 How do you freeze an estate?

There are many different approaches to an estate freeze, some of them very complex. The following example is one of the simplest types:

**Example**

Lucas owns all of the common shares of his business, X Corp. His original share investment in X Corp. was $100, and it is now worth $10 million. Lucas expects it to increase in value significantly over the next several years. Lucas has two children, both in their early 20s, who work in the business.

First, Lucas exchanges his common shares of X Corp. for 10,000 new preferred shares (a step that can be taken without triggering any income tax). The preferred shares are voting shares. They are also retractable at any time, at his option, for $1,000 per share. In other words, Lucas can demand that the corporation pay him $10 million for his shares at any time.

Each of Lucas's children then subscribes for 50 new common shares in X Corp., paying $1 per share. Since X Corp. is worth $10 million, and Lucas's preferred shares are retractable for $10 million, the common shares have negligible value at the moment.

Over the next few years, the value of X Corp. rises to $10.5 million. Now Lucas's preferred shares are still worth only $10 million, but the common shares are worth $500,000. Lucas has thus transferred the post-freeze "growth" in the corporation to his children at no tax cost to him.

Note also that since Lucas's preferred shares are voting shares, he has kept control of the corporation. Lucas has 10,000 votes and his children together have only 100.

The mechanics of an estate freeze are complex, and numerous income tax rules have to be considered. The basic concept, however, is generally as outlined above. Often you would set up a holding company and a family trust (see 21.5.4) as part of the freeze, rather than having your children subscribe directly for shares in the operating company.

**Look into the potential benefits of an estate freeze.**

An estate freeze can significantly reduce the tax payable on your death, if the value of your business is "frozen" sufficiently early. The value of the business is fixed at the time of the freeze, so the tax on the subsequent capital appreciation is deferred until your children sell the business (or until their deaths). You can also multiply the availability of the capital gains exemption for certain "small business corporation" shares (see 6.4.1), if it is still available when your children eventually dispose of the shares. At the same time, you do not need to give up control of the business.

You can also continue to receive income from the corporation, either by declaring dividends on the preferred shares or by drawing a salary if you continue to work in the business.

If you use a trust to acquire the common shares, you can retain flexibility for allocating the shares of the business among your children later.

When you set up the freeze, you can trigger part or all of the accrued capital gain on your shares to date. This may allow you to use your lifetime capital gains exemption (see 6.4.1), for example. Be aware of the various restrictions on claiming the exemption (see 6.4.3).

Depending on how the freeze is structured, you can achieve income splitting (see Chapter 5) by directing income into the hands of your children for tax purposes. Note that certain attribution rules do not apply if your corporation qualifies as a "small business corporation" (see 6.2.3) or your children have reached the age of 18 (see 5.2.5). However, existing arrangements may be affected by the income-splitting tax on certain income received by minor children (see 5.2.4).

If you have carried out an estate freeze but the value of the frozen shares has gone down due to economic conditions, you may benefit from carrying out a "refreeze", which would fix a lower value on the business and your preferred shares. This lower value would further decrease the tax payable on your death and allow greater future growth for the common shares held by your children or a trust.

Whether an estate freeze or refreeze is useful to you depends very much on your business, your financial position, your future plans and your goals. You should obtain qualified professional advice before undertaking this type of planning.

## 21.7 Life insurance

Life insurance plays many roles in estate planning. For example, it can:

- provide replacement income for your dependants
- provide a fund for emergency expenses or children's education in future years
- pay for final expenses such as funeral costs
- assist in funding the succession of a business in a closely held corporation
- fund capital gains tax liability that arises on death (see 22.2.3)
- allow you to accumulate funds on a tax-sheltered basis to supplement retirement income.

Insurance proceeds received on the death of the life insured are not taxable. Similarly, the premiums you pay for your life insurance are generally not tax-deductible.

If your corporation is the beneficiary of a policy on your life, the corporation may be able to distribute the life insurance proceeds to your estate and other shareholders without any tax applying. Stricter rules apply for policy benefits received after March 22, 2016 to prevent what the government considers to be artificial increases in tax benefits.

Some business owners may own a holding company that owns an operating company. If you own such a holding company and it is the beneficiary of your life insurance policy but the operating company pays the premiums, the holding company may be assessed a shareholder benefit. You may want to consult your professional adviser about how to structure the ownership of the insurance policy to avoid the shareholder benefit.

**Make sure you have sufficient life insurance.** Your need for insurance changes as factors such as your income, investment portfolio and dependants change. Therefore, a regular review of your coverage is important.

There are many different life insurance products available. These products can generally be divided into two types: term insurance and permanent insurance.

Term (or "pure") insurance policies usually have lower premiums at younger ages. You are paying the cost of insuring against the risk of your death in the current year and nothing more. As long as you continue to pay the premiums, your coverage continues; many policies guarantee renewal without additional medical evidence. However, the cost of premiums increases dramatically in later years for normal renewable policies. Most term policies terminate at age 70 to 75, which is lower than the current average life expectancy, though many companies offer "term to age 100"-type policies, which can be acquired for level premiums over life.

A permanent insurance policy (often called "whole life" or "universal life") combines pure insurance coverage with an investment fund. As a result, the cost of premiums is often much higher than term insurance though much of this cost forms part of the investment fund. Many permanent insurance policies offer fixed premiums for guaranteed maximum terms (say, 10 or 20 years). At the end of the term, the policy is often fully paid up. The policy can be designed so that the investment fund or cash surrender value accumulates tax-free. Such a fund can be borrowed against or "cashed out" in later years. However, doing so would have a tax cost.

Permanent insurance products are usually desirable for the following purposes:

- capital gains tax funding
- estate equalization (to allow for an even distribution of your estate, such as where you wish to leave business assets to beneficiaries active in a family business and non-business assets to those family members not active in the business)
- business succession planning

- long-term, tax-effective investment strategies.

When buying insurance, consider who should be the beneficiary. If your estate is the beneficiary, the insurance proceeds would form part of your estate on your death and be subject to any claims that creditors have on your estate. The proceeds would also be subject to probate fees (see 21.4 above). You may therefore want to have the insurance proceeds payable directly to your spouse, another beneficiary or an insurance trust, in order to bypass the estate. The investment fund or cash surrender value of a policy can also be protected from creditors during your lifetime where certain beneficiaries are named.

New rules affecting the taxation of whole and universal life insurance policies took effect January 1, 2017 (see 7.3.3). Existing policies are generally not affected. You may want to consult your professional advisers to discuss how these changes may affect any estate planning with life insurance that you may be considering.

## 21.8  Business succession

If you own and manage a business, it could well be your family's largest asset. After your death, the business may be crucial for meeting your family's financial needs. Taking steps to ensure your business's ongoing profitability and management can be just as important as considering the planning opportunities available to reduce taxes on your death.

One of the first issues you must resolve is what will happen to the business when you die. You could plan for the business to be kept in the family, sold to a buyer outside the family or liquidated. The option you choose depends on things such as the nature of the business, the likelihood of its continued success after your death and the abilities of your family members and/or key employees to run the business's operations.

Plan for the succession of your business.

If the family is not capable or does not want to run the business, it may be in everyone's best interests to sell or liquidate the business on or before your retirement. If some family members are quite active in managing the business while others are not, dividing ownership equally among your family might seem fair but it could disrupt the business and create tension in the family. Often in these cases, you could use other family assets or life insurance to ensure fairness for all family members.

If you decide to keep the business in the family, you should seek professional advice to help you decide whether to transfer ownership during your lifetime or on death, who will receive the business's shares and in what proportion, whether the shares will be gifted or sold, and the most tax-effective way to structure the transfer.

If you do not own 100% of your company's shares, the transfer of its legal control may be addressed by a carefully drafted shareholders' agreement (see 14.4).

Life insurance owned by you or your company can facilitate the sale of your shares of the company and help to fund any tax liability arising on death. The tax rules may allow you to maintain certain tax advantages associated with life insurance-funded arrangements if your company was the beneficiary of a life insurance policy held for this purpose on or before April 25, 1995, or if there was an agreement in place at that time relating to the disposition of your shares. These tax advantages would remain available if you cancel the pre-April 26, 1995 life insurance policy and replace it with another policy or you increase the amount of insurance coverage.

## 21.9  Planning for the succession of wealth

In some cases where a family business has been sold, the family's largest asset after the sale is the net sale proceeds. In other cases, wise investment decisions have resulted in the accumulation of significant wealth. Since the bulk of such estates may ultimately accrue to your children, you should assess the age at which you feel they should have access to this wealth and whether you should put controls or restrictions on the use of these resources for certain periods of time.

*Inter vivos* and testamentary family trusts (see 21.5.4) can facilitate the transfer of wealth to children over pre-determined ages. Such trusts are also useful in situations where the child is dependent by reason of mental or physical infirmity. They can also be beneficial if your children lack an appreciation for the value of money.

If you will be passing on a sizeable estate to your children, you should consult with your legal and tax advisers to develop a plan to transfer the wealth into their hands.

## 21.10 Pre-paid funeral and cemetery arrangements

Planning and paying for your funeral and cemetery arrangements in advance can go a long way toward easing the stress on your survivors at a difficult time. Many funeral and cemetery service providers offer plans through which you can deposit funds as pre-payment for their services.

Consider a pre-paid plan to finance your funeral and cemetery arrangements.

To help Canadians finance these arrangements, the tax rules provide a special tax exemption for the investment income earned on eligible pre-paid amounts. Like the deferred income plans discussed in Chapter 3, the sooner you contribute to a pre-paid funeral or cemetery arrangement, the longer your funds will benefit from the effect of tax-free compounding of income.

You can contribute up to $35,000 to an arrangement that covers both funeral and cemetery services. If the funeral and cemetery services will be provided by separate businesses, you can contribute up to $15,000 to an arrangement that covers only funeral services and up to $20,000 to an arrangement that covers only cemetery services. The funds in your account can be used to cover your own funeral and cemetery arrangements or those of anyone you choose; the limits only restrict the amount that any one person can contribute to such plans over his or her lifetime.

Although the amounts of your lump-sum or periodic contributions are not tax-deductible, any income earned on the deposited amounts is not subject to tax while they are in the plan. If you withdraw the funds and use them for other purposes, any amounts that exceed your total contributions are taxable in the year of withdrawal.

Any amounts left over after the funeral and cemetery expenses have been paid for will be refunded to the contributor or the contributor's estate. The tax payable on the refund is calculated with a formula that ensures that only the fund's investment income is subject to tax.

## 21.11 References

There is little published information on estate planning that is easily understood by the layperson. As well, every individual's case is different. Consult a qualified tax professional for advice.

Interpretation Bulletin IT-531, Archived – "Eligible funeral arrangements" is available on the CRA's website at *www.cra-arc.gc.ca* or by telephone request at 1-800-959-8281 for individual income tax and trust-related enquiries.

# Chapter 22

## If you are an executor or estate trustee

- Take steps to reduce the tax burden on the estate (22.1.3)
- Consider realizing selected capital gains and losses on assets left to a spouse or spousal trust (22.2.3)
- Consider filing separate income tax returns to multiply credits (22.2.4)
- Obtain a clearance certificate before distributing assets (22.2.5)
- Watch out for the effects of foreign estate taxes (22.5)

*If you are an executor or estate trustee, your responsibilities for the deceased's estate include filing all tax returns required and ensuring that all taxes have been paid. To fulfill these responsibilities, you need to know about the tax rules that apply on death. In this chapter, we provide an overview of these rules and some steps you may be able to take to minimize the taxes owed by the deceased and the estate.*

> *Caution: The tax planning ideas discussed in this chapter may be affected by the federal government's proposed new tax regime for private companies, as outlined in the Department of Finance's July 2017 consultation paper and draft legislation. See Appendix I for details.*

## 22.1 What happens on death?

When a person dies, the executor or administrator of the person's estate (called the "estate trustee") is responsible for taking charge of the individual's affairs and distributing assets as set out in his or her will. The executor's responsibilities include determining the assets and liabilities of the estate, filing all income tax returns for the deceased and the estate, paying the debts outstanding at the date of the individual's death (including all taxes), and letting the beneficiaries know which of the amounts they receive from the estate are taxable.

If there is no will or the will is invalid, provincial law determines how the deceased's assets are distributed. The deceased's representatives or heirs must apply to the court to appoint an administrator to administer and distribute the estate according to a formula set out in legislation (see 21.2.1).

### 22.1.1 Applying for probate

The executor normally applies to the court for "letters probate", which will give court approval for the executor to take over the deceased's property, manage it and distribute it to the beneficiaries of the estate.

Probate fees are charged by the courts in each province (except Quebec) to grant letters probate. The probate charge generally applies to the total value of an estate's assets at the time of death, without any deduction for debts other than those encumbering real property. (See 21.4 for estate planning steps you may be able to take to minimize probate fees.)

### 22.1.2 Notifying government agencies

If the deceased received Canada Pension Plan (CPP) or Old Age Security (OAS) payments, the executor or legal representative should contact Service Canada to cancel the deceased's benefits and determine the death benefits due to a surviving spouse or the estate.

### 22.1.3 Post-mortem tax planning

Take steps to reduce the tax burden on the estate.

Tax planning does not necessarily stop on death. There may be many opportunities for post-mortem planning available to the deceased's estate to lessen the tax burden on the estate or the deceased taxpayer to the benefit of the beneficiaries. Post-mortem planning begins shortly after death and is usually complete within the first year.

For example, in certain circumstances, more than one income tax return may be filed for the deceased taxpayer (see 22.2.4). If the deceased has a surviving spouse, the executor may be able to make a contribution to a spousal RRSP before the deadline (60 days after the end of the year of death).

In more complicated situations, the deceased's representative may choose to wind up a corporation owned by the estate during the first fiscal period of the estate or make certain elections relating to capital losses arising in the estate (see 22.2.3).

If you are an executor and estate trustee, you should seek advice on how to manage the tax burden on the estate that has been left under your care. If you do not, you could be sued by the beneficiaries. The courts have found executors liable for failing to take active steps to structure the estate's affairs to reduce income tax.

## 22.2 Taxes on death

### 22.2.1 Tax payable by the deceased taxpayer

When a person dies, the executor must file a "terminal return" for the deceased to report income up to the date of death. Although the regular T1 and Quebec TP1 return forms are used, there are special rules for these returns. For example:

- charitable donations, which can normally be claimed for the year of donation or carried forward to future years (see 8.1), can be carried back and claimed in the year prior to death (subject to the limits discussed in 8.1) or, starting in 2016, claimed by the estate (see 8.2), if not of use in the terminal return
- medical expenses paid, which can normally be claimed for a 12-month period ending in the year (see 2.7.1), can be pooled for any 24-month period that includes the day of death
- the full amount of the deceased's RRSP (see 3.1) or RRIF (see 20.4.4) is brought into income for the year of death, unless the beneficiary of the plan is the deceased's spouse or certain dependants (see 22.4.1); if the funds are not transferred to the spouse's own RRSP or RRIF, the spouse must report the funds as income for tax purposes
- any balance borrowed by the deceased from an RRSP under the Home Buyers' Plan (see 3.3.6) or Lifelong Learning Plan (see 3.3.7) and not yet repaid must be included in income unless an election is made to have the liability assumed by the surviving spouse
- the fair market value of the property held in the deceased's TFSA (see 4.1) at the time of death is not taxable to the deceased but any investment income earned in the TFSA after the holder's death is generally no longer tax-exempt (see 22.4.2)
- minimum tax (see 7.6) does not apply to the year of death
- capital property not left to a surviving spouse (either outright or through a spousal trust) is deemed disposed of at its fair market value, resulting in either a capital gain or a capital loss (see 22.2.3)
- capital losses, which are normally only allowed to offset capital gains (as discussed in 6.2.2), may be deducted from other income (except to the extent you have previously claimed the capital gains exemption)
- certain kinds of income earned but not received by the deceased before death can be reported on a separate return (against which the deceased's personal credits can be claimed a second time) (see 22.2.4)
- for deaths after 2015, the terminal return may include income deemed to have been received from certain testamentary spousal trusts (see 22.2.3).

The terminal return for the deceased is due by the usual deadline (see 9.1.1) or six months after death, whichever is later. For example, if the date of death is March 10, 2018, the deceased's 2018 return is due by April 30, 2019 (or June 15, 2019 if the deceased or spouse had self-employment income). Any balance of tax owing is due on April 30 of the year after the year of death or six months after death, whichever is later.

A similar extension is allowed for filing of the return for the year before the year of death if the individual dies before the return's normal due date. Continuing our example above, the deceased's 2017 tax return would be due by September 10, 2018 instead of the usual April 30, 2018 deadline.

If the deceased person was paying tax by instalments, no further instalment payments have to be paid after his or her death. The only instalments required are those that were due before the date of death.

Note that life insurance proceeds received as a result of an individual's death are not subject to income tax. Life insurance is discussed in more detail in 21.7.

If you are an active or retired partner of a professional partnership, see 16.2.6.

### 22.2.2 Tax payable by the estate

Any income earned after death is subject to tax as part of the estate. The estate is treated as a separate person that must file a return as a trust each year until all of the assets are distributed. (Sometimes this distribution can take several years, but some estates can be wound up within one year.)

Before 2016, an estate could pay tax at the same graduated income tax rates as an individual for as long as the estate existed. Starting in 2016, an estate paying tax at graduated rates is only entitled to do so for the first 36 months of its administration. After that, the estate's income is subject to tax at the top federal and provincial rate.

Income earned by the estate on all of its assets (whether administered under one or more wills) is eligible to be taxed at graduated tax rates, whereas income earned by a testamentary trust created by a will is taxed at the top rate after 2015.

A graduated rate estate may use a non-calendar year-end for tax purposes during the first 36 months of its administration. Once the 36-month period ends, the estate must use a calendar year-end.

The estate trustee should ensure that the estate does not undertake transactions that could cause it to prematurely lose its graduated rate estate status during its first 36 months, for example, incurring certain debts to pay a beneficiary or certain other persons. If the estate loses its graduated rate estate status, it would prematurely lose the benefit of graduated income tax rates and other adverse tax consequences may arise.

Any income paid to beneficiaries of the estate may be taxed in their hands directly, instead of in the estate. Tax can generally be deferred on any capital distribution from the estate to a beneficiary resident in Canada. When an estate distributes property to a beneficiary who is not resident in Canada, different rules apply. The requirements for distributions to non-resident beneficiaries are complex—consult your professional adviser to ensure that you obtain proper tax advice before the distribution.

### 22.2.3 Capital gains on death

Canada has no federal estate tax or inheritance tax, nor do any of the provinces. To the extent you simply have cash in the bank and you leave it to your family, there would be no tax to pay at all (other than probate fees, discussed in 21.4).

Many people, however, have capital assets such as stocks, real estate and jewellery. As a general rule, capital assets are deemed for tax purposes to have been sold immediately before death at their fair market value, thus triggering a capital gain on all of the increase in value that has accrued since the assets were purchased. This prevents gains from accruing indefinitely without ever being taxed. The normal capital gains rules apply to this deemed disposition, together with the availability of exemptions, such as the lifetime capital gains exemption (see 6.4).

> **Example**
>
> Jane dies in March 2018. Her only capital assets are her house, which has a cost base of $50,000 and is now worth $600,000; a diamond ring, which has a cost base of $5,000 and is now worth $10,000; and a stock portfolio, which has a cost base of $10,000 and is now worth $100,000.
>
> The house is deemed sold at fair market value just before Jane's death, but there is no capital gain because it was her principal residence. The ring and the stocks are also deemed sold at their current values, for a total gain of $95,000. One-half of the capital gain, or $47,500, is taxed as a taxable capital gain on Jane's terminal return.

Any accrued capital losses are also realized at death. If you own depreciable property, recaptured capital cost allowance or a terminal loss may also be triggered.

The main exception to the "deemed disposition" rule is where you leave assets to your spouse (including a common-law or same-sex spouse—see 2.2.1) or to a spousal trust (a trust that meets certain requirements, as outlined in 21.5.2). In such a case, you are deemed to have sold your assets immediately before your death at their cost, so no capital gain results, as long as your spouse or a spousal trust obtains ownership and unfettered rights to the property. Your spouse (or the trust) then inherits that cost for tax purposes along with the assets. When your spouse (or the trust) sells the assets, or on your spouse's death, the full capital gain or loss from your original purchase price will be taxed.

If you establish a spousal trust, any capital gains on the assets in the trust at the time of your spouse's death would be taxed in the trust. It may be possible to elect to have the gains taxed in your spouse's estate in certain limited circumstances. A professional adviser can help you review your options in this area.

*Consider realizing selected capital gains and losses on assets left to a spouse or spousal trust.*

There is a special rule under which an estate executor may elect to realize a capital gain or loss on a property-by-property basis when assets are left to a spouse (or a spousal trust) on the deceased's death. This election may be beneficial if the estate executor elects to trigger a capital gain in order to use loss carryforwards or a capital gains exemption.

Alternatively, triggering a capital loss may recover tax in the year prior to death, since capital losses in the year of death may be carried back to the immediately preceding year and used against any income, except to the extent that the deceased previously claimed the capital gains exemption (see 6.4).

Capital losses can also be carried back to offset capital gains in the previous three years.

If you transfer assets during your lifetime to an alter ego or joint partner trust, the assets pass to the ultimate beneficiaries according to the terms of the trust document and do not pass through your estate. Special rules apply to the trust on the death of the settlor of an alter ego trust or the second partner of a joint partner trust (see 21.5.5).

If you are an active or retired partner of a professional partnership, see 16.2.6.

### 22.2.4  Separate income tax returns

The executor or legal representative must file an ordinary income tax return reporting the income of the deceased from January 1 of the year of death to the date of death. In certain circumstances, the executor may exclude specific types of income from the ordinary return and report them on separate, optional income tax returns.

*Consider filing separate income tax returns to multiply credits.*

Certain tax credits such as the age credit, basic personal tax credit, spousal tax credit, wholly dependent person tax credit and caregiver credit that apply in the ordinary return for the year of death may also be deducted in each of the separate returns filed, making it advantageous to file these separate returns. Certain other tax credits and certain deductions may be used in either the separate returns or the ordinary return or split between the returns.

The executor may choose to file up to three separate returns aside from the ordinary return. These optional returns are for income from:

- rights or things
- a business as a partner or proprietor
- a graduated rate estate.

Rights or things are amounts that were not paid at the time of death and that, had the person not died, would have been included in his or her income when received. There are rights or things from employment and other sources such as certain investments—for example, uncashed matured bond coupons and unpaid dividends declared before the date of death.

If the deceased was a partner or sole proprietor of a business, business income may be reported on a separate return if the fiscal period of the business was not the same as the calendar year and the death occurred after the end of the fiscal period but before the end of the calendar year, among other conditions. The executor may use this return to report income for the time from the end of the fiscal period to the date of death.

Similarly, if the deceased was a beneficiary of a graduated rate estate and the estate does not report its income on a calendar-year basis, any income from the end of the estate's last fiscal period to the date of death may be reported on a separate return. Income from *inter vivos* trusts and, as of January 1, 2016, from testamentary trusts does not qualify for this special treatment.

### 22.2.5 Clearance certificates

As executor or legal representative, you may want to get a clearance certificate from the CRA before you distribute all of the property under your control. A clearance certificate indicates that all taxes for which the deceased is liable have been paid. If you do not get a certificate, you would be liable for any tax the deceased owes. A final clearance certificate covers all tax years to the wind-up of the estate. A separate clearance certificate is needed for a trust such as a spousal trust, which is deemed to have disposed of its assets immediately before the spouse's death.

Obtain a clearance certificate before distributing assets.

## 22.3 Death benefits

A death benefit is an amount paid in recognition of a deceased employee's service. Death benefits may be paid by the deceased's employer to the surviving spouse, other family members or to the estate. Up to $10,000 of such benefits may be received tax-free.

The first $10,000 of death benefits paid for any one employee is exempt from tax. The employee's spouse gets the exemption; to the extent there is no spouse or the spouse receives less than $10,000 and other taxpayers receive such funds, any remaining amount of exemption can be split among the other recipients. "Spouse" includes common-law and same-sex spouses who meet the criteria outlined in 2.2.1.

Note that life insurance proceeds are completely different from death benefits, and are not taxed at all when received.

## 22.4 RRSPs, RRIFs and TFSAs on death

### 22.4.1 RRSPs and RRIFs

On death, a taxpayer is normally taxed on the entire amount of any RRSPs or RRIFs, except where the funds are left to the taxpayer's spouse or financially dependent child or grandchild, in which case they are included in the spouse, child or grandchild's income. To the extent the funds come from an RRSP, they can be transferred to the spouse's own RRSP or RRIF for a deduction that offsets the income inclusion. The spouse can also use these funds to acquire an annuity. To the extent the funds come from a RRIF, if the spouse is named as a successor annuitant to the RRIF, the payments under the deceased's plan would continue to be paid to the spouse. If the spouse is named as beneficiary of the RRIF, amounts under the deceased's plan can be transferred to the spouse's own RRSP or RRIF, or he or she can use the funds to acquire an annuity.

If the RRSP or RRIF funds are left to a financially dependent child or grandchild, the RRSP or RRIF funds can either be taxed in the hands of the child or grandchild or used to buy a term annuity to age 18. Other options are available for financially dependent children or grandchildren with mental or physical infirmities. The executor should obtain professional advice on these matters.

If the value of the RRSP or RRIF decreases after the taxpayer's death and before the assets are distributed to the beneficiaries, a deduction for the loss may be allowed on the taxpayer's terminal return, as long as the distribution is made by the end of the year following the year of death.

### 22.4.2 TFSAs

On the death of a TFSA holder, the fair market value of the TFSA is not taxable to the deceased, though other tax implications may arise.

The TFSA would continue to exist after the holder's death if the surviving spouse is named as the successor account holder. The successor would not have to pay tax on the TFSA's value on his or her spouse's death or on any future income earned in the account. This rollover of the account to the successor does not affect the successor's unused TFSA contribution room.

If no successor holder exists but the account holder has designated beneficiaries, these beneficiaries would receive the TFSA's value at the account holder's death tax-free. Any income earned in the account after the account holder's death would be taxable to the beneficiaries. If the beneficiaries have unused TFSA contribution room, they can roll over the amount received to their own TFSAs. If the beneficiary is the spouse, he or she may transfer the TFSA's value at the date of death (but not any subsequent income) to their TFSA without affecting their unused TFSA contribution room.

If the TFSA does not have a successor holder or designated beneficiary, the TFSA would pass to the deceased holder's estate.

## 22.5 Foreign estate taxes

If you own assets in other countries, estate, inheritance or succession taxes of those countries (or their states or provinces) may apply on your death.

Estate taxes and succession duties imposed by other jurisdictions are not normally eligible for a foreign tax credit in Canada, even though you may have a Canadian income tax liability as a result of the deemed disposition described in 22.2.3. Double taxation can result. You may need to plan for this possibility ahead of time.

> Watch out for the effects of foreign estate taxes.

If you are a U.S. citizen, see our discussion of U.S. estate tax in 18.8.3.

If you are not a U.S. citizen but own assets legally located in the U.S., including real estate, debts owed to you by U.S. citizens or shares in U.S. corporations, see the planning options to deal with U.S. estate tax discussed in 19.4.5.

## 22.6 References

The following publications and more information, including forms and brochures, can be obtained on the CRA's website at *www.cra-arc.gc.ca* or by telephone request at 1-800-959-8281 for individual income tax and trust-related enquiries or 1-800-959-5525 for business and self-employed individual enquiries.

Guide T4011, "Preparing Returns for Deceased Persons"
Information Sheet RC4111, "What to Do Following a Death"
Interpretation Bulletin IT-210R2, Archived – "Income of deceased persons—Periodic payments and investment tax credit"

Interpretation Bulletin IT-212R3, Archived – "Income of deceased persons—Rights or things" and Special Release IT-212R3SR

Interpretation Bulletin IT-234, Archived – "Income of deceased persons—Farm crops"

Interpretation Bulletin IT-278R2, Archived – "Death of a partner or retired partner"

Interpretation Bulletin IT-305R4, Archived – "Testamentary spouse trusts"

Interpretation Bulletin IT-313R2, Archived – "Eligible capital property—Rules where a taxpayer has ceased carrying on business or has died"

Interpretation Bulletin IT-326R3, Archived – "Returns of deceased persons as 'another person'"

Interpretation Bulletin IT-349R3, Archived – "Intergenerational transfers of farm property on death"

Interpretation Bulletin IT-407R4 Consolidated, Archived – "Disposition of cultural property to designated Canadian institutions"

Interpretation Bulletin IT-508R, Archived – "Death benefits"

Also, see the following selected topics on the CRA's website:

"Final return"
"Optional returns"

# Appendix I

## New Tax Regime for Private Company Tax Planning

Before you consider some of the tax planning advice in this book, it is important that you are aware that Canada's Department of Finance has proposed significant changes that would affect the effectiveness of some of these strategies. The government released a detailed public consultation paper and proposed legislation on July 18, 2017 that would prevent you from using some tax plans commonly used in the past. The proposals would generally apply for 2018 and later tax years (though some of the rules could have effect as of July 18, 2017 or even earlier). At the time of writing, the government has not yet finalized or enacted these changes.

Specifically, the government's proposals address:

- using private corporations to have income taxed in the hands of family members who are subject to lower personal tax rates (known as "income sprinkling"—for example, see 16.1.2)
- income sprinkling by multiplying the lifetime capital gains exemption across multiple family members (for example, see 14.1)
- holding a passive investment portfolio inside a private corporation (see 14.6)
- converting a private corporation's dividend income into capital gains that are taxed at a lower rate.

Below is a general overview of the consultation paper and proposed legislation, as released on July 18, 2017. Before implementing any of the planning ideas in this book, you should ask your tax adviser about the status of any proposed legislation and its effective dates. That way, you will not be caught unaware by any legislation enacted after this book's publication. You should then decide whether to unwind any existing tax planning to avoid adverse tax consequences.

## Income sprinkling using private corporations

"Income sprinkling" generally involves reducing a family's combined income taxes by having income that would otherwise be taxable to an individual at a high personal income tax rate to be taxable to other family members who are subject to lower personal tax rates.

To address income sprinkling, the government has proposed to extend the tax on split income (i.e., "kiddie tax"—see 5.2.4) to certain adults but generally only where the amount of split income they receive is considered "unreasonable" in the circumstances. Amounts determined to be unreasonable would be taxed at the top marginal rate.

The reasonableness test would apply to split income amounts derived from a business of a related Canadian-resident individual or a corporation over which a related Canadian-resident individual has influence (e.g., a family operating company). Factors that would be considered to determine the reasonability of split income received by (or allocated to) the individual (e.g., an adult child or spouse) include the individual's labour and capital contributions to the business, risk assumed and previous returns or remuneration. These new rules would be more restrictive for family members age 18-24. The rules also apply to extended family members, including aunts, uncles, nieces and nephews.

Currently, the tax on split income does not apply to "compound" or secondary income (i.e., income earned from an initial investment of income that is itself subject to the tax on split income). This compound income is taxed at the lower rate that applies to the family member who earned it. Under the proposals, compound income would also be subject to the tax on split income for family members under age 25.

The proposed measures expand the types of income that are considered to be split income, but they would not generally apply to any income you receive as salary, wages or certain inherited property.

These proposed measures generally would apply for 2018 and later tax years.

## Multiplying the lifetime capital gains exemption

The government's proposed legislation also addresses income sprinkling strategies that multiply the lifetime capital gains exemption across family members.

Specifically, the proposed rules generally would deny the exemption for:

- capital gains realized or accrued before the taxation year in which the individual turns 18

- gains that accrued during the time that property was held by a trust (such as a family trust), subject to exceptions for, among others, spousal or common-law partner trusts, alter ego trusts and certain employee share ownership trusts

- taxable capital gains from the disposition of property that is included in an individual's split income.

These proposals would apply to sales (i.e., dispositions) of shares after 2017. Special transitional rules would allow you to elect to realize, on a day in 2018, a capital gain on eligible property by way of a deemed disposition for proceeds up to the fair market value of the property. This special election would be available for property you owned continuously from the end of 2017 until the day of the deemed disposition.

Capital gains triggered by the election generally would be eligible for the lifetime capital gains exemption under the current tax rules. However, the government proposes to relax the eligibility tests for qualified small business corporation shares and farming or fishing property where the election is made.

## Holding a passive investment portfolio inside a private corporation

The government's consultation paper also contemplates changes to the tax treatment of passive investment income earned inside a private corporation, although no proposed legislation has been released to date. The government is reviewing options for eliminating the financial tax deferral advantages of earning, retaining and passively investing business income in a private corporation.

The consultation paper's goal is to solicit public feedback on potential tax policy approaches. It is likely that the government will consider this feedback before legislation is drafted, and it is not yet known when any new rules would take effect.

Since corporate tax rates are generally lower than personal tax rates, owners of private corporations may choose to earn business income in a corporation and then retain the after-tax earnings in the corporation to earn passive income. The current tax system already applies additional refundable corporate taxes on passive income to ensure that the tax paid on the passive income approximates the tax an individual in the top tax bracket would pay. However, the government says there is no tax provision to align the earnings available to fund the passive investment within the corporation with the after-tax amount that would be available to the individual if they earned such business income directly. So, in these circumstances, the use of a corporation increases the funds available for passive investment or savings.

In the paper, the government contemplates replacing the current regime with a new one that would tax passive investment income earned through a private company at the same rate as the salary of someone in the top personal tax bracket. The government says it intends the new regime to apply on a "go-forward basis" but has not released any transitional rules.

The new approach could also change how passive income is taxed at the individual level when distributed as dividends by the corporation. For example, the new regime could affect dividends that a private company receives from publicly traded stocks, which can currently be distributed to shareholders as eligible dividends. The government notes that in some cases, dividend income from publicly traded stocks could no longer be treated as eligible dividends but as non-eligible dividends instead.

The government also says that the non-taxable portion of capital gains would no longer be credited to the capital dividend account where the source capital of the investment is income taxed at corporate income tax rates.

## Converting a private corporation's income into capital gains

The consultation paper and draft legislation set out specific proposals that may affect the planning discussed in this book directly. You should be sure to review these changes before implementing any planning you might be considering.

### Anti-surplus stripping rule tightened

The government has proposed changes to prevent individual taxpayers from using non-arm's-length transactions that "step-up" the cost base of shares of a corporation and avoid the "anti-surplus stripping" rule. If you sell shares of a corporation to a non-arm's-length corporation, this rule aims to prevent you from extracting surplus income retained in a corporation at the lower tax rates on capital gains instead of the higher dividend tax rates. If certain conditions are met, the purchaser corporation is deemed to have paid (and you as the seller are deemed to have received) a dividend. The effect is to deny capital gains treatment if you receive non-share consideration that exceeds the shares' tax attributes (e.g., cost base and paid-up-capital).

> Capital gains are taxed at a lower rate than regular income and eligible and non-eligible dividends. Capital gains are taxed at only half the rate of regular income, providing potential tax savings of about 25%. Compared to eligible dividends, tax on capital gains can be about 6.5% to 17% lower. For non-eligible dividends, the tax on capital gains can be about 16% to 20% lower, depending on your province of residence.

Specifically, the government has proposed to reduce the cost base of an individual's share by the total of all capital gains realized on previous dispositions of the share by that person and any non-arm's-length individual. This cost base reduction would apply regardless of whether you claimed a capital gains exemption on the previous disposition.

Currently, this rule only applies to reduce an individual's cost base where the capital gains exemption was previously claimed (or where the gain is a tax-free pre-1972 gain). The government has said that although this change could give rise to both a capital gain on a step-up transaction and a taxable dividend on a later non-arm's-length disposition, the change is ultimately intended to discourage taxpayers from trying to avoid this anti-surplus stripping rule.

### Intergenerational transfers of shares

As part of these changes, the government is looking into ways to facilitate intergenerational transfers of shares of a small business corporation to an adult child's corporation by ensuring these transfers would not be caught by the anti-avoidance rules. Although no proposed rules have been released, the government has asked taxpayers to provide feedback on whether, and how, to better accommodate genuine business transfers from one generation to the next.

### New anti-surplus stripping rule

Finally, a new, separate anti-surplus stripping rule is proposed to address tax planning that the government believes circumvents the rules on the conversion of a private corporation's surplus into tax-exempt, or lower-taxed, capital gains. This rule generally would apply to non-arm's-length transactions where it is reasonable to consider that "one of the purposes" of a transaction or series of transactions is to pay an individual shareholder/vendor non-share consideration (e.g., cash) in a manner that involves a "significant disappearance" of the corporation's assets. In these cases, the non-share consideration would be treated as a taxable dividend, instead of a capital gain, and subject to the higher tax rate on dividend income.

These changes would apply to shares disposed of (and amounts received or that become receivable) on or after July 18, 2017.

# Appendix II

## Federal and Provincial Income Tax Rates and Brackets for 2017

| | Tax Rates | Tax Brackets | Surtax Rates | Thresholds |
|---|---|---|---|---|
| Federal[1] | 15.00% | Up to $45,916 | | |
| | 20.50 | 45,917–91,831 | | |
| | 26.00 | 91,832–142,353 | | |
| | 29.00 | 142,354–202,800 | | |
| | 33.00 | 202,801 and over | | |
| British Columbia[2] | 5.06% | Up to $38,898 | | |
| | 7.70 | 38,899–77,797 | | |
| | 10.50 | 77,798–89,320 | | |
| | 12.29 | 89,321–108,460 | | |
| | 14.70 | 108,461 and over | | |
| Alberta[3] | 10.00% | Up to $126,625 | | |
| | 12.00 | 126,626–151,950 | | |
| | 13.00 | 151,951–202,600 | | |
| | 14.00 | 202,601–303,900 | | |
| | 15.00 | 303,901 and over | | |
| Saskatchewan[4] | 10.75% | Up to $45,225 | | |
| | 12.75 | 45,226–129,214 | | |
| | 14.75 | 129,215 and over | | |
| Manitoba[5] | 10.80% | Up to $31,465 | | |
| | 12.75 | 31,466–68,005 | | |
| | 17.40 | 68,006 and over | | |
| Ontario[6] | 5.05% | Up to $42,201 | | |
| | 9.15 | 42,202–84,404 | 20% | $4,556 |
| | 11.16 | 84,405–150,000 | 36 | 5,831 |
| | 12.16 | 150,001–220,000 | | |
| | 13.16 | 220,001 and over | | |

358

| | Tax Rates | Tax Brackets | Surtax | |
|---|---|---|---|---|
| | | | Rates | Thresholds |
| Quebec[7] | 16.00% | Up to $42,705 | | |
| | 20.00 | 42,706–85,405 | | |
| | 24.00 | 85,406–103,915 | | |
| | 25.75 | 103,916 and over | | |
| New Brunswick[8] | 9.68% | Up to $41,059 | | |
| | 14.82 | 41,060–82,119 | | |
| | 16.52 | 82,120–133,507 | | |
| | 17.84 | 133,508–152,100 | | |
| | 20.30 | 152,101 and over | | |
| Nova Scotia[9] | 8.79% | Up to $29,590 | | |
| | 14.95 | 29,591–59,180 | | |
| | 16.67 | 59,181–93,000 | | |
| | 17.50 | 93,001–150,000 | | |
| | 21.00 | 150,001 and over | | |
| Prince Edward Island[9] | 9.80% | Up to $31,984 | | |
| | 13.80 | 31,985–63,969 | | |
| | 16.70 | 63,970 and over | 10% | $12,500 |
| Newfoundland and Labrador[10] | 8.70% | Up to $35,851 | | |
| | 14.50 | 35,852–71,701 | | |
| | 15.80 | 71,702–128,010 | | |
| | 17.30 | 128,011–179,214 | | |
| | 18.30 | 179,215 and over | | |
| Yukon[8] | 6.40% | Up to $45,916 | | |
| | 9.00 | 45,917–91,831 | | |
| | 10.90 | 91,832–142,353 | | |
| | 12.80 | 142,354–500,000 | | |
| | 15.00 | 500,001 and over | | |
| Northwest Territories[8] | 5.90% | Up to $41,585 | | |
| | 8.60 | 41,586–83,172 | | |
| | 12.20 | 83,173–135,219 | | |
| | 14.05 | 135,220 and over | | |
| Nunavut[8] | 4.00% | Up to $43,780 | | |
| | 7.00 | 43,781–87,560 | | |
| | 9.00 | 87,561–142,353 | | |
| | 11.50 | 142,354 and over | | |

## Notes

1) The federal tax brackets are indexed each year by a calculated inflation factor, which is based on the change in the average federal inflation rate over the 12-month period ending September 30 of the previous year compared to the change in the rate for the same period of the year prior to that. The federal inflation factor is 1.4% for 2017.

2) British Columbia indexes its tax brackets using the same formula used federally but uses the provincial inflation rate rather than the federal rate in the calculation. The province's inflation factor is 1.8% for 2017. B.C. residents are also required to make monthly payments under the province's Medical Services Plan.

3) Alberta indexes its tax brackets using the same formula used federally but uses the provincial inflation rate rather than the federal rate in the calculation. The province's inflation factor is 1.3% for 2017.

4) Saskatchewan indexes its tax brackets using the same formula used federally. The inflation factor is 1.4% for 2017. Saskatchewan's 2017 budget suspends the annual indexation of the personal income tax system starting with the 2018 taxation year. Saskatchewan reduced its personal tax rates by 0.5%, as of July 1, 2017. The rates in the table are the average for 2017.

5) Manitoba indexes its tax brackets using the same formula used federally but uses the provincial inflation rate rather than the federal rate in the calculation. The province's inflation factor is 1.5% for 2017.

6) Ontario indexes its tax brackets and surtax thresholds using the same formula used federally but uses the provincial inflation rate rather than the federal rate in the calculation. The province's inflation factor is 1.6% for 2017. Ontario resident individuals with taxable income over $20,000 are also required to pay a Health Premium each year.

7) Quebec indexes its tax brackets using the same formula used federally but uses the provincial inflation rate, excluding changes in liquor and tobacco taxes, rather than the federal rate in the calculation. The province's inflation factor is 0.74% for 2017. Residents of Quebec are required to pay a health contribution and to make payments to the province's Health Services Fund.

8) New Brunswick, Northwest Territories, Nunavut and the Yukon index their tax brackets using the same formula used federally. The inflation factor is 1.4% for 2017.

9) Nova Scotia and Prince Edward Island do not index their tax brackets or surtax thresholds.

10) Newfoundland and Labrador indexes its tax brackets using the same formula used federally but uses the provincial inflation rate rather than the federal rate in the calculation. Newfoundland and Labrador's inflation factor is 2.0% for 2017.

# Combined Top Marginal Tax Rates for Individuals[1] – 2017

| | Interest and Regular Income | Capital Gains[2] | Eligible Dividends | Non-eligible Dividends[3] |
|---|---|---|---|---|
| British Columbia[4] | 47.70% | 23.85% | 31.30% | 40.95% |
| Alberta[5] | 48.00 | 24.00 | 31.71 | 41.24 |
| Saskatchewan[6] | 47.75 | 23.88 | 30.33 | 39.62 |
| Manitoba | 50.40 | 25.20 | 37.79 | 45.74 |
| Ontario | 53.53 | 26.76 | 39.34 | 45.30 |
| Quebec | 53.31 | 26.65 | 39.83 | 43.84 |
| New Brunswick[7] | 53.30 | 26.65 | 33.51 | 46.25 |
| Nova Scotia | 54.00 | 27.00 | 41.58 | 46.97 |
| P.E.I. | 51.37 | 25.69 | 34.23 | 43.87 |
| Newfoundland and Labrador | 51.30 | 25.65 | 42.62 | 43.62 |
| Yukon[8] | 48.00 | 24.00 | 26.91 | 40.67 |
| Northwest Territories | 47.05 | 23.53 | 28.33 | 35.72 |
| Nunavut | 44.50 | 22.25 | 33.08 | 36.35 |

*Notes*

1)   The combined top marginal tax rate is the rate an individual pays on income that falls within the highest tax bracket in the province or territories of residence.

2)   The lifetime capital gains exemption limit for qualified farm property, qualified fishing property and qualified small business corporation shares increased to $835,716 (from $824,176) for 2017. An additional lifetime capital gains exemption of $164,284 is available for qualified farm or fishing property disposed of in 2017.

3)   The 2016 federal budget announced that the dividend tax credit (DTC) rate on non-eligible dividends will remain at 10.5% after 2016. The DTC rate was previously scheduled to decrease to 10% in 2017, 9.5% in 2018 and 9% in 2019.

The 2016 federal budget announced that the gross-up factor for non-eligible dividends will remain at 17% after 2016. The gross-up factor was previously scheduled to decrease to 16% in 2018 and 15% in 2019.

4)   British Columbia decreased its DTC rate for non-eligible dividends to 2.18% (from 2.47%) of taxable dividends, as of January 1, 2017.

5)   Alberta decreased its DTC rate for non-eligible dividends to 2.19% (from 3.08%) of taxable dividends, as of January 1, 2017.

6)   Saskatchewan decreased its personal tax rates by 0.5% and its DTC rate for eligible dividends, as of July 1, 2017. The rates in the table are the average for 2017.

7)   New Brunswick decreased its DTC rate for non-eligible dividends to 3.245% (from 3.625%) of taxable dividends and increased its DTC rate for eligible dividends to 14% (from 13.5%) of taxable dividends, as of January 1, 2017.

8)   Yukon decreased the province's DTC rates that apply to non-eligible dividends and eligible dividends, as of July 1, 2017. The rates in the table are the average for 2017.

# Appendix III

## Federal and Provincial Non-Refundable Tax Credit Rates and Amounts for 2017[1]

| | Federal | B.C. | Alta. | Sask. | Man. |
|---|---|---|---|---|---|
| Tax rate applied to credits | 15.00% | 5.06% | 10.00% | 10.75% | 10.80% |
| Indexation factor[2] | 1.40% | 1.80% | 1.30% | 1.40% | 1.50% |
| Basic personal | $11,635 | $10,208 | $18,690 | $16,065 | $9,271 |
| Spousal/partner and wholly dependent person[3,5] | 11,635 | 8,740 | 18,690 | 16,065 | 9,134 |
| *Net income threshold* | — | *874* | — | *1,607* | — |
| Dependants[4,5] | | | | | |
| 18 and over and infirm | See | 4,467 | 10,820 | 9,464 | 3,605 |
| *Net income threshold* | Caregiver | *7,115* | *7,147* | *6,715* | *5,115* |
| Caregiver[5] | 6,883 | 4,467 | 10,819 | 9,464 | 3,605 |
| *Net income threshold* | *16,163* | *15,117* | *17,202* | *16,164* | *12,312* |
| Child[6] (max) | — | 250 | — | 6,094 | — |
| Adoption[7] (max) | 15,670 | 15,670 | 12,783 | — | 10,000 |
| Disability[8] | 8,113 | 7,656 | 14,417 | 9,464 | 6,180 |
| Disability supplement[9] | 4,733 | 4,467 | 10,819 | 9,464 | 3,605 |
| Pension[8] (max) | 2,000 | 1,000 | 1,439 | 1,000 | 1,000 |
| Age 65 and over[8,10] | 7,225 | 4,578 | 5,208 | 4,894 | 3,728 |
| *Net income threshold* | *36,430* | *34,075* | *38,772* | *36,430* | *27,749* |
| Medical expense threshold[11] | 2,268 | 2,122 | 2,415 | 2,268 | 1,728 |
| Employment[12] | 1,178 | — | Refundable | — | — |
| Canada Pension Plan[13] (max) | 2,564 | 2,564 | 2,564 | 2,564 | 2,564 |
| Employment Insurance[13] (max) | 836 | 836 | 836 | 836 | 836 |
| Children's fitness[14] and arts[15] (max) | — | 500 | — | — | 500 |
| Home buyers[16] (max) | 5,000 | — | — | 10,000 | — |
| Home accessibility[17] (max) | 10,000 | Refundable | — | — | — |
| Tuition fees[18] | Yes | Yes | Yes | Partially | Yes |
| Education[18] | | | | | |
| Full-time—per month | — | 200 | 727 | 400 | 400 |
| Part-time—per month | — | 60 | 218 | 120 | 120 |
| Charitable donations[19] | | | | | |
| Credit rate on first $200 | 15.00% | 5.06% | 10.00% | 10.75% | 10.80% |
| Credit rate on balance | 29.00/ 33.00% | 14.70% | 21.00% | 14.75% | 17.40% |
| Public transit pass costs[20] | — | — | — | — | — |

| | Ont. | N.B. | N.S. | P.E.I. | Nfld. |
|---|---|---|---|---|---|
| Tax rate applied to credits | 5.05% | 9.68% | 8.79% | 9.80% | 8.70% |
| Indexation factor[2] | 1.60% | 1.40% | n/a | n/a | 2.00% |
| Basic personal | $10,171 | $9,895 | $8,481 | $8,160 | $8,978 |
| Spousal/partner and wholly dependent person[3,5] | 8,636 | 8,402 | 8,481 | 6,931 | 7,336 |
| *Net income threshold* | *864* | *841* | *848* | *693* | *734* |
| Dependants[4,5] | | | | | |
| 18 and over and infirm | See | 4,673 | 2,798 | 2,446 | 2,851 |
| Net income threshold | Caregiver | *6,630* | *5,683* | *4,966* | *6,127* |
| Caregiver[5] | 4,794 | 4,673 | 4,898 | 2,446 | 2,851 |
| *Net income threshold* | *16,401* | *15,959* | *13,677* | *11,953* | *13,933* |
| Child[6] (max) | — | — | 1,200 | 1,200 | |
| Adoption[7] (max) | 12,409 | — | — | — | 12,116 |
| Disability[8] | 8,217 | 8,011 | 7,341 | 6,890 | 6,058 |
| Disability supplement[9] | 4,792 | 4,673 | 3,449 | 4,019 | 2,851 |
| Pension[8] (max) | 1,406 | 1,000 | 1,173 | 1,000 | 1,000 |
| Age 65 and over[8,10] | 4,966 | 4,831 | 4,141 | 3,764 | 5,731 |
| *Net income threshold* | *36,969* | *35,968* | *30,828* | *28,019* | *31,405* |
| Medical expense threshold[11] | 2,302 | 2,239 | 1,637 | 1,678 | 1,955 |
| Employment[12] | — | — | — | — | — |
| Canada Pension Plan[13] (max) | 2,564 | 2,564 | 2,564 | 2,564 | 2,564 |
| Employment Insurance[13] (max) | 836 | 836 | 836 | 836 | 836 |
| Children's fitness[14] and arts[15] (max) | — | — | — | — | — |
| Home buyers[16] (max) | — | — | — | — | — |
| Home accessibility[17] (max) | — | Refundable | — | — | — |
| Tuition fees[18] | Partially | No | Yes | Yes | Yes |
| Education[18] | | | | | |
| Full-time—per month | 547 | — | 200 | 400 | 200 |
| Part-time—per month | 164 | — | 60 | 120 | 60 |
| Charitable donations[19] | | | | | |
| Credit rate on first $200 | 5.05% | 9.68% | 8.79% | 9.80% | 8.70% |
| Credit rate on balance | 11.16% | 17.95% | 21.00% | 16.70% | 18.30% |
| Public transit pass costs[20] | Refundable | — | — | — | — |

*Notes*

1) The table shows the dollar amounts of federal and provincial non-refundable tax credits for 2017 (except for Quebec, see the table "Quebec Non-Refundable Tax Credit Rates and Amounts for 2017"). In order to determine the credit value, each dollar amount must be multiplied by the tax rate shown, which is the lowest tax rate applicable in the particular jurisdiction. For example, the Ontario basic personal credit amount of $10,171 is multiplied by 5.05% to determine the credit value of $514.

   Income earned by the taxpayer or dependant, as applicable, over the net income thresholds shown in the table reduces the availability of the credit on a dollar-for-dollar basis. The only exception to this is the age credit, which is reduced by 15% of the taxpayer's net income over the threshold.

2) The indexation factors shown in the table are used to index the credits in each jurisdiction. The calculation of these factors is based on the change in the average federal or provincial inflation rate over the 12-month period ending September 30 of the previous year compared to the change in the rate for the same period of the year prior to that.

   British Columbia, Alberta, Manitoba, Ontario and Newfoundland and Labrador use the applicable provincial inflation rate in their calculations, while Saskatchewan and New Brunswick uses the federal inflation rate. Nova Scotia and Prince Edward Island do not index their credits. The Saskatchewan 2017 budget temporarily suspended the personal income tax indexation factor starting with the 2018 taxation year.

3) The spousal/partner and wholly dependent person amounts are calculated by subtracting the spouse/partner and wholly dependant's net income from the maximum amount.

   The spousal/partner credit may be claimed for a common-law partner as well as for a spouse. Taxpayers who are single, divorced or separated, and who support a dependant in their home, may claim the wholly dependent person credit. The credit can be claimed for dependants under age 18 who are related to the taxpayer, for the taxpayer's parents or grandparents, or for any other infirm person who is related to the taxpayer (see note (5)).

4) The 2017 federal budget introduced a new Canada caregiver credit that will replace the existing caregiver credit, infirm dependant credit, and family caregiver tax credit. The 2017 Ontario budget introduced a new Ontario caregiver tax credit that will replace the existing caregiver credit and infirm dependant credit. See note (5).

5) The caregiver credit is available to taxpayers who care for a related dependant. Generally, the dependant must be over age 18 and infirm or, in the case of a parent or grandparent, over age 65 (except for federal and Ontario purposes, where the credit is not available for non-infirm dependants).

   For the federal Canada caregiver credit, the credit amount is $6,883 for infirm dependants who are parents, grandparents, brothers/sisters, aunts/uncles, nieces/nephews, adult children of the claimant or of the claimant's spouse or common-law partner, and $2,150 for an infirm dependent spouse or common-law partner for whom the individual claims the spouse or common-law partner amount, an infirm dependant for whom the individual claims an eligible dependant credit, or an infirm child who is under age 18 years at the end of the year.

   For Ontario, the credit amount is $4,794 for relatives who are infirm dependants, including adult children of the claimant or of the claimant's spouse or common-law partner.

6) British Columbia provides a back-to-school tax credit amount of $250 per child to individuals with school-aged children age 5 to 17. Nova Scotia and Prince Edward Island provide a credit for children under age 6. If certain conditions are met, an individual can claim $100 per eligible month for up to $1,200 per year. Unused credit amounts may be transferred between spouses.

Saskatchewan provides a credit for children under age 18 if certain conditions are met. Unused credit amounts may be transferred between spouses.

7) The adoption credit is available on eligible adoption expenses incurred in the year and not reimbursed to the taxpayer, up to the maximum amount shown in the table.

8) The disability, pension and age credits are transferable to a spouse or partner. The amounts available for transfer are reduced by the excess of the spouse's or partner's net income over the basic personal credit amount. The disability credit is also transferable to a supporting person other than a spouse or partner; however, the amount of the credit is reduced by the excess of the disabled person's net income over the basic personal credit amount.

9) The disability supplement may be claimed by an individual who is under age 18 at the end of the year. The amount in the table is the maximum amount that may be claimed, and it is reduced by certain child and attendant care expenses claimed for this individual.

10) Saskatchewan provides an additional non-refundable tax credit for individuals age 65 or older in the year, regardless of their net income amount. The amount for 2017 is $1,292.

Nova Scotia provides an additional non-refundable tax credit for individuals age 65 or older in the year if their taxable income is less than $24,000. The amount for 2017 is $1,000.

11) The medical expense credit is calculated based on qualified medical expenses exceeding 3% of net income or the threshold shown in the table, whichever is less. Medical expenses incurred by both spouses/partners and by their children under age 18 may be totalled and claimed by either spouse/partner.

Taxpayers can also claim medical expenses for other eligible dependants to the extent the amount exceeds the lesser of 3% of net income of the dependant or the threshold shown in the table. Ontario is currently the only province with a maximum allowable medical expense for other eligible dependants. The limit is $12,409 for 2017.

12) The federal employment credit may be claimed by individuals based on the lesser of the amount shown in the table and the amount of employment income earned in the year.

Alberta offers a refundable family employment credit for Alberta residents with children under age 18 who meet the income eligibility criteria. The credit is paid in January and July of each year.

13) Self-employed taxpayers can deduct 50% of their Canada or Quebec Pension Plan premiums in calculating net income and claim the balance as a non-refundable tax credit. Self-employed taxpayers can also claim Employment Insurance premiums paid.

14) British Columbia and Manitoba are the only provinces that provide fitness tax credits.

In British Columbia, taxpayers can claim up to $500 for fees paid on enrolment in an eligible program of physical activity for children under age 16 (or 18 if eligible for the disability tax credit) at the beginning of the year. Fifty per cent of the children's fitness credit can be claimed as children's fitness equipment credit. For children who are under age 18 at the beginning of the year and eligible for the disability tax credit, taxpayers can claim an additional $500 if at least $100 is paid for registration or membership fees for a prescribed program of physical activity.

In Manitoba, taxpayers can claim up to $500 for fees paid on registration or membership for an eligible program of physical activity for children under age 18 at the end of the year, spouse or common-law partner age 18 to 24 at the end of the year, and self if under age 25 at the end of the year. For children or young adults eligible for the disability tax credit, taxpayers can claim an additional $500 if at least $100 is paid for registration or membership fees for a prescribed program of physical activity.

15) British Columbia and Manitoba are the only provinces that provide children's arts tax credits.

Taxpayers in British Columbia and Manitoba can claim up to $500 for fees paid relating to the cost of registration or membership in an eligible program of artistic, cultural, recreational or developmental activity for children under age 16 (or 18 if eligible for the disability tax credit) at the beginning of the year. For children who are under age 18 at the beginning of the year and eligible for the disability tax credit, taxpayers can claim an additional $500 if at least $100 is paid for registration or membership fees for an eligible artistic program.

16) First-time home buyers who acquire a qualifying home during the year may be entitled to claim a federal non-refundable tax credit up to $5,000 and worth up to $750 ($5,000 × 15%).

To qualify, neither the individual nor their spouse or common-law partner can have owned and lived in another home in the calendar year of the new home purchase or in any of the four preceding calendar years. The credit can be claimed by either the purchaser or by their spouse or common-law partner.

The credit is also available for certain home purchases by or for the benefit of an individual eligible for the disability tax credit.

Saskatchewan's First-Time Home Buyers Tax Credit provides a non-refundable income tax credit of up to $1,075 (10.75% × $10,000) to eligible taxpayers. Persons with a disability also qualify for the purchase of more accessible homes, with eligibility rules similar to those for the federal first-time home buyers credit. The Saskatchewan credit generally applies to qualifying homes acquired after December 31, 2011.

17) The home accessibility tax credit provides a credit for qualifying expenses incurred for work performed or goods acquired for a qualifying renovation of an eligible dwelling of someone who is age 65 or older before the end of the taxation year or eligible for the disability tax credit. British Columbia and New Brunswick provide a refundable credit of up to $1,000 for similar expenses.

18) The eligible portion of the tuition and education tax credits are transferable to a spouse or common-law partner, parent or grandparent. Any amounts not transferred may be carried forward indefinitely by the student.

New Brunswick eliminated the province's tuition and education tax credits, as of January 1, 2017. Saskatchewan eliminated its tuition and education tax credits, as of July 1, 2017. Ontario eliminated its tuition and education tax credits, as of September 5, 2017. Ontario education tax credits can be claimed for months of study before September 2017. Individuals may still claim credit amounts carried forward from prior years.

The federal government eliminated the education tax credits, as of January 1, 2017. British Columbia's 2017 budget proposed to eliminate the province's education tax credits, as of January 1, 2018.

19) Charitable donations made by both spouses/partners may be totalled and claimed by either person. The maximum amount of donations that may be claimed in a year is 75% of net income. However, all donations may be carried forward for five years if they are not claimed in the year made.

A temporary charitable donor's super credit supplements the existing charitable donation tax credit. A first-time donor is entitled to a one-time 40% federal credit for money donations of $200 or less, and a 54% federal credit for donations between $200 and $1,000. An individual is considered a first-time donor if neither the individual nor the individual's spouse or common-law partner has claimed the charitable donations tax credit or first-time donor's super credit in any taxation year after 2007. This credit may be claimed once in the first-time donor's 2013 to 2017 taxation years.

The federal government introduced a new tax rate of 33% on income over $200,000 starting January 1, 2016. The rate of 33% applies to charitable donations made after 2015 over $200 to the extent of the claimant's income that is subject to the top tax bracket. Otherwise, the rate of 29% applies to the donations over $200.

20) Individuals can claim a federal tax credit for the cost of monthly transit passes (or passes of a longer duration) incurred for travel by the individual, their spouse or partner, or dependent children under age 19. The cost of certain electronic payment cards and weekly public transit passes may also be eligible. The 2017 federal budget eliminated the public transit credit, as of July 1, 2017.

The 2017 Ontario budget announced a refundable Ontario seniors' public transit credit for all Ontarians age 65 and over. This new credit covers eligible public transit costs, as of July 1, 2017.

# Appendix IV

## Quebec Non-Refundable Tax Credit Rates and Amounts for 2017

| | |
|---|---|
| Tax rate applied to credits[1] | 16% |
| Indexation factor[2] | 0.74% |
| Basic personal amount | $14,890 |
| Amounts for dependants: | |
|    Child under 18 engaged in full-time training or post-secondary studies[3] | 2,682 |
|    Child over 17 who is a full-time student[4] | |
|    Other dependants over 17[5] | 3,907 |
| Person living alone or with a dependant:[6,7] | |
|    Basic amount | 1,707 |
|    Single-parent amount (supplement) | 2,107 |
| Age 65 and over[6] | 3,132 |
| Experienced workers (age 63 and over)[8] | |
|    Age 63 | 4,000 |
|    Age 64 | 6,000 |
|    Age 65 and over | 8,000 |
| Pension[6] (max) | 2,782 |
| Disability | 3,307 |
| Union and professional dues[9] | 10% |
| Tuition fees[10] | 8% |
| Interest paid on student loans[11] | 20% |
| Medical expenses[1,12] | |
| Charitable donations[13] | |
|    Credit rate on first $200 | 20% |
|    Credit rate on balance | 24/25.75% |

*Notes*

1)    The 2017 Quebec budget lowered the general rate used to calculate most personal tax credits to 16% (from 20%), for the 2017 and later taxation years.

   The province's budget also announced that each amount used for calculating personal tax credits will automatically be indexed annually, as of the 2018 taxation year.

   In order to determine the credit value, each dollar value must be multiplied by the Quebec's tax credit rate. For example, the basic personal credit amount of $14,890 is multiplied by 16% to determine the credit value of $2,383.

The unused portion of all non-refundable credits may be transferred from one spouse/partner to another, but only after all credits have been taken into account in calculating the individual's income tax otherwise payable.

2) Quebec indexes its tax credits each year by using an inflation factor that is calculated based on the provincial rate of inflation, excluding changes in liquor and tobacco taxes. The Quebec inflation factor is 0.74% for 2017.

3) This credit is available for a dependent child who is under age 18 and is engaged in full-time professional training or post-secondary studies for each completed term, to a maximum of two semesters per year per dependant. The credit is also available for infirm dependants who are engaged in such activities part-time.

4) An eligible student can transfer to either parent an amount relating to an unused portion of their basic personal credit amount for the year (transfer mechanism for the recognized parental contribution). Each taxation year, the amount that can be transferred must not exceed the limit for that year ($9,582 for 2017).

5) This credit is available if the dependant, other than the spouse, is related to the taxpayer by blood, marriage or adoption and ordinarily lives with the taxpayer. The taxpayer must not have benefited from a transfer of the recognized parental contribution from this dependant.

6) The total of the credit amounts for individuals age 65 or older, for living alone or with a dependant, and for receiving retirement income is reduced by 18.75% of the amount by which net family income exceeds $33,755.

7) This credit is available if the individual lives in a self-contained domestic establishment that they maintain and in which no other person lives other than themself, a minor person or eligible student. If the individual lives with an eligible student, for the purposes of the transfer mechanism for the recognized parental contribution (see note (4)), the individual may be able to add an amount for a single-parent family of $2,107 to the basic amount for a person living alone.

8) The 2016 Quebec Budget lowered the eligibility age from 64 to 63 for 2017 and further reduced it to age 62 in 2018. The budget also increased the maximum amount of "eligible work income" to $10,000 for all workers age 65 and over, as of 2018.

For 2017, this credit is available for workers who are 63 years of age or older. For workers age 63, the credit applies at a 16% rate to $4,000 of "eligible work income" over $5,000. For workers age 64, the credit applies at a 16% rate to $6,000 of "eligible work income" over $5,000. For workers age 65 and over, the credit applies at a 16% rate to $8,000 of "eligible work income" over $5,000. The credit for workers age 63 or older is reduced by 5% of eligible work income over $33,755. Eligible work income includes salary and business income but excludes taxable benefits received for a previous employment as well as amounts deducted in computing taxable income, such as the stock option deduction.

Any unused portion of the tax credit cannot be carried forward or transferred to the individual's spouse.

9) The credit for union and professional dues is calculated based on the annual fees paid in the year. The portion of professional dues relating to liability insurance can be deducted from income, so it is not included in calculating the credit amount.

10) The tuition credit is calculated based on tuition, professional examination and mandatory ancillary fees paid for the calendar year. Tuition fees qualify for an 8% non-refundable credit for Quebec tax purposes. The student may transfer the unused portion of the tuition credit to a parent or grandparent. The portion of this credit that is not transferred will be available for future use by the student.

11) The 2017 Quebec budget announced that interest paid on student loans will continue to qualify for a 20% tax credit. Interest not claimed in a year may be carried forward indefinitely.

12) The medical expense credit is calculated based on qualified medical expenses over 3% of family income. Family income is the total income of both spouses/partners. The 2017 Quebec budget announced that eligible medical expenses and eligible expenses to obtain medical care not provided in the region where an individual lives will continue to qualify for a 20% tax credit.

13) Charitable donations made by both spouses/partners may be totalled and claimed by either person. The maximum amount of donations that may be claimed in a year is 100% of net income. However, all donations may be carried forward for five years (or 10 years for certain donations) if they are not claimed in the year of donation.

Quebec's tax credit is 20% on the first $200 of eligible gifts and 24% for amounts over $200. As of 2017, a 25.75% donation tax credit can be claimed to the extent the donor's income exceeds $103,915.

# Quebec Refundable Tax Credit Rates and Amounts for 2017[1]

| | Tax Rate | Max expense | Max credit |
|---|---|---|---|
| **Medical expenses**[2]<br>Reduced by 5% of family income over $22,725[3] | 25% | only certain medical expenses qualify | $ 1,175 |
| **Child care expense credit**[4] | 26%–75% | | |
| The lesser of expenses incurred or: | | | |
| For a child who has a severe or prolonged mental or physical impairment | | 11,000 | |
| For a child under age seven | | 9,000 | |
| For a child under age seventeen | | 5,000 | |
| **Adoption expense credit**[5] | 50% | 20,000 | 10,000 |
| **Infertility treatment credit**[6] | 20%–80% | 20,000 | 16,000 |
| **Informal caregivers of related adults**[7] | | | |
| Basic amount | | | 647[3]/1,007 |
| Supplement | | | 529[3] |
| Reduced by 16% of eligible relative's income over $23,505[3] | | | |
| **Respite of caregivers**[8] | 30% | 5,200 | 1,560 |
| Reduced by 3% of caregiver's family income over $56,935[3] | | | |
| **Home support of elderly persons living alone**[9] | | | |
| Not recognized as dependant seniors | 35% | 19,500 | 6,825 |
| Recognized as dependant seniors | 35% | 25,500 | 8,925 |
| Reduced by 3% of the individual's family income over $56,935[3] | | | |
| **Short-term transition of seniors in rehabilitation centre**[10] | 20% | costs incurred in maximum 60-day period | |
| **Safety equipment for seniors**[11] | 20% | costs incurred over $500 | |
| **Eco-friendly renovations**[12] | 20% | costs incurred over $2,500 | 10,000 |
| **Residential waste water treatment system**[13] | 20% | costs incurred over $2,500 | 5,500 |

## Notes

1) Quebec's credit rates, maximum expenses eligible and methods of calculating credits vary from one type of refundable credit to another. Quebec's credit rate is applied to the dollar amounts in the table to determine the maximum credit value. For example, the adoption expense credit amount of $20,000 is multiplied by 50% to determine the maximum credit value of $10,000. Some refundable credits are reduced when thresholds are exceeded.

2) Quebec provides a refundable tax credit equal to the total of 25% of medical expenses eligible for the non-refundable credit (see the table "Quebec Non-Refundable Tax Credit Rates and Amounts for 2017") and 25% of the amount deducted for impairment support products and services. A minimum amount of earned income has to be earned in order to claim the refundable tax credit: $3,005 for 2017.

3) Quebec indexes various tax credits each year by using an inflation factor that is calculated based on the provincial rate of inflation, excluding changes in liquor and tobacco taxes. The Quebec inflation factor is 0.74% for 2017.

4) Unlike the federal treatment of qualifying child care expenses, which are eligible for a deduction in computing net income, Quebec provides a refundable tax credit for such expenses. The rate of credit falls as net family income rises.

   The maximum amount of expenses eligible for the credit is generally the lesser of:

   - $11,000 for a child of any age who has a severe or prolonged mental or physical impairment, plus $9,000 for a child under age seven, plus $5,000 for a child under age 17, or

   - actual child care expenses incurred in the year.

   Eligible expenses include costs incurred during the period an individual receives benefits under the Quebec Parental Insurance Plan or the Employment Insurance Plan. The child care expenses are not limited by the earned income of the parent. The definition of "eligible child" for the purposes of the refundable tax credit for childcare expenses has changed. As of the 2017 taxation year, an eligible child of an individual for a taxation year is a child of the individual or the individual's spouse, or a child who is dependent on the individual/spouse and whose income for the year does not exceed $9,582, if the child is under age 16 years of age at any time during the year or is dependent on the individual or the individual's spouse and has a mental or physical infirmity.

5) Qualifying expenses include court and legal fees paid to obtain a final adoption order, travel and accommodation expenses for foreign adoptions, translation expenses, and fees charged by foreign and domestic social agencies.

6) The applicable credit rate varies from 20% to 80% of eligible infertility expense, depending on family situation and income. The credit can be claimed on infertility expenses of up to $20,000.

7) There are three components to this credit. The first component applies to caregivers who house an eligible relative in their home where the relative is age 70 or older or is an adult with a severe and prolonged mental or physical impairment. The second component applies to informal caregivers who live in an eligible relative's home and a physician has attested that the relative is unable to live alone due to a severe and prolonged mental or physical impairment. The third component applies to caregivers whose spouse is age 70 or older or has a severe and prolonged mental or physical impairment, and the couple lives in their own home other than in a seniors' residence.

   The amount of the basic credit increases to $1,007 for 2017 if the caregiver cares for an elderly spouse. Caregivers caring for an elderly spouse are not entitled to the supplement amount.

   For the purposes of this credit, an eligible relative is a child, grandchild, nephew, niece, brother, sister, uncle, aunt, great-uncle, great-aunt or any other direct ascendant of the individual or the individual's spouse.

8) Caregivers can also claim a refundable tax credit for respite services. Qualifying expenses include specialized respite services for the care and supervision of an eligible person. If the expense has been used in calculating another refundable or non-refundable credit, it cannot be claimed for this credit as well.

9) The home support tax credit can be claimed by persons age 70 and over living in their home. For seniors recognized as a dependant, and when this credit is determined for a couple as soon as one of the members of the couple is recognized as a dependant, no reduction is allowed. If the expense also qualifies for the non-refundable medical expense credit (see the table "Quebec Non-Refundable Tax Credit Rates and Amounts for 2017"), the expense cannot be claimed for this credit as well.

10) The rehabilitation centre tax credit can be claimed by seniors age 70 or older for costs incurred for the first 60 days of any given stay in a public or private "functional rehabilitation transition unit". There is no limit to the number of stays that can be claimed.

11) The safety equipment tax credit can be claimed by seniors age 70 or older for the purchase or rental of equipment (including installation costs) used to improve their safety and security in their principal residence. Examples of qualifying equipment include remote monitoring systems, GPS tracking devices for persons, and walk-in bathtubs and showers.

12) The temporary RénoVert tax credit can be claimed for qualifying eco-friendly home renovations done by a qualified contractor under a contract entered into before April 1, 2017 and paid for by an individual before April 1, 2018 (extended from October 1, 2017). Eco-friendly renovation work includes work involving insulation, sealing exterior doors, windows, heating, air conditioning, water heating and ventilation systems, as well as work to maintain or improve water or soil quality. Eco-friendly renovation work excludes any work eligible for the credit for the upgrading of residential waste water treatment system, since a new refundable tax credit applies to such work as of April 1, 2017 (see note (13)). The work must relate to existing parts of an individual's eligible dwelling.

13) Quebec's 2017 budget introduced a new temporary refundable tax credit for upgrading the residential waste water treatment systems of an eligible dwelling. Qualifying work includes the construction, renovation, modification or rebuilding of a system for the discharge, collection and disposal of waste water, toilet effluents or grey water. The work must be carried out by a qualified contractor and paid for under a service agreement entered into after March 31, 2017 and before April 1, 2022.

# Index

# KPMG offices across Canada

KPMG LLP, an Audit, Tax and Advisory firm (kpmg.ca) and a Canadian limited liability partnership established under the laws of Ontario, is the Canadian member firm affiliated with KPMG International Cooperative ("KPMG International"). KPMG member firms around the world have more than 189,000 professionals, in 152 countries.

The independent member firms of the KPMG network are affiliated with KPMG International, a Swiss entity. Each KPMG firm is a legally distinct and separate entity, and describes itself as such.

| | | | |
|---|---|---|---|
| **Abbotsford** 604-854-2200 | **Kelowna** 250-979-7150 | **Prince George** 250-563-7151 | **Toronto** 416-777-8500 |
| **Calgary** 403-691-8000 | **Kingston** 613-549-1550 | **Québec** 418-577-3400 | **Toronto – Vaughan** 905-265-5900 |
| **Chilliwack** 604-793-4700 | **Langley** 604-455-4000 | **Regina** 306-791-1200 | **Vancouver** 604-691-3000 |
| **Edmonton** 780-429-7300 | **Lethbridge** 403-380-5700 | **Saint John** 506-634-1000 | **Vancouver – Burnaby** 604-527-3600 |
| **Fredericton** 506-452-8000 | **London** 519-672-4880 | **Saskatoon** 306-934-6200 | **Vernon** 250-503-5300 |
| **Halifax** 902-492-6000 | **Moncton** 506-856-4400 | **Sault Ste. Marie** 705-949-5811 | **Victoria** 250-480-3500 |
| **Hamilton** 905-523-8200 | **Montréal** 514-840-2100 | **St. Catharines** 905-685-4811 | **Waterloo** 519-747-8800 |
| **Kamloops** 250-372-5581 | **North Bay** 705-472-5110 | **St. John's** 709-733-5000 | **Windsor** 519-251-3500 |
| **Kanata** 613-212-5764 | **Ottawa** 613-212-5764 | **Sudbury** 705-675-8500 | **Winnipeg** 204-957-1770 |

# Tax planning for you and your family 2018

### Reduce your family's tax bill and increase your family's wealth

This book offers practical, easy-to-understand strategies that can help you keep more of your hard-earned dollars and boost your family's net worth, whether you're a married or single parent, a student, an executive, or the owner-manager of your own business.

Updated for 2018 by the tax and financial planning team at one of Canada's largest professional services firms, KPMG, this year's guide gives you the latest on:

- Creating a sound financial plan for your family's future and your retirement.

- Making the most of the special tax breaks available for students, working parents, first-time home buyers, seniors and people with disabilities.

- Planning for investments in tax-effective vehicles like stocks, bonds, mutual funds and life insurance products.

- Deferring taxes through popular savings vehicles like RRSPs, Tax-Free Savings Accounts and Registered Pension Plans.

- Reducing taxes on your income from your job by maximizing your claims for items like automobiles, moving costs and home office expenses.

- Structuring your charitable donations to help maximize the value of the gift to the charity and the tax benefits to you or your estate.

- Shielding your earnings and property from US income and estate taxes.

- Creating a tax-effective estate plan through strategies such as estate freezing, family trusts and business succession planning.

- Providing a high-level summary of the proposed new tax regime for private companies.

A comprehensive index, complete cross-references, current tables of federal and provincial tax rates and credits, and summaries of key tax planning points in each chapter make it easy to quickly pinpoint the information you need.

*Tax planning for you and your family* – your guide for saving money at tax time and all year round.

ISBN 978-0-7798-7829-1

$28.95

9 780779 878291